A Brief History of
Ancient Greece

A Brief History of Ancient Greece

POLITICS, SOCIETY, AND CULTURE

THITD EDITION

Sarah B. Pomeroy
*Hunter College and the City University of
New York Graduate Center, Emerita*

Stanley M. Burstein
California State University, Los Angeles, Emeritus

Walter Donlan[†]
University of California, Irvine, Emeritus

Jennifer Tolbert Roberts
City College and the City University of New York Graduate Center

David W. Tandy
University of Leeds

New York   Oxford
OXFORD UNIVERSITY PRESS

Oxford University Press is a department of the University of Oxford.
It furthers the University's objective of excellence in research,
scholarship, and education by publishing worldwide.

Oxford   New York
Auckland   Cape Town   Dar es Salaam   Hong Kong   Karachi
Kuala Lumpur   Madrid   Melbourne   Mexico City   Nairobi
New Delhi   Shanghai   Taipei   Toronto

With offices in
Argentina   Austria   Brazil   Chile   Czech Republic   France   Greece
Guatemala   Hungary   Italy   Japan   Poland   Portugal   Singapore
South Korea   Switzerland   Thailand   Turkey   Ukraine   Vietnam

For titles covered by Section 112 of the US Higher Education
Opportunity Act, please visit www.oup.com/us/he for the latest
information about pricing and alternate formats.

Published by Oxford University Press
198 Madison Avenue, New York, NY 10016
http://www.oup.com

Library of Congress Cataloging-in-Publication Data
Pomeroy, Sarah B.
A brief history of Ancient Greece : politics, society, and culture / Sarah B. Pomeroy, Hunter
College and the City University of New York Graduate Center, Emerita; Stanley M. Burstein,
California State University, Los Angeles, Emeritus; Walter Donlan, University of California, Irvine,
Emeritus; Jennifer Tolbert Roberts, City College and the City University of New York Graduate
Center; David W. Tandy, University of Leeds.—Third Edition.
     pages cm.
   Includes index.
   Revision of: Ancient Greece. Second edition.
   ISBN 978-0-19-998155-7
1. Greece—Civilization—To 146 B.C. —Textbooks.   I. Burstein, Stanley Mayer.   II. Donlan,
Walter   III. Roberts, Jennifer Tolbert, 1947-   IV. Tandy, David W.   V. Ancient
Greece.   VI. Title.
   DF77.P65 2013
   938—dc23
                                                                          2013014874

About the cover: Temple of Athena, Lindos. Photograph by Eliot Porter, 1981.

Printing number: 9 8 7 6 5 4

Printed in Canada

For
Lee Harris Pomeroy
Dorothy F. Burstein
Page Tolbert
Gustav and Aphra Tandy

CONTENTS

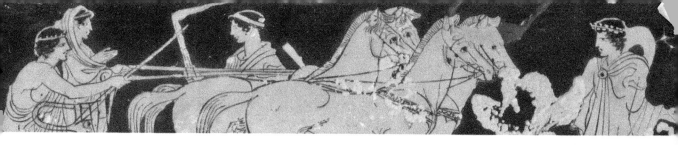

LIST OF MAPS

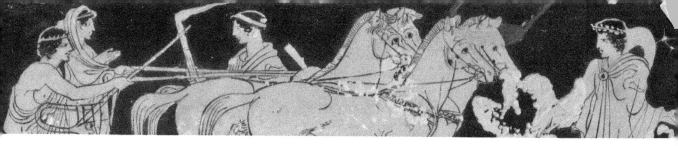

TRANSLATIONS USED
BY PERMISSION

Arrowsmith, William. 1959. *Orestes*, from *The Complete Greek Tragedies*, David Grene and Richmond Lattimore, eds. Chicago: University of Chicago Press.

Barker, Ernest. 1973. *The Politics of Aristotle*. Oxford: Oxford University Press.

Benardete, Seth. 1959. *Persians*, from *The Complete Greek Tragedies*, David Grene and Richmond Lattimore, eds. Chicago: University of Chicago Press.

Blanco, Walter. 2013. *The Histories*, from *Herodotus: The Histories*, 2nd ed., Walter Blanco and Jennifer Roberts, eds. New York: W. W. Norton.

———. 1998. *The Peloponnesian War*, from *Thucydides: The Peloponnesian War*, Walter Blanco and Jennifer Tolbert Roberts, eds. New York: W. W. Norton.

Burstein, Stanley M. 1985. *The Hellenistic Age from the Battle of Ipsos to the Death of Kleopatra VII*. Cambridge, UK: Cambridge University Press.

Cornford, F. M. 1945. *The Republic of Plato*. Oxford: Oxford University Press.

Fowler, Harold N. 1914. *Plato, Euthyphro, Apology, Crito, Phaedo. Phaedrus*. Loeb Classical Library. Cambridge, MA: Harvard University Press.

———. 1936. *Plutarch, Moralia*. Vol. X. Loeb Classical Library. Cambridge, MA: Harvard University Press.

Gagarin, Michael and Paul Woodruff, eds. 1995. "Encomium of Helen," in *Early Greek Political Thought from Homer to the Sophists*. Cambridge, UK: Cambridge University Press.

Green, Peter. 1997. *The Argonautica of Apollonios Rhodios*. Berkeley and Los Angeles: University of California Press.

Hanson, Ann. 1975. "Hippocrates: Diseases of Women," *Signs* 1: 567–584.

Jameson, M. 1996. "A Decree of Themistocles from Troizen," *Hesperia* 29 (1960): 200–201, modified by P. Green. 1996. *Xerxes at Salamis*. New York and London: Praeger.

Lattimore, Richmond. 1959. *Agamemnon*, from *The Complete Tragedies*, David Grene and Richmond Lattimore, eds. Chicago: University of Chicago Press.

Lombardo, Stanley. 1997. *Homer, Iliad*. Indianapolis, IN: Hackett Publishing Company.

Lombardo, Stanley. 2000. *Homer, Odyssey*. Indianapolis, IN: Hackett Publishing Company.

Marincola, John. 2009. *The Hellenika*, in *The Landmark Xenophon's Hellenika*, Robert B. Strassler, ed. New York: Random House.

Murray, A. T. 1936. *Pseudo-Demosthenes, Against Neaera*, from *Demosthenes*. Vol. VI. Loeb Classical Library. Cambridge, MA: Harvard University Press.

New American Standard Bible. 1995. La Habra, CA: The Lockman Foundation.

Nisetich, Frank. 1980. *Pindar's Victory Songs*. Baltimore: Johns Hopkins University Press.

————. 2005. *The New Posidippus: A Hellenistic Poetry Book*, Kathryn Gutzwiller, ed. Oxford: Oxford University Press.

Pomeroy, Sarah B. 1994. *Xenophon: Oeconomicus, A Social and Historical Commentary*. Oxford: Clarendon Press.

Pomeroy, Sarah B. 2002. *Spartan Women*. New York: Oxford University Press.

Rhodes, P. J. and Robin Osborne. 2003. *Greek Historical Inscriptions 404–323 BC*. Oxford: Oxford University Press.

Saunders, A. N. W. 1975. *Demosthenes and Aeschines*. Harmondsworth, UK: Penguin.

Tandy, David W. and Walter C. Neale. 1996. *Hesiod's Works and Days*. Berkeley and Los Angeles: University of California Press. (© by the Regents of the University of California)

Todd, O. J. 1968. *Xenophon: Memorabilia and Oeconomicus*. Cambridge, MA: Harvard University Press.

Warner, Rex. 1959. *Medea*, from *The Complete Greek Tragedies*, David Grene and Richmond Lattimore, eds. Chicago: University of Chicago Press.

Waterfield, Robin. 1994. *Plato. Symposium*. Oxford: Oxford University Press.

Waterfield, Robin. 1998. *Plutarch. Greek Lives*. Oxford: Oxford University Press.

West, M. L. 1991. *Greek Lyric Poetry*. Oxford: Oxford University Press.

————. 2005. "A New Sappho Poem." *Times Literary Supplement*, June 26.

Wyckoff, Elizabeth. 1959. *Antigone*, from *The Complete Greek Tragedies*, David Grene and Richmond Lattimore, eds. Chicago: University of Chicago Press.

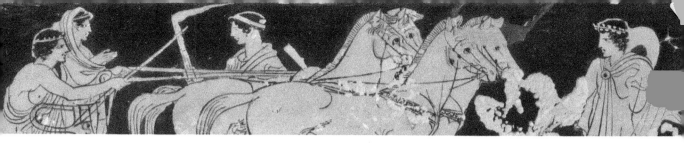

PREFACE

The history of the ancient Greeks is one of the most improbable success stories in world history. A small people inhabiting a country poor in resources and divided into hundreds of squabbling mini-states created one of the world's most remarkable cultures. Located on the periphery of the Bronze Age civilizations of Egypt and Mesopotamia, the Greeks absorbed key technical skills such as writing and metallurgy in the process of developing a culture marked by astonishing creativity, versatility, and resilience. Finally, having spread from Spain to the borders of India, Greek culture was gradually transformed as it became an integral part of other civilizations: Latin, Byzantine, and Islamic. In the process, the Greeks left a rich legacy in every area of the arts and sciences that is still alive in contemporary civilization.

Almost two decades ago the authors of this book set out to write a new history of the country the English poet Byron called "the land of lost gods." The goal of *Ancient Greece. A Political, Social, and Cultural History* (Oxford, 1999) was to flesh out the romantic images of Greece with the new understanding of the realities of history gained from the patient scholarship of a half-century of talented historians. We also hoped to change the teaching of ancient history in North America and elsewhere by giving full recognition to the significance of the Dark Age and of the Hellenistic period in the formation of Greek civilization, incorporating into the story of Greece the experiences of those who did not belong to the elite (such as women and slaves), and using archaeological and artistic evidence as primary sources—not as mere illustrations of what was already known from written texts.

Since the publication of that book, Oxford University Press has afforded us four opportunities to build on our work. In 2004 we published the first edition of *A Brief History of Ancient Greece*, which, although shorter than our first work, placed greater emphasis on social and cultural history. In 2008, we published a second edition of the original book and in 2012 a third; the brief version was released in a second edition in 2009. On each occasion, every paragraph and sentence was carefully reviewed. The readings were updated, and suggestions and corrections sent to us by our readers were incorporated into the text. The maps have been completely redesigned and new translations selected or prepared wherever necessary. We have doubled the color plates in this edition, enabling readers to see images as the Greeks saw them.

This book has drawn on all the improvements made in our earlier work; the art program, for example, combines photos from the earlier editions of this book with some from the second and third editions of the larger book and includes new images as well. We have expanded our discussions of religion, childhood, marriage, and funeral customs. Scholarship does not stand still, however, and we have continued to incorporate new knowledge in this edition as we did in its predecessors, especially in the first three chapters. Finally, we would particularly call the readers' attention to three features of our book: the timeline at the beginning, which provides a brief but comprehensive overview of Greek history; the extensive glossary at the end, which provides capsule descriptions of many of the terms that occur in the book; and the color plates, which bring our readers closer to the physical reality of the remarkable objects and buildings the Greeks created.

All synthetic works depend on the work of innumerable scholars, whose names do not appear in our text. We would like to thank them and our generous readers and students, from whose comments and suggestions we have greatly benefited. We are indebted to Charles Cavaliere and his always helpful staff at Oxford University Press who have been generous with their support and assistance throughout the gestation of this project. We wish also to thank Barbara McManus and Lee Harris Pomeroy for their help and advice with images. The late Walter Donlan's contributions to the previous editions of this book were great, and his ongoing participation has been missed. Fortunately, another historian of early Greece, David Tandy, has joined our team, and he has thoroughly revised the chapters dealing with prehistoric and Archaic Greece in the light of the best contemporary scholarship.

Finally, we would also like to thank the various publishers who have granted us permission to reprint translations. All unattributed translations in the text are by the authors except for those of Herodotus, which are from the translation of Walter Blanco that appears in Walter Blanco and Jennifer Tolbert Roberts, eds., *Herodotus: The Histories*, 2nd ed. (New York: W. W. Norton & Company, Inc., 2013); and Thucydides, which are from the translation of Walter Blanco that appears in Walter Blanco and Jennifer Tolbert Roberts, eds., *Thucydides: The Peloponnesian War* (New York: W. W. Norton & Company, Inc., 1998). Abbreviations for standard works follow those used in *The Oxford Classical Dictionary*, 4th ed. (Oxford: Oxford University Press, 2012).

Jennifer T. Roberts, *New York City*   Sarah B. Pomeroy, *New York City*
Stanley M. Burstein, *Los Alamitos, California*   David W. Tandy, *Leeds, UK*

REVIEWERS OF THE THIRD EDITION

Radcliff Edmonds, Bryn Mawr College
Philip Holt, University of Wyoming
Timothy Howe, St. Olaf College
Susan Hussein, Montclair State
    University

Andrew Nichols, University
    of Florida
Lawrence Okamura, University of
    Missouri-Columbia

NEW TO THE THIRD EDITION

- Full rewriting of treatment of early Greece
- Expanded treatment of military history
- Expanded discussion of archaeology
- New documents and new translations of documents
- Revised and expanded art program, including a second color insert

T I M E L I N E

PERIOD	MILITARY EVENTS	POLITICAL/SOCIAL EVENTS	CULTURAL DEVELOPMENT
7000–3000 Neolithic		Permanent farming villages	Domestication of plants and animals; pottery
3000–2100 Early Bronze Age		Social ranking emerges; villages and districts ruled by hereditary chiefs	Widespread use of bronze and other metals in the Aegean
2100–1600 Middle Bronze Age	2100 Lerna and other sites destroyed	2100 (?) Incursions of Indo-European Speakers into Greece	2100 (?) Indo-European gods introduced into Greece 1900 First palaces in Crete 1900 Mainland contacts with Crete and the Near East 1800 Cretans develop Linear A writing
1600–1200 Late Bronze Age	1500–1450 Mycenaeans take over Crete 1375 Knossos destroyed 1250–1225 "The Trojan War" (?) 1200 Invaders loot and burn the palace centers	1600 Mycenae and other sites become power centers; small kingdoms emerge 1400–1200 Height of Mycenaean power and prosperity 1200–1050 Palace- system collapses	1600 Shaft graves 1500 Tholos tombs 1450 Linear B writing 1400 New palaces in Greece 1200 Cultural decline

continued

PERIOD	MILITARY EVENTS	POLITICAL/SOCIAL EVENTS	CULTURAL DEVELOPMENT
1200–900 Early Dark Age (Submycenaean 1125–1050) (Protogeometric 1050–900)		1050 Small chiefdoms established; migrations of mainland Greeks to Ionia 1000 Dorian Greeks settled in the mainland and the islands	Iron technology 950 Monumental building at Lefkandi
900–c. 750/700 Late Dark Age (Early Geometric 900–850) (Middle Geometric 850–750)		900 Population increases; new settlements established; trade and manufacture expand 800 Rapid population growth	800 Greeks develop an alphabet; earliest temples built 776 Traditional date of first Olympian games
c. 750/700–480 Archaic Period (Late Geometric 750–700)	730–700 First Messenian War; Lelantine War 700–650 Evolution of hoplite armor and tactics 669 Battle of Hysiae 650 Second Messenian War	750–700 City-states emerge 750 Overseas colonization to the West begins 670–500 Tyrants rule in many city-states 650 Colonization of Black Sea area begins; earliest known stone inscription of a law; "Lycurgan" Reforms at Sparta; the "Great Rhetra" (?) 632 Cylon fails in attempt at tyranny in Athens 620 Law code of Draco in Athens 600 Lydians begin to mint coins	750–675 *Iliad* and *Odyssey* composed 720 "Orientalizing period" in art begins 700 Hesiod. Period of lyric poetry begins 650 Temples built of stone and marble; Corinthian black-figure technique 600 Beginnings of science and philosophy (the "Presocratics") 582–573 Pythian, Isthmian, Nemean games inaugurated

continued

PERIOD	MILITARY EVENTS	POLITICAL/SOCIAL EVENTS	CULTURAL DEVELOPMENT
		560–514 Pisistratus and his sons tyrants of Athens	Pisistratus expands religious festivals at Athens
		550 Sparta dominant in the Peloponnesus	
			530 Athenian red-figure technique
		507 Cleisthenes institutes political reforms in Athens	5th-century rationalists and scientists; Hippocrates; advances in medicine; increase in literacy
	499 Ionian Greeks rebel from Persian Empire		
	490 Battle of Marathon		Classical style in sculpture
		486 Decision to choose Athenian archons by lot	
		482 Ostracism of Aristides	
	480–479 Persian invasion of Greece		
480–323 Classical Period		477 Foundation of Delian League Growth of democracy in Athens	470–456 Construction of temple of Zeus at Olympia
	464 Helot rebellion in Sparta	461 Reforms of Ephialtes at Athens	
	460–445 "First" Peloponnesian War		458 Aeschylus' *Oresteia*
		454 Athenians move treasury from Delos to Athens Flourishing of Greek trade and manufacture	451 Pericles carries law limiting citizenship at Athens
			Herodotus at work on his *Histories*
	431–404 Peloponnesian War	445 Thirty Years' Peace	447–432 Construction of Parthenon at Athens Sophists active in Athens
		429 Death of Pericles	Thucydides begins his *History*
			c. 428 Sophocles' *Oedipus Tyrannus*
		423 Thucydides exiled from Athens	425 Aristophanes' *Acharnians*
		421 Peace of Nicias	
	415–413 Sicilian campaign		415 Euripides' *Trojan Women*

continued

PERIOD	MILITARY EVENTS	POLITICAL/SOCIAL EVENTS	CULTURAL DEVELOPMENT
		411–410 Oligarchic coup in Athens; establishment of Council of 400; regime of the 5,000	411 Aristophanes' *Lysistrata*
	403–377 Sparta the most-powerful state in Greece	404–403 Regime of the Thirty Tyrants in Athens	
	395–387 Corinthian War	399 Trial and execution of Socrates	399–347 Dialogues of Plato; foundation of the Academy
		Fourth century: Rise of class of *rhetores* at Athens; economic inequalities and social *stasis* throughout Greece	399–360 Writings of Xenophon
	377–371 Athens the most powerful state in Greece	Serious population decline in Sparta; impoverished class of "Inferiors" at Sparta; increasing amount of property in hands of Spartan women	375–330 Works of Praxiteles
	371–362 Thebes the most powerful state in Greece		368–347 Aristotle studies at Academy
	359 Defeat of Perdiccas III	359 Accession of Philip II	
		357 Marriage of Philip II to Olympias	
		356 Birth of Alexander the Great	356 Philip II's Olympic victory
		356–346 Third Sacred War; Peace of Philocrates	355 Demosthenes' first speech
			347 Death of Plato
			346 Isocrates' *Philippus*
	338 Battle of Chaeronea	338 Assassination of Artaxerxes III; foundation of Corinthian League; marriage of Philip II and Cleopatra	338 Death of Isocrates
	336 Invasion of Asia by Philip II	336 Accession of Darius III; assassination of Philip II; accession of Alexander III	

continued

PERIOD	MILITARY EVENTS	POLITICAL/SOCIAL EVENTS	CULTURAL DEVELOPMENT
	335 Revolt of Thebes	335 Destruction of Thebes	335 Aristotle returns to Athens; founding of Lyceum
	334 Battle of Granicus		
	333 Battle of Issus	333 Alexander at Gordium	
	331 Battle of Gaugamela	331 Foundation of Alexandria	331 Visit to Siwah by Alexander
	330–327 War in Bactria and Sogdiana	330 Destruction of Persepolis; death of Philotas	
		329 Assassination of Darius III	
		328 Murder of Cleitus	
	327–325 Alexander's invasion of India	327 Marriage of Alexander and Roxane	
	326 Battle of the Hydaspes		
323–30 Hellenistic Period	323–322 Lamian War	323 Death of Alexander III; accession of Philip III and Alexander IV	
		322 Dissolution of the Corinthian League	322 Deaths of Aristotle and Demosthenes
	321 Invasion of Egypt	321 Death of Perdiccas; Antipater becomes regent	321–292 Career of Menander
	318–316 Revolt against Polyperchon		
	315–311 Four-year war against Antigonus	315 Freedom of Greeks proclaimed by Antigonus the One-Eyed	
	307 Demetrius invades Greece	311 Peace between Antigonus and his rivals	307–283 Foundation of the Museum
	306 Battle of Salamis	306 Antigonus and Demetrius acclaimed kings	306 Epicurus founds Garden
		305 Ptolemy, Seleucus, Lysimachus, and Cassander declare themselves kings	
	301 Battle of Ipsus	301 Death of Antigonus; division of his empire	301 Zeno founds Stoa

continued

Period	Military Events	Political/Social Events	Cultural Development
			300–246 Construction of the Pharos
		283 Death of Ptolemy I; accession of Ptolemy II	283–222 Works of Theocritus, Callimachus, Apollonius of Rhodes
	281 Battle of Corupedium	281 Deaths of Lysimachus and Seleucus	
	279 Invasion of Gauls		
		235–222 Reign of Cleomenes III at Sparta	246 Eratosthenes becomes librarian at Alexandria
	222 Battle of Sellasia	222 Exile of Cleomenes III; end of his reforms at Sparta	
	200–197 Second Macedonian War	196 Romans proclaim freedom of the Greeks at Isthmian games	
	171–168 Third Macedonian War	167 End of the Macedonian monarchy	167 Polybius comes to Rome
	31 Battle of Actium		
		30 Suicide of Cleopatra VII; Rome annexes Egypt	

A Brief History of
Ancient Greece

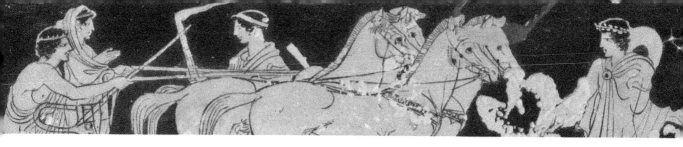

Introduction

Historians who study ancient civilizations have the daunting task of following the path of societies and cultures on the basis of scant sources. Actually, as past civilizations go, ancient Greece has left us a comparatively rich record. Even so, we possess only a tiny fraction of what was originally there. Inevitably, then, many aspects of society and culture, even in the most well-documented periods of Greek antiquity, cannot be viewed in bold relief. Yet there is good news, too. Every year new discoveries are made that continue to enlarge our fund of information, and new ways of looking at the old sources have broadened our perspectives.

SOURCES: HOW WE KNOW ABOUT THE ANCIENT GREEKS

Sources are the raw material of history out of which historians weave their stories. Just about everything preserved from the ancient world is a potential source for the history of antiquity. Our sources fall into two broad categories: the physical remains, which include anything material, from bones to buildings; and the written remains, which include the words of the Greeks themselves or of others who wrote about them in antiquity. Of course, the line between the material and the written is often blurred, as in the case of words scratched on a piece of pottery or an inscription carved on a stone pillar.

Given that our primary sources are at least two thousand years old, and in many cases much older, it is not surprising that most of them require rehabilitation or reconstruction even before they can be of substantial use. Fortunately,

1

historians do not have to examine them from scratch. They rely on archaeologists to excavate, classify, and interpret most of the material evidence; paleographers to decipher and elucidate the texts written on papyrus and parchment; and epigraphists and numismatists to interpret inscriptions on stones and coins. Without the expertise of those specialists who process the raw sources, the work of historians would not be possible.

Archaeologists study past societies primarily through the material remains—buildings, tools, and other artifacts. They create a history of the material culture on the basis of the changing patterns that they discern in the physical record. Historians, on the other hand, primarily use documents, inscriptions, and literary texts to construct a narrative of events and the people who were involved in them: what they did, why they did it, and the changes brought on by their actions. Nevertheless, both disciplines are engaged in a single collaborative project, the reconstruction of the lifeways of the Greek peoples over time.

RETRIEVING THE PAST: THE MATERIAL RECORD

Ancient Greece lies underground. Except for a few stone buildings, mostly temples, that have survived above ground, everything we have has been dug up from beneath, very often from dozens of feet below the present surface. Materials decay, and the soil of Greece is not good for preserving things. Accordingly, artifacts made of wood, cloth, and leather are rarely found. Metals fare better: Although iron is subject to corrosion, gold and silver last almost forever, and bronze is fairly durable. Another material that is virtually indestructible is terra-cotta, clay baked at very high temperatures. Clay was used in antiquity for many different objects, including figurines and votive plaques; but most of the clay objects that have been preserved are vessels that have been found by the thousands in graves and other sites. It was mainly on the basis of pots that archaeologists were able to construct a chronology for prehistoric and early historic Greece that could be translated into actual dates.

Clay pots were made wide-bellied or slender-bodied; long-necked or wide-mouthed; footed or footless; with one, two, or no handles. Some pots, such as the perfume flasks called *aryballoi,* stood only two or three inches high; others, like the *pithoi* used for storing olive oil and grain, were often as big as a human being. In the ancient world, clay vessels had to be made in all sizes and shapes because they served virtually every purpose that a container can serve. They were our bags, cartons, and shipping crates; our cooking pots, bottles, and glasses; our fine stemware and "good" china bowls. Their basic shapes remained much the same, but they underwent gradual changes in style and decoration so that pots can be placed in relative chronological sequences. Earthenware from one site is cross-dated with examples from other sites, thus confirming that site A is older or younger than sites B and C. The big breakthrough for establishing "absolute" or calendar dates, however, comes about when a datable object from an outside culture is found amidst the Greek material. Such an object might be a scarab inscribed with the name of an Egyptian king. Because the actual dates of his reign are known independently (from the Egyptian king lists), it follows that the Greek objects found with it in that deposit belonged to approximately the same time. Through the repeated process of establishing key cross dates, a workable chronology emerges that allows us to place an object, or grave, or building in real time: "late fourteenth century BC" or "around 720 BC." Today's archaeologists also have at their disposal more scientific techniques for dating objects and sites, such as measuring the radioactive decay of organic materials (carbon-14 dating).

Yet, notwithstanding the considerable success that modern archaeology has had in bringing the ancient past to light, wordless objects can tell us only so much about how people lived, what they experienced, or what they thought.

Retrieving the Past: The Written Record

Ancient writings were inscribed on many different materials including clay, stone, metal, and papyrus (and, beginning in the second century BC, parchment). Most of the written sources that have come down to us were composed in the Greek alphabet, which was introduced in the eighth century BC, but we also have clay tablets from a very brief time in the second millennium BC that were written in a syllabic script called Linear B. (We discuss Linear B writing in Chapter 1 and the Greek alphabet in Chapter 2.)

With the rapid spread of the alphabet came a torrent of written texts that would continue unabated throughout the rest of antiquity. Unfortunately, most of this material has been lost; that so much has survived is something of a miracle in itself. We may lament that of the more than 120 plays written by Sophocles, one of the most famous of the fifth-century BC dramatists, only seven have come down to us whole. We are grateful, however, to have as much as we do. After all, 20 million words are stored in the electronic database of Greek literary texts written down from the late eighth century BC to the second century AD.

The most common medium for writing in the ancient Mediterranean was papyrus (the paper of antiquity), which had been used in Egypt since the third millennium. Papyrus sheets were made by bonding together layered strips sliced from the papyrus reed; these were then glued together to form a long roll, twenty or more feet long. Words were written horizontally to form columns, which the reader isolated by scrolling back and forth along the roll. A papyrus roll could hold, on average, a play of about 1,500 lines or two to three "books" of Homer's *Iliad* or *Odyssey* (see Figure I.1). Every text had to be copied by hand (usually by slaves), a time-consuming and expensive proposition. The ancient Greeks were fairly assiduous in preserving the authors from their past. A reader visiting the great library at Alexandria during the first century BC would have had access to about 500,000 book-rolls, and the collection at Pergamum is said to have exceeded 200,000 rolls.

Already by this time the process of selection had begun. The Alexandrian scholars themselves appear to have used the term "those included" to denote

Figure I.1. A papyrus of Homer, *Iliad* 24, lines 693–711. London, The British Museum (Papyrus 114).

a list of authors who were deemed most worthy of being studied in schools. Naturally, the "included" writers had the best chances for survival. As literary tastes continued to change during later antiquity, many manuscripts ceased to be copied and crumbled into dust. Fortunately, papyrus endures well in a hot, dry environment, as in the desert sands of Egypt, where many thousands of Greek papyri, dating from the fourth century BC onward, have been found. Most of these are contemporary documents; however, papyri rescued from desert dumps have also preserved major literary works from all periods of Greek antiquity that otherwise would have been lost completely. In addition to texts originally written on papyrus, hundreds of inscriptions on stone and metal, including coins, survive, ranging in subject matter from private funerary epitaphs and dedications to public decrees, treaties, and laws. The latter are especially valuable because they preserve information about public life that is seldom recorded elsewhere.

Our sources vary in both quantity and quality according to time and place. For the Mycenaean Age (c. 1600–1200 BC), we have a wealth of material evidence (including the Linear B tablets) that permits a fairly detailed picture of the society. For the subsequent period, the Dark Age, down to the eighth century BC, material remains are very sparse and there are no written records. After the seventh century BC, however, when both material and literary remains start to proliferate, we begin to have a dynamic picture of change and continuity. The picture will show how the Greeks responded to environmental pressures with ideas and technological innovations, how they interacted as individuals within communities and as communities within communities, and how they developed a distinctive culture while preserving individual distinction.

Our literary sources are a diverse group, written in many different genres, or categories of composition defined by form and content. These include various types of poetry such as epic, lyric, tragedy, and comedy, as well as the prose genres of history, biography, oratory, and philosophy. Naturally, modern historians rely especially on the writings of ancient historians and biographers; but the other genres, both of poetry and of prose, are no less essential as sources.

Of course, there is a significant distinction between mythical and historical narratives of the past. We do not expect historical veracity from Homer's account of the Trojan War. At the same time, not even a historian who strives for veracity can give us a truly objective and unbiased account of the past. The ancient historians, no different from us really, aimed to convey only what they deemed historically significant. Because they selected some facts to the exclusion of others, even two roughly contemporary historians—the fifth-century Herodotus and Thucydides, for example—would necessarily produce different accounts of the same past events. Another limitation of our written sources is that, with very few exceptions, they are all produced by a privileged group: urban men, mostly from the upper class. To illuminate the lives of women, the very poor, and slaves, who do not generally speak for themselves, historians employ a variety of strategies, often drawing on gender studies, anthropology, cultural studies, and other interdisciplinary approaches.

A Synopsis of Written Sources by Periods 3000–750/700 BC

As we have seen, the Greeks of the Bronze Age (c. 3000–1200 BC) left no written records except for the Linear B tablets near the end of the Late Bronze Age. The long silence that followed baffled the efforts of even ancient Greek historians to describe the centuries before the reappearance of writing in the eighth century. Their source material was a body of orally transmitted myths and legends, some of which probably went back to the second millennium. The Greeks of the historical period generally regarded these stories as their ancient history. The central event of their distant past was the Trojan War, which, if it really happened, would have taken place in the thirteenth century BC. The Trojan War and its immediate aftermath are the setting for the earliest texts that we have, Homer's *Iliad* and *Odyssey*, which are believed to be the end product of a tradition of oral poetry going back many centuries. It is currently thought that they were committed to writing in the later eighth century or early in the seventh century. The use of these two very long epic poems as historical sources has been debated since the end of antiquity and is still a matter of controversy. Do they reflect a real society? If so, of what era? Or do they reveal, rather, the values and norms of later Greeks, who contrasted their own time with a former "age of heroes"?

750/700–480 BC

Hesiod (c. 700 BC) stands at the beginning of the Archaic Age. The two texts that have come down under Hesiod's name, the *Theogony* and the *Works and Days*, are, like the *Iliad* and the *Odyssey*, lengthy poems composed in the epic meter. In content, however, they differ not only from Homer but also from each other. Whereas the *Theogony* reaches back in time to tell about the origins of the Greek gods and the creation of the universe, the *Works and Days* is set in the poet's own day and is our earliest source that directly addresses contemporary social concerns.

The Archaic Age poets—who composed in the variety of forms we lump together under the rubric of lyric—abuse their enemies, praise the gods, argue politics, and pine over unrequited love in their verses. Even in the fragmentary shape in which we have them, the poems let us glimpse the political, social, and intellectual movements that distinguished the seventh and sixth centuries BC.

Yet in a sense the Archaic Age is still prehistory, for there are no historical writings from this period. The fifth-century historians Herodotus (c. 484–420 BC) and Thucydides (c. 460–395 BC), however, provide us with much valuable information about the development of the early city-states, especially Athens and Sparta. Sources for early Athens, although meager, are not quite as sparse as they are for Sparta. By good fortune, a papyrus from Egypt has preserved part of *The Athenian Constitution*, written by the philosopher Aristotle (384–322 BC) or one of his students. This document, as well as Plutarch's *Life of Solon*, quotes fragments of the poetry of the lawgiver Solon (c. 600 BC), who is our earliest source for Athenian society. The bulk of what we know about early Sparta and its institutions, however, comes from later writers, particularly the fourth-century BC historian Xenophon and the biographer Plutarch (c. 46–120 AD). Because the Spartans themselves left almost no written records and the accounts of later writers tended to idealize or criticize their culture, it is particularly challenging for historians to separate the real Sparta from the fictional one.

480–323 BC

What modern historians call the Classical period of Greece begins in 480 BC with the unsuccessful Persian invasion of Greece and ends with the death of Alexander the Great. The sources for this period are fuller than for any other period of ancient Greece and are drawn from all over the eastern Mediterranean world, not from Greece alone. The wars of these two centuries formed the themes of our first extant Greek historians. *The Histories* of Herodotus (c. 484–420 BC) asks the question, "Why did Greeks and non-Greeks go to war?," and responds with a chain of mutual wrongful acts and cultural misunderstandings reaching far back in time and space. Herodotus is our primary source for the Persian wars from the Greek perspective and provides much information about relations among Greek city-states in the sixth and early fifth centuries, especially Athens and Sparta.

The principal source for the actions that led to the Peloponnesian War between Athens and Sparta and their allies and for the war itself is the *History* of Thucydides (c. 460–395 BC). Thucydides aimed for accuracy; his account is informed by contemporary documents as well as by interviews with witnesses on both sides. But, as we have noted, no historian is ever truly impartial. As an interpreter of events, he couldn't help making judgments with every selection or arrangement of his "facts." Xenophon (c. 428–354 BC), who began his *Hellenica* almost exactly where Thucydides left off and continued his history down to 362 BC, seems to have made an effort to practice what he understood as "Thucydidean historiography." Fragments of several other fourth-century historians who wrote about the Peloponnesian War and its aftermath survive in the biographies of Plutarch and the historical books of Diodorus of Sicily (first century BC).

During these two centuries of alternating war and uneasy peace, poetry, philosophy, and the visual arts flourished; and the extant works reflect changing ideas, tastes, concerns, and lifestyles, particularly in Athens, from which most of our evidence comes. Of the hundreds of dramas that were produced during this period, only the tragedies of Aeschylus, Sophocles, and Euripides and the comedies of Aristophanes and Menander have survived (and even their works are mostly lost). With the exception of Menander's comedies, the plays do not attempt to mirror society; nor, like today's "docudramas," can they be seen as "history with the boring parts taken out." Yet, social historians can extrapolate from them evidence about many aspects of Athenian life. The tragedians Aeschylus, Sophocles, and Euripides use plots and characters from ancient myths, but their dramas often offer insights into the contemporary concerns of the citizenry. Unlike the characters in the tragedies, those of the comic playwright Aristophanes are represented as contemporary Athenians. Some of them are well-known public figures whom he makes the butt of parody and abusive satire. Although it is difficult for us to tell how Aristophanes really felt about the people he attacked in verse, his comedies do show us what made male audiences in a democracy laugh.

Philosophers were among the numerous intellectuals in the fourth century who were voicing their dissatisfaction with traditional democracy and suggesting new models of government. The surviving works of Plato (428–347 BC) and Aristotle (384–322 BC) not only fault the fundamental ideals of democracy, liberty, and equality but even undertake to redefine them. Yet philosophical writings, no less than drama, defy our attempts to fasten down their viewpoints. Plato, for example, conveniently detaches himself from his arguments by expressing them in the form of dialogues in which he does not appear himself. Nevertheless, their theories about statecraft are evidence for the debate among the intellectual elite over the viability of democracy as they knew it in their day.

Varied aspects of Athenian public and private life in the fourth century are made vivid to us by the dozens of extant speeches. Lysias, Andocides, Isocrates, and Demosthenes were among the influential politician-orators (*rhētores*) who composed speeches for delivery in the law courts and the popular assembly.

Because they were constructed to dazzle their audiences and persuade them with clever rhetoric, the "facts" brought forth in their arguments (e.g., the wording of a particular law) must be regarded with some skepticism. Demosthenes (384–322 BC) was most famous for his "Philippics," orations against the ruler of Macedon, Philip II, who was then threatening to become the master of all the Greek states.

323–30 BC

The conquests of Philip's son, Alexander III (the "Great"), extended as far as the borders of India. Curiously, the huge number of books written about Alexander after his death in 323 BC survive only in fragments. We are left with five ancient biographies—Plutarch's *Life of Alexander* is one—written three hundred to five hundred years later and thus subject to the biases of their own times. The sources for Alexander's successors, who ruled over the various parts of the huge empire, are equally scanty. Except for Diodorus' account (first century BC) of the final decades of the fourth century and scraps of other later writings that yield some information about the two generations after Alexander, little else remains to tell their story.

Fortunately, ample sources exist that illuminate everyday life and the administrative, military, and economic apparatus of the various Hellenistic kingdoms. In Egypt, for example, numerous inscriptions and thousands of public and private documents preserved on papyrus record all aspects of urban and village life. Among the papyri we find private letters, marriage contracts, wills, tax assessments, and records of legal proceedings.

New philosophies such as Stoicism and Epicureanism (whose precepts are preserved in later sources) offered advice on how to cope with the sense of dislocation produced by this vastly enlarged, culturally diverse universe. Not surprisingly, the surviving works of the Hellenistic poets Callimachus, Theocritus, and Apollonius of Rhodes expressed a double urge: to re-create the past so that it conformed to the needs of a complex world and at the same time to preserve the past exactly as it was.

THE PHYSICAL CONTEXT: THE LAND OF GREECE

The material and written sources are only part of the story, however. History does not occur in a vacuum, but in particular places. Greek historians, therefore, must also consider the character of the land of Greece itself, for the natural environment of a people—the landscape, the climate, and the natural resources—is a major factor in determining the way they live and how they develop socially. *Hellas*, the homeland of the Greeks, ancient and modern, covers the southern portion of the Balkan peninsula and the islands that lie to the west and east of the mainland. The Greek islands to the east, in the Aegean Sea, are numerous; some are closer to the coast of Anatolia (modern Turkey) than to the mainland. The largest Greek island, Crete, lies to the south, about midway between the Greek mainland and North Africa. A place of myth and legend, Crete will have a prominent role in the early part of our narrative.

In terms of square miles, Greece is about the size of England in Great Britain or the state of Alabama (c. 51,000 square miles) in the United States. The landscape is very rugged, with mountains covering almost 75 percent of the land. Only about 30 percent of the land can be cultivated at all, and only about 20 percent is classified as good agricultural land. Except in the northern mainland, where there are extensive plains, the mountains and lower hills cut the land into many narrow coastal plains, and upland plains and valleys. Except for Mt. Olympus in Thessaly (nearly 10,000 feet), the mountain ranges are not terribly high (3,000–8,000 feet), but they are quite steep and craggy, which made overland travel in antiquity difficult and somewhat isolated the small valleys and their people from one another.

By far the easiest way to travel was by sea, especially in the islands and the southern mainland, where the coast is never more than forty miles away. The chains of islands in the Aegean Sea facilitated sea voyages. Although the coastlines of the mainland and the islands are generally quite rugged, sailors could usually find a safe landfall where they could beach their boats for the night or wait out a threatening storm. The few locations that offered a good harbor became ports early on, destinations for the exchange of trade goods. Throughout antiquity, the narrow Aegean tied the Greeks to the Near East and Egypt, commercially, culturally, politically, and militarily. The commercial contacts were vital, for with the exception of building stone and clay, Greece is not well endowed with raw materials. The necessity to trade overseas for raw materials, especially for bronze, destined the Greeks very early in their history to take to the sea and mingle with people from the other, older civilizations to the east and south.

The Mediterranean climate is semiarid, with long, hot, dry summers and short, cool, moist winters when most of the rain falls. This general pattern varies from region to region in Greece. Northern Greece has a more continental climate, with much colder and wetter winters than the south. More rain falls on the western side of the Greek mainland than on the eastern side, and the Aegean islands receive even less. The generally mild weather permitted outdoor activity for most of the year. The soil in Greece, although rocky, is fairly rich, the most fertile plowland being in the small plains where, over the ages, earth washed down from the hills has formed deep deposits. The lower hillsides, which are rockier, can be cultivated through terracing, which prevents the soil from washing farther down the slope and captures soil from above. The mountains, with their jagged limestone peaks and steep cliffs, support only wild vegetation, but some enclose mountain valleys suitable for farming and grazing animals. Wood, essential for fuel and construction, especially shipbuilding, was originally abundant in the highland areas. As time went on, however, forests became depleted, and by the fifth century BC the more populous regions were forced to import timber. Water, the most precious natural resource, is scarce in Greece, because there are very few rivers that flow year-round and few lakes, ponds, and springs. Unlike in the huge river valleys of Egypt and Mesopotamia, irrigation on a large scale was not possible; farming depended on the limited annual rainfall.

It should be emphasized that this description of the land and resources of Greece is a generalized one. Although small in area, Greece has a variety of local landscapes and microclimates in which the rainfall and the quantity and quality of farmland, pastureland, and raw materials are decidedly different. On the whole, however, the land, which the Greeks called *Gaia* ("Mother Earth"), allowed the majority of the farmers a decent although modest living, but she offered no guarantees. Drought, especially in the more arid regions, was a constant and dreaded threat. A dry winter meant a lean year, and a prolonged drought meant hunger and poverty for entire villages and districts. Torrential rainstorms, on the other hand, could send water rushing down the hillsides and through the dry gullies, suddenly wiping out the terraces, flooding the fields, and destroying the crops. Life on the sea was equally unpredictable. The Aegean, although often calm with favoring winds, could just as suddenly boil up into ferocious storms, sending ships, cargo, and sailors to the bottom. (Drowning at sea, unburied, was a hateful death for the Greeks.) It is no wonder, considering the extent to which the Greeks were at the mercy of the land, sky, and sea, that the gods they worshiped included personifications of the elements and forces of nature.

Food and Livestock

In general, the soil and climate amply supported the "Mediterranean triad" of grain, grapes, and olives. Bread, wine, and olive oil were the staples of the Greek diet throughout antiquity and for long afterward. Grains—wheat, barley, and oats—grow well in Greek soil, having been cultivated from native wild grasses. Olive trees and grapevines, also indigenous to Greece, flourished in their cultivated state. Legumes (peas and beans) and several kinds of vegetables, fruits (especially figs), and nuts rounded out and varied the basic components of bread, porridges, and olive oil. Cheese, meat, and fish, which are rich in proteins and fat, supplemented the diet. Meat, however, provided a very small part of the average family's daily food intake and was consumed primarily at feasts and festivals. The Greeks did not care for butter and drank little milk. Their beverages were water or wine (usually diluted with water). Honey was used for sweetening, and various spices enhanced the flavor of food. Although it might appear monotonous to modern tastes, the Greek diet was healthful and nourishing.

The pasturing of small animals did not interfere with agriculture. Flocks of sheep and goats grazed on hilly land that could not be farmed and on the fallow fields, providing manure in return. As suppliers of wool, cheese, meat, and skins, these small animals had great economic importance. The Greeks also kept pigs, relished for their meat, and fowl. The two largest domesticated animals, horses and cattle, occupied a special niche in the economy and the society. Oxen (castrated bulls) or mules (hybrids of the horse and donkey) were necessary for plowing and for drawing heavy loads. A farmer without ready access to a yoke of oxen or a pair of mules would be classified as poor. Herds of cattle and horses did compete with agriculture, as the stretches of good grazing land they required were also prime farmland. Practically speaking, there could be large-scale ranching of cattle and horses (except in the northern plains) only in times of low population density. Because they require so much in the way of resources, only the wealthy could afford the luxury of keeping cattle and horses in large numbers. As the most prestigious animals for sacrifices and feasts, cattle were a status symbol for the rich. Horses, though, were the prime markers of high rank: beautiful creatures, very expensive to maintain, and useful only for riding and for pulling light chariots.

This agricultural and pastoral way of life remained essentially unchanged throughout antiquity. The fundamental economic fact that ancient Greece was essentially a land of small-scale farmers (most of whom lived in farming villages and small towns) governed every aspect of Greek society, from politics to war to religion. It has been estimated that even in the fifth to third centuries BC, the peak population periods, possibly as many as 80 to 90 percent of the male citizens of a city-state were engaged in agriculture in some degree while their wives worked inside the house. One of the major unifying forces within the Greek city-states was the citizen-farmers' devotion to their small agricultural plain and its surrounding hillsides and their willingness to die defending their "ancestral earth," as the poet Homer called it. The primary disunifying force throughout Greek history was the perpetual tension between those citizens who had much land and those who had little or none.

SUGGESTED READINGS

Bodel, John, ed. 2001. *Epigraphic Evidence: Ancient History from Inscriptions*. London: Routledge. Collection of essays concerning the value of epigraphic evidence for reconstructing the history of Greece and Rome.

Easterling, P. E. and E. J. Kenney, eds. 1985. *The Cambridge History of Classical Literature*. Cambridge, UK: Cambridge University Press. Separate chapters on individual authors and genres by distinguished critics cover the entirety of ancient Greek literature, from Homer to the period of the Roman Empire.

Erskine, Andrew, ed. 2009. *A Companion to Ancient History*. Oxford, UK: Blackwell. Forty-nine articles by leading historians surveying the basic approaches and themes of ancient history.

Hedrick, Charles W., Jr. 2005. *Ancient History: Monuments and Documents*. Oxford, UK: Blackwell. Lucid introduction to the sources used by ancient historians and how to analyze them.

Luce, T. J. 1997. *The Greek Historians*. London: Routledge. Brief introduction to the major ancient Greek historians and their works.

Morley, Neville. 1999. *Writing Ancient History*. Ithaca, NY: Cornell University Press. Introduction to the methods and goals of contemporary ancient historiography.

———. 2000. *Ancient History: Key Themes and Approaches*. London: Routledge. Useful survey of the principal concepts and theories of contemporary ancient historiography.

Renfrew, Colin and Paul Bahn. 1991. *Archaeology: Theories, Methods, and Practice*. New York: Thames and Hudson. Comprehensive introduction to the discipline of archaeology today: what it is, what it does, and how it is done.

Runnels, Curtis and Priscilla M. Murray. 2001. *Greece Before History: An Archaeological Companion and Guide*. Stanford, CA: Stanford University Press. A brief history of the archaeology of Greece from the Old Stone Age to the end of the Bronze Age, written by experts for the general reader.

van Andel, Tjerd and Curtis Runnels. 1987. *Beyond the Acropolis: A Rural Greek Past*. Stanford, CA: Stanford University Press. A description of the topography, flora, fauna, and subsistence strategies of ancient Greek farming life.

CHAPTER ONE

Early Greece and the Bronze Age

Before the late nineteenth century, when archaeologists unearthed three famous cities from the mythical Age of Heroes, no one knew that advanced civilizations had existed in the Aegean during the Bronze Age. First, in 1871, came the excavations of **Heinrich Schliemann** in Turkey. An eccentric German businessman-turned-archaeologist, Schliemann rejected the view prevalent among scholars of his day who dismissed the Greeks' war against Troy as just another mythical tale. Convinced that the Trojan War had actually taken place just as it was recounted in the *Iliad* and the *Odyssey*, the early epic poems attributed to Homer, Schliemann followed the advice of Frank Calvert, a British diplomat and experienced amateur archaeologist, who had already conducted trial excavations at Hissarlik, on the northwest coast of Anatolia, and began large-scale diggings at the site. In 1872–1873 his labors bore fruit, revealing the massive ruins of a Bronze Age walled citadel, which he identified as the fabled Troy. The news electrified the scholarly world and captured the public's imagination. Schliemann's own imagination led to the adornment of his wife in the earrings and necklaces that were part of "Priam's Treasure" (Figure 1.1b).

Later scholarship showed that "Priam's Treasure" had been buried much earlier than Schliemann believed, but the fact remains: there really had been a Troy just where Homer said it was located!

In 1876, Schliemann turned to the site of Mycenae in southern Greece, which tradition held to be the city of King Agamemnon, the leader of the Greek siege of Troy. Because of Mycenae's importance in myth and, as we now know, in history, the Late Bronze Age in Greece (1600–1200 BC) is commonly referred to as the Mycenaean period. Oddly, although the site of Mycenae had been known

Figure 1.1a. German businessman-turned-archaeologist Heinrich Schliemann (1822–1890), excavator of Troy and Mycenae.

since antiquity, and some of its ruins were still above ground, no one had systematically excavated there. Here Schliemann's luck also held: almost immediately he discovered buildings and royal graves rich in gold. He apparently believed that he had found Agamemnon's death mask (although the story that he sent a telegram out to the King of Greece exclaiming, "I have gazed upon the face of Agamemnon!" is almost certainly fictitious). The pioneering Schliemann's finds are not themselves conclusive evidence of a large-scale war between Troy and Mycenae. Nevertheless, the impressive ruins unearthed at both sites (especially at Troy in the last 25 years), with their immense wealth in gold and other costly things, do prove correct the Greeks' memory of their Heroic Age as a time of fabulous wealth and splendor.

No less spectacular was **Sir Arthur Evans'** discovery in 1900 of a huge complex at **Cnossus** on the island of Crete. Evans became obsessed with the palace, and he spent much of his personal fortune on restoring significant portions of it. Although some of his restorations have been shown to be inaccurate, the size and magnificence of the palace gave credence to the legend that Cnossus had been the center of a powerful naval state. Evans called this first Aegean civilization

Figure 1.1b. Sophie Schliemann, née Sophia Engastromenou, decorated at Troy by pieces of "Priam's Treasure." See Plate IIa.

Figure 1.1c and d. Two of the gold masks found in early shaft graves at Mycenae. On the left is the mask Schliemann thought was Agamemnon's. Athens, National Archaeological Museum.

Minoan, after Minos, the mythical king of Cnossus, who lived, according to Homer, three generations before the Trojan War. Just as the **Mycenaean civilization** was associated with pioneering archaeological work by Heinrich Schliemann, the **Minoans** belonged to Arthur Evans, who built an ample personal residence for himself in Cnossus. Schliemann and Evans added more than a thousand years to the history of Greece and showed that the ancestors of the historical Greeks lived in a totally different world from that of classical Greece. But that was only the beginning. More than a century of additional work by numerous talented archaeologists—Greek and non-Greek—has extended the history of Greece back thousands of years farther and revealed that its history was even more remarkable and complex than Schliemann and Evans could have imagined.

When exactly did Greek history begin? In the third century BC, an anonymous Greek historian living on the island of Paros began his history in 1582 BC, when Greek tradition claimed that kings began to rule in Athens.

DOCUMENT 1.1

The Parian Marble (IG 12.5 444)

Set up publicly in a gymnasium where it could be easily read, the Parian Marble provided the citizens of Paros with a summary of Greek history from the earliest rulers to the author's own lifetime. The selections translated here include the origins of kingship at Athens and the reign of Deucalion, who was believed to have created the ancestors of the Greeks after the flood by throwing stones behind his back. These earliest entries are more myth than history; the flood myth, found all over the Greek world, was borrowed at an early date from the Near East.

From all kinds of records and common histories, I have recorded our times from the beginning, starting with Cecrops, who became the first king of Athens, until [*. . .] yanax was archon at Paros and Diognotus was archon at Athens. {264/3 BC}

   1. Since Cecrops became king of Athens and the place took the name Cecropia, which was previously called Actica from Actaeus, who was born from the earth, 1,318 years. {1582}

   2. Since Deucalion became king by Mt. Parnassus in Lycoreia, when Cecrops was king of Athens, 1,310 years. {1574}

   4. Since the flood in Deucalion's lifetime happened and Deucalion fled the rains from Lycoreia to Athens to the side of Cranaus and he laid the foundation of the temple of Zeus the Olympian and made sacrifice for safety, 1,265 years, when Cranaus was king of Athens. {1529}

   6. Since Hellen son of Deucalion became king of Phthiotis and the Hellenes took their name who were previously called Graeci and. . . ., when Amphictyon was King of Athens, 1,257 years. {1521}

*Square brackets indicate that the text is missing letters or words.

Until recently, modern historians preferred a more recent date, 776 BC, the year the Olympic games were founded. Despite these differences, however, there had been agreement that Greek history began with the appearance of reliable written records. Today, historians take a more radical view, for the archaeological revolution that Schliemann and Evans began has pushed the beginning of history back to about 40,000 years ago and revealed a history different from anything ancient and modern historians of Greece imagined.

Greece in the Stone Ages

Humans have lived in Greece for at least 40,000 years, since the Middle Paleolithic (Old Stone) Age. These early inhabitants lived mainly by hunting and some gathering of wild plants, using finely crafted tools and weapons of stone, wood, and bone. At the end of the Ice Age, when the glaciers that had covered much of Europe were receding (c. 12,000 BC), the climate of Greece warmed considerably; in the process, the landscape and its plants and animals evolved into their present forms. Evidence from a cave at Franchthi in the Peloponnesus shows that the inhabitants at the end of the Ice Age hunted red deer and smaller game; caught fish in the coastal waters; and gathered wild cereals, wild peas and beans, and nuts.

Early in the **Neolithic (New Stone) Age** (c. 7000 BC), the inhabitants began to cultivate domesticated plants; to use domesticated animals, which had been introduced from the Near East; and to weave cloth on a loom. Soon artisans began creating figurines in clay and marble of animals and human beings (mostly females) and elegantly shaped, brightly decorated pottery. Agriculture allowed people to settle down permanently. Small farming villages sprang up made of one-room, mud-brick houses similar to those of the Near East. Under the favorable conditions of the warm New Stone Age, villages grew larger and new village communities were formed.

The society of the small Stone Age villages was probably egalitarian, with no inequality outside of sex, age, and skill. Families cooperated and shared with their neighbors, most of whom were kinfolk. Leadership was probably temporary, assumed now by this man, now by another, as the need for a decisive voice arose. With the growth of population, however, a more lasting leadership role emerged. Anthropologists call such a leader the "big man" or the "head man," the one who is better at "getting things done." His wisdom, courage, generosity, skill in solving disputes, and similar qualities propel him to the forefront and keep him there as long as people have confidence in him. In time, this position becomes a sort of "office" into which a new man, having demonstrated that he is better suited than other would-be leaders, steps when the old head man retires or dies (or is pushed out).

Greece in the Early and Middle Bronze Ages (c. 3000–1600 bc)

Nearly four thousand years after the adoption of agriculture, another fundamental technological innovation was introduced into the villages of Greece: bronze. Neolithic craftsmen in southeastern Europe and western Asia were already skilled at smelting and casting copper, but because it is a soft metal, its usefulness was limited. The pivotal step of adding 10 percent tin or arsenic to copper to produce bronze, a much harder metal, was taken in the Near East during the fourth millennium and arrived in Greece about 3000 BC. This was a momentous technical advance, for tools and weapons of bronze were considerably more efficient than those made of stone, bone, or copper. By 2500 BC, metal workers in Greece and the Balkans had mastered not only the use of bronze, but other metals such as lead, silver, and gold. High-ranked families, those with greater surpluses of wealth, would have had the greatest access to scarce metals and metal products. Possession of these and other prestige items further distinguished them from the mass of the population. Their increasing demand for metal goods created a need for more specialists and workshops and accelerated trade for copper, tin, and other metals throughout the Mediterranean region. As the economy expanded and the settlements grew larger, so did the wealth, power, and authority of their

Figure 1.2. Cycladic marble figurine of a male figure playing double pipes from Keros (c. 2500–2200 BC). This highly abstracted human image was once enlivened with painted details. Athens, National Archaeological Museum.

leaders, now probably established as hereditary chiefs ruling for life and accorded exceptional honors and privileges.

The Civilizations of the Near East

In contrast to Greece and the Balkans in the Early **Bronze Age** (c. 3000–2100 BC), the Near East had already progressed to that higher level of organization of the natural and social environment termed "civilization." The Aegean civilizations of **Crete** and mainland Greece, as we shall see, owed their rise in the second millennium to their close contact with the palace kingdoms of the East.

Around 3500 BC in the wide fertile plain the Greeks named Mesopotamia, "the land between the rivers" Tigris and Euphrates (in what is now southern Iraq), there appeared, for the first time in history, the markers of civilization: large-scale irrigation, cities with thousands of inhabitants, bureaucratic government, wide trade networks, written documents, legal systems, and science. Egyptian civilization, which arose around 3200 BC along the long, narrow valley of the Nile, followed a trajectory similar to that of Mesopotamia, except that very early on it became a united kingdom under a single ruler, the pharaoh.

In Mesopotamia, however, and in the rest of western Asia, societies evolved in the form of discrete polities centered around great cities that drew the surrounding towns and villages into a single political unit—the city-state—administered from the capital. During the third millennium the more powerful city-states conquered their weaker neighbors, giving rise to territorial kingdoms that were ascendant for a time, only to be conquered in turn by rival kingdoms.

Within individual kingdoms society was highly stratified; the population was dependent on and subject to an elite ruling class, headed by a hereditary monarch. The kings and the high nobles—deploying a huge amount of surplus wealth from agriculture, manufacture, and trade and millions of hours of human labor—built massive defensive walls and temples, as well as luxurious palaces and elaborate tombs for themselves and their families. Art and architecture especially served religion, which became the most important means of control, for it connected the will of the ruler with the will of the gods. Vast wealth and increased population allowed the frequent wars of conquest and retribution to be fought on a huge scale by well-organized armies.

These early civilizations would exercise a profound influence on the political and cultural development of the Greeks; and increasingly, as time went on, the histories of the Near Eastern and Aegean peoples became more and more entwined.

The First Greek Speakers

Although far less politically and technologically sophisticated than the Near East, Greece attained a fairly high level of social complexity during its Early Bronze Age. The remains of **Lerna** in Argolis, for example, show that it was a large town with stone fortification walls and monumental buildings, of which the largest (83 feet by 40 feet), known as the House of the Tiles, had two stories, a corridor along

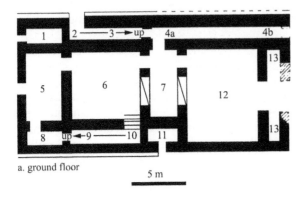

a. ground floor

5 m

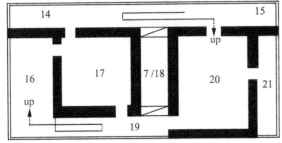

b. upper floor

Figure 1.3. Plan of the House of the Tiles at Lerna (c. 2200 BC). Note the several access points from the outside. It is uncertain exactly what the building was used for, but there are several examples of this building type to be found at this time on the mainland.

one side, a monumental entrance as well as several sections accessible only from the exterior, and a roof of tiles rather than thatch. (See plan in Figure 1.3.) The "corridor house" is a distinctive type that has also been found at at least three other sites on the mainland at this time. Archaeologists speculate that it served several functions: as the dwelling of the chief and his family, as a feasting hall, and also as a place for communal storage; the corridor houses are clear signs of sociopolitical hierarchy, as larger towns came to dominate surrounding villages and hamlets. Toward the end of this period (c. 2250 BC), Lerna and similar sites in southern and central Greece were destroyed. Many historians associate the destruction and the cultural stagnation that followed during the Middle Bronze Age (c. 2100–1600 BC) with the incursion of a new people, who spoke an early form of Greek. That dating is by no means certain, however, and the questions of when the first Greek speakers arrived and the route they took remain open today.

More certain is that the newcomers were part of a great and lengthy ancient migration of peoples, known collectively as the **Indo-Europeans**. In the late eighteenth century AD, Sir William Jones, a British official in India, observed that ancient Greek bears many similarities to other ancient languages, such as Latin and Sanskrit (the language of ancient India), as well as to entire families of spoken languages, such as the Germanic and Slavic. Take for example our word "mother": Greek *mētēr*, Latin *māter*, Sanskrit *māta* (stem *mātar-*), Anglo-Saxon *mōdor*, Old Irish *mathir*, Lithuanian *mote*, and Russian *mat'* (stem *māter*).

The close likenesses in vocabulary and grammar among these ancient languages and their descendants led scholars to conclude that they had all sprung from a common linguistic ancestor, which they termed "Proto-Indo-European." A current hypothesis is that Greek and the other Indo-European languages evolved during the long waves of emigrations from an original Indo-European homeland, located perhaps in the vast steppes north of the Black and Caspian seas. Over the course of many centuries (beginning perhaps in the fourth millennium BC) the Indo-European languages spread across Europe and Asia, from Ireland to Chinese Turkestan and into the Indian subcontinent.

The Greeks

Eventually, the Greek language completely submerged the non-Indo-European "Aegean" languages. The relatively few words that survived from the old language were chiefly names of places (e.g., Korinthos, Parnassos) and of native plants and animals, such as *hyakinthos* ("hyacinth") and *melissa* ("bee"). During the nineteenth century of our era, there was considerable conjecture about the social organization and culture of the Indo-Europeans. Many assumed that they were a superior race of horse-riding "Aryan" warriors who swept into southern Europe and obliterated the cultures of the weak, unwarlike, agrarian natives. No scholar today accepts this myth of Aryan superiority that was the pretext for so many crimes against humanity in the nineteenth and twentieth centuries, culminating in the horrors perpetrated by the Nazis and Fascists in the 1930s and 1940s. The imposition of their language does suggest that the Greek speakers came in as conquerors and initially dominated the indigenous populations. It is likely, however, that by the end of the Middle Bronze Age, the two peoples had merged into a single people and their two cultures had fused into a single Hellenic culture that contained elements of both. This development was easier because the newcomers were not wild horse-riding nomads, fresh out of the steppes, as they were once portrayed to be (although they likely introduced horses to Greece). Like the indigenous peoples, they subsisted as herders and farmers and practiced metallurgy and other crafts, such as pottery and cloth making. Indo-European society was patrilineal (descent is reckoned from the father, *patēr* in Greek) and patriarchal (the father is the supreme authority figure, and political power is in male hands).

The Minoans

First settled around 7000 BC by Neolithic farmers and stock raisers, who may have come from Anatolia and spoke a non-Indo-European language, Crete followed the regional path of slow growth helped along by technological innovation. During the fourth millennium, some of the small farming villages had grown into large towns. Eventually, the chiefs of these early centers emerged as leaders over other chiefs and people in their districts. Thus Crete became a land of small city-kingdoms.

   The earliest large, multiroom complex with a central courtyard (which Evans named the "Palace of Minos") was built about 1900 BC at Cnossus, by then a town

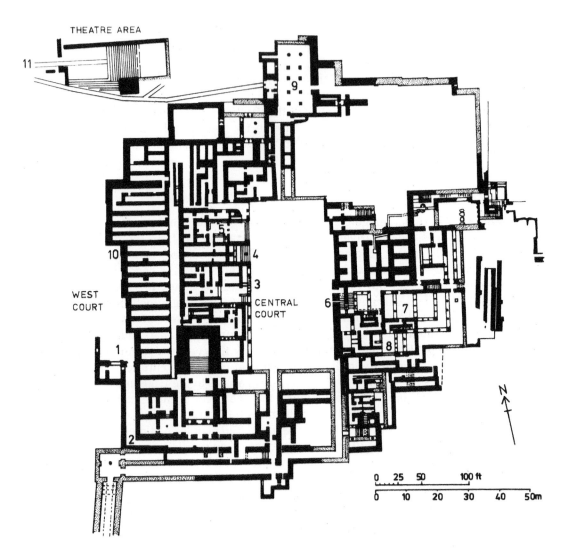

THEATRE AREA

11

9

10

4

3

WEST
COURT

CENTRAL
COURT

6

7

1

8

2

N

0   25   50   100 ft
0   10   20   30   40   50m

The Palace at Cnossus

1 West Porch
2 Corridor of the Procession
3 Palace Shrine
4 Stepped porch
5 Throne Room
6 Grand Staircase

7 Hall of the Double Axes
8 'Queen's Megaron'
9 Pillar Hall
10 Store-rooms
11 Royal Road, to Little Palace

Figure 1.4a. Plan of the Minoan palace at Cnossus, Crete (c. 1400 BC).

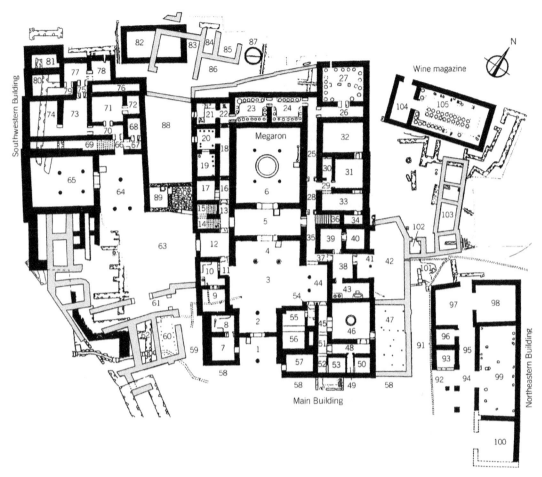

Figure 1.4b. Plan of the Mycenaean palace at Pylos (c. 1200 BC). Note the distinctive megaron in the center of the complex, in contrast to the open central court at Cnossus.

with several thousand inhabitants. Other major palaces, not as grand as Cnossus, followed at Phaistos, Mallia, Zakro, and elsewhere, each center controlling an area of a few hundred square miles. The political and cultural flowering in Crete (and on other Aegean islands as well) probably can be attributed to their involvement in international trade. The island's location and natural harbors made it an important crossroad in the trade routes across the Mediterranean Sea. The palace-centered economies that emerged in Crete were replicas, on a much smaller scale, of the economies of the Near Eastern states. It has not been established, however, whether Cnossus ever became the center of a unified island-wide kingdom or was the largest and most powerful among a number of self-ruling states.

The Cnossian palace we see today was built around 1700 BC, after the first palace was destroyed by an earthquake. Cnossus and the other smaller Cretan palaces consisted of a maze of rooms—residential quarters, workshops, and storerooms—clustered around a large central courtyard (Figure 1.4a). This impressive residence of the ruler and a few high-ranking subordinates was the political, economic, and administrative center and indeed the focal point of state ceremony and religious ritual for the entire kingdom. The population at Cnossus at its height has been estimated at 17,000 persons.

The palace economies were based on storage and redistribution. Food and other products from the palace's lands and from private farms and herds, paid as taxes, were collected and stored in the palace. The income both sustained the palace and its crafts workers and was redistributed back to the villagers as rations and wages. The palace's reserves of grain and olive oil could also be distributed to the population during famines. Another use of the royal surplus, however, was for trade. Produce and goods manufactured in the palace went out on ships along the wide Mediterranean trade network in exchange for goods from foreign lands, especially metal and luxury items.

To administer their complicated economies the Cretans developed a writing system (in a script Evans named **Linear A**) comprised of specific signs that stood for the sounds of spoken words and syllables. Linear A writing, preserved on small clay tablets found on Crete but also in other Aegean islands, remains untranslated. It is clear, however, that its main purpose was for keeping economic and administrative records.

As in the Near East, there was an enormous gulf between the ruling class and the people. The multitude of ordinary Cretan farmers and crafts workers paid for the opulent lifestyles of the few with their labor and taxes, while they themselves lived very modestly, in small mud-brick houses clustered together in the towns and villages. To be sure, the people received benefits in the form of protection from famine and from outside aggressors, but their compliance with the rigid hierarchy suggests something more—a positive identification with the center, that is, the king. In Crete, as in all ancient civilizations, whoever was in power or the head of state was a symbol as well as the actual political leader. He was the embodiment of the state: supreme war leader, lawgiver, and judge and, most important, the intermediary between gods and the land and people.

Minoan Art and Architecture

Minoan art and architecture owe a large debt to the civilizations of the Near East, and especially **Egypt**, as they even adapted Egyptian conventions for depicting the human form to Minoan tastes. Yet, even as the Minoans borrowed extensively from the techniques and styles of the older civilizations, the Cretans developed their own distinctive style and spirit. Visitors to the ruins of Cnossus are dazzled by its size and complexity—the palace covered 3.2 acres with perhaps three hundred rooms—and the elegance of its architecture.

The palace was constructed of stone and mud brick and stood two and three stories high with basements beneath. Numerous porticoes, balconies, and loggias, all brightly painted, gave the exterior a theatrical look. Light wells brought daylight and fresh air into the interior of the palace. A system of conduits and drains provided many of the rooms with running water and waste disposal. On the walls and passageways there were brilliantly colored depictions of plant and animal life and scenes of human activity, often religious processions or rituals. Similar subjects and motifs are found not only at other Cretan palaces but also in wealthy private homes in the towns and villages. One scene that was particularly associated with the palace was bull-leaping, in which lithe young men and women jumped over charging bulls.

Minoan art is much admired today for its sophistication, vitality, and exuberance. The frescoes, vase paintings, and small sculptures give us a glimpse into how the inhabitants of the palaces and villas saw themselves. Both men and women are represented as youthful, slender, and graceful. The men are smooth shaven and wear only a short kilt, similar to the Egyptian male dress. The women are shown wearing elaborate flounced skirts and a tight, sleeved bodice that exposes their breasts. Both men and women have long hair, stylishly curled, and wear gold bracelets and necklaces.

A remarkable example of Minoan cultural influence was discovered in 1967 at Akrotiri on the small island of **Thera** (modern Santorini), north of Crete. A prosperous city of several thousand inhabitants, Akrotiri was destroyed by a powerful volcanic eruption around 1628 BC, which preserved it, nearly intact, under a deep layer of volcanic ash. Its remains show how extensively the Therans absorbed Cretan art, architecture, religion, dress, and lifestyles into their own island culture. (See Plate III.) Nevertheless, the distinctly "local" features in the architecture, urban layout, wall paintings, and pottery manufacture on Thera and the other Cycladic islands suggest that they were independent societies, trading partners, not colonial outposts of a Cretan empire.

Greece and the Aegean in the Late Bronze Age (c. 1600–1200 bc)

Cretan influence also extended to southern and central Greece by way of trading contacts, which began as early as 2000 BC. That relationship played a major role in the development of the Mycenaean Greek civilization. The Greeks did not just borrow individual elements from the Minoan cultural repertoire; they even adopted wholesale the model of the Cretan state, right down to the writing system. When they had become powerful in their own right, however, the Mycenaeans repaid their teachers by invading Crete and taking over the Cretan palace centers. Then their civilization, too, came crashing down at the end of the Late Bronze Age.

The Early Mycenaeans (c. 1600–1400 bc)

During the course of the Middle Bronze Age, Greece was gradually transformed. In the Peloponnesus and other areas of mainland Greece, population rose, productivity increased, and trade with the outside expanded, all of which led to a further strengthening of the economic and political power of the leaders. Warrior chiefs were now evolving into monarchs.

Hundreds of Bronze Age settlements have been found in mainland and island Greece, many of which can be identified by name from the ancient legends. Archaeology has confirmed that the famous mainland cities of epic poetry—such as Mycenae, Tiryns, Pylos, Thebes, and Athens—were in fact the major Bronze Age centers. Their grand palaces, however, were not built until the fourteenth and thirteenth centuries, over the remains of older, less imposing structures. Accordingly, what we know of the early stage of the **Mycenaean civilization** (roughly 1600–1400 BC) is revealed chiefly through graves and the offerings interred with the bodies of the deceased men, women, and children.

In **Mycenae**, these **shaft graves**—deep rectangular pits into which the bodies were lowered—cover more than a century of burials, from a little before 1600 to about 1500. The earlier graves yielded many bronze weapons (swords, daggers, spearheads, and knives) and quantities of local pottery, but little gold or jewelry. By comparison, a single later grave, containing the bodies of three men and two women, held an arsenal of weapons (43 swords, for example) and hundreds of other expensive objects, including gold jewelry adorning the corpses of the women. The increase in luxury imports during this period—from Crete, Cyprus, Egypt, Mesopotamia, Syria, Anatolia, and western Europe—attests both to the growth of Mycenaean trade and to greater control by the ruling class over the economy and the society. Around 1500 BC the noble families began to inter their dead in the more impressive *tholos* tomb, a very large stone chamber, shaped like a beehive. With their high corbel vaulted interiors and long stone entrance-ways, the *tholoi* (plural) were conspicuous signs of the ever-increasing power and resources of the leaders (Figures 1.5b and c.).

Shortly after the tholos tombs came into fashion, Greeks from the mainland gained control of Crete, destroying a majority of the palace centers but leaving Cnossus mostly intact. Wealthy Crete was a juicy prize and the Mycenaeans had

a

Figure 1.5a. A bronze dagger inlaid with a scene of a lion hunt, from shaft grave IV at Mycenae. Athens, National Archaeological Museum.

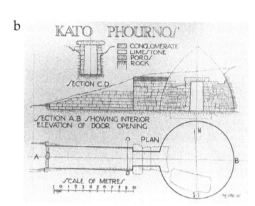

Figure 1.5b. Plan and cross-section of a Mycenaean tholos tomb.

Figure 1.5c. Interior vault of a tholos tomb at Mycenae (the so-called Treasury of Atreus).

come to stay. This takeover, however, which occurred around 1490 BC, probably did not bring great changes in Cretan society and culture. Life under their new Greek rulers went on much as before, except that now they paid their taxes to kings who spoke Greek. The new kings ruled and lived in the manner of Cretan kings, although they did keep to certain mainland ways, for example, their burial rites.

Their prosperity, however, was short-lived. Around 1375 BC, Cnossus was burned and looted; and although the ruined palace continued to be occupied, Mycenaean Crete sank in importance as Mycenae and the other mainland centers reached the zenith of their prosperity and influence in the Aegean. It is not known who destroyed Cnossus and set off the irreversible decline of the Cretan economy and culture. The most likely suspects are other mainland Mycenaeans lured by the riches of the Cretan palaces and perhaps eager to get rid of their biggest rival in the Mediterranean trade.

The Linear B Tablets

We know that it was Greeks who took over Crete in 1490 BC because of the work of **Michael Ventris**, an amateur linguist who served as a cryptographer during World War II. As we saw earlier, the Minoans had devised a writing system made up of linear signs incised on clay tablets, which they used to keep palace records. The archaeologist Evans had discovered a few tablets with this script at Cnossus, but he also found three thousand clay tablets inscribed with a more elaborate version of the linear script, which he named **Linear B** to differentiate it from the earlier Linear A script. He assumed without question that the language of both was Cretan. The discovery in 1939 of an archive room full of Linear B tablets in the Mycenaean palace of **Pylos** on the Greek mainland seemed to strengthen Evans' theory that mainland Greece had been controlled by the Minoans throughout the Late Bronze Age.

In the 1950s, however, Ventris broke the code. Building on the work of earlier scholars such as the American Alice Kober, Ventris demonstrated that the language of the Linear B tablets was not in fact Cretan, but an early form of Greek. With more than four thousand tablets to work with, he and other linguists were able gradually to obtain the phonetic values of the signs. For example, a combination of three signs—*ti-ri-po*—yields the syllabic equivalent of the Greek word *tripous*, "tripod." This reading was supported by the fact that these signs on one of the tablets were accompanied by a drawing of a tripod cauldron. Today, the Linear B inscriptions have given up many of their secrets. The decipherment of Linear B has illuminated not only the historical relationship between Greece and Crete but also the workings of the Mycenaean palace system and has confirmed that the Mycenaean palaces were ruled by kings.

The Later Mycenaeans (c. 1400–1200 BC)

The palace complexes whose ruins we see today were built in the fourteenth and thirteenth centuries, during the final phase of Mycenaean wealth and power. Their architecture and decoration closely imitated the Minoan style but with some notable differences. They were much smaller and, unlike the unfortified Cretan palaces, they were usually located on a commanding hill, encircled by high, thick walls. We may infer that protection from invasion by rival kingdoms was a primary concern of Mycenaean rulers. The walled citadels served also as a refuge for the inhabitants of the unfortified towns below. (At Mycenae, the eighty-acre town at the foot of the citadel was home to about 6,400 persons.) Later Greeks called them Cyclopean walls, as though they had been built by the mythical race of giant Cyclopes. Indeed, such massive works were probably as much a boast of the king's wealth and power as they were a defense for his palace and people.

The Mycenaeans also utilized space within their palaces differently from the Minoans. In place of the open central courtyard of the Cretan complexes, they made the focus of their palaces the **megaron**, a large rectangular hall (Figures 1.4b and 1.6b). The megaron was the ceremonial center used for feasts, councils, and receptions of visitors. One entered it through a courtyard, which led into a portico and a small anteroom. In the middle of the great hall stood a large, raised circular hearth, flanked by four columns that supported an open balcony. The megaron room would survive in the form of a chieftain's house during the long Dark Age that followed and as the essential plan of the Greek temple from the eighth century onward. Although Mycenaean palaces had fewer rooms and lacked

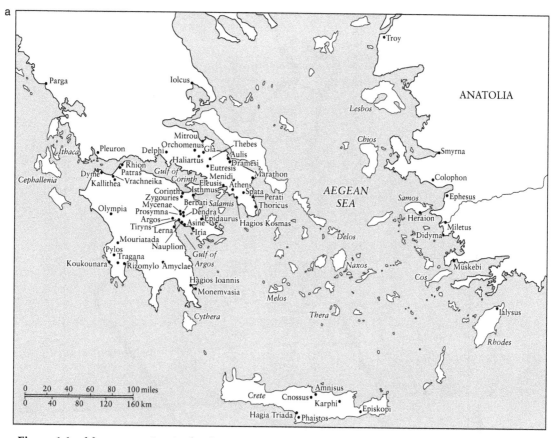

Figure 1.6a. Mycenaean sites in the thirteenth century BC.

some of the architectural embellishments of their Cretan counterparts, they offered such Minoan amenities as indoor plumbing and beautiful wall paintings. The frescoes are completely Minoan in style, although they show a preference for martial themes, such as personal combats, sieges, and hunting scenes.

Despite their cultural similarities, the Mycenaeans were not unified politically but were divided into separate small kingdoms. Moreover, they were relatively few in number compared to the vast populations of the **Hittite empire**, which covered Anatolia and Syria, and of Egypt during its brilliant and aggressive "New Kingdom" period (c. 1575–1087 BC). Yet despite their political fragmentation, the Mycenaeans appear to have been a significant presence in the Mediterranean world. Archaeology points to the existence of Mycenaean colonies on a number of the Aegean islands and even at the sites of later Greek cities like Miletus in western Anatolia. Not surprisingly, inscriptions and finds of Aegean-style frescoes in Syria and Palestine also suggest that they had diplomatic relations with most of the powers of the region. Their closest contacts, however, were with the Hittite empire in Anatolia.

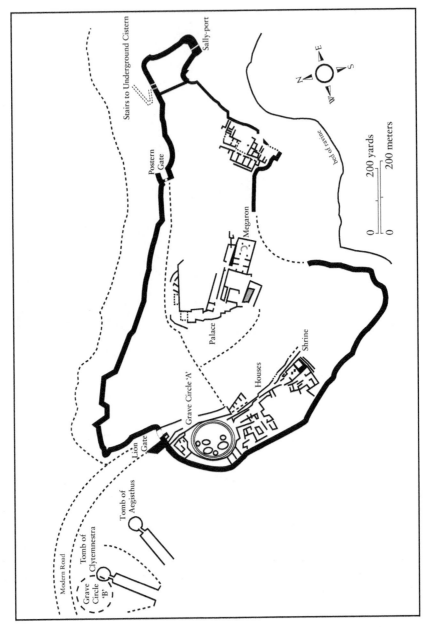

Figure 1.6b. Plan of the citadel at Mycenae. Note the distinctive megaron in the center of the complex. The "Lion Gate" is the western entrance.

Figure 1.6c. The "Lion Gate" entrance to the citadel of Mycenae.

The Hittite archives of the fourteenth and thirteenth centuries record diplomatic contacts and even military confrontations at various places in western Anatolia including possibly Troy between the Hittite kings and kings of a people they called "**Ahhiyawa**," which phonetically resembles "Achaeans," the most frequent name in the Homeric epics for the Greeks who conquered Troy—an event that, if true, would have occurred in the later thirteenth century. Mycenaean activity was not, however, limited to the Aegean basin. Mycenaean pottery and metalwork are found also in Egypt, Sicily, and southern Italy. It is quite possible, too, that a good portion of the immense wealth found in the graves and tombs of these warrior kings and nobles came not only from peaceful trade but also from the Mycenaeans' prowess as seafaring marauders.

The Administration of a Mycenaean Kingdom

A memorable figure for readers of the *Iliad* and the *Odyssey* is the aged warrior Nestor, who, Homer tells us, lived in a magnificent many-roomed house in a town called Pylos, from which he ruled over a large area of Messenia. The discovery of the "palace of Nestor" by the American archaeologist Carl Blegen in 1939 confirmed that the Pylos of the legends had been an actual Bronze Age center.

Figure 1.7a. A Linear B tablet from Mycenaean-ruled Cnossus. On this tablet we can see the numbering system: circles stand for hundreds, horizontal lines for tens, and vertical lines for units.

Figure 1.7b. Drawing of a chariot tablet from Cnossus recording the assignment of weaponry to a chariot warrior. The tablet, which contains the man's name written in Linear B syllabic signs followed by ideograms for his weapons, may be translated as follows: "To Opilimnios 1 corselet 1 wheeled chariot 1 horse."

Even more important was Blegen's find of large numbers of Linear B tablets. Clay tablets were not intended to be permanent records; they were preserved only because they were baked hard in the fires that destroyed the palace. What we have, in fact, are just scribes' temporary records from the final year of Pylos' existence. Yet these terse lists (supplemented by the Linear B tablets from Cnossus and other centers) tell us much about the economy and society of Mycenaean Greece.

Like other regional centers, Pylos reached its zenith between 1400 and 1200. Nestor's palace, which lay undisturbed since its destruction around 1200, had been built around 1300 over the ruins of an earlier, smaller complex of buildings. The kingdom of Pylos was large and highly organized. It contained around two hundred villages and towns, spread out over an area of about fourteen hundred square miles, and was divided into two "provinces," each subdivided into several "districts." The clay tablets give us some idea of Mycenaean social structures. At the apex of the pyramid stood the king (*wanax*). Next in rank, apparently, was the *lawagetas*, whose title may be loosely translated as "leader of the army." Below them was a large bureaucracy of military and administrative officers and minor officials who oversaw the functioning of the palace and the outlying areas.

The centralized production and distribution system ensured a luxurious standard of living for the highest officials and perhaps some portion of the minor ones. The majority of people, however, the ones who produced the wealth—the farmers, herders, artisans, and laborers—lived modestly, in small one- or two-room houses, with few luxuries. Many families farmed as tenants on land belonging to the nobles; others held plots of land in their own names. Craftsmen, herders, and priestesses, for example, are listed as "owners" of private land. Just as in later times, most agricultural producers lived in rural villages, whereas the majority of the crafts specialists were concentrated in the regional centers and the larger settlements. The palace strictly supervised production. Officials were sent out into the countryside for regular assessments, and the taxes in produce and animals levied on individuals and villages were meticulously recorded. One tablet from Mycenaean Cnossus reports "Men of Lyktos 246.7 units of wheat; men of Tylisos 261 units of wheat; men of Lato 30.5 units of wheat." Similarly, any deficiencies in the assessments were reported. The administrative reach of the palace was truly impressive: one set of Linear B documents at Cnossus, all entered in the handwriting of a single scribe, indicates the monitoring of about 100,000 sheep. This pervasive reach of the palace, however, does not mean that the free masses were oppressed peasants toiling in misery on the estates of the rich. The men of the village farmed their plots and tended to their trees, vines, and livestock; they paid their taxes, contributed some labor to the palace, and served in the army. The women performed the domestic tasks of spinning and weaving, food preparation, and child care. A number of the village women were also engaged as textile workers for the palace, for which they received rations of wool and flax.

The truly oppressed were the slaves. References to "captives" and "bought" show that the Mycenaean warrior aristocrats were active in the slavery business. Tablets from Pylos, for example, record more than six hundred slave women, along with their children, who labored as grinders of grain, bath attendants, flax workers, weavers, and so on. The gods and high-ranking individuals also owned slave workers. It is possible that some of the lowest-status workers on the tablets were not true slaves (i.e., foreigners captured or bought) but native individuals or families who, for whatever reasons, were reduced to a state of permanent dependence on the palace.

The palace complex was the hub of the kingdom's economy, employing large numbers of workers who turned raw materials into finished products for both domestic consumption and export. Tasks were highly specialized; women were engaged mostly in the textile sector, making cloth goods of wool and linen, whereas men were listed as carpenters, potters, metalsmiths, leather workers, perfume makers, and more. The wanax kept a close eye on the workshops and the storage areas, and his scribes scrupulously wrote down how much raw material the crafts specialists were given, the objects they produced, and the rations of food they received in return. Nothing escaped their attention. Dozens of entries go like this: "one ebony footstool inlaid with figures of men and a lion in ivory." Even chariot wheels are listed individually, and a note is made of their condition: "serviceable," or "unfit for use."

The leading exports were textiles and metalwork, to which we may add olive oil (both plain and perfumed), wine, hides, leather, and leather products. Fine pottery, jewelry, and other costly items also competed well in the international luxury trade. In return, the palaces imported things lacking in Greece, such as copper, tin, gold, ivory, amber, dyes, and spices as well as foreign varieties of items that they did have, such as wine and jewelry. Needless to say, few luxury goods made their way into the houses and graves of the common people.

Religion

The belief in supernatural forces and beings that control the natural world is probably as old as humankind. Nearly as old are cult and ritual—the acts of devotion

Figure 1.8a. Engraved gold ring from Minoan Cnossus showing women worshiping a goddess. These female figures with bare breasts wear the flounced skirts characteristic of Minoan dress. Heraclion, Archaeological Museum.

Figure 1.8b. A similar scene on a gold ring from Late Bronze Age Mycenae, indicating Minoan influence on Mycenaean religious rituals. Athens, National Archaeological Museum.

to the gods—and religious myths, the suppositions about the gods told in story form as part of ritual activity. Among agrarian peoples, the relationship of mortals to immortals revolves around the continuation of the fertility of the land, animals, and humans. To appease the gods, who can bestow or remove the blessings of nature at will, the people make communal displays of respect, including sacrifices of food and animals and even humans at times. The Minoans and Mycenaeans were no exception; they honored their gods with processions, music, and dance and propitiated them with gifts and sacrifices. The slaughter and butchering of animals on outdoor altars was the most solemn ritual. The Minoans may even have practiced human sacrifice during times of crisis.

In Minoan art the principal recipient of worship is a goddess, dressed in the Cretan style and placed in outdoor settings that feature trees and other vegetation and animals. Similar scenes appear on Mycenaean frescoes, vases, and gold and silver rings. The ubiquitous goddess figures depicted in Minoan-Mycenaean art are thought to be representations of an ancient Aegean mother goddess, who presided over nature and fertility. In that case, we must infer that the fertility goddesses brought in by the Indo-European speakers were assimilated into the artistic form of the Aegean nature mother.

There are, however, notable differences between Minoan and Mycenaean religious practices. For example, the Minoans frequently performed their rituals in caves and in sanctuaries built on mountain peaks, whereas the Mycenaean shrines are mainly confined to the palace centers. The Linear B tablets also reveal that the Mycenaeans worshipped many of the gods of later Greek religion, including Zeus, Hera, Poseidon, Hermes, Athena, Artemis, Dionysus, and possibly Apollo and Ares. Zeus, the supreme god of the later Greeks, is plainly the ancient Indo-European "sky-father" and was brought in by the earliest Greek speakers. *Zeus patēr*, "Zeus the father," is the same deity as the Sanskrit *Dyaus pitar* and Roman *Iuppiter*. The names of Hera, Poseidon, and Ares are also formed from Indo-European roots.

The palace was the center of religious activity. The gods, their sanctuaries, and their priests and priestesses received gifts of land, animals, and precious objects as well as human labor, which were requisitioned by the wanax from the people. A ruler with such coercive powers as the wanax could claim that his sovereignty was divinely sanctioned and that he was the special representative of the community to the gods. There is no evidence, however, to suggest that a wanax was considered divine either in his lifetime or after death or that he functioned as a priest king over a theocratic state, as in Egypt and Mesopotamia.

Warfare

The wanax was, above all, a warrior king, who took part in the fighting along with his military commander (lawagetas) and subordinate commanders. In fact, throughout ancient Greek history, most political leaders would also be the commanders-in-chief and many would meet death on the battlefield or on

a

b

Figure 1.9a. Bronze plate armor and boar's tusk helmet from Dendra in Argolis (c. 1400 BC). Nauplion, Museum.

Figure 1.9b. A vase from thirteenth-century Mycenae showing a line of ordinary soldiers on the march armed with helmets, shields, and long spears and a mourning woman who watches their departure. Athens, National Archaeological Museum.

the sea. Mycenaean warriors were heavily armored. Officers wore helmets of bronze or of boars' tusks, corselets of bronze plates, and bronze greaves (knee and shin protectors). The soldiers were equipped with leather and padded linen versions of these. All combatants carried large shields made of ox hide stretched over a wooden frame. Weapons were bronze swords and daggers, heavy thrusting spears and light throwing spears, bows and arrows, and slings. The Mycenaeans' most impressive weapon was the chariot. Scholars are still not certain whether the Greeks adopted the chariot from the Near East about 1600 BC or already had it when they first settled in Greece. A lightweight platform set atop two high, spoked wheels, and pulled by two horses, the chariot could carry two men for many miles at a pace previously unknown in land travel. Throughout the Near East, the chariot corps was the primary military arm, used for massed chariot charges against an enemy's chariots and infantry, one man driving and the other shooting arrows. Because the rough terrain of Greece is, however, unsuited for such tactics, many believe that the Mycenaeans employed chariots only to convey heavily armored elite warriors to and from the fighting. On the other hand, it is conceivable that small-scale versions of eastern chariot warfare took place on the plains that lay below the Mycenaean fortresses. In any case, the significance of the chariot was probably not so much its use in battle but rather its prestige value.

Like other material borrowings, such as the grand palaces and the tholos tombs, chariotry proclaimed the Mycenaean rulers to be the equals of the great kings of Asia and Egypt. Mycenaean art depicts the elite employing chariots also for hunting, racing, and ceremonial processions, as upper-class Greeks would for many centuries after the chariot had ceased to have any military function.

The End of the Mycenaean Civilization

At the apparent height of its prosperity, Mycenaean civilization suffered a fatal blow. Beginning a little before 1200 BC, almost all the palace centers and many of their outlying towns and villages were attacked and destroyed or abandoned. Order gave way to turbulence and restless wanderings. Many centers were never reoccupied after the initial devastation. Others recovered and even enjoyed a brief resurgence but soon succumbed to further attacks. A few, like Mycenae and Tiryns, lived on as small villages huddled below the ruined fortifications of their once-mighty palaces. By shortly after 1100, the Mycenaean kingdoms and the complex systems that had supported them no longer existed.

It was not just Mycenaean civilization that suffered: The entire eastern Mediterranean region was overwhelmed by catastrophe at this time. The mighty Hittite empire, which encompassed Anatolia and Syria, fell apart around 1200 BC, crushed by invaders from the north. Egypt was attacked several times by an assortment of warrior bands from all around the Mediterranean. Quite possibly Mycenaeans were among these marauders, who are referred to as the "sea peoples" in Egyptian records. It was also during this period that the fall of Troy occurred (c. 1250–1200). There is no way of knowing, however, whether those who besieged and burned the city were really the Mycenaean Greeks, as the legend of the Trojan War tells.

Until fairly recently it was thought that the Dorians were responsible for destroying and looting the Mycenaean palaces. The modern "Dorian invasion" hypothesis is largely based on the legends of later Doric speakers. Doric was one of the three main dialects of ancient Greek, spoken during historical times in the Peloponnesus, Crete and other Aegean islands, and parts of the Anatolian coast. Dorians claimed ancestry from the mythical hero Heracles (Hercules), whose sons, so the story went, were expelled from the Peloponnesus after his death. Several generations after the Trojan War, Heracles' descendants returned south to reclaim by force their rightful ownership of their ancient homeland. The invasion hypothesis was popular because it accounted well for both the initial destructions and the dominant presence of Doric speakers in the Peloponnesus during historical times. Moreover, it seemed to be corroborated by the ancient Greeks themselves. Against the theory, however, is the fact that no material trace of such invaders can be seen in the archaeological record.

Because no single cause could have had such widespread and profound effects, many have explained the breakdown in terms of a web of negative socio-economic agents, which together brought about a disequilibrium that disabled the "subsystems" of the entire palace system (its various spheres of activity, such as trade, agricultural production, metallurgy, and the crafting of artifacts). Marauding bands of "sea peoples" could have provided one catalyst, by obstructing sea trade in the Aegean, which in turn would have cut off the supply of tin and copper for bronze production. If external trade ceased, not only goods but social contacts would be lost; ideas as well as objects could not be exchanged. At the same time, natural disasters, like prolonged drought, soil exhaustion, and earthquakes, could have put pressure on the food-distribution subsystem, which may have already been undermined by the inefficiency of the top-heavy palace bureaucracies. As food and other crucial resources became scarce, the people might have turned against one another. At this point, when the system had already become weak and vulnerable, internecine warfare, popular uprisings, or slave revolts might have precipitated the final collapse.

Along with the destruction of the palaces, the centralized, rigidly hierarchical states disappeared forever from Greece. Underneath the veneer of great wealth and stability, the Mycenaean economy and government were shallowly rooted, essentially fragile systems. With the end of this stage of Greek history would come the beginning of a new era, so different that when the Greeks looked back on their own Bronze Age past they could only imagine it as a kind of mythical dreamworld, a time when gods and humans mingled together.

KEY TERMS

Ahhiyawa	Lerna	Pylos
Bronze Age	Linear A	shaft graves
Central court	Linear B	Sir Arthur Evans
Cnossus	megaron	Thera
Crete	Michael Ventris	tholos
Egypt	Minoans	wanax
Heinrich Schliemann	Mycenae	
Hittite empire	Mycenaean civilization	
Indo-Europeans	Neolithic Age	

Suggested Readings

Barber, Elizabeth Wayland. 1994. *Women's Work: The First 20,000 Years. Women, Cloth, and Society in Early Times*. New York and London: Norton. The history of textile manufacture as women's work and art from the Paleolithic through the Iron Age, including weaving techniques and myths about weaving. A major study of women's principal contribution to the ancient economy.

Bryce, Trevor. 2006. *The Trojans and Their Neighbors*. London: Routledge. Lucid history of Troy in the context of second-millennium BC Anatolia by an outstanding Hittite historian.

Castleden, Rodney. 1993. *Minoans: Life in Bronze Age Crete*. London: Routledge. Written for the nonspecialist, the book re-creates the society and culture of the Cretan civilization.

Chadwick, John. 1967. *The Decipherment of Linear B*. 2nd ed. Cambridge, UK: Cambridge University Press. The story of how the Linear B tablets were deciphered as told by one of the principal investigators.

———. 1987. *Linear B and Related Scripts*. Berkeley and Los Angeles: University of California Press. This little monograph describes the relationship between the Linear A script and Linear B and tells how Linear B was used by the Mycenaeans.

Cline, Erich H., ed. 2010. *The Oxford Handbook of the Bronze Age Aegean*. Oxford: Oxford University Press. Over 900 pages comprising 66 chapters written by 61 scholars.

Davis, Jack L, ed. 1998. *An Archaeological History from Nestor to Navarino*. Austin: University of Texas Press. (Reprinted with new introduction, Princeton, NJ: American School of Classical Studies: 2008.) The history of Pylos. The first half focuses on the Bronze Age site, its environment, and its spare occupation after the Catastrophe.

Dickinson, Oliver. 1994. *The Aegean Bronze Age*. Cambridge, UK: Cambridge University Press. Detailed account of the Bronze Age cultures of the Aegean basin.

Drews, Robert. 1993. *The End of the Bronze Age: Changes in Warfare and the Catastrophe ca. 1200 B.C.* Princeton, NJ: Princeton University Press. An overview and detailed analysis of the latest theories of the fall of the great civilizations of the Late Bronze Age.

Duhoux, Yves and Anna Morpurgo Davies, eds. 2008/2011. *A Companion to Linear B: Myceanean Greek Texts and their World*. 2 vols. Louvain-la-Neuve, Belgium: Peeters. Up-to-date contributions by top-notch scholars on various aspects of the Mycenaean world using the Linear B tablets as their starting point.

Finkelberg, Margalit. 2005. *Greeks and Pre-Greeks: Aegean Prehistory and Greek Heroic Tradition*. Cambridge, UK: Cambridge University Press. Brilliant analysis for the evidence for Bronze Age society in Greek legend and myths.

Fitton, J. Lesley. 1996. *The Discovery of the Greek Bronze Age*. Cambridge, MA: Harvard University Press. A sparkling survey of the pioneering excavators, their excavations, and the controversies that swirled around their discoveries of Bronze Age Aegean cultures.

Fox, Margalit. 2013. *The Riddle of the Labyrinth: The Quest to Crack an Ancient Code*. New York: Ecco. The exciting story of three people who worked to decipher Linear B. These include Sir Arthur Evans (whose attempts failed) and Alice Kober, a heretofore unnoticed scholar whose meticulous work enabled Michael Ventris to finally crack the code.

Friedrich, Walter L. 2000. *Fire in the Sea, the Santorini Volcano: Natural History and the Legend of Atlantis*. Trans. Alexander R. McBirney. Cambridge, UK: Cambridge University Press. Lucid, beautifully illustrated account of the geology and archaeology of Santorini/Thera.

Preziosi, Donald and Louise A. Hitchcock. 1999. *Aegean Art and Architecture* (Oxford History of Art). Oxford, UK: Oxford University Press. A comprehensive introduction to the art and architecture of Greece, Crete, and the Cycladic islands from 3300 to 1000 BC.

The "Dark Age" of Greece and the Eighth-Century "Renaissance" (c. 1200–750/700 BC)

In the middle of the twelfth century BC there were still a few places in Greece where the palaces survived, but these signs of economic and cultural vitality soon fade from the archaeological record. By the early eleventh century, the Greek world had settled into its **Dark Age**, a period of steep decline and slow recovery that lasted until the eighth century. During those obscure centuries, new social and political patterns were formed, out of which would emerge, in the eighth century, a new type of political organization, the city-state (*polis*).

DECLINE AND RECOVERY (c. 1200–900 BC)

There were no more kings, officials, scribes, palace staffs, or state armies; gone was the elaborate redistributive system. Monumental stone buildings were no longer erected, elaborate frescoes and fine furniture were no longer commissioned, and even the art of writing was lost. Bronze, gold, and other luxury imports dwindled to a trickle, as vital trade links were broken. All across the Greek world, towns and villages were left abandoned, their inhabitants either dead or gone to other places, some as close as Achaea and Arcadia, some as far away as Palestine and **Cyprus**. It is true that movements and dislocations of people can exaggerate an impression of overall depopulation; yet it is safe to say that in the two centuries following 1200 BC, Greece emptied out far more than it filled up. By 1050 BC its population was probably the lowest in a thousand years, perhaps only 30 percent of what it had been in 1200.

For the early-twentieth-century historians who coined the phrase "Greek Dark Age," the four centuries that lay hidden between the fall of Mycenae and the birth of the city-state were a period of total obscurity coupled with utter poverty and stagnation. Recent archaeological findings, however, indicate that some regions within Greece recovered much sooner than others and that recovery took different forms. Areas bordering on the Aegean Sea appear to have suffered a briefer period of decline and to have bounced back sooner than regions in western Greece. In fact, at several major centers, including Athens, occupation continued without interruption; many were reoccupied within a generation or two after their destruction.

What survived from the world of the thirteenth century into the world of the eleventh, and what was lost? For those who remained in Greece, life was simpler than it had been during the palace period, but that does not mean that Greece lapsed into a primitive state. Farmers continued to farm, growing the same crops they had always grown; herders tended their flocks as before; women spun and wove their wool and flax. Potters, metal workers, and carpenters still practiced their crafts (although at a lower level of skill and refinement), and the people kept worshiping their gods and performing religious rituals. In short, the timeless rhythm and activities of the agricultural year and the farming village remained unchanged and would remain constant over the following centuries.

Even when the material culture appears to have been at its nadir, important technological innovations appeared. Around 1050 BC the combination of several new techniques and small inventions produced a superior pottery that was well

Figure 2.1. A Late Protogeometric belly-handled *amphora* (storage jar; c. 950–900 BC) from the Ceramicus cemetery, with compass-drawn concentric circles foreshadowing the Geometric style. Athens, Ceramicus, Oberländer Museum.

proportioned and finely decorated. A faster potter's wheel improved the shape of the vases. For the first time, potters were using a compass, to which several brushes were attached, to draw perfect arcs, half-circles, and concentric circles. Lines were drawn with a ruler instead of freehand. New shapes and designs emerged, enhanced by more lustrous glaze achieved by firing at a higher temperature. This new style, called **Protogeometric** (c. 1050–900), seems to have originated in Attica and spread to other regions.

It was also at about this time that Greek metal workers mastered the difficult process of smelting and working **iron**. Iron weapons and tools were harder than bronze and kept their edge better. Iron technology was long known in the East, but the Mycenaeans had not exploited the sources of iron ore available in Greece. When the disruption of trade largely cut off access to copper and tin, however, necessity proved the mother of invention. From 1050 on, small local iron industries sprang up all across the mainland and the islands. By 950, almost every weapon and tool found in graves is made of iron, not bronze.

Beginning around 1050, there was an accelerated movement from the Greek mainland across the Aegean Sea to the Anatolian coast. During this time a number of settlements were established—among them Miletus (the earliest), Ephesus, and Colophon—that would become thriving cities. These population shifts created what the Mycenaeans had not—a large permanent presence in the East—and ensured that the Aegean Sea would one day be known as the "Greek Sea." On the mainland during this time, some major settlements, like Athens and Corinth, might have had populations in the low thousands; however, most sites held no more than a few dozen to a few hundred people.

Society in the Early Dark Age

With the dissolution of the intricate ties that had bound the outlying settlements to the palace complexes and to one another, the former centers and peripheral villages found themselves largely on their own, politically and economically. Nevertheless, at the same time that early Iron Age Greeks were transforming the Mycenaean past into a Heroic Age, and had forgotten what a redistributive system was and how it worked, they remembered one thing: They had always had kings. Two types of evidence indicate that the new communities were led by a paramount figure; one is linguistic and one is archaeological. The Linear B tablets refer to an official called *qa-si-re-u*. The *qa-si-re-u* seems to have been a minor official, a sort of mayor or head of a town or village within a Mycenaean kingdom. The later Greek form of this term, **basileus**, however, is usually translated as "king" and designates the paramount figure in a state, suggesting that after the disappearance of the great Bronze Age citadels, the local officials like the old *qa-si-re-u* became the leaders of the new, smaller Greek communities of the Dark Age.

The archaeological evidence for the survival of the idea of kingship is the presence in Dark Age communities of relatively large apsidal (curved at one end) structures referred to as "chieftains' houses" or the "houses of the local basileus." Such a local basileus may have presided over the Dark Age village of **Nichoria** in southwestern Peloponnesus, which was excavated in the 1970s. Originally a large subsidiary town of the kingdom of Pylos, Nichoria was abandoned around 1200 and came back to life about 1075 as a much smaller village cluster, with a peak population of about two hundred in the early ninth century BC. Dark Age Nichoria was fairly prosperous in a humble way. The forty or fifty families dwelt on a ridge overlooking a plain. There was an abundance of good farmland and plenty of open pasture for animals, notably cattle.

At the center of the ridge top, excavators uncovered a large tenth-century building, consisting of a spacious megaron and a small porch (Room 2 in Figure 2.2a), which they identified as the "village chieftain's house." A remodeling in the ninth century added another room at the rear (Room 3) and a bigger courtyard in front, enlarging the house to an impressive 52 feet by 23 feet wide. It is suggested that the chieftain's house also functioned as the religious center and perhaps as a communal storehouse. This is where the elders gathered to feast and talk about local affairs. Although much better constructed than the surrounding houses, it had the same shape and was made of the same materials; its floor was packed earth and its walls were of mud brick, supporting a steep thatched roof. Clearly, the family that lived there enjoyed very high status in Nichoria itself and in the surrounding countryside. Yet they lived in a style that was not much different from that of their neighbors. In fact, the small, later additions to the front (Room 2) and rear (Room 3) of the chief's house are the only design differences between it and the other houses in the community (Figure 2.2c).

At the other side of Greece from Nichoria—at **Lefkandi** on the island of Euboea—stood a much wealthier settlement that is still yielding up its secrets today. Like Nichoria, Lefkandi had been a bustling Mycenaean town that revived

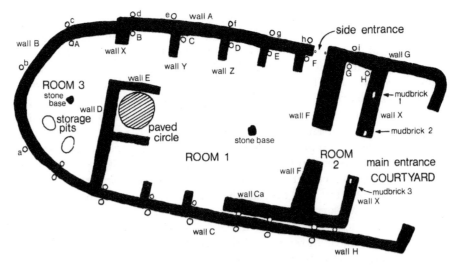

Figure 2.2a. Plan of the ninth-century "village chieftain's house" at Nichoria.

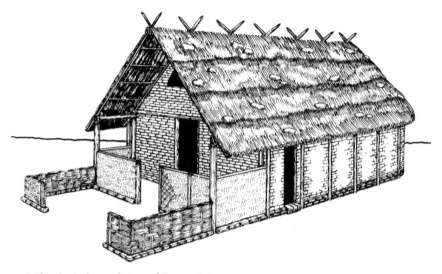

Figure 2.2b. Artist's rendition of Figure 2.2a.

Figure 2.2c. Artist's conception of an "ordinary" Dark Age house.

after the collapse of the palace system and prospered during the Dark Age. In 1981, preliminary emergency excavations indicated an enormous structure, but as excavators began planning a major discovery, the local developer's bulldozer abruptly removed much of the top of the hill. Even this unfortunate removal of a full third of the structure did not prevent the archaeologists from completing their discovery: the largest Dark Age building yet found. Dated to about 950 BC, the long narrow structure (150 by 30 feet) covered more than twice the area of that of any contemporary building. Whether this was a chief's house or his mausoleum, or even a communal dwelling akin to the longhouses of archaic North American

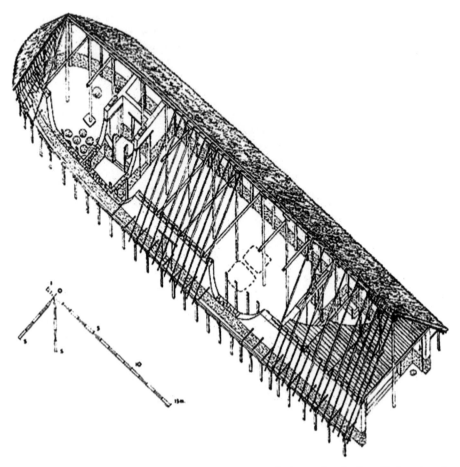

Figure 2.2d. Axonometric reconstruction of the "chief's house" at Lefkandi showing the grave of the basileus of Lefkandi and his consort (c. 950 BC). This is the largest Dark Age building yet discovered.

native groups is uncertain. But the biggest surprise of all was the discovery of two burial shafts sunk into the building's central room.

In one of the shafts lay two pairs of horses, one on top of the other—reminiscent of the grave offerings given to exceptional warriors during the Late Bronze Age, centuries earlier. The other compartment held the remains of two humans: a cremated man (a warrior) and an inhumed woman, apparently his wife. The man's ashes were well preserved in a large bronze amphora that had been made in Cyprus about a century before the funeral. Next to it lay an iron sword, a spearhead, a razor, and also a whetstone for sharpening the weapons: the toolkit of a fighting man. The horse sacrifices and the costly imports deposited in the couple's grave suggest to some scholars that this man had been a wealthy, hereditary chief with Eastern contacts. Others posit that he belonged to an elite "warrior class."

The woman whose skeleton was found beside the warrior has aroused at least as much curiosity as her spouse. Gold-plated coils flanked her head, broad gold rings decorated her fingers, and her breasts were covered with large disks made of fine gold foil. Around her neck, the excavators found the gold beads and central pendant of an elaborate necklace believed to have been fashioned in the Near East at least 650 years before the time of the burial. This necklace might have been a family heirloom, or it might have been purchased from Near Eastern traders roaming the Aegean Sea. All her adornments reveal that the woman's social status was equal to the man's. But how can we explain the ivory-handled dagger that had been positioned beside her head? Was this woman offered as a sacrifice to the man along with the horses? Or did she die suddenly while attending the funeral rites for her cremated husband? We cannot tell the whole story here: there is no archaeological certainty that she was buried at the same time as the warrior.

Soon after the funeral the whole building was demolished and covered over with a mound of earth and stones so huge that its construction must have required the labor of the entire community; as soon as the building was filled in, a cemetery sprang up next to mound, though there had been no graves there when the building had been standing. For all its uncertainties, this central building, with its spectacularly rich graves and the presence of high-quality local and imported pottery, much of it from Athens and northern Greece, indicates clearly that by the mid-ninth century BC, the society had become stratified, with the basileus and his supporters enjoying access to exotic luxuries and able to mobilize the labor of the community for large-scale projects.

REVIVAL (C. 900–750 BC)

Around 900 BC, as the conservative Protogeometric style evolved into the **Geometric style** (c. 900–700), a new artistic and aesthetic spirit becomes evident. There was no dramatic break with tradition, and in some regions the old style continued for some time. Nevertheless, new shapes and new decorative features mark the Geometric as a distinctly new period. Circles and semicircles gave way to linear angular motifs, such as the famous "meander pattern" (Figures 2.7a and 2.7b).

Eventually painters would fill up the entire surface of a vase with zones of meanders, zigzags, triangles, and crosshatches, alternating them with solid bands and lines. Ninth-century craftsmen were now producing costly luxury items like fine gold jewelry, ivory carvings, and bronze vessels, both for domestic consumption and long-distance trade. This development attests to the renewed availability of raw materials from abroad, including bronze, which began to appear in larger quantities.

Homer and Oral Poetry

An oral poet was a skilled storyteller who sang or chanted in verse before an audience to the accompaniment of a stringed instrument called the *kitharis*. Later

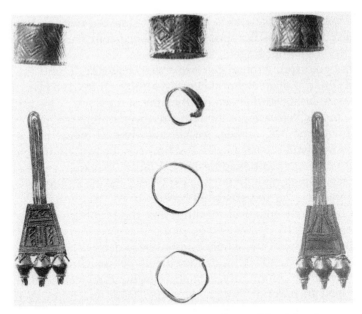

Figure 2.3. Gold jewelry from the cremation grave of a wealthy Athenian woman
(c. 850 BC). In addition, she was buried with a number of fine vases, bronze and iron pins,
ivory seals, and a faience necklace. Athens, Agora Museum. (See Plate IV.)

Figure 2.4. Blind Homer. Roman
marble copy of the head of a
Hellenistic imaginary portrait
(c. 200 BC). Boston, Museum of
Fine Arts.

Greeks revered **Homer**, the composer of the *Iliad* and the *Odyssey*, as their greatest poet, although they knew nothing about his life aside from the tradition that he was blind and from Ionia.

The two poems are generally dated to between the later eighth and early seventh century BC, about the time writing reappeared in Greece. It is possible that Homer, an illiterate bard, dictated his long epics to persons who could write. To us it seems impossible that works of such artistry and length—the *Iliad* is around 16,000 lines and the *Odyssey* 12,000—could have been created without writing. Yet modern comparative studies of traditional **oral poetry** have shown that bards can in fact compose long, complex narratives as they perform.

Homer and other Greek oral poets would have had at their disposal a store of traditional plots, characters, and themes that they had learned from previous generations of singers, who in turn had learned them from their elders, and so on, back in time. In retelling the ancient stories that were familiar to their audiences, poets could also draw on an inherited stock of "formulas" (fixed phrases, lines, and blocks of text), which they had memorized and could vary as the occasion demanded. Over a lifetime of private rehearsals, "writing" and "rewriting" the poetry in his mind, a skilled poet like Homer would have crafted and perfected the poems that bore his personal signature. At the same time, the traditional narrative framework was flexible enough to permit the changing and varied concerns of his audiences to be incorporated into the bard's performances; each performance would be fresh and "updated." When the epics were finally committed to writing—probably within the poet's lifetime—they were frozen, so to speak, and thus lost this ability to be continuously re-created; yet they gained the advantage of some degree of protection from further modification.

The epics are set in the Age of Heroes, which encompasses a generation or two before, and one generation after, the legendary **Trojan War**. The tale of the Trojan War is a classically simple folk saga. **Paris**, the son of King Priam of **Troy**, seduced and brought back to Troy the beautiful **Helen**, the wife of **Menelaus**, ruler of the Spartans. To avenge the insult, Menelaus and his brother, **Agamemnon**, wanax of Mycenae, gathered a huge army of Achaean warriors. The Achaeans sailed to Troy, destroyed the city after a ten-year siege, and then dispersed, each contingent to its own homeland.

The hope that archaeology could prove the historicity of the Trojan War has inspired archaeologists since Schliemann's pioneering excavations in the 1870s and 1880s and led to important discoveries. For most of the second millennium BC, a mighty walled citadel, which archaeologists call Troy VI, occupied the hill of Hisarlik; discoveries of Mycenaean pottery at the site indicate that it was in contact with Greece. Moreover, excavations in the 1990s by a combined German and American expedition discovered traces of a walled settlement south of the citadel, suggesting that Troy VI may have been the center of a great city such as Homer described. At the same time Hittite texts have revealed that Troy (Hittite Taruisa) was the capital of a kingdom in northwest Anatolia named Wilusa (Greek Ilion, an alternate name for Troy) that was the cause of hostilities on at least one occasion between the Hittites and the Greek kingdom of Ahhiyawa.

In the end, archaeology cannot prove that the Trojan War as Homer described it actually occurred, but the new discoveries make it increasingly possible that a conflict involving Troy VI was the origin of the oral tradition that culminated in the *Iliad* and *Odyssey*. For the Greeks, however, the Trojan War was the pivotal event of their early history. Yet the epics, although set in this distant past, are not really about history, nor are they about the Trojan War. History and war are the background for the enactment of social dramas, whose protagonists are caught up in the kinds of dilemmas that every generation experiences and must deal with.

The nagging question for historians is this: Do the epics tell us anything about actual Greek society, whether of Homer's own day (late eighth or early seventh century) or of some earlier date? Or are they pure fictions that have only symbolic meaning? The answer, of course, is somewhere in the middle. The Homeric world was a past world that was in every way bigger, better, and more fantastic than the environment of the contemporary audiences. For instance, Hector, the Trojan leader, picks up a stone to use as a weapon, "which two men, the best in the land, could not easily lift from the ground onto a wagon, men such as mortals are today" (*Iliad* 12.445–449). Such a scene serves the purpose of "epic distancing," which gives the aura of a long-ago heroic society. The poet deliberately leaves out innovations that were known to him, such as the reintroduction of writing. Nevertheless, aspects of that imaginary world—its interests, passions, ideologies, and to some degree its social institutions—must have conformed to the audience's real-life experiences. The norms and values of Homeric society are internally consistent and coherent enough to be given a place in the not-so-long-ago past, which we may assign roughly to the end of the Greek Dark Age.

HOMERIC SOCIETY

Homer's Greece is divided geographically into independent regions of various sizes, each one constituting a *demos*, a word that denotes both the territory itself and the "people" who inhabit it. A typical demos would contain several settlements—towns and villages—along with their adjoining farmlands and pastures. For example, in the catalogue of the contingents that make up the Greek army at Troy there is this entry for the large region of Aetolia.

> The Aetolians were led by Andraemon's son,
> Thoas. They lived in Pleuron, Olenos, Pylene,
> In seaside Chalcis by-the-sea, and rocky Calydon. . . .
> Forty black ships followed Thoas to Troy.
> (*Iliad* 2.638–644 Lombardo)

The official title borne by warrior leaders like Thoas is basileus. As already mentioned, the word occurs in the Linear B tablets as the title of a minor local official within a Mycenaean kingdom. Although basileus is normally translated as "king," in Homeric society, basileis (plural) in the *Iliad* and the *Odyssey* clearly are not kings in the sense of monarchs who hold absolute sway over their subjects.

Thoas is the paramount chief in Aetolia, superior in authority to the local chiefs of the villages listed and the leader of all those who called themselves Aetolians. Elsewhere he is described as "Thoas, who in the whole of Pleuron and steep Calydon ruled over the Aetolians, and was honored like a god by the people" (*Iliad* 13.216–218). The "people" is the demos (a root of many English works, such as demo-cracy, demo-graphics, and epi-demic). Demos, which in the Linear B tablets (in the form *damo*) apparently referred to a village community, signifies, from Homer on, both a territorial unit and the people who lived in it. Thus, demos in this passage indicates both Aetolia, the region, and the Aetolians, the people.

A good-sized demos often contained other chiefs, lower in rank, but called by the same title of basileus. When Odysseus enters the magnificent house of Alcinous, ruler of the island of Scheria, he finds the basileus and his wife Arete, the basileia, entertaining the other basileis. In Alcinous' own words, "twelve renowned basileis hold sway as leaders in the demos, and I myself am the thirteenth" (*Odyssey* 8.390–391). There is no question that Alcinous is supreme among them—the "paramount chief"—yet he must also take counsel with them, for they are not merely subordinates but men of power in their own local districts. It is against this background of loosely centralized territorial units that we may envisage social life in the **Homeric epics**.

Community and Household

Social and economic life at the end of the ninth century was centered in the local communities, most of which were still quite small. The Greeks did not live in isolated farmsteads but clustered together in small settlements. Farmers would walk out each morning to their plots and return to the village at dusk. Communities were closely knit through generations of intermarrying with other families within the village and in other villages of the same demos.

The separate settlements were likewise bound together to ensure the survival of the territorial demos. Individual villages within the demos might quarrel with one another, but they united against threats from outside. Inside the boundaries of the demos all who shared the demos name—the "Ithacans," or the "Megarians"— could live and move safely. Once outside the homeland, one was "in the demos of others," in an alien country, so to speak, where the protection of tribal ties ended, and one was a stranger, without rights. In Homer, when a stranger appears in an alien demos, he is asked to identify himself by naming his "demos and polis." By polis, the questioner means the main town of the demos, the most populous settlement, the place where the paramount basileus lived, and where the assembly of the demos met.

From Homer we may infer that the smallest unit of Dark Age society was the household (*oikos*). The oikos was the center of a person's existence, and every member was preoccupied with its preservation, economic well-being, and social standing. The word oikos signified not only the house itself but also the family, the land, livestock, and all other property and goods, including slaves. Greek society was patrilineal and patriarchal. The father was supreme in the household by custom and later by law. Descent was through the father, and on his death the property was divided equally among his sons. Although daughters did not inherit directly, they received a share of their parents' wealth as a dowry. Because daughters in Homer are prized, suitors customarily give *hedna* (courting gifts) to the bride's father as part of the marriage contract. The new bride took up residence in the house of her husband; thus their children belonged to the husband's oikos, not to hers.

Among chieftain families—which are the only ones described in Homer—married sons continue to reside in the paternal oikos with their wives and children. Not infrequently, though, the custom is reversed. A powerful chief brings his daughter's new husband into his own household instead. In this way, he gets to keep his daughter and acquires a new man to fight and work for the oikos. Another means of increasing the oikos is for the father to beget additional children by slave women. That could cause friction in the family, however. Odysseus' father did not sleep with a newly bought slave woman and so "avoided his wife's anger" (*Odyssey* 1.443). Although the male children of slaves are inferior to the legitimate sons in respect to inheritance rights, they are otherwise full members of the family and part of its fighting force and workforce. Illegitimate daughters seem to have the same status as their legitimate half-sisters.

All members of a basileus' oikos do a share of the work. Odysseus, Homer tells us, built a bedroom and bed for him and his wife Penelope all by "himself and no one else" (*Odyssey* 23.189). The sons of basileis tend the flocks and herds, the main wealth of the family. Homeric wives work alongside the women slaves in the tasks of spinning and weaving; and young daughters do other tasks, such as fetching water from the communal fountain, or washing clothes by the river. Most of the labor of a wealthy household, however, was provided by female and male slaves (either bought or captured), and by *thētes* (singular, *thēs*), poor, landless free men who worked as hired hands.

The main economic resource for each of the families in a village or town was its ancestral plot of farmland called a **klēros** (literally an "allotment"). Without a kleros a man could not marry. A lotless man (*aklēros*) had two options: He could eke out a precarious existence on a poor patch of unclaimed marginal land, or worse, hire on as a thes. The latter was a galling life, not only because it was hard work for very little pay (essentially his keep), but also because working for another man's family was felt to be an indignity.

The economies of ordinary and elite households in the Dark Age differed primarily in scale. An ordinary farmer would probably have owned a yoke of oxen for plowing, and perhaps a mule. No doubt he pastured enough sheep and goats for the family's consumption of wool, cheese, and meat. The rich man had more of everything, particularly animals, but also more farmland and workers. Even with many more mouths to feed, a wealthy oikos produced a large surplus in good years, whereas the average family, if it was a good year, would have had just a little extra to spend on its wish list, another ox, for example, or a pair of gold earrings.

A wealthy oikos, though, could exchange its surplus production of woolen goods and leather for slaves, metal, and expensive ornaments of the sort that increasingly show up in the ninth-century graves. By this time, we observe such signs of increasing stratification in more and more places. In the ninth century socioeconomic divisions into an elite group and a commoner mass become quite clear.

Chiefs and Followers

In Homer, the office and title of basileus passes from father to son as in **chiefdom** societies everywhere, but inheritance alone is not enough to secure the title. In accordance with the aristocratic ethos that permeates the poems, a basileus must be competent to fulfill his role as leader of the people in war and peace. He should be both a good warrior and a persuasive speaker. When Peleus, basileus of the Myrmidons, sends his son Achilles off to the Trojan War, his advice is, "Be both a speaker of words and a doer of deeds" (*Iliad* 9.443). Above all, it is the deeds, "the works of war," that make a leader. In Homer, a chief's status is measured by how many warriors follow him, and few will fight with a leader who is not a good warrior.

In Homer's world, raiding is a way of life. Any chief may raise his own following of *hetairoi* ("companions") and go on raids against the villages of another demos, either to even the score in some ongoing quarrel or just to steal or plunder their livestock, valuables, and women.

In recruiting men for a raid, a warlord draws on his large surplus of animals to provide them feasts, thereby showing himself to be a generous leader. Odysseus, for example, describes how he outfitted ships and gathered a following:

> I feasted them [*hetairoi*] for six days, giving them
> All the animals they needed for sacrifice—
> Enough for the gods and for their own banquets.
> On the seventh day we set sail for Crete. . . .
> (*Odyssey* 14.248–253 Lombardo)

Heroes express themselves by raiding the livestock of others. Whether on a raid or in a war, the basileus is the one most severely tested, for he is literally the leader, stationing himself "among the front-fighters." Because the leader risks his life fighting in the thick of battle, his people are obligated to repay him with honors and gifts.

Reciprocity—mutual and fair exchange—governs all social relationships in the Homeric world. Accordingly, fairness rules the distribution of the spoils of war. Following a raid, the loot is gathered together. First the chief takes his share, including something extra as his special "prize"; only then is the rest given to the men "to divide up, so that no one may go cheated of an equal share" (*Odyssey* 9.549).

A leader who keeps more than his due risks losing the respect of his followers. He cannot afford not to appear generous and openhanded. Similarly, in their relations with one another, chiefs constantly exchange gifts and feasts. In this way basileis show off their wealth, cement alliances, win new friends, and collect obligations that will have to be paid back later.

Despite the great authority given him by his position, a basileus has limited ability to coerce others to do his bidding. He is a chief, not a king. Once, when Odysseus' followers decide to do exactly the opposite of what he has ordered them, he responds that as "one man alone" he must abide by the will of the many.

In a society in which performance is more important than descent, a weak successor will be challenged by rivals eager to replace him as head chief. That is the situation confronting Odysseus' son Telemachus in his father's twenty-year-long absence from Ithaca. Telemachus is barely twenty years old, with no experience of leadership, and he has only a few supporters, as his father's hetairoi have gone to Troy with him. Meanwhile, a group of young chiefs and sons of chiefs have permanently camped out in his courtyard, feasting on his livestock, seducing the slave girls, and wooing his mother, Penelope, now presumed a widow. The suitors assume that the one who succeeds in marrying Penelope will take over as basileus, even though they admit that the office belongs to Telemachus by his "paternal birthright." In the end, Odysseus returns, kills the suitors, and assumes his rightful place as the basileus of Ithaca and the nearby islands. In most instances, however, weakened ruling dynasties would not have fared as well as the house and lineage of Odysseus.

Government and Foreign Relations

Governmental institutions in Homeric society were few and simple. A council, the *boulē,* made up of chiefs and other influential men, met in the great hall (megaron) of the ruling chief to formulate policy for the demos. The leader had the decisive voice, but usually heeded the advice and counsel of the "elders," as the boule members were called (though many were actually younger men). Their deliberations were presented to an assembly of the people, held outdoors in the *agora* or "place of gathering." Attending were all the men of fighting age and older; women did not attend. In the Homeric assembly, only men of high rank could bring up a matter for discussion, and although it was permissible for any member of the demos to respond, only rarely did an ordinary man speak out. The demos made its will known by shouting, muttering, or total silence.

Besides being the military and political leader, the top basileus played a religious and judicial role in the life of the community. He was not a priest, nor did he claim to have prophetic powers. But his position was divinely sanctioned; Homer firmly emphasizes that Zeus upholds the ruling authority of the office of basileus. When the basileus presided over public sacrifices, he was the spokesman for the people, similar to a father sacrificing on behalf of his family.

Chiefs played a lesser role in judicial matters, as the only law was custom, that is, the community's traditions regarding right and wrong in particular situations. (Systems of formal, written laws would not emerge until the seventh century.) Even the most antisocial act, murder within the demos, was not a crime in the sense that it required arrest and trial of the alleged murderer by the society at large. Rather, it was the custom that the families of the killer and the victim should come to an agreement on a material penalty as compensation, thus avoiding a socially destabilizing feud between the families. When the parties could not reach a private agreement, the dispute went before a court. Homer describes a dispute over payment of murder compensation, which is heard and decided by a group of elders (probably chiefs), one of whom will receive an award of gold for speaking the "straightest judgment." The lawsuit takes place in an assembly, with the people pushing and shoving and shouting (*Iliad* 18.497–508). The council, assembly, and law court are all there is to government in Homer, but they were sufficient. They would remain the essential organs of government, in a more highly evolved form, in the later city-states.

Foreign relations among epic heroes are often conducted personally through the institution of *xenia* ("guest friendship"). Appearing first in Homer, xenia occurs frequently in works by Greek authors from all periods of antiquity. Xenia was a mutual bond of friendship and trust between individuals who belonged to separate *dēmoi*, often very far apart. *Xenoi* ("guest friends") would provide each other entertainment, lodging, and valuable parting gifts whenever they received one another into their demoi (plural) and homes. Xenia was more than just hospitality, however; its duties extended to protection, diplomatic aid, and even intervention to save a guest friend's life. In some ways, the obligations of xenia are more like those of kinship than friendship. Once the bond was established, it was assumed to be perpetual, and the relationship was passed down from generation to generation through the male line.

In the *Iliad*, Diomedes, a Greek, and Glaucus, a Lycian ally of the Trojans, encounter one another in battle. Hostility, however, turns into amity when Diomedes recalls to Glaucus that his grandfather Oeneus had hosted Glaucus' grandfather Bellerophon for twenty days and that to cement the xenia bond Oeneus gave a scarlet belt, and Bellerophon a two-handled golden cup. Now, two generations later, Diomedes proposes that they renew the old ties, saying "Let us exchange armor with each other so that these men [i.e., the Greeks and Trojans] may know that we declare that we are ancestral guest-friends" (*Iliad* 6.231–232).

Social Values and Ethics

The code of behavior followed by Homeric males is typical of warrior societies. A man is called "good" (*agathos*) when he exhibits bravery and skill in fighting and athletic contests. He is "bad" (*kakos*) if he is a coward or useless in battle. A "good man" should honor the gods, keep promises and oaths, and be loyal to friends and fellow warriors. He should exhibit self-control, be hospitable, and respect women and elders. It is proper to show pity even toward captured warriors and to refrain from defiling corpses of the enemy. These gentler qualities, although they are desirable, are not required; a man may be merciless and cruel and still be agathos.

Being good at slaughtering and pillaging brings honor and glory, as well as wealth, and so warriors compete with one another in the art of killing. The purpose of this excessive striving is to enhance and preserve one's *timē*, one's value and worth, respect and honor. The spirit of competition permeates every facet of life and is not bounded by class or gender. The highest good is to win and be called "best" (*aristos*), whether in spear throwing, running, playing ball, or chariot racing; in speaking or in displays of cunning; or in weaving or crafting pots. A poor farmer is roused to work hard when he sees his neighbor getting rich, says **Hesiod** (c. 700 BC), and "potter resents potter and carpenter resents carpenter, and beggar is jealous of beggar and singer of singer" (*Works and Days* 19–25).

Elite males especially insist that their value be recognized publicly, whether by a seat of honor at a feast or a choice item from the plunder. Not to be honored when honor is due, or worse, to be dishonored, are unbearable insults. In the *Iliad,* when Agamemnon takes back Achilles' "prize of honor," the captive girl Briseis, Achilles is so keenly stung by the assault against his worth that he refuses to fight.

It is more difficult to access the feelings of Homeric women, because their behavior and motives are revealed to us through a male lens. What the poems do accurately describe is a male-dominated society in which women's roles and the range of behaviors deemed socially acceptable are constructed for them by men. Needless to say, their assigned roles as housewives and mothers dictated a different set of expectations. Like men, women also compete, though only within the few arenas of excellence allowed them; for example, this one or that one "surpassed her age-mates in beauty and work [e.g., weaving] and intelligence." They are expected to act modestly in public and in the company of men, and above all to be chaste. Although men are permitted to have concubines, adulterous women bring great disgrace and dishonor on themselves and their families.

DOCUMENT 2.1

Andromache mourns over the body of her husband Hector, slain by Achilles. Her lament centers on the fate of the helpless women and children.

> White-armed Andromache led the lamentation
> As she cradled the head of her man-slaying Hector:
> "You have died young, husband, and left me
> A widow in the halls. Our son is still an infant,
> Doomed when we bore him. I do not think
> He will ever reach manhood. No, this city
> Will topple and fall first. You were its savior,
> And now you are lost. All the solemn wives
> And children you guarded will go off soon
> In the hollow ships, and I will go with them.
> And you, my son, you will either come with me
> And do menial work for a cruel master,
> Or some Greek will lead you by the hand
> And throw you from the tower, a hideous death,
> Angry because Hector killed his brother,
> Or his father, or son."

(*Iliad* 24.723–737 Lombardo)

Despite the severe limitations placed on them by male society, Homeric women are included in the public space. They go freely about the village and countryside, participate in festive and religious events, and serve as priestesses. Nor are they without power. Strong women abound in Homer. Clytemnestra puts a dagger through her husband Agamemnon; Arete, the wife of the Phaeacian basileus, shares some of his authority; and Penelope is as cunning and resourceful as her husband, Odysseus. Nevertheless, in the Dark Age, as in later Greece, women from birth to death were dependent on and under the control of males: fathers and brothers, and then their husbands and grown sons. However much Greek women may have contributed to public opinion, they possessed no political rights of their own, apart from the protection they enjoyed as members of an oikos.

Gods and Mortals

By the eighth century, the Greek pantheon had attained much the same form it was to have throughout the rest of pagan antiquity. Hesiod's ***Theogony*** gives a genealogical "history" of the gods. From ancient Mesopotamian narratives Hesiod derives the idea that creation was essentially the separation of an originally undifferentiated mass into its component forces, conceived as deities. This division provoked a series of generational wars among the primordial gods until the last generation, the Olympians led by Zeus, gained control and brought order to the universe.

The Olympian gods, therefore, were not the creators of the universe, but rather the offspring of three and four generations of sexual unions, beginning with Earth and Sky. As the descendants of the physical universe, the gods embodied the forces of nature; Zeus in effect *was* the sky and all its phenomena. But the Greeks anthropomorphized their deities, portraying them as idealized men and women with special powers to control and direct nature.

The divine world mirrors the human condition. So, for example, Ares, the god of war, is the spirit of blood lust that enters a warrior and makes him eager to kill and destroy. Aphrodite, the goddess of love, is the irresistible force of sexual desire. Athena represents the sphere of practical wisdom (weaving, carpentry, metalworking, technology in general), while Apollo's wisdom extends to music, poetry, and philosophy. Artemis, like Athena, is a perpetual virgin; but whereas Athena is a friend and helper of warrior-heroes, Artemis shuns all contact with males and lives in the forests, as both hunter and protector of animals.

What sets the gods unbridgeably apart from humans is that they are immortal, ageless, and not subject to disease; and they have the power to manipulate the mortal world. In Homer, humans are the playthings of the gods, who vie with one another to aid their own favorites and to thwart those whom other gods favor.

In Homer, the gods insist on their proper honors, but not much else. Acts that are condemned as sins by many religions—such as homicide, stealing, or adultery—do not arouse the wrath of the Homeric gods. The gods do, however, condemn oath breaking and mistreating strangers, suppliants, and beggars. In both Homer and Hesiod, humans look to Zeus to keep order and justice in the community at large. Thus, Zeus is said to send severe wind and rain storms against those "who make crooked decrees, using force in the assembly, and drive out justice, heedless of the watchfulness of the gods" (*Iliad* 16.384–388).

In many religions, earthly sorrow and suffering are eased by the promise of a paradise after death for those who have lived righteously. The Greeks did not have this consolation: Their conceptions of a personal afterlife remained vague and undeveloped throughout the Archaic and Classical periods. For most Greeks, existence in any meaningful sense ended when the soul (*psyche*) left the body at the moment of death. Most souls carry on a dreary afterlife in the nether world. There is punishment for some in Hades, but it is reserved for those who have insulted or tricked the gods. Later, however, through the influence of mystery cults (such as the worship of Demeter at Eleusis) and philosophical speculation, ideas of a blissful afterlife for the morally good and eternal torment for the bad would become more highly developed.

The prayers, rituals, and sacred objects associated with the cult of a god were in the care of priests and priestesses. Although there existed no priestly caste as in the Near East and Egypt, Homeric priests and priestesses were not ordinary members of the community but were drawn from the noble families. Their official duties generally took up very little time and required little in the way of preparation and training.

THE END OF THE DARK AGE (C. 750–700 BC)

For many parts of Greece, the eighth century was a period of population growth, technological innovations, and increasing political centralization. The eighth century was dubbed by modern historians the "Greek Renaissance" because it appeared to be a revival of the glories of the Mycenaean Age. During this period, trade links multiplied, communication with the East intensified, writing was reintroduced into Greece, and prosperous new communities were established in the West. As the Mediterranean world became increasingly more interlinked, even the more isolated areas of Greece were drawn into networks of cultural exchange.

People of neighboring areas were meeting together more regularly to celebrate religious rituals, which included competitions among athletes and bards. Communities also vied with one another in the production of luxury items, such as finely decorated pottery and bronze tripods, and in building monumental temples. Still, we should not view the eighth century as a radical break from the past but rather as an acceleration of trends visible already in the tenth century.

The Rise of a Landowning Aristocracy

Population growth put pressure on the land. Although pasture land was nominally open to all, in reality the elite families had long before appropriated the best for themselves, in particular the lush grassy meadows where they grazed their large herds of cattle and horses. They converted more and more of this fertile soil to growing grain and other crops, a much more productive use of land. In this way, the already land-rich oikoi (plural) were able to acquire more arable land until, in the course of a few generations, they came to own a disproportionate amount of the total land. No doubt prior occupancy enabled some oikoi to claim some legal right to plow and plant the traditional pasture lands, but quite possibly chicanery and even use of force were employed by the elite in this land grab. In any case, by the early seventh century the elite minority had transformed themselves into an aristocracy of large landowners, and the majority continued to live off small-to-medium farm plots and a few animals.

We should, however, be careful to put scarcity of land into perspective. Nowhere in eighth-century Greece did the population approach the carrying capacity of the land. In fact, the countryside continued to be filled in throughout the seventh and into the sixth century. The problem was not that there was no land but rather that the most productive land was concentrated in the hands of a minority of the families. Sons whose inherited share of their paternal kleros was insufficient for their growing families would be compelled to seek marginal land in the outskirts of the demos (where they had to work harder for less return). For the ambitious, there was another solution to the problem of land hunger: relocation abroad.

Colonization and the Growth of Trade

In the second half of the eighth century substantial numbers of people left Greece to establish new farming communities in southern Italy and Sicily. These colonizers followed the trail blazed by earlier adventurers, who sailed west with **Phoenicians**, not to farm but to trade. Overseas trade, which had been increasing gradually since the tenth century, expanded considerably in the eighth. In about 825, Greeks from Euboea joined the international trading post of Al Mina in northern Syria (though the jury is still out on whether the Greeks were there as traders or mercenaries, residents or visitors). A Greek trading colony was founded shortly after 800 at Pithecusae, an island in the Bay of Naples in southern Italy. Working with their more experienced Phoenician partners, the Euboeans soon established a trading circuit that stretched between Al Mina in the east and Pithecusae in the west. By the early seventh century, Greeks had once again become important participants in the Aegean and in the wider Mediterranean trade. The new Greek opportunities that sprang up in the West offered the settlers not only a good-sized kleros on good soil but also opportunities to trade their own products and those of old Greece for raw materials, especially metal, with the inhabitants of southern Europe.

Colonization and the expansion of trade and commerce had broad economic effects throughout the towns and villages of the Greek world. There was more work for craftsmen, sailors, shipbuilders and outfitters, and haulers. Even small farmers took advantage of the economic opportunities offered by this expanded world. Hesiod takes it for granted that a farmer will put part of his surplus production in a boat that will travel a fair distance for "profit." The big landholders benefited most, however, because they could produce large surpluses for the market and could subsidize the costs and bear the losses of long sea voyages.

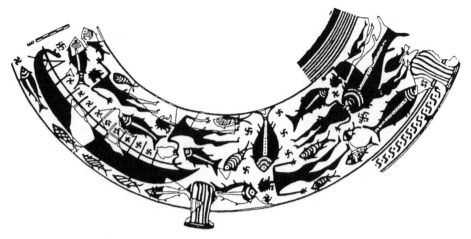

Figure 2.5. Drawing of Late Geometric *crater* (mixing bowl) showing a shipwreck (c. 725–700 BC) from Ischia, Italy. Ischia Museum.

The Alphabet and Writing

The increased contacts with the East led to the most significant cultural achievement of the late Dark Age, the Greek **alphabet**. Somewhere—most likely in the eastern Mediterranean—Greeks borrowed letters from the Phoenician alphabet, a Semitic script that consisted primarily of signs for consonants. They adapted certain of the Phoenician characters to represent the sounds of the Greek consonants and changed the value of other consonant signs, making them into vowels. Thus was born an alphabet that was largely phonetic. It is generally believed that this occurred in the early eighth century BC. Scholars continue to debate why the Greeks took up a writing system at this time and not earlier. Some propose that the alphabet was adopted for the express purpose of writing down epic poetry, whereas others cling to the older explanation that it was first used for commercial and other utilitarian purposes. Either theory is plausible, although so far no specimen of eighth-century commercial writing has been found.

The earliest known examples of connected Greek words are bits of epic-like verse scratched on vases dated to the second half of the eighth century. These graffiti do not prove, as some propose, that the alphabet was devised to preserve orally composed poems in written form. Whatever the initial motive for it, once writing was established, it was put to many different uses. The earliest specimen of a civic use of writing is a stone inscription of laws from Dreros on Crete, carved around 650.

Writing spread quickly throughout the Greek-speaking world, although not as one standard alphabet but rather as numerous local scripts, with variations in the forms and numbers of characters and in the sounds they represented. The alphabetical script of about twenty-four letters was a huge advance over

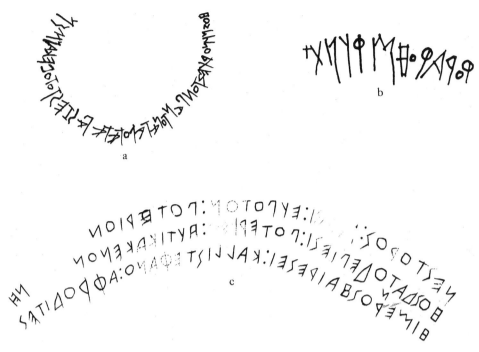

Figure 2.6a. Examples of graffiti on eighth-century vases. The readable portion of inscription (a) says, "He who, of all the dancers, now dances most gracefully" [? will win this pot?]. Inscription (b) identifies the owner: "I am the cup of Qoraqos." Inscription (c) reads, "I am the drinking cup of Nestor, good to drink from. Whoever drinks this cup, immediately the desire will seize him of beautiful-crowned Aphrodite."

the cumbersome Linear B syllabic system of eighty-seven signs. Because most of the alphabetical characters stood for a single spoken sound, it was fairly easy to learn to read and even to write Greek. Yet, although the numbers of people who could read and write increased over time, mass literacy was never achieved in ancient Greece. Indeed, through the eighth and most of the seventh century, Greece was almost as completely oral and aural as it had been in the Dark Age. Even in the Classical and Hellenistic periods, when literacy was most widespread, most information passed from mouth to ear.

Art and Architecture

A new direction in artistic representation becomes apparent in the pottery of the Late Geometric period (c. 750–700 BC). Except for an occasional horse or a bird, or, even rarer, a human figure, Greek vases had been essentially without images from the eleventh to the eighth century, when suddenly depictions of animals and humans became frequent. Then, around midcentury, artists began to paint action scenes such as battles, shipwrecks, funerals, and chariot processions. On massive Late

Figure 2.6b. Late Geometric *oinochoe* (wine jug) from Athens (c. 740 BC) on which graffito (a) in Figure 2.6a was inscribed. Athens, National Archaeological Museum.

Geometric amphorae from Athens that were commissioned as funeral monuments for the wealthy, these pictorial narratives occupy a prominent position among the abstract geometric motifs. Eventually the geometric designs become mere decorative frames for the figure scenes. Vase painters add new pictorial elements, and the figures become increasingly more naturalistic. Other media, such as small bronze sculptures and engraved metalwork, also feature dynamic action. Distinct regional and local styles emerged, as craftsmen experimented with, adapted, and discarded homegrown and imported trends and techniques. Around 720 BC, Greek art begins to feature a variety of ornamental motifs such as rosettes, griffins, and sirens, which are associated with the "orientalizing style." This phase, during which Greeks deliberately used elements of Near Eastern and Egyptian art, sculpture, and architecture, would continue for the next hundred years or so.

The monumental temple, the signature Greek architectural form, emerged in the eighth century. The earliest known examples from around 800 BC were small, with mud-brick walls, wooden columns, and thatched roofs, and looked very much like regular houses (Figure 2.8). A rectangular temple to Hera on the island of Samos, constructed a few decades later, was the first to make a clear distinction between divine and human houses. Although still made of the same materials as the earlier temples, it was several times larger: 100 feet long compared to 25 feet. A little later, architects added a wooden colonnade or peristyle all around the long

Figure 2.7a. Middle Geometric crater from Athens (c. 800 BC) with meander, zigzag, and other geometric patterns. Note the flanking horses, which enliven the severe geometric decoration, and the jug-shaped knob on the lid. Paris, The Louvre.

Figure 2.7b. Large Late Geometric grave amphora (c. 750 BC) that was used as a monument on the grave of a woman in the Dipylon cemetery at Athens. At the level of the vase's handles is a scene with human figures: mourners surrounding the body of the deceased woman, who is lying on a funeral bier. Height: 61 inches. Athens, National Archaeological Museum.

but narrow shell, and the Greek temple as we know it was born. By 700 BC, there were dozens of them, built along similar lines, in all parts of the Greek world.

The appearance of large temples shows that people wanted to and were able to expend their wealth, time, and labor on projects that brought honor to the whole community: the community's temple began to replace the chief's house as the focal point of the settlement. In Athens at this time, votive offerings placed in the temples of the gods—most notably bronze tripods and cauldrons, figurines, and bronze dress pins—greatly exceed the amount of metal objects found in upper-class burials. In this way the elite could give to the community and flaunt their wealth at the same time—a pattern that was to hold throughout the life of the Greek city-state.

Thick brick and stone defensive walls, another major architectural feature, first appear in Ionia and the Aegean islands. Smyrna in Anatolia had an impressive circuit wall by around 850, and a number of Cycladic island sites were also fortified in the ninth century. On the mainland, however, the earliest circuit walls date to a little before 700. The construction of massive defensive walls may mean that actual warfare, as opposed to raiding expeditions, was growing more frequent; they also attest to growing wealth and communal pride.

Panhellenism and the Heroic Revival

Another eighth-century phenomenon was the rise of religious sanctuaries and festivals that were not merely local but **Panhellenic** (*pan* = "all"), attracting worshippers from all over the Greek world. The most famous early sanctuaries were those of Zeus and Hera at Olympia, of Apollo and Artemis at Delos, and the oracles (places of divine prophecy) of Zeus at Dodona and of Apollo at Delphi. Tradition has it that in 776 BC, athletic contests became part of the festival of Zeus at Olympia. Held every four years, the Olympian games at first attracted

Figure 2.8. Clay model of a house or temple from Argos (c. 725–700 BC). Athens, National Archaeological Museum.

contestants and visitors only from the vicinity; but by century's end their fame had spread widely, and by the sixth century contestants and spectators would be drawn from all over the Greek world. Panhellenic festivals fostered a sense of Greek identity, reinforcing a feeling that Greeks everywhere shared a common heritage, language, and religion.

The eighth century also saw a new interest in the Bronze Age "ancestors." Quite suddenly, around 750, Greeks everywhere began to express their connection to the heroic past in new and dramatic ways. Numerous ancient tombs (mostly Mycenaean) that had been largely ignored throughout the Dark Age began to receive votive offerings, and their anonymous inhabitants were now worshiped as "heroes." Some cult heroes were identified with legendary figures and honored not at graves but at special shrines set up to them, such as the precincts sacred to Agamemnon at Mycenae and to Menelaus and Helen near Sparta. We can add a third new behavior: wealthy Greeks of the late eighth century began to bury their dead as warriors. These burials resemble those of both Achilles' great hetairos Patroclus in the *Iliad* and of the warrior at Lefkandi: the corpse was cremated and bones were put in a bronze urn; weapons were placed in the grave, and occasionally the bodies of sacrificed horses as well. All this suggests that the leading families were proclaiming descent from the heroes of old.

As the eleventh to the eighth centuries come more clearly into view, it becomes increasingly apparent that the Dark Age was the cradle of the city-state society and culture that was to follow. The basic structures and institutions of later Greek society were firmly in place before 800 BC. And so it was during the eighth century that Greece emerged from the Dark Age into the renaissance of the Archaic period. This cultural watershed, which not so long ago was seen as a sudden and revolutionary phenomenon, appears now more like a rapid evolution in response to swiftly changing conditions. The swift transformation of traditional chieftain politics into the city-state government and the turbulent history of the early city-states are the subjects of the next chapter.

KEY TERMS

Agamemnon	Homer	Paris
alphabet	Homeric epics	Phoenicians
basileus	iron	Protogeometric style
chiefdom	kleros	*Theogony*
Cyprus	Lefkandi	timē
Dark Age	Menelaus	Trojan War
demos	Nichoria	Troy
Geometric style	oikos	*Xenia*
Helen	oral poetry	
Hesiod	Panhellenic	

Suggested Readings

Burkert, Walter. 1985. *Greek Religion*. Cambridge, MA: Harvard University Press. A classic history of ancient Greek religion from the Minoan-Mycenaean Age to the Hellenistic period.

Cairns, Douglas L., ed. 2001. *Oxford Readings in Homer's* Iliad. Oxford, UK: Oxford University Press. Seventeen excellent, recent essays, plus a rich general introduction by the editor.

Carter, Jane B. and Sarah P. Morris, eds. 1995. *The Ages of Homer*. Austin: University of Texas Press. Informative collection of essays on the historical and literary background of Homer's poems.

Coldstream, J. N. 2003. *Geometric Greece*. 2nd ed. London: Routledge. A comprehensive presentation and analysis of the archaeological evidence from 900 to 700 BC.

Finkelberg, Margalit, ed. 2011. *The Homer Encyclopedia*. Oxford, UK: Blackwell. Five-volume, comprehensive collection featuring work by leading specialists writing for specialists and nonspecialists alike.

Finley, Moses I. 1978. *The World of Odysseus*. 2nd ed. New York: Viking Press. First published in 1954, this book revolutionized the study of Dark Age society and institutions.

Griffin, Jasper. 1980. *Homer on Life and Death*. New York: Oxford University Press. An insightful literary exploration of the Homeric characterization of the epic hero.

Heitman, Richard. 2005. *Taking Her Seriously: Penelope and the Plot of the Odyssey*. Ann Arbor: University of Michigan Press. Fascinating analysis of the return home of Odysseus: Does Penelope recognize the disguised-as-beggar Odysseus from his very arrival?

Hurwit, Jeffrey M. 1985. *The Art and Culture of Early Greece, 1100–480 B.C.* Ithaca, NY: Cornell University Press, Chaps. 1–3. A keen analysis of Dark Age art in relation to the changing social scene. Chapters 4 to 6 are also recommended reading for art and culture in the Archaic period.

Latacz, Joachim. 2004. *Troy and Homer: Towards a Solution of an Old Mystery*. Oxford, UK: Oxford University Press. A new effort at finding history embedded in the traditions of the Trojan War.

Thomas, Carol G. 2005. *The Trojan War*. Westport, CT: Greenwood Press. Lucid introduction to the problems concerning the Trojan War and its aftermath.

Thomas, Carol G. and Craig Conant. 1999. *Citadel to City-State: The Transformation of Greece, 1200–700 B.C.E.* Bloomington: Indiana University Press. Written with the general reader in mind, this book traces the processes of change that led from the destruction of Bronze Age civilization to the emergence of the city-states. Each chapter is devoted to a specific site, among which are Nichoria and Lefkandi.

Whitley, James. 1991. *Style and Society in Dark Age Greece: The Changing Faces of a Preliterate Society 1100-700 BC*. Cambridge, UK: Cambridge University Press. Clear and concise overview of the changing social circumstances of Dark Age Greeks.

CHAPTER THREE

Archaic Greece
(c. 750/700–480 BC)

The forces of change that had swept over Greece in the eighth century continued at an accelerated pace in the seventh and sixth. Population continued to rise, and in response Greeks founded more colonies, spreading across the shores of the Mediterranean and Black Seas. Trade, helped by colonization, dispersed Greek goods far beyond the limits known to the Bronze Age traders. The Panhellenic shrines, festivals, and oracles grew in number and importance, further fostering the sense of a common Greek identity. The **Archaic period** also saw new forms of literary, artistic, and intellectual expression.

The Archaic period did have its dark side. Wars among Greeks became more frequent, and warfare itself became more lethal. Worse, strife within a demos became commonplace, as the leaders wrangled among themselves over power sharing and the poorer citizens fought for economic relief and their civic rights. All this movement for good or for bad took place within a new social and political framework, the city-state, which by 700 BC had replaced the old chieftain system in many parts of the Greek world.

THE FORMATION OF THE CITY-STATE (POLIS)

The term "city-state" is a modern coinage, yet city-states themselves are ancient political formations, going back to the Early Bronze Age in Mesopotamia. Basically, a city-state is a defined geographical area comprising a city and its adjacent territory, which together make up a single, self-governing political unit. The Greeks called this arrangement a *polis*, which gives us "political," "politics," and "policy."

As we saw in Chapter 2, the essential elements of the Greek city-states were already in place during the later Dark Age. The capital cities of what became city-states existed all through the Dark Age, and most of them had been the major centers of their regions during the Mycenaean period. The territorial community, the demos in its joint sense as the land and the people, appears fully developed in the Homeric epics, as are the two primary governmental organs of the Greek city-state: the assembly of men of fighting age and the council of "elders." All that was lacking to make the demos communities of 800 BC into the polis-states of 700 BC were certain necessary formalities: formal political unification of the demos and the creation of a central government.

Political Unification (Synoecism)

In all city-states, from ancient Mesopotamia to Renaissance Europe, the capital city is the focal point of the state. In most Greek city-states, all male inhabitants of a city's territory, whether they lived in the capital or the countryside, were called *politai* (members of the polis) as if they all lived together in the polis (the city). So, for example, the inhabitants of the several settlements in the plain around the main town of Megara called themselves (and were called by others) "the Megarians."

Later Greeks referred to the process of political unification of states as **synoecism**, the anglicized form of the Greek *sun-oik-ismos* ("uniting the oikoi"). The vast majority of new city-states were quite small (25 to 150 square miles in area), often consisting of a single main town and its adjacent plain holding a couple of outlying villages. In such cases, political unification was a simple matter because polis (the state) and polis (the town) were almost identical entities. Everyone lived within a few miles of everyone else, and many of the few hundred families in the demos would have been interrelated. Drawing them together into a single political unit was merely a matter of making formal the ancient ties of kinship and neighborliness.

Political unification of regional territories, those that contained several important towns and villages besides the central town, was a more complex process and is not well understood. Scholarly opinion is that the unification of the regional territories was a drawn-out development, beginning possibly in the late ninth century BC and crystallizing between about 750 and 700. Regional unification appears for the most part to have been voluntary and peaceful. For some places, however, there is evidence that intimidation and even force were used to integrate reluctant towns and villages into a political union. Such was the case in the region of Laconia, where the four original villages of Sparta absorbed the village of Amyclae, three miles to the south, into the Spartan polis against its will. Synoecism was also incomplete in some regions. Argos, for example, never fully succeeded in unifying the whole of the large region of Argolis. Several small, independent city-states continued to exist outside the plain of Argos, and even in the plain itself some villages retained a good deal of local autonomy.

By the early seventh century, dozens of independent city-states had been established all across the Mediterranean, from Ionia in the east to Sicily and southern Italy in the west, and many more would be added as the Greeks further expanded their geographical horizons. Not all Greeks lived in city-states, however. In a number of large regions of the Peloponnesus and central and northern Greece, the inhabitants opted for a different form of political organization. The *ethnos*, as the city-state Greeks called it, consisted of a people and its territory (a demos) but without a capital polis, or a central government, or formal political union. The separate towns and villages of an ethnos were independent and autonomous, yet they also had a strong sense of common identity: "the Aetolians" as distinct from "the Phocians" to their east, and so on. They were united in religious cult, and they had institutions for reaching common decisions and unified action when necessary, as in the case of attack from outsiders, for example.

GOVERNMENT IN THE EARLY CITY-STATES

Political union could not have occurred unless the local basileis, the leaders of the districts, towns, and villages of the demos, wished it. These men, the new landowning **aristocracy**, were the planners and architects of the new centralized government of the emerging city-states. The key decision was to eliminate the position of the paramount basileus and rule collectively, a relatively easy matter, as the paramount chief had little power over the other chiefs to begin with. The governmental structures of the early poleis differed in specifics, yet all followed a similar pattern: (1) the office of paramount basileus was either abolished completely or was greatly reduced in power; (2) the governing functions formerly exercised by the basileus were distributed among several officials; (3) the importance of the council of aristocratic "elders" increased, and that of the assembly of the people decreased. Of course, these decisions were not arrived at in a single year or even a single generation. The sources make it clear, however, that the process of determining which villages and districts were to be included in the polis and what kind of government it probably took no more than two or three generations.

For a unified polis to be strong and to compete successfully against other unified poleis, it had to create a more powerful and more intrusive central government than it had possessed before unification. A more complex system of organization and social control was a necessary response to the new conditions of rapidly growing populations, greater exploitation of the land and resources, increasing productivity and wealth, expanding trade, and more complicated relationships with neighboring states. Especially pressing was the need for ways to mobilize manpower and resources efficiently for warfare, for as population increased and land became scarcer, poleis fought each other over territory, a more serious business than the raids and counterraids for animals and booty that characterized "war" in the Dark Age. Firm control from the center was therefore both necessary and good for a polis as a whole, but it was especially good for the large landowners who made up the government and, like all dominant groups in human history, were highly motivated to preserve their economic and political power.

The basileus did not disappear completely. In a few poleis, a type of the traditional hereditary chiefdom, with severe limits on the paramount leader's power, appears to have continued on through the Archaic period. The Spartans retained the chieftain system the longest, though in a unique form, with two hereditary, lifelong basileis ruling as equals. In this "dual kingship" the Spartan basileis exercised considerable authority, especially in the military sphere, but their powers were curbed by five annually elected magistrates, called *ephoroi* ("overseers"). Their job was to make sure that the basileis ruled lawfully and to prosecute them if they did not.

In most poleis, however, the title "basileus" became just the name for one of a number of officials who made up the collective leadership of a city-state. The powerful families divided up the spheres of authority—administrative, military, religious, and judicial—among themselves, creating magistracies and boards. Later Greeks called this form of government **oligarchy** or "rule by the few" (*oligoi* = few). Unlike in the previous system, positions of authority could not be inherited, and their tenure was brief. In most states, by the middle of the seventh century, a term of office was limited to a single year and could not be held again until a stipulated number of years had passed. In this way, the power of single magistrate was checked, and honors were shared among the whole of the aristocratic community. Each city-state developed its own system of magistracies according to its own needs and circumstances. Obviously, small poleis needed fewer officials than large ones.

In general there was no hierarchy among the major offices, although many states did have a principal official who was regarded as the chief administrator. The most common titles for the chief officer were *archon* (e.g., at Athens and elsewhere in central Greece) and *prytanis* (e.g., at Corinth and poleis in Ionia). The chief magistrate sometimes retained the old title of basileus. In some poleis—Athens, for example, and Megara—an officer called the *polemarchos* ("war leader") was in charge of military operations. Supervision of religious activities fell to another magistrate or, more often, a board of magistrates, which also judged crimes having to do with religion, such as homicides, which polluted the community. The common use of the title basileis to designate these officials is evidence of the reverence that was still attached to the name.

The real center of power in the early city-states, however, resided not in the officials and boards but in the council of elders. The boule in the Archaic poleis had even more power than the boule in Homeric society. The members were normally recruited from the highest magistrates, who entered the council after their terms of office. Membership in the council was usually for a long term or even for life. The archons and other magistrates, by contrast, had limited terms and would hesitate to oppose the august body of prominent men whose ranks they wished some day to join. The aristocratic council met more frequently than in the pre-state period and assumed for itself the task of making policies and drafting laws for the polis.

As the authority of the council increased, the limited power of the old assembly of adult male citizens to influence policy was further reduced in the oligarchic city-state. Some states excluded the poorest citizens from membership in the assembly by imposing a property qualification. Some restricted the number of assembly meetings and the business to be brought before it, or they curtailed free discussion of the issues. The sovereignty of the aristocratic council, however, would be relatively short-lived; as time passed, the authority of the assembly to decide policy would increase.

THE COLONIZING MOVEMENT

The widespread emigration of Greeks from their Aegean homelands that had begun in the mid-eighth century continued for more than two centuries. When it ended, around 500 BC, the Greek world extended from Spain in the west to Colchis at the furthest point of the Black Sea in the east and from the northern coast of Africa in the south to Ukraine in the north. As was pointed out in Chapter 2, the primary causes of this remarkable expansion were two: the search for sources of metal to satisfy the Greeks' growing need and the hope of acquiring the land required to live the life of a citizen in the new poleis as opportunities for land at home dwindled. Founding a **colony** required careful preparation. The "mother" polis (*mētropolis*) had to choose a site for the colony, obtain divine approval for it, plan the new settlement, and choose its *oikistēs* (founder). It is also becoming clear to historians that the sponsorship of a colony is often to be interpreted loosely, as there appear to be colonies that were in all likelihood private enterprises; although most of the individuals involved may have come from one particular city-state, there was manifestly no city-state organizing the foundation.

It was the oikist who was responsible for leading out the colonists, laying out the city's defenses, establishing the sanctuaries of the gods, and assigning the kleroi to the settlers. If his leadership proved successful, the oikist would become the guardian hero of the new polis after his death, although it is easy to imagine that many an honored oikist was in fact a later invention designed to facilitate a relationship between colony and "metropolis." The colony itself would remain linked to its metropolis by bonds of kinship and cult, symbolized by the fire the oikist brought from the metropolis' hearth to kindle the hearth of the new polis. To ensure that cult practices be carried out in keeping with ancestral custom, a priest or priestess also migrated from the metropolis. Otherwise, however, the colony was a new and completely independent polis, as the Greek term for colony, apoi-kia, indicates: "a home away [from their old home]" for the colonists.

The colonizing movement had two phases, each lasting a little over a century. The first began in the mid-eighth century BC and was directed to Italy and the western Mediterranean; the second started about a century later and was concentrated on the north Aegean and the Black Sea. The pioneers in the colonization of Italy were Euboeans, the same people who had helped maintain contact between Greeks and the Near East during the Dark Age. Following routes that had been blazed by Phoenician traders, they founded a trading settlement in the early eighth century on the island of Pithecusae (modern Ischia) in the Bay of Naples. It was a huge success, attracting not only other Greeks but also Phoenicians, who made up 15 percent of the more than ten thousand inhabitants that eventually occupied this tiny island. With its good harbor, Pithecusae was well situated to

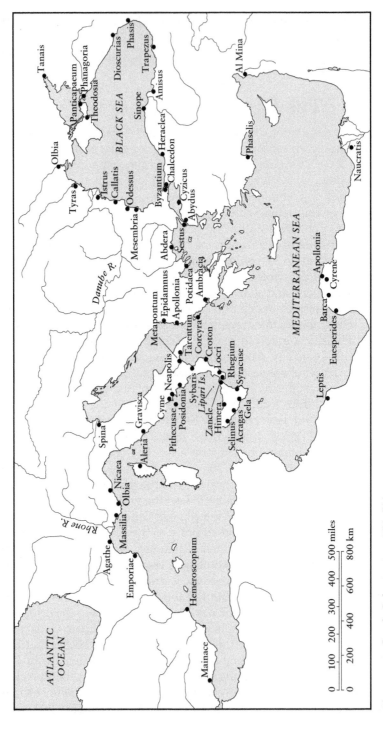

Figure 3.1. Greek Colonization: 750–500 BC.

exploit the iron deposits on the nearby island of Elba and to trade with the Italic populations of the mainland.

The Euboeans followed up their success at Pithecusae with additional poleis: Cumae (757) on the Italian mainland near modern Naples, and four in Sicily between 734 and the end of the century. Poleis in the Peloponnesus, plagued by problems caused by unequal distribution of land at home, also sent out colonists to the fertile areas of Italy and Sicily. The Corinthians, for example, settled the Adriatic island of Corcyra (modern Corfu; c. 734) and a year later founded Syracuse, which would become the major city-state in Sicily and a famous center of culture in the Greek world. Toward the very end of the century, the Spartans established their one and only overseas colony, Taras in southern Italy, settled by exiled dissidents.

Colonization of the West continued into the seventh century as the early colonies spun off daughter settlements and newcomers from other parts of old Greece came looking for farmland and trading opportunities. For example, about 600 BC, colonists from Phocaea on the coast of Anatolia founded Massilia (modern Marseilles) on the coast of southern France. Its location at the mouth of the Rhone River afforded the Massilians easy access to the lucrative trade with the Celtic inhabitants of the upper Rhone Valley. By then, however, opportunities for further Greek expansion in the West were disappearing. Besides, the western Greeks had rivals: Phoenicians who had colonized Carthage (in modern Tunisia) and had been partners with the Greeks up to this time were establishing their own empire in western Sicily, southern Spain, and the islands of Corsica and Sardinia.

There were other places to go, however. For example, the people of the tiny island of Thera, feeling the pinch of land shortage, founded Cyrene in Libya (c. 630). It was the areas around the Hellespont and the Black Sea, though, with their good fishing grounds, rich soil, mineral wealth, and trading possibilities, that lured the Greeks the most. And they went at it with gusto: Miletus alone is credited in the ancient sources with having founded ninety colonies. Having no rivals in this area (unlike in the Mediterranean basin), the Greeks were able to establish new colonies throughout the Archaic and Classical periods until the Black Sea was almost entirely ringed by Greek poleis. Many colonies became rich and powerful, among them Byzantium (founded by Megarians c. 660), which a thousand years later, under its new name, Constantinople, would become the capital of the Roman Empire. The transplanted city-states proudly proclaimed their Greekness, building monumental temples, patronizing Panhellenic institutions such as the Delphic oracle and the Olympic games, and eagerly staying abreast of cultural developments in the Aegean. (The earliest example of the Greek alphabet is from the town of Gabii near Rome and the earliest surviving hexameter verse in fact comes from Pithecusae.)

Relations with the people into whose lands the colonists came were complex. On one hand, the colonies were gateways through which various peoples of southern Europe and the Black Sea areas obtained access to the products and culture of the Greeks and other Mediterranean societies. The Etruscans in Italy, for example, adapted the Greek alphabet and avidly embraced Greek art and even religious cult. (See Plate Xa.) On the other hand, the Greeks were intruders, and conflict with the native inhabitants occurred frequently. Occasionally Greeks even became virtual subjects of their non-Greek neighbors, as in Egypt where the only Greek settlement, Naucratis, was founded c. 625 BC as a trading post under strict Egyptian supervision by a consortium of twelve eastern Greek cities. A few new cities, such as Syracuse, Byzantium, and Heraclea Pontica, ultimately succeeded in expelling or enslaving their non-Greek neighbors. For the most part, however, the colonists made accommodations with their non-Greek neighbors, trading and intermarrying with them and sometimes even sharing their territory. Nor indeed was the cultural exchange all in one direction. For instance, cults such as those of the Thracian goddess Bendis and the divine musician Orpheus spread throughout the Aegean and beyond.

Economic and Social Divisions in the Archaic Poleis

The colonizing movement was only a partial remedy for the disparity in land ownership. Not every family could emigrate, and as the population at home continued to grow, each new generation of oikoi found it increasingly difficult to gain access to good land. The result was a widening of the existing economic and social gulf between the small group at the top—comprising perhaps no more than 20 percent of the families—and all the rest.

The economic power of aristocratic families rested on their inherited landholdings. As a group they controlled a disproportionate share of the total agricultural land in the demos and an even greater share of the good land, including lush meadows for grazing their horses and cattle. They became even richer by concentrating on cash crops, such as wine and olive oil. Most significant for their profits was their ability to exploit the plight of the poorest farmers, who made up a third or more of the demos. Some of them mortgaged their kleroi to the rich, paying off the debt with a portion of their crops; others became sharecroppers on rich men's lands. Many were reduced to the status of thetes. The majority of citizens in a polis, however—perhaps 50 percent of households—although far from wealthy, were economically self-sufficient and therefore economically neither rich nor dependent on the rich. The fourth-century philosopher Aristotle in his *Politics* called this group "the middlers" (*hoi mesoi*), the portion of the polis that was between the very rich and the very poor and possessed a moderate amount of wealth.

These three divisions of rich, middling, and poor were not monolithic, of course; within each there were gradations of wealth and social rank. The small upper class was dominated by a still smaller number of families that were preeminent because of their nobler bloodlines and greater wealth: an aristocracy within an aristocracy. Moreover, the hierarchy was subject to shifts; one family might rise into the ranks of the upper nobility and another might drop down into the lesser nobility. Nevertheless, the propertied class as a whole remained clearly marked off from the groups below them. They protected their economic and social exclusiveness by marrying only among themselves. Moreover, they cultivated an image of group superiority, calling themselves "the good" (*hoi agathoi*) on the basis of their wealth and ancestry, while lumping together those outside the landed nobility as "the bad" (*hoi kakoi*) and "the many" (*hoi polloi*).

Within the middle group there was greater economic and social gradation. Some non-noble oikoi shared in the increasing prosperity of the Archaic Age and were fairly well off; at the other end of the scale were those barely keeping out of debt. The differences in economic status—and therefore in social status—among the independent farmers and craftsmen prevented them from perceiving themselves as a class with their own interests, like the rich landowners. Upward mobility, even for the top of this group, was not easy. Yet if a commoner family became wealthy enough, it could marry into the nobility. The sixth-century aristocratic poet Theognis complains that although men take pains to make their animals "well-born" by careful breeding, a "good man" (agathos) will not hesitate to marry the daughter of a "bad man" (kakos) if she brings with her a good dowry. "Wealth," he laments, "corrupts a lineage" (*Theognidea* 183–192). Downward mobility, on the other hand, was more common, as unmanageable debt frequently reduced farmers to the condition of a thes. The erosion of the independent farmer group in the seventh century became a serious problem within the city-states.

The gradations of the bottom group would have been only in the degree of abjectness, as the chances for economic betterment for the very poor were slight. It was not just poverty that made the lives of thetes miserable. They lacked even the limited protection that slaves received from belonging to an oikos and also had to endure the stigma of working for others, which for the Greeks connoted loss of freedom. It is understandable that when Homer wished to emphasize the utter misery of death, he had the dead Achilles tell Odysseus that he would rather be alive and the thes of a landless man—the poorest of the poor—than king of the dead (*Odyssey* 11.489–491).

From a number of poleis come various slang terms denoting persons of inferior status: "the naked ones" (Argos), "dusty-feet" (Epidaurus), "wearers of sheep-skins" (Sicyon), "wearers of dog-skin helmets" (Corinth). In addition to the thetes, there existed in some areas of Greece another category of laborers, characterized as "between free persons and slaves." Among those who endured this sort of semislavery were the Spartan helots. These were the original inhabitants of parts of Laconia and most of Messenia who were conquered by the Spartans in war and made to work for the Spartan citizens as serfs on what had been their own land. The helots were given some human rights—they could marry and raise a family and keep a portion of their production—but in most respects they were property, as we shall see in the next chapter.

The only persons of lower status than these were, of course, the actual slaves, males and females acquired from the outside by capture or purchase who had no freedom whatever and no human rights and were legally classed as property. Their children too were slaves, owned by their parents' owner. It was not until the sixth century that slaves began to pour into the poleis in large numbers. Some have argued that the increased use of slaves was the result of political reforms abolishing debt bondage within the polis, which forced the rich, who had found it profitable to exploit the labor of impoverished citizens, to turn to slave labor.

Citizenship

Although all free-born members of the polis were citizens (*politai*), they were far from equal in their citizen rights. Aside from their public role in religion, female citizens were denied any participation in political affairs. This was the exclusive domain of male citizens who were over eighteen years of age. Each man's share of civic responsibilities and rights, however—to vote and speak in the assembly, hold office, serve as judges, and fight in the army—was determined unequally along economic and social lines. In the early city-states, as we have seen, only the rich and well born possessed the full range of citizen privileges. Non-noble citizens of moderate means were barred from holding office, and in many cases the poorest citizens had no vote in the assembly. Full participation by all citizens in the governance of their poleis would be achieved only at the end of the Archaic period and then only in the democratic states; in oligarchic states, the poorest members would continue to be second-class citizens. Even in the most democratic poleis, citizenship would be denied to ex-slaves and resident aliens.

Women, however, always played important roles in the Greek state. Religion was an integral part of the polis, where the proper worship of the gods was key to good order, prosperity, and success in battle should war come calling. Many priesthoods were held by women. In addition, as an aggregate of oikoi, from an early date the polis depended on women for the stability of the household in terms of the bearing and rearing of children, the production of clothing, and in the case of the more affluent households, the management of slaves.

Resentment from Below and the Beginnings of Social Change

There was strong popular resentment against the wealth, power, and arrogance of the self-styled agathoi in the seventh century. The rallying cry among the have-nots must have been "redistribution of the land!" The middling oikoi—those that produced enough to live on or enough and some extra—also had cause for resentment. Because the aristocratic households successfully held on to most of the fertile soil, the independent farmers had few opportunities to acquire good land. They could choose to emigrate abroad, which many did, or else acquire marginal land far from their villages, which yielded poorer return for extra labor and increased travel time. The middle group also chafed at being shut out of positions of power and prestige by the oligarchy's lock on the magistracies, boards, and particularly the council, where political decisions were formulated. The well-off farmers were just as liable to be cheated in the law courts as the poorer ones and just as helpless against "crooked judgments." In the assembly, the one organ of government to which they were admitted, the people's voice carried little weight against the concentrated power of the rich.

Yet, despite the strength of the ruling oligarchs and the apparent weakness of the rest of the demos, absolute domination by the former was destined to be short-lived. By the early sixth century, the oligarchic hold was weakening and more inclusive forms of government were emerging that would eventually give political power to the mass of people, including the poor. Spearheading the protest against aristocratic excess was the middle group of independent farmers over whom the oligarchs had the least control. We are fortunate to have a very early voice for this group, **Hesiod**.

Hesiod: The View from Below

In addition to the *Theogony*, Hesiod is credited with another long hexameter poem (828 lines), about farming, called *Works and Days*. Unlike the Homeric epics, which are set in a distant Age of Heroes and tell of the triumphs and tragedies of great warrior chiefs, *Works and Days* is set in the present (c. 700 BC) and tells about ordinary people and their ordinary lives. In the *Iliad* and the *Odyssey*, common folk are visible only as part of the social background. They are given collective roles as the mass of soldiers or citizens in the assemblies; or they appear in vignettes about farmers, housewives, shepherds, and craftsmen. These Hesiod puts in the foreground.

Hesiod tells us that he and his brother, Perses, lived in the small Boeotian village of Ascra (part of the polis of Thespiae, five miles away), and when their father died a dispute arose over the division of the kleros. Perses cheated or tried to cheat Hesiod of a portion of the inheritance by bribing the judges (basileis). After the judgment, Hesiod intimates, Perses became a loafer and a spendthrift and reduced himself to such poverty that he found it necessary to go to his poet-brother for help. Whether this is the literal truth or a fiction, such family situations must have been common.

The quarrel provides the pretext for the poem's form—a sermon to his erring brother. Sermonizing poetry, so different from that of the Homeric narrative, was clearly influenced by the ancient genre of Near Eastern "wisdom literature," which consisted of exhortations, instructions, and admonitions addressed to a son or other relative, or even to a king, and was spiced with stories and proverbs about right and wrong. Though ostensibly Hesiod was advising Perses, the real audience was the whole group to which he and Perses belonged, namely, the upper level of the independent farmers, the middlers. At other points in the poem, however, he speaks on behalf of his peers and directs his sermonizing to the ruling group, whom he calls basileis.

Hesiod addresses the basileis very sternly, not at all deferentially. He calls them "gift-eating" basileis and accuses them straight out of habitually rendering their verdicts "with crooked judgments." He tells them that Zeus himself is watching over his daughter Dike ("Justice") and avenges unjust acts against her committed by those in power. Thus, the basic civil moral that justice through law is the foundation of good government appears already fully formed in Hesiod.

DOCUMENT 3.1

Hesiod lectures the aristocrats.

O basileis, you too observe well this judgment, for the deathless ones, who are near among people, observe all those who wear each other out with crooked judgments, paying no attention to the vengeance of the gods. . . . There is the virgin Dike, born from Zeus, majestic and revered among the gods who hold Olympus. And whenever somebody hurts her by scorning her crookedly, she straightway seats herself at the side of father Zeus, the son of Cronus, and tells him about the unjust thinking of people, until the demos atones for the outrages of the basileis who, by thinking pernicious thoughts, veer off the right track by pronouncing judgments crookedly. . . . O basileis, straighten your words, gift-eaters, and forget entirely crooked judgments.

(*Works and Days* 248–264 Tandy, adapted)

A moralistic tone pervades the entire poem. Hesiod has a whole litany of proverbial dos and don'ts that we could find in any peasant society. He counsels a strict reciprocity in all dealings. When you borrow from a neighbor, he says, "pay it back well, with the same measure, or better if you can, so that you may later find him reliable should you need him" (349–351).

At the core of Hesiod's moral program is the ethic of work, arduous manual labor:

> It is from work that men are many-sheeped and rich, and the man
> who works is much dearer to the deathless ones. Work is no reproach;
> idleness is a reproach. If you work the idler will quickly envy you as
> you become wealthy. Success and renown attend upon wealth.
>
> (*Works and Days* 308–313 Tandy)

Here, Hesiod asserts that through work the ordinary farmer may win the three prizes of wealth, divine favor, and glory, which in the Homeric epics only heroes could attain. The prizes of work, of course, are pared down to suit the humble life of a rural village. For Hesiod and his neighbors wealth meant not golden goblets, but "having their granaries full of the sustenance of life" at harvest time and not having to borrow; renown was being admired and respected by all the folk in the village.

As a social document of the peasant-farmer's values, *Works and Days* also allows us to appreciate class differences in outlook toward institutions such as marriage. Among the upper class, marriage was primarily a means of establishing political alliances and enhancing family prestige. Noble families often sought advantageous marriages outside their polis. Hesiod's vantage point, rather, is that of a village farmer. It is not a wife who will bring him political connections that he seeks, but a local girl who will not sully his reputation if she should turn out to be a glutton or lazy or unfaithful.

Marry a virgin so that you may teach her devoted ways, and marry
especially one who resides near you, lest you marry a source of laughter
for the neighbors. For a man carries off nothing better than a good wife,
and in turn there is nothing more chilling than an evil one. . . .

(Works and Days 699–703 Tandy)

This misogyny was an attitude frequently expressed in the Archaic period
and it continued throughout Greek antiquity. The best-known illustration of this
way of thinking is the myth of Pandora, the first woman, as it is told in both the
Theogony (571–612) and *Works and Days* (60–105). Zeus, Hesiod says, commanded
this "beautiful evil" to be created as a punishment for the crime of Prometheus,
who stole fire from the gods and gave it to humans. Pandora opened the lid of
a jar containing all the plagues and diseases of the world and let them out. All
womankind inherited Pandora's "shameless mind and deceitful nature," her "lies
and coaxing words" (78). Women live off men like the drones among the bees.
"Do not let a woman wiggling her behind deceive you with her wheedling words.
She is after your granary. The man who trusts a woman trusts thieves" (373–375).

Hesiod's class of middling farmers resembled the wealthy class in one important respect: They exploited the labor of others. Hesiod takes for granted that the
farmers he addresses can afford to own at least one slave woman or man, or take
on a regular hired hand (thes), and employ day workers at busy times. The farmer
keeps his eye on the bottom line. The day's food for a hired plowman is to be carefully measured out—just enough to keep up his energy level. He advises hiring
a thes who has no oikos (he will work for less) and a childless female worker ("a
worker with a child at her breast is a bother" 603).

However much he railed against the wealthy and powerful, Hesiod, then, was
not a "champion of the oppressed," as some historians have called him. Rather
his was the indignant voice of the middle: Zeus will look favorably on those who
are pious, hard working, and just and in the end will punish those who are not. A
hundred years later in Athens, another thunderous voice would be raised against
the evil greed and violent actions of the aristocrats—this time not from below but
from a member of the aristocracy, the statesman Solon, whose reforms would pave
the way for Athenian democracy.

THE HOPLITE ARMY

Battles between poleis were fought by men like Hesiod and his neighbors, average
farmers and craftsmen. Developments in military equipment and organization
altered the nature of warfare in the early city-states. It is in this new type of
military organization that we most clearly observe the polis ideology that the
citizen is the slave of the common good. Beginning about 650 BC polis armies were
increasingly made up of heavily armored foot soldiers called **hoplites**, arranged
in a tightly packed formation—the **phalanx**—which apparently evolved from
the looser type of mass formation depicted in the *Iliad*. The transition to the new
form of fighting was gradual; but in the fully developed phalanx, as we see it in

fifth- and fourth-century BC sources, the soldiers lined up shoulder to shoulder with each rank, almost treading on the heels of the one in front of it.

Battle tactics were quite simple: Opposing phalanxes formed, charged at one another, and collided. The hoplite's weapons were a long heavy spear, used for thrusting and jabbing, and a short slashing sword for close-in fighting. For protection he wore a helmet, breastplate, and greaves (shin and knee protectors), all made of bronze and covering as much of the body as possible. The most important piece of equipment was a new type of shield called the *hoplon*, which was quite different from the shields carried by the Homeric warriors. It was round, made of wood covered with a thin sheet of bronze, and was held by inserting the left arm through a central band and gripping a strap at the rim, which gave it maneuverability. Its large size (about three feet in diameter) gave cover to the man on the left, allowing hoplites to fight close together with half of their bodies protected by the adjacent man's shield. Seen from the front, a phalanx presented nearly a solid wall of shields, helmeted heads, and spears. (See Plate VIa.)

A hoplite battle was a ferocious affair. When the opposing front lines collided, the ranks behind, stacked up to eight rows deep, shoved against those in

Figure 3.2. Bronze votive offering, first quarter of the seventh century, said to have been found near Thebes. This hoplite has lost his right arm and spear, as well as his shield, which would have been attached to his left forearm. The inscription on his legs contains two hexameter lines: "Mantiklos dedicated me to the farshooter, silver-bowed Apollo from his share; and may you too, Phoebus [=Apollo], give a generous return." Boston, Museum of Fine Arts.

front—the maneuver was called "the pushing"—using their weight to break the enemy's ranks. It took considerable courage to keep place in the ranks when all around you was the sight, sound, and smell of iron piercing into flesh and bone, all this while carrying up to 70 pounds of equipment! Heartened by the presence of friends and family members close by, though, most men did stand fast, "biting their lip with their teeth," as the Spartan poet Tyrtaeus (c. 650 BC) says, out of personal pride and sense of duty as a citizen.

> It benefits the whole community and state,
> when with a firm stance in the foremost rank
> a man bides steadfast, with no thought of shameful flight.
> (Tyrtaeus fr. 9.15–17 West)

Although the fighting was savage, hoplite battles were usually brief, seldom lasting more than an hour, and casualties were relatively light for both losers and victors, seldom over 15 percent. Once the enemy broke ranks and fled, there was not much pursuit, so massacres were rare. Campaigns, too, were brief; usually, a single set battle ended the fighting for the summer. Farmer-hoplites, whether winners or losers, could not stay long away from their fields and animals.

Not all citizens fought in the phalanx, however. The very wealthiest citizens (perhaps 10 percent of all citizens) could afford horses for themselves and so they served as cavalry, although the Greek terrain was no more hospitable for cavalry than it had been for chariots. Because hoplites had to furnish their own arms and armor, which were fairly expensive, the poorest men were excluded and served instead as light-armed troops. The proportion of the nonhoplite oikoi in the Archaic period would have varied from polis to polis: perhaps 20 or 30 percent of all citizen families. Although disparities in wealth and social status separated phalanx fighters from light-armed skirmishers, there were no such distinctions within the phalanx itself. In the ranks, where high-born nobles and men from the middle fought side by side, strict equality prevailed. Under these conditions it would become increasingly difficult for the nobles to claim that they alone were competent to wield political power and formulate policy for their poleis.

THE ARCHAIC AGE TYRANTS

The first serious challenge to oligarchic rule came not from below but from within the elite group itself, in the form of a new political phenomenon the Greeks called **tyranny** (*tyrannis*). The "age of tyrants" lasted from about 670 to 500 BC, affecting a great many of the Greek states. The Archaic Age tyrant (*tyrannos*) was what we call today a dictator or strongman, a single ruler who, however, lacked the legitimacy of the old paramount basileus. Indeed, the Greeks had no name for such a figure; the title tyrannos was likely borrowed from the Lydians, an Anatolian people. Tyrants were only later regarded as evil despots. Their subsequent ill repute stemmed partly from propaganda spread by the aristocrats themselves, who naturally resented the domination of a single man, and partly from the popular sentiment that dictatorial rule posed a threat to the freedom of all. Yet the early tyrants were probably viewed more favorably by their nonaristocratic contemporaries.

Very few of the dozens of tyrants who grabbed power in their poleis are known in any detail, but we can discern a general pattern. First, most tyrants arose from the elite group, although not necessarily from the top-ranked families. Cypselus of Corinth (c. 657–627), for instance, was marginalized within the prominent "clan" of the **Bacchiads**, because his mother, a Bacchiad, had married outside the clan. In addition to noble birth, would-be tyrants were distinguished in their poleis for their personal achievements. Cypselus, prior to seizing control, had held the post of polemarch (military commander) in Corinth, as had another famous tyrant, Orthagoras of Sicyon (mid-seventh century). Cylon of Athens, whose attempted coup in 632 failed, had won fame as a victor in the Olympic games. Finally, despite attempts to form dynasties by passing on their rule to their sons, few tyrannies lasted more than three generations and most collapsed after one or two.

Continual feuding among the major aristocratic factions certainly contributed to the emergence of the tyrants. Each faction was associated with a preeminent lineage (*genos*) that extended an umbrella of fictive kinship over less prestigious families, who supported the leading family in its political ambitions. The frequent bouts of violence and bloodshed among what were basically rival gangs of hotheaded young aristocrats were politically disruptive. The intervention of a strongman who could keep them in check would be welcome to the people, if not to the aristocrats.

The would-be tyrant also needed armed followers. These might be disaffected aristocrats within the polis who were frozen out of the ruling circle, or a mercenary force from outside the polis. Such aid was sometimes supplied by a friendly tyrant (for his abortive coup, the Athenian Cylon received troops from his father-in-law Theagenes, tyrant of Megara). Pisistratus of Athens had a variety of resources in his three attempts to seize power, including local bodyguards, mercenaries, and troops donated by powerful outsiders. His story is told in Chapter 5.

Yet no tyrant, however great his resources, could have overthrown the oligarchs without the tacit support of the citizens themselves, particularly the heavily armed farmer-hoplites. These need not have actively helped him; they could just stand aside and refuse to defend the nobles. Those at the bottom of the social pyramid would naturally have supported a coup against the group that was exploiting them. Indeed, the tyrants seem to have presented themselves as champions of the demos against the oligarchs. Aristotle in the fourth century put it concisely:

> A tyrant is set up from among the demos and the multitude to oppose the nobles so that the people may suffer no injustice from them. This is clear from the facts of history. For almost all the tyrants have arisen from being leaders of the people [*dēmagōgoi*; hence "demagogue"], so to speak, having gained their confidence by slandering the nobles.
>
> (*Politics* 1310b 12–17 Rackham, adapted)

By and large, the tyrants did favor the poor over the rich, sometimes confiscating the land of the wealthy and redistributing it to the poor and making laws that limited aristocratic privilege. They initiated the construction of temples, harbors, and fortifications—as well as improvements in the water supply, drainage systems, and the like—all of which provided work for poor citizens. Moreover, they encouraged trade and commerce. For example, Periander, the son of Cypselus, built a stone trackway across the Isthmus of Corinth (where a canal runs today), allowing ships and cargoes to be hauled between the Saronic and Corinthian gulfs. Under tyranny, cultural activities also thrived. New religious cults and festivals were established, and tyrants made special efforts to attract the best artists, architects, poets, and thinkers in Greece to their poleis.

The founding tyrants had won popular support because of their charisma and achievements. Their sons, however, as heirs to a nonexistent office, were quite vulnerable to opposition. Although some succeeded on their own merits, most resorted to increasingly "tyrannical" measures, which only exacerbated resentment against them. So, the second- or third-generation tyrants were overthrown, and their exiled opponents returned, usually to reestablish oligarchic rule. Rarely, however, were the poleis the same after a tyranny. The farmer-hoplites were no longer willing to vote for leaders whom they could not hold accountable. Nor could the nobles now refuse their inclusion in the process of public decisions or take back from the poor the benefits that the tyrants had bestowed on them to make their lives easier. So it is paradoxically possible to view tyranny as a transitional structure that led to democracy.

THE ARTS AND SCIENCES

In art as well as in literature, philosophy, and science, Archaic Greece experienced a burst of creativity unsurpassed in any comparable time period of the ancient world. Building on the achievements of the Late Geometric period, the craftsmen of the seventh and sixth centuries attained new heights of excellence in all forms of visual art. With the development of the city-state, differences in style among the various poleis became more distinct. This is most evident in the pottery, which continues in the Archaic period to be the most ample source for measuring artistic evolution.

Art and Architecture

During Cypselus' reign as tyrant, Corinth emerged as the leading commercial center of Greece. Corinthian potters dominated the trade in finely painted pottery, exporting huge quantities of their specialty item, tiny perfume flasks—exquisitely decorated in the fashionable orientalizing style—filled with scented olive oil. The enterprising Corinthians also invented a widely imitated technique called "black-figure," which permitted the rendition of minute details. In this technique the vase painter first applied to the pale yellowish Corinthian clay a slip composed of clay particles suspended in water; on this field, he created silhouetted figurative and decorative forms. He then used a sharp point to incise linear details into the clay surface. The decoration was generally further enhanced with red and white colors. When the vase was fired, the areas covered with the clay slip turned black. Corinthian black-figure ware was enormously popular, but as often happens, success led to mass production and a consequent decline in quality, as the famous animal motifs were monotonously and carelessly repeated.

By 550, Athenian black-figure pottery, featuring differently shaped and larger vessels, had driven Corinthian vases from the export market. Around 530, the Athenians, in turn, invented a new style called "red-figure," which reversed the black-figure technique. The artist drew outlines first and then painted the background with a gloss (clay slip) that fired black, leaving the outlined areas in the orange-red color of the Attic clay itself. Afterward he painted on the details with a fine brush. This allowed a more subtle and refined rendering of detail than the incised black-figure technique. Portraits of contemporary daily life were added to the standard mythological and heroic scenes; athletics, horsemanship, and rowdy drinking parties are favorite themes. On some vases erotic acts, both heterosexual and homosexual, are represented graphically. In such scenes, the men are citizens, but the women are all prostitutes (slaves or foreigners). Citizen women appear in domestic settings, often accompanied by their female slaves.

Figure 3.3. These two views of an Attic *amphora* (storage jar) showing the heroes Achilles and Ajax playing a board game are attributed to the Andocides Painter and to the Lysippides Painter (c. 530 BC). We call this vase "bilingual" because it is decorated in the new red-figure technique on one side and in traditional black-figure on the other. Boston, Museum of Fine Arts.

Monumental sculpture (life-size or larger) in both marble and bronze statues was an innovation of the Archaic period. From the Egyptians the Archaic Greeks learned the techniques of making large freestanding sculptures. Most Greek Archaic statues are in the form of either a naked "young male" (*kouros*) or a clothed "young maiden" (*korē*). Gradually, sculptors departed from the rigidly stylized, static Egyptian model toward a more naturalistic representation of the human body. From the very beginning these sculptures were brightly painted, enhancing their lifelike qualities. (See Plate XIIb.) Kouroi and korai were commonly set up by wealthy families as grave monuments or as offerings in the sanctuary of a god or goddess. Often bearing an inscription with the dedicator's name, they were highly public advertisements of a family's or an individual's status in the community.

The architecture of the Archaic period still centered on religious buildings, the monumental temple, and (beginning in the sixth century) smaller edifices, such as the "treasuries," which housed dedications to the gods. A significant advance in temple architecture occurred around the middle of the seventh century, when limestone and marble replaced mud brick and wood. Here again, the Greeks were indebted to the Egyptians from whom they learned the engineering skills necessary for handling huge stone blocks. By the early sixth century, the two main types or "orders" of architecture, the Doric and the Ionic (see Figure 7.4), were well-established, and Greek temples looked much as they would for the next five hundred years. As other stone buildings were added in the sixth century, all the capital poleis (except Sparta) began to resemble true urban centers. Most construction was in and around the *agora*, "the gathering place," a large open space at or near the center of the city. The agora became the marketplace and public space of the city and therefore of the whole polis. It was the place where male citizens congregated to do business, gossip, and make political deals. Market stalls were sheltered in shaded colonnades called stoas. Official buildings, such as the council house, distinguished the agora as the state center; sanctuaries, fountain houses, and public monuments gave it grace and dignity.

Lyric Poetry

Although heroic epics continued to be produced during the Archaic period, most talented poets preferred to express themselves in other genres, which we lump together under the rubric of **lyric poetry**. Indeed the seventh and sixth centuries BC are often referred to as the "lyric age" of Greece. Only a tiny fraction of all the verses composed then are extant today, most in fragmentary form, yet what we have provides an ample enough doorway into the thought and concerns of the Archaic Greeks.

The roots of lyric poetry extend far back in time to folk songs created for special occasions, such as harvests, weddings, funerals, and coming-of-age rituals, or to hymns, fables, drinking songs, and love songs—everything, in other words, that pertained to communal and private life. With the advent of literacy, songs could now be preserved and circulated; poets could attain not merely local but Panhellenic fame by competing with their more carefully crafted songs composed and polished in writing. Some kinds of poems were performed to the

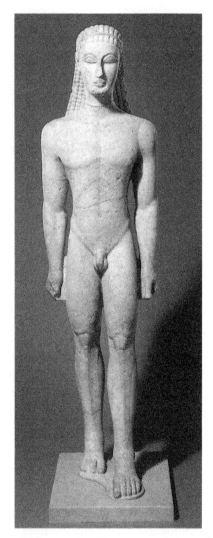

Figure 3.4. Statue of Khonsuiraa, an Egyptian nobleman (early seventh century BC). Boston, Museum of Fine Arts.

Figure 3.5. Marble kouros, said to be from Attica (c. 600–480 BC). Height without plinth, 6' 9". Whereas the stiff and stylized pose as well as the carving methods employed in Egyptian stone statuary were sources of inspiration, the Archaic Greek sculptor has created a freestanding, nude male figure. New York, The Metropolitan Museum of Art.

Figure 3.6. This marble kouros with an inscribed base stood on the grave of Aristodicus in Attica (c. 510–500 BC). Although naturalistically proportioned and fluidly modeled, this statue of a short-haired athletic youth still conforms to the traditional kouros pose. Athens, National Archaeological Museum.

Figure 3.7. Late Archaic korē from the acropolis of Athens (c. 490 BC), dedicated by Euthydicus. Athens, Acropolis Museum.

accompaniment of a lyre (*lyra*, hence "lyric"), others to a flute-like instrument (*aulos*). A major distinction is made by modern scholars between solo songs and songs performed by a chorus of young men or women who sang and danced to the music of the lyre. Solo poetry could be presented before large public audiences or small private gatherings of upper-class males at a drinking party (*symposium*). Choral odes might run to several hundred lines, whereas solo poems were usually much shorter, sometimes just a few lines.

Most Archaic lyric poetry was not choral; it was personal, sometimes extremely so, in subject and tone. The poets sang about drinking, friends and enemies, sexual love, old age and death, politics, war, and morality. The poet's tone could range from lighthearted to bitter to contemplative. They not only give us rare insights into feelings about private matters but also, because private life and polis life were so closely intertwined, reflect sentiments and attitudes about their society. Further, the poetry presents, from a strictly male point of view (Sappho's verses excepted), the social attitudes of both the elite and the middle strata. Although we have fragments from about two dozen poets of this period, we can sample only a few of them here. We shall meet other Archaic poets in later chapters.

Some Lyric Poets

Archilochus of Paros (mid-seventh century) represents himself as both a soldier of fortune and an inspired poet. He writes of drinking bouts, his sex life, his comrades and enemies, battles, and shipwrecks. He delights in skewering pretentiousness.

> I don't like an army commander who's tall, or goes at a trot,
> or one who has glamorous wavy hair, or trims his beard a lot.
> A shortish sort of chap, who's bandy-looking around the shins,
> he's my ideal, one full of guts, and steady on his pins.
>   (Archilochus fr. 114 West)

The Spartans found these next couplets—which mock the ideal of heroic self-sacrifice—so outrageous that they forbade the recitation of Archilochus' poetry at Sparta.

> Some Thracian sports my splendid shield:
> I had to leave it in a wood,
> but saved my skin. Well, I don't care—
> I'll get another just as good.
>   (Archilochus fr. 5 West, adapted)

Some lyric poets also derided aristocratic display of luxury. For example, the philosopher-poet Xenophanes (c. 570–475 BC) censured the elite of his native Colophon who went to the assembly in their all-purple cloaks, "proud in the splendor of their finely coiffured hair/and sleek with unguents of the choicest scent" (fr. 3 West). Hipponax of Ephesus (late sixth century) took a more cynical approach toward wealth. He adopted the persona of an urban hustler, always broke and engaging in drunken brawls and escapades. He revels in the low life of the city and even makes fun of his poverty. "And Wealth—he's all too blind—he's never come/to my house, never said, 'Hipponax, here's/three thousand silver drachmas, and a heap/of other stuff besides.' No, he's a dimwit" (fr. 36 West). There are also voices that sound Hesiodic, promoting the commonsense values held by ordinary citizens of middling means. A collection of homespun maxims, attributed to Phocylides of Miletus, is made up of sayings such as, "Many things are best in the middle; I want to be middle (*mesos*) in the *polis*"; and "What good is noble birth for those who lack grace in words and counsel?"

Most of the surviving poetry, however, appeals more openly to an audience that has wealth and leisure. Much of it was composed specifically for recitation at drinking parties. Partisan politics was naturally a favorite topic. Just as often, however, symposiastic poetry celebrates the pleasures of wine and love (both heterosexual and homosexual) and laments the sad necessity that these joys must fade with old age. This poem by the seventh-century Ionian poet Mimnermus is typical:

> What's life, what's joy, without love's heavenly gold?
> I hope I die when I no longer care
> for secret closeness, tender favors, bed,
> which are the rapturous flowers that grace youth's prime
> for men and women. But when painful age
> comes on, that makes a man loathsome and vile,
> malignant troubles ever vex his heart;
> seeing the sunlight gives him joy no more.
> He is abhorred by boys, by women scorned:
> so hard a thing God made old age to be.
>
> (Mimnermus fr. 1 West)

Similar in style and tone is Ibycus (mid-sixth century) from Rhegium in Italy, who spent some years in Samos under the patronage of the tyrant Polycrates. Ibycus wrote long choral narratives on traditional epic and mythological themes, but he was most famous in antiquity for his homoerotic poetry, full of sensuous imagery. In one poem, Eros ("Love") comes like the north wind from Thrace, and with "parching madness, dark and fearless, shakes me to the bottom of my heart with his might" (fr. 286.6–13). In another poem, on falling in love late in life, he compares himself to an old champion racehorse that unwillingly drags his chariot to the contest (fr. 287.6–7).

Sappho (late seventh century) is the only known woman poet from the Archaic period, in fact, one of the few in all of ancient Greek literature (women were not encouraged to write). A member of a prominent aristocratic family from Mytilene on the island of Lesbos, Sappho was greatly admired throughout antiquity; later critics listed her among the top nine lyric poets, and hailed her as the "tenth Muse." Sappho appears to have been the leader of a close-knit circle of young upper-class women in Lesbos (hence the modern term "lesbian") who shared their lives for a brief period before marriage. Sappho wrote wedding songs (*epithalamia*) to be performed by choruses of young girls, as well as political verses, but most of what has survived is solo song, highly personal in tone, with erotic love between women as its main theme.

DOCUMENT 3.2

Nine "books" (i.e., papyrus rolls) of Sappho's work were collected in the Alexandrian period, but only four poems survive intact or nearly so. Here is a selection of shorter fragments:

> Honestly I wish I were dead.
> She was covered in tears as she went away,
> left me, saying, "Oh it's too bad!
> How unlucky we are! I swear,
> Sappho, I don't want to be leaving you."
> This is what I replied to her:
> "Go, be happy, and think of me.
> You remember how we looked after you;
> or if not, then let me remind. . . ."

Sappho fr. 94 West

> Atthis, you've come to hate the thought of me,
> you fly to join Andromeda.

Sappho fr. 131 West

> I have a pretty child, like flowers,
> of gold her form, my precious Cleis;
> whom I would not exchange
> for all of Lydia, or the lovely land. . . .

Sappho fr. 132 West

Previously unknown texts, or some known only through fragments, still turn up among the papyri. In 2004 scholars deduced that part of a papyrus roll from Egypt in the collection of the University of Cologne in Germany contained fragmentary poems of Sappho. Like Mimnermus, Sappho talks of growing old. The girls who remain in her circle for a few years, however, are always young and desirable, for younger ones replace their elders who leave for marriage. She cites the mythic example of Tithonus who had been granted immortality in response to the prayer of Eos, the dawn goddess who loved him. Because Eos forgot to ask that Tithonus be given eternal youth, he grew older and more frail without being able to die, while she remained forever young.

> You for the fragrant-bosomed Muses' lovely gifts
> be zealous, children, and the clear melodious lyre:
> but my once tender body old age now
> has seized; my hair's turned white instead of dark;
> my heart's grown heavy, my knees will not support me,
> that once on a time were fleet for the dance as fawns.
> This state I oft bemoan; but what's to do?

> Not to grow old, being human, there's no way.
> Tithonus once, the tale was, rose-armed Dawn,
> love-smitten, carried off to the world's end,
> handsome and young then, yet in time grey age
> o'ertook him, husband of immortal wife.
>   Sappho fr. 58 + P. Köln 21351 West 2005, adapted

One of Sappho's fellow aristocrats, Alcaeus, also achieved lasting fame as a poet. Like the other symposiastic poets, he wrote of love and wine and the myths of old, but he was most famous for his political poems. Alcaeus puts us in the center of the complicated power relations among the aristocratic factions in Mytilene: the political deals and betrayals, the partisan hatred and violence, which were wracking the polis. Here is his description of his predicament, having been exiled from his society and family's property:

> Plunged in the wild chaste-woods I live
> a rustic life, unhappy me,
> longing to hear Assembly called
> and Council, Agesilaidas!
>
> From lands my grandfather grew old
> possessing, and my father too,
> among these citizens who wrong
> each other, I've been driven away.
>
> An outland exile. . . .
>   (Alcaeus fr. 130b.1–9 West)

The largest chunk of symposiastic poetry that we have is a compilation of fourteen hundred lines of poetry all attributed to Theognis of Megara (mid-sixth century), but actually containing poems written by a number of different authors, dating from the late seventh to the early fifth century. In a stridently elitist tone Theognis vilifies the base-born kakoi while singing the praises of the high-born agathoi. The poet's contempt for non-noble citizens—whom he deems innately incapable of achieving excellence—reflects the frustration of the minority elite as they watched their power and privilege being eroded as the nonelite made political and economic gains. Aristocratic resentment over their reversal of fortune comes through in verses such as these (addressed to the young lover of "Theognis"):

> Cyrnus, those who were *agathoi* once are now *kakoi*, and those who were *kakoi* before are now *agathoi*. Who could bear seeing this, the *agathoi* dishonored and the *kakoi* getting honor?
>   (*Theognidea* 1108–1111)

Although aristocrats would continue to proclaim their innate superiority, the movement toward political leveling that had begun in the seventh century was essentially completed by the early decades of the fifth.

Philosophy and Science

The sixth century saw the beginning of philosophy (literally "the love of wisdom"). The early Greek philosophers—who may have been the first to write in prose—are called the Presocratics, that is, the thinkers who lived before Socrates (c. 469–399 BC) and his disciple, Plato. Plato (c. 429–347) set the course that Western philosophical thought follows up to today. The Presocratics are also clearly differentiated from the Socratics in that the former concentrated on the structure and development of the physical universe, whereas the latter were more interested in ethics, in the role human beings play in relation to one another and to the larger society.

The study of astronomy and mathematics had flourished in Mesopotamia since the early second millennium; and the first Presocratics, who were from Miletus in Ionia, built on the achievements of their eastern neighbors. Greeks had always studied the night sky, of course. They named the planets, stars, and star groups after their gods and characters in their myths, like Orion the hunter and the girls he pursued and never caught, the Pleiades. Basic knowledge of the celestial motions had always been essential in daily life: In *Works and Days*, Hesiod's agricultural calendar is addressed to farmers who learned when it was time to perform their seasonal chores by the position of the constellations. When Greeks sailed, they plotted their location by the position of celestial objects. What the Presocratics introduced to the Greeks was "scientific" astronomy. Thales of Miletus, for example, was said to have predicted the solar eclipse of 585 BC; and his fellow Milesian, Anaximander, was credited with drawing a plan of the heavens (as well as the first geographical map).

The Milesians were also the first to abandon mythical-religious explanations for the origins of the universe and instead to seek purely physical causes. Thales theorized that the origin of all matter was water (for it could be transformed into both gas and solid forms), and that the earth was flat and floated on water. In contrast, Anaximander called the original principle "The Boundless," or "The Indefinite," a limitless entity that governs the material world, harmonizing such opposites as wet and dry and cold and hot. He postulated that the earliest creatures arose out of the sea from slime warmed by the sun's heat. Another Milesian, Anaximenes, thought that everything had evolved from air: It became fire when it was rarefied, could change to wind and cloud, and when condensed was transformed into solid substances. Like Thales, Anaximenes believed that the earth was flat, but he thought that it floated on air.

Pythagoras, one of the most influential cosmologists, is familiar to us from the geometric theorem that still bears his name. Around 531 BC, he left his native Samos because of the tyranny of Polycrates and settled in southern Italy with a group of disciples, both male and female. The doctrines of the Pythagoreans combined mysticism (they believed in the transmigration of the soul), political theory, cosmology, and mathematics. Pythagoras taught that arithmetic was the key to understanding the universe. He postulated that the earth was a sphere in the center of a series of hollow spheres. The stars were fixed on the outer spherical shell and the planets on smaller shells within. The movements of the celestial spheres, dictated by strict arithmetical ratios, gave the universe a musical harmony, but because the sound is always with us, we are unable to hear it.

Xenophanes' ideas about the development of the cosmos were based more on personal observation. For example, when he noticed fossil imprints of marine life and seaweed in three different locations inland, he theorized that they were produced when the earth was covered with the mud created by the primal mixture of seawater and earth. We have fragments of his poems in which he attacks conventional religious and ethical beliefs, including two that make provocative suggestions about gods having been created by humans rather than the other way around:

> The Ethiopians say that their gods are snub-nosed and black and the Thracians that their gods have light blue eyes and red hair.

> But if cattle and horses and lions had hands or drew with their hands and completed works like men, horses would draw images of their gods that were like horses and cattle like cattle, and they would make their bodies like the bodies each of them had.
>
> (Xenophanes frs. 16, 15)

The writings of the early Greek scientists were circulated all around the Greek world and thinkers freely criticized each other's theories. Heraclitus of Ephesus (late sixth century), for example, rejected Pythagoras' notion of an orderly and regulated cosmos, maintaining instead that everything was constantly changing like a river: You cannot step into the same river twice. To reach understanding of this process of change, we must learn the hidden principle, which he calls "logos." Heraclitus taught that the world is not what it appears to be. A similar idea was at the core of Parmenides' (early fifth century) attempt to analyze what it means to say that something is or exists. According to Parmenides, all you can say and think is that "being" exists but that "nonbeing" does not exist. Change is logically impossible because if something changes it is no longer the same and does not exist. Such questions as these, first posed by the Presocratics, would preoccupy philosophers for the rest of antiquity: What do we mean when we say that something exists, and what is the relationship between the world as we perceive it through our senses and what it "really" is?

Panhellenic Institutions

The ease with which poets, thinkers, artists, and ideas moved from city to city shows how culturally unified the Greek world was even as it remained politically divided. The Panhellenic gatherings played a prominent part in forging a common Hellenic identity, as ever-greater numbers came to worship, consult oracles, and attend musical and athletic competitions.

The oracle of Apollo at Delphi drew Greeks and non-Greeks alike from all over the Mediterranean (See Plate XV). For a hefty fee individuals could consult Apollo for prophetic advice on marriage, careers, voyages, and so on. Poleis too sought the god's guidance and sanction on serious matters of state, such as colonizing, religion, and laws. Apollo responded through a priestess, called the Pythia, who, in a self-induced trance, divulged his messages, which were put into coherent (although frequently ambiguous) verses by "interpreters" (*prophētai*). Because so many tyrants, foreign kings, and aristocratic leaders consulted the oracle, the sanctuary at Delphi became a storehouse of information about political conditions across the Mediterranean.

The greatest attraction, however, was the sanctuary of Zeus at Olympia. By the end of the seventh century the quadrennial games in Zeus' honor—inaugurated, according to tradition, in 776 BC—were drawing spectators and contestants from the entire Greek world. The success of the Olympics soon spawned three new Panhellenic athletic festivals: in honor of Apollo at Delphi (582 BC), for Poseidon at Isthmia near Corinth (581 BC), and for Zeus at Nemea in Argolis (573 BC). These festivals were integrated into the four-year Olympiad to form an athletic "circuit," staggered so that there would be one major game each year, two in alternate years, with the Olympics remaining the premier event. Other Panhellenic festivals modeled on the Olympic games were inaugurated at Athens, Thebes, and elsewhere during the sixth century.

The Panhellenic contests and rituals brought Greeks together in peaceful celebration. For the month in which the Olympic games were held, for example, poleis observed a sacred truce that guaranteed safe passage for all participants and spectators while traveling to and from Olympia. The sacred precincts themselves became places for poleis to flaunt their wealth and achievements with costly dedications of statuary and marble "treasuries," commemorating both athletic and military victories.

Yet there were no team events, only individual contests. Thus the games kept alive the ancient ideal of the individual hero: to be declared the best (*aristos*) by gaining victory over a worthy opponent. The content and spirit of the Panhellenic games had changed very little since the games in the *Iliad*. The events still tested speed, strength, dexterity, and endurance, precisely the qualities desired in a Homeric warrior.

The main events at the Olympic games were the foot races, the most prestigious of which was the short sprint, called the stade (*stadion*, hence stadium), a distance of about 210 yards. In this contest alone—at a separate festival honoring Hera—maidens participated; their course was one-sixth shorter than the men's stade. The young women did not race completely nude, as the males did, but their tunics barely reached the knees and covered only one side of the chest (see Figure 4.5).

Male athletes competed in a variety of events, including wrestling, boxing, and the *pankration*, a vicious combination of boxing and wrestling with no holds barred except biting and eye gouging. In the *pentathlon* opponents competed in five events: the stade, javelin and discus throws, the long jump, and wrestling. Most spectacular of all was the four-horse chariot race, a contest dating back to the Late Bronze Age. (The wealthy owner of the horses and chariot, not the charioteer, was declared the winner.) (See Plate XIV.) A number of festivals also featured competitions in choral and solo poetry and in instrumental performances.

The prizes were just tokens of glory, wreaths of foliage: at Olympia olive leaves, at Delphi laurel, at Nemea wild celery, and at Isthmia pine. (The rewards at the less notable festivals were more substantial.) On their return home, however, victors could expect lavish rewards: triumphal processions, civic honors, statues, and even prizes of money.

RELATIONS AMONG STATES

Cultural exchange was only one means of interaction among the Greek poleis. Throughout history states have interacted in two additional areas: trade and warfare.

Trade was brisk in archaic Greece, with many products traveling by sea. Yet money as we know it was largely absent. Both at home and away, Greeks continued to rely on the barter system familiar from earlier eras. Wealthier traders might pay for their purchases with solid pieces of gold, silver, bronze, or iron; but of course these always had to be weighed and their purity verified, which was burdensome. Had nobody thought to mint coins? In fact, by the end of the archaic period someone had. A twentieth-century find in the kingdom of Lydia in western Asia Minor turned up coins that date to the late seventh century. They were made of **electrum**, an alloy of gold, silver, and a trace of copper, and stamped with a symbol that indicated their weight and hence their value. The idea soon caught on in Greece as well. Most early coins, however, were of such high value as to be of limited use in commerce; and it is likely that the principal function of early coinage was to proclaim the authority (not to mention the independence) of the government that issued them. It was not until the classical period that coins were issued in a wide variety of denominations and began to play a large role in commercial life.

Figure 3.8. Electrum coin from eastern Greece with a stag on the obverse and a punch mark on the reverse. Early sixth century BC. The earliest inscribed Greek coin, it was made from the natural alloy of gold and silver known as electrum. Athens, Numismatic Collection.

With the emergence of the city-states, the external problem of coexistence became much more complicated. What had been raids among neighboring communities turned into serious warfare. There were several reasons for the heightened tensions. As states began to run out of land, they attempted to extend their boundaries, and disputes often erupted over borderlands that had not required strict definition when populations were still small. Moreover, quarrels of mother poleis were often taken up by their colonies, with new enmities arising among poleis hundreds of miles away. On the mainland territorial wars between poleis began as early as the late eighth century, when Chalcis and Eretria in Euboea fought over possession of the rich Lelantos River plain that lay between them. In the Lelantine War, as it is called, both sides were said to have had distant allies from much farther away—possibly indicating the involvement of rival colonial networks.

Interstate tensions were especially high in the Peloponnesus, which contained three of the major Greek city-states—Sparta, Argos, and Corinth. After their conquest of Messenia in the late eighth century, the Spartans warred against their rivals, the Argives, with some success, although they were badly beaten by them in 669 BC in a battle at Hysiae in Argolis. The Argives in the meantime were trying to expand their own landholdings and influence within the Peloponnesus, particularly around Corinth; the Corinthians themselves were fighting over territory with their smaller neighbors, Megara and Sicyon. Such costly and deadly squabbles over land continued in the Peloponnesus until the middle of the sixth century, when the Spartans began using diplomacy and forming alliances to maintain their supremacy in southern Greece.

In the sixth century the Greek states began in earnest to establish formal mechanisms for avoiding war. Most of these cooperative institutions had their genesis in the pre-state period, but it was not until the later Archaic Age that they were refined and regularized. At the same time that formal means were being instituted, diplomatic relations were still being conducted much as they had been in the Dark Age. The tyrants especially conducted foreign policy this way, making pacts of friendship or marriage alliances with other tyrants or with the top aristocrats. For example, Periander (c. 627–587), who succeeded his father Cypselus as tyrant of Corinth, developed a political friendship with Thrasybulus, tyrant of Miletus, ending an old enmity between the two poleis going back to the Lelantine War. The pact aided both Corinthian traders in Egypt and the Black Sea and Milesian traders in the West. Periander was also asked by Athens and Mytilene to arbitrate a dispute over control of Sigeum, an important way station on the route to the Black Sea.

Temporary military alliances are as old as war. In the Archaic period they became more formal and longer lasting. States began to make written treaties, pledging friendship and cessation of aggression for a stipulated time. The earliest formal pact we know of comes from the polis of Sybaris in southern Italy (c. 550 BC). An inscription reads, "The Sybarites and their allies and the Serdaioi made an agreement for friendship faithful and without guile, for ever. Guarantors: Zeus, Apollo, and the other gods, and the *polis* of Poseidonia." There were also several new types of multistate alliance. One was the amphictyony or "association of neighbors," whereby several independent city-states cooperated to maintain and protect a common sanctuary of a god. Although an amphictyony did not prevent its members from warring against one other, at least it mitigated hostility. Member states might pledge, for example, not to destroy each other's cities or cut off their water supply.

It was also in the sixth century that ethnē (plural) began to form loose unions among their separate towns and villages. These differed from the amphictyonies in that they had an overarching central body that coordinated community action. Nevertheless, the authority of central governments over the independent entities would remain relatively feeble until the creation in the fifth century of true "federal states."

The mid-sixth century also saw the first of the mega-alliances, the Peloponnesian League created by Sparta. The history of the fifth century would be shaped by the rivalry and then the hatred between the Spartans and the Athenians. They would conduct their wars and diplomatic skirmishes as the hegemons of two huge alliances of city-states, the Peloponnesian and Delian Leagues, respectively, which together comprised the Greek world. We turn next to Sparta.

KEY TERMS

agora	Hesiod	metropolis
Archaic period	*hoi agathoi*	oligarchy
aristocracy	*hoi kakoi*	phalanx
Bacchiads	hoplite	polis
colony	*korē*	Sappho
electrum	*kouros*	synoecism
ethnos	lyric poetry	tyranny

SUGGESTED READINGS

Aubet, Maria Eugenia. 2001. *The Phoenicians and the West: Politics, Colonies, and Trade.* Trans. Mary Turton. 2nd ed. Cambridge, UK: Cambridge University Press. Comprehensive account of the trading and colonizing activities of the Greeks' chief rivals in the Mediterranean.

Boardman, John. 1974. *Athenian Black Figure Vases.* London: Oxford University Press.

———. 1975. *Athenian Red Figure Vases.* London: Oxford University Press.

———. 1978. *Greek Sculpture: The Archaic Period.* London: Oxford University Press. These three volumes make up a valuable set of handbooks on Greek art of the Archaic period, lavishly illustrated, with concise and informative commentary.

———. 1999. *The Greeks Overseas: Their Early Colonies and Trade.* 4th ed. London: Thames and Hudson. An excellent introduction, with many illustrations, to Greek colonization and the economic and cultural interactions between the Greeks and their neighbors in other lands.

Burkert, Walter. 1992. *The Orientalizing Revolution: The Near Eastern Influences on Greek Culture in the Early Archaic Age.* Trans. Margaret E. Pinder and Walter Burkert.

Cambridge, MA: Harvard University Press. Illuminating analysis of the interaction between Greek and Near Eastern culture in the Archaic period.

Edwards, Anthony. 2004. *Hesiod's Ascra*. Berkeley and Los Angeles: University of California Press. Reconstruction on the basis of Hesiod's *Works and Days* of life in a Greek town in the Archaic period.

Forsdyke, Sara. 2005. *Exile, Ostracism, and Democracy: The Politics of Expulsion in Ancient Greece*. Princeton, NJ: Princeton University Press. An excellent survey of the political instability generated by aristocratic violence and its legacies into the Classical period.

Gagarin, Michael. 2008. *Writing Greek Law*. Cambridge, UK: Cambridge University Press. A fresh review of the evidence and the arguments for the writing down of the first Greek laws.

Greene, Ellen. 1999. *Reading Sappho: Contemporary Approaches*. Berkeley and Los Angeles: University of California Press. Anthology of essays discussing the oral tradition, women's erotics, myth, ritual, and more using feminist and gender theory approaches.

Hansen, Mogens Herman. 2006. *Polis: An Introduction to the Ancient Greek City State*. Oxford, UK: Oxford University Press. Important summary of the results of recent scholarship on the nature of the *polis*.

Hanson, Victor Davis. 1995. *The Other Greeks: The Family Farm and the Agrarian Roots of Western Civilization*. New York: Free Press. A wide-ranging, meticulously detailed study of the "yeoman" farmer-hoplite and his role in the formation of the city-state.

Redfield, James M. 2003. *The Locrian Maidens: Love and Death in Greek Italy*. Princeton, NJ: Princeton University Press. Brilliant and riveting account of life in Epizephyrian Locri, a Greek colony in southern Italy.

Ridgway, David. 1992. *The First Western Greeks*. Cambridge, UK: Cambridge University Press. Lucid survey of the archaeological evidence for early Greek settlement in Italy.

Rose, Peter W. 2012. *Class in Archaic Greece*. Cambridge, UK: Cambridge University Press. Rich in detail and relentless in argument, an analysis of the Archaic period from a Marxist perspective.

Seaford, Richard. 2004. *Money and the Early Greek Mind: Homer, Philosophy, Tragedy*. Cambridge, UK: Cambridge University Press. The best treatment of the significance of the arrival of coinage into the Greek world.

Snodgrass, Anthony. 1980. *Archaic Greece: The Age of Experiment*. Berkeley and Los Angeles: University of California Press. The first major book on Archaic Greece written by an archaeologist, and an important reappraisal of the importance of the Archaic period to Greek history.

Tandy, David W. 1997. *Warriors into Traders*. Berkeley and Los Angeles: University of California Press. An innovative revisionist analysis of the economic history of Greece in the Archaic period.

Tandy, David W. and Walter C. Neale, eds. 1996. *Hesiod's* Works and Days: *A Translation and Commentary for the Social Sciences*. Berkeley and Los Angeles: University of California Press. A very useful commentary that looks at Hesiod's world through the perspectives of sociologists, anthropologists, and social economists.

Wees, Hans van. 2004. *Greek Warfare: Myths and Realities*. London: Duckworth. Brilliant reinterpretation of the development of Greek warfare in the Archaic period.

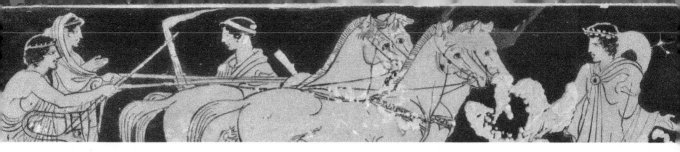

CHAPTER FOUR

Sparta

Admired in peace and dreaded in war, for much of the Archaic and Classical periods Sparta was the most powerful city in the Greek world. It was also different from other poleis. To be sure, the Spartans shared many basic institutions with other Greeks: Their society was patriarchal and polytheistic, servile labor played a key role, agriculture formed the basis of the economy, law was revered, and martial valor was prized. Nonetheless, Sparta was unique in many important ways. No other Greek state ever defined its goals as clearly as Sparta or expended so much effort in trying to attain them. The intrusion of the state into the lives of individuals was substantial in all Greek states, but no state surpassed Sparta in the invasive role it played in daily life. Spartans took enormous pride in their polis, and other Greeks were impressed by the patriotism and selflessness the Spartan system entailed. The Spartans' denial of individuality fostered a powerful sense of belonging that other Greeks envied, and Sparta continues to cast a spell over historians, philosophers, feminists, and political scientists.

Despite the interest the Spartans sparked in Greek intellectuals, it is difficult to write about Sparta and its surrounding territory, **Laconia**. The problem is not lack of sources; the volume of ancient writing on Sparta is large. The difficulty lies in the fact that many of our sources are tainted by their acceptance of an idealized image of Sparta that historians call the "Spartan mirage." This idea of Sparta was a vision of an egalitarian and orderly society characterized by patriotism, courage in battle, and tolerance for deprivation.

Figure 4.1. View of Sparta.

THE DARK AGE AND THE ARCHAIC PERIOD

Laconia was an important center in the Bronze Age. Like much of the rest of Greece, Laconia experienced a sharp drop in population at the end of the Mycenaean period. Sometime in the tenth century BC, Dorian newcomers entered the territory. By the eighth century BC, trends similar to those documented elsewhere in Greece had begun to appear in Laconia as well. New villages were founded as population gradually increased, and four of those villages near the Eurotas River in the center of the Laconian plain united to form the city of Sparta. Early in the eighth century, the town of Amyclae, three miles from the original four villages, was added to the city. Thus, the Spartan polis was the city center plus the territory of the plain. Increased contacts with the rest of Greece were reflected in the emergence of a distinctive Spartan version of geometric art.

Like other early Greek poleis, Sparta (or **Lacedaemon**, as it was often called in antiquity) began to experience difficulties in satisfying its needs from its own territory. Sparta was located inland, with the nearest port, Gythium, twenty-seven miles to the south. This atypical location encouraged the city to seek a novel solution to the need for land to feed a growing population, a solution that would determine the course of Spartan development. Unlike other Greek cities, which repeatedly founded colonies overseas in an effort to alleviate the pressure on resources caused by population expansion, the Spartans founded only one colony, Taras, in southern Italy. Instead of looking abroad for a solution to their difficulties, the Spartans sought a military answer to their problem through conquest of

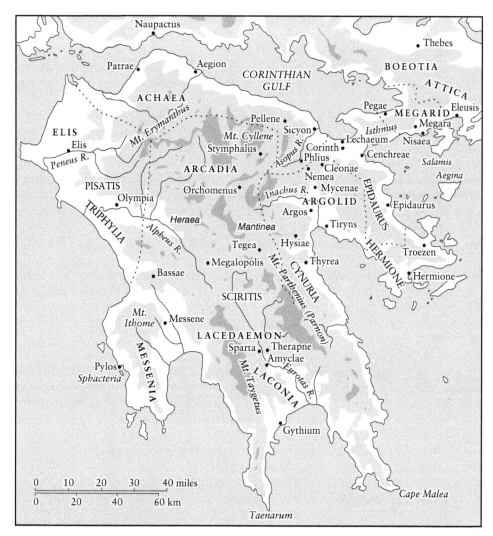

Figure 4.2. Peloponnesus.

their neighbors, and by the end of the eighth century, they had gained control of the plain of Laconia.

Helots and the Social Hierarchy

To ensure control of the Laconian plain, its inhabitants were reduced to the status of **helots**, hereditary subjects of the Spartan state. The rest of the inhabitants of Laconia, who occupied the area surrounding the city of Sparta, became *perioeci* ("those who dwell around [Sparta]," or "neighbors"). Unlike the helots, who were in essence slaves, the perioeci remained free. Although they were obligated to serve in the army, they were not permitted to participate in the government. They did enjoy some local autonomy, however, and in many ways lived like the majority of Greeks who were not Spartans, working as homemakers, farmers, craftsmen, and merchants. Thus they constituted an essential part of the Spartan economic system.

The Spartans also coveted the fertile Messenian lowlands, and at some time in the third quarter of the eighth century they invaded **Messenia**, beginning what modern historians call the First Messenian War. According to tradition, the war lasted twenty years and ended about 720 BC. Messenia became subject to Sparta, and like the Laconians, some of the Messenians became perioeci, but most became helots, bound to their land and obliged to work it for their Spartan masters with no consolation but the promise that they would not be sold out of Messenia. The Spartan poet Tyrtaeus gloatingly described them as "burdened like asses, bringing to their masters under harsh compulsion one half . . . of the fruits of the land" (fr. 6 West).

The conquest of Laconia and Messenia made Sparta one of the largest of Greek states, controlling a territory of over three thousand square miles (about three times the size of the Athenian state). Sparta was also one of the richest states. Spartan pottery and metalwork were among the finest in Greece. The beauty of Spartan women was widely celebrated, and Sparta's female choruses were famous. A vivid impression of the wealth and elegance of Spartan life is provided by a few surviving fragments of the works of the seventh-century BC poet Alcman, whose hymns, written for choruses of unmarried Spartan girls to sing on ceremonial occasions, mention luxury items including racehorses, purple textiles, and gold jewelry in the shape of serpents. (See Plate VIII.)

> There is no abundance of purple sufficient to protect us, nor
> our speckled serpent bracelet of solid gold, nor our Lydian cap,
> adornment for tender-eyed girls, nor Nanno's hair, (70) nor Areta
> who looks like a goddess, nor Thylacis and Cleesithera. Nor will
> you go to Ainesimbrota's and say "I wish Astaphis were mine," and
> (75) "I wish Philylla would look at me, and Demareta, and lovely
> Vianthemis"—no, it is Hagesichora who exhausts me with love. . . .
> (fr. 1.65–78 Alcman; Pomeroy 2002)

Spartan prosperity, however, rested on insecure foundations. Civil unrest in the late eighth and early seventh centuries was avoided by exiling dissidents, who founded Sparta's only colony, Taras. The growing desperation of the Messenians was a more serious threat. Greek political theorists considered it a mistake to enslave people in their own home territory, especially when the enslaved significantly outnumbered their masters, as the Messenians did the Spartans. Not surprisingly, the Messenians rebelled in the wake of a major Spartan military defeat by the Argives at the Battle of Hysiae in 669 BC.

As is true of the First Messenian War, little is known of the details of the Second Messenian War. The poems Tyrtaeus wrote celebrating Spartan courage in the war became Sparta's classics. The following excerpt is from the same poem that is quoted in Chapter 3:

> This is the man of worth in time of war.
> Soon he turns back the foemen's sharp-edged battle lines
> and strenuously stems the tide of arms;
> his own dear life he loses, in the front line felled,
> his breast, his bossed shield pierced by many a wound,
> and of his corselet all the front, but he has brought
> glory upon his father, army, town.
> His death is mourned alike by young and old; the whole
> community feels the keen loss its own.
>   (Tyrtaeus fr. 9 Diehl; West 1991, p. 26)

In the end Sparta prevailed and the Messenians had no choice but to resign themselves to the rigors of their former helot status.

The Second Messenian War had been a terrifying revelation of the potential risks of the helot system. As a result of the conquest of neighboring regions, the helots outnumbered Spartan citizens by a ratio that may have been seven to one or even higher. The Spartans were forced to find a way to preserve their domination over their helots. The solution they found was drastic, and its implementation gradually transformed Sparta and eventually created the unique regimented society known to us from Classical sources. Simply stated, the Spartans realized that if all potential hoplites could be trained to the highest degree of skill possible, Sparta would enjoy an overwhelming military advantage over its helots and other enemies. Therefore the Spartans reformed their institutions with a view toward achieving two goals: freeing male citizens from all but military obligations, and socializing them to accept the regimentation and discipline required of a Spartan soldier. Until the fourth century and the Hellenistic period, the Spartans were the only real professional soldiers. In effect they waged a perpetual war against the helots and were consequently always prepared to deploy their military force when necessary.

THE SPARTAN SYSTEM

Little is known about the actual development of the Spartan system. Greek historians followed Spartan tradition and ascribed its creation to **Lycurgus**, a shadowy figure who may or may not really have lived. Scholars today are agreed that many of the institutions whose creation Greeks ascribed to Lycurgus, such as men's dining groups, organization of the population by age cohorts, and the use of iron money, had, in fact, once existed in other Greek communities. These practices survived at Sparta because their place in Spartan life had been redefined to aid in the production of the ideal Spartan hoplite.

However this evolution occurred, the evidence indicates that the main features of the Spartan system were in place by the end of the seventh or the early sixth century BC. The Spartan regime may be called totalitarian, for it touched on almost every aspect of life, including those we in modern Western society consider private: how to wear our hair, the choice of whether and when to marry, the conditions of conjugal intercourse, and the decision whether to rear a child.

The Education and Upbringing of Boys

As the poetry of Tyrtaeus made plain, the Spartan ideal for a man was to be skilled and courageous in battle, neither to run away nor surrender but to stand his ground and give up his life for his city. Training was designed to produce men who conformed to this pattern alone. The Spartan was liable for military service to the age of sixty and needed to stay fit; hence he never was trained for any other profession or way of life. The educational system, like much else that was unique to Sparta, received legitimacy from the tradition that was created by Lycurgus.

The process of creating invincible warriors began at birth, for the state took upon itself the right to determine a new baby's viability. Whereas other Greek poleis left the choice to the father, at Sparta officials appointed by the government examined the newborns. The vitality of male infants and their potential as soldiers determined whether they would be raised or abandoned. (Female babies, apparently, were not subjected to official scrutiny, for their physical prowess did not directly affect the outcome of battles.) Fathers did not decide how to raise their children. Rather, all children received the same education under state supervision. Education in Sparta, as elsewhere, was organized by age groups: children, boys, youths (**ephebes**), young men, and adults. From the age of seven, boys left home to be trained in groups called "herds" according to principles designed to encourage conformity, obedience, group solidarity, and military skills.

The emphasis in the boys' education was not on reading and writing but rather on practicing to endure hardships and to fend for themselves as would be necessary when they became hoplite soldiers. To toughen their feet, they went barefoot, and they often went naked as well. When they were twelve, their hair was cut short. They never wore a tunic and were each allocated only one cloak yearly to wear in all kinds of weather. Unlike the rest of the Greeks, who made war only in the summer, the Spartans were perpetually at war with the helots and therefore needed to be prepared to fight year round. Magistrates called **ephors** ("overseers") inspected the boys daily and examined them in the nude every ten days. The boys slept in groups on rough mats that they had made themselves. To develop cunning and self-reliance, they were encouraged to supplement their food rations by stealing. Whipping awaited anyone who revealed his lack of skill by getting caught.

From the ages of fourteen to twenty, the ephebes performed their preliminary military service. At twenty they grew their hair long (unlike men in other parts of the Greek world) and shaved themselves in the distinctive Spartan style—a long beard and no mustache. Between ages twenty and thirty they were permitted to marry but had to continue to live with their army groups until the age of thirty.

Acceptance into a *syssition* ("dining group," "mess") was an essential stage in reaching adulthood. The Spartan man ate his meals with about fifteen members of his army group, an experience that fostered the loyalty and cooperativeness essential to successful hoplite warfare. Each member of the syssition was obliged to contribute a fixed quantity of food and drink. The *syssitia* (plural) were in some ways analogous to the *symposia* ("drinking parties") enjoyed by Greeks elsewhere, but the fact that the Spartan was purposely schooled to drink in moderation points to an important difference. Greeks usually mixed their wine with water. Helots, however, were forced to consume undiluted wine and to perform vulgar and ridiculous songs and dances to exemplify the consequences of lack of control. Young Spartans, who were invited to the syssitia as part of their education, were encouraged to laugh at the spectacle of the drunken helots. The lesson was a double one: From this experience, youths were expected to learn both to be wary of drinking to excess—for inebriation could lead to death in conditions of perpetual warfare—and to view the helots as pathetic creatures, patently inferior to the Spartan soldiery.

Inevitably, the success rate in forging soldiers according to the prescribed mold was less than 100 percent. Although the harsh treatment of those perceived as cowards discouraged failure, some boys failed to develop as expected. Because martial valor offered the sole path to the honor and respect of one's peers, life was wretched for boys who were unable to cope with the rigors of military life. When cowards were identified, they were stigmatized and called "tremblers." Their ridiculous appearance announced their disgrace: They were obliged to wear cloaks with colored patches and to only partially shave their beards. Humiliated in public, they were despised even by their own kinsmen, whom they were believed to have dishonored. They could not hold public office, nor was it likely that anyone would marry them or their sisters, with the consequence that their family would die out and the eugenic goals of the state be well served.

Becoming a Spartan Woman

Sparta's military ethos had implications for females as well as males. Just as boys were brought up to become brave fighters, girls were raised to bear stalwart soldiers-to-be. Spartans were the only Greek women whose upbringing was prescribed by the state and who were educated at state expense. For example, unlike other Greek women, who spent most of their time indoors and were regularly given less food than men and no wine, Spartan females exercised outside, were well nourished, and drank wine as part of their daily diet. Childbearing was their only social obligation. Although, like all Greek women, they did know how to weave, they were free from the obligation to engage in any other form of domestic labor.

Specific lines of development were prescribed for Spartan girls much as they were for boys. The educational system for girls was also organized according to age classes. Girls were divided into the categories of children, young girls, maidens who had reached puberty, and married women. Hairstyles announced a woman's passage through the life cycle. As a maiden, she wore her hair long and loose; as a bride, her hair was cropped; as a married woman, her hair was covered. (See Plate VIIb.) As with so much else in their way of life, Spartans ascribed the customary upbringing of Spartan girls to Lycurgus:

DOCUMENT 4.1

Excerpt from Plutarch's *Life of Lycurgus*

He made the girls exercise their bodies by running and wrestling and throwing the discus and javelin so that their children in embryo would have a strong start in strong bodies and would become stronger, and the women themselves would also have the strength to bear their pregnancies and to experience childbirth more easily. He did away with prudishness, sitting indoors, and all kinds of effeminacy. He made it customary for young girls no less than boys to be nude when they walked in processions, and when they danced and sang at certain festivals with the young men present and looking on. Sometimes the girls would make fun of individual young men, helpfully criticizing their mistakes. On other occasions they would sing the praises which they had composed about those deserving them, so that they inspired them with great enthusiasm and love of glory. . . .

There was nothing shameful in the girls' nudity. They were modest, and not wanton. Nudity encouraged simple habits and an enthusiasm for physical health, as well as giving the female sex a taste of noble feelings. . . . Therefore the women tended to speak and think in the way that Leonidas' wife Gorgo is reported to have done. When some woman, probably a foreigner, said to her "You Spartans are the only women who rule men," she replied "That is because we are the only ones who give birth to men."

(14.2–4 Plutarch, *Life of Lycurgus*)

As is the case in many warlike societies, the perpetual absence of men who were on military duty created a division of labor in which women managed domestic affairs. Aristotle, writing in the fourth century BC and considering some four hundred years of Spartan history, complained that for this reason Spartan women enjoyed altogether too much freedom, power, and prestige. The constitution of Lycurgus, he believed, was flawed from the start because only men conformed to it, whereas women escaped its regulations. He was convinced that Spartan women indulged in "every kind of luxury and intemperance," promoting greed and an attendant degeneration of the Spartan ideal of equality among male citizens. He also wrote that the Spartans' freedom to bequeath their land as they wished and the size of dowries led to two-fifths of the land in his own time having fallen into the hands of women. Spartan daughters received as dowries one-half the amount of their parents' property that their brothers received as inheritance. (In contrast, in Athens daughters received approximately one-sixth the amount that their brothers inherited.) Yet Aristotle no doubt exaggerates when he complains that Sparta was ruled by women, for they had no share in the government. Clearly, however, their ownership and control of property gave Spartan women far more authority than their counterparts in the rest of Greece.

Sex and Marriage

As elsewhere in Greece, marriages in Sparta might or might not entail a close emotional attachment between husband and wife. The Spartan requirement that married men continue to live in barracks until the age of thirty meant that young couples did not live together even in peacetime.

According to **Plutarch**, Spartan marriages often took on a strikingly clandestine character that struck other Greeks as worthy of comment.

> They used to marry by capture, not when the women were small or immature, but when they were in their prime and fully ripe for it. The so-called "bridesmaid" took the captured girl. She shaved her head to the scalp, then dressed her in a man's cloak and sandals, and laid her down alone on a mattress in the dark. The bridegroom, who was not drunk and thus not impotent, but was sober as always, having dined with his mess group, then would slip in, untie her belt, lift her, and carry her to the bed. After spending only a short time with her, he would depart discreetly so as to sleep wherever he usually did with the other young men. And he continued to do this thereafter. While spending the days with his contemporaries, and going to sleep with them, he would cautiously visit his bride in secret, embarrassed and fearful in case someone in the house might notice him. His bride at the same time was scheming and helping to plan how they might meet each other unobserved at a suitable time. They did this not just for a short period, but for long enough that some might even have children before they saw their own wives in the day. Such intercourse was not only an exercise in self-control and moderation, but also meant that partners were fertile physically, always fresh for love, and ready for intercourse rather than being satiated and impotent from unlimited sexual activity. Moreover some lingering spark of desire and affection always remained in both.
>
> (Plutarch, *Life of Lycurgus* 15.3–5; trans. Pomeroy 2002)

In addition to the secret marriage, other reported customs include the random selection of spouses by cohorts of potential brides and bridegrooms groping in a dark room. In a system of aristocratic endogamy (i.e., marriage within the group), the haphazard selection of spouses is a symptom of equality, for one spouse is as

Figure 4.3. Laconian bronze mirror with support in form of a nude female figure standing on a lion; the winged griffins on her shoulders help support the mirror's originally shiny and reflective disk, c. 520 BC. Unusual depictions of nude young women made at Sparta like this one may depict the goddess Artemis Orthia or celebrants of her cult. Because female nudity is rare in early Greek art, mirror supports like this one have also been associated with Aphrodite, the goddess of love. New York, The Metropolitan Museum of Art.

good as the next. Because the sole purpose of marriage is reproduction, the secret, or trial, marriage permits the couple to find other spouses if their union proves to be infertile. If these customs were ever practiced, they apparently had died out by the Classical period. The absence of adultery at Sparta, however, continued to evoke comment among non-Spartans. **Xenophon** also mentions a combination of practices that satisfied both the private desires of individual women and men and the state's eugenic goals and insatiable need for citizens:

> He [Lycurgus] took away from men the right to take a wife whenever they wanted to, and ordered that they marry in their prime, believing that this too was conducive to the production of fine children. If, however, it happened that an old man had a young wife—seeing

Figure 4.4. Laconian cup, attributed to the Naucratis Painter, c. 570–560 BC. These five reclining men served by a naked boy holding a wine pitcher are probably shown at a *syssition*, the Spartan version of the Greek *symposion*. Two winged male demons and two sirens hover above them. Paris, The Louvre.

that men of that age guard their wives—he thought the opposite. He required the elderly husband to bring in some man whose body and spirit he admired to beget children. On the other hand, in case a man did not want to have intercourse with his wife but wanted children of whom he could be proud, he made it legal for him to choose a woman who was the mother of a fine family and wellborn, and if he persuaded her husband, he produced children with her. Many such arrangements developed. For the wives want to get possession of two oikoi, and the husbands want to get brothers for their sons who will share their lineage and power, but claim no part of the property.

(Xenophon, *Spartan Constitution* 1.7–10; Pomeroy 2002)

Homosexuality and Pederasty

Like other ancient Greeks, Spartans lacked the binary division modern society tends to impose between people who are considered homosexual and those who are viewed as heterosexual, and same-sex erotic relationships did not preclude their participants entering into heterosexual marriages, with which the homosexual relationship might exist simultaneously. Ancient homosexuality differs from the modern version in several respects. The origins of many same-sex relationships lay in the educational system. Erotic relationships between members of the same sex were considered potentially educational for both women and men as long as the element of physical attraction was not primary. Single-sex education was the norm in the Greek world, and older men and women often functioned as "teachers" or informal guides to younger members of society. The disapproval that attaches today to romantic connections between teachers and students or between old and young would have puzzled the ancient Greeks, who viewed the erotic element in the teacher–pupil relationship as a constructive building block in the education of the young. The attraction of teachers to their youthful pupils was considered to have social utility, encouraging the enamored teacher to work hard at educating the student, who in turn was offered an inspiring role model in an older, wiser, more accomplished suitor. The pupils in question were generally in early adolescence. This pattern of same-sex relationships was evident not only in the context of education but in life as a whole. How much physical sexual activity actually was involved is unclear, because many Greek intellectuals who left written records of social customs tended to be embarrassed about sex and were eager to stress the cerebral element in same-sex romantic connections. We know less about the homoerotic bonds between women, but Plutarch in his *Life*

Figure 4.5. Bronze statuette of a Spartan girl running, wearing a racing dress that exposes her right breast, c. 525–500 BC. London, The British Museum.

of Lycurgus reported that "sexual relationships of this type were so highly valued that respectable women would in fact have love affairs with unmarried girls," and the erotic element in the songs of female choruses (like the poem of Alcman quoted previously) is not hidden.

For males and females alike, liaisons with members of the same sex provided much of the companionship, sexual pleasure, and sense of spiritual well-being that many people in modern Western society nowadays associate with marriage. Homosexuality was integrated into the system. The idealized model of the same-sex relationship involved an older person and an adolescent and consequently was time-limited. With boys it was considered inappropriate to continue the relationship after the teenager's beard began to grow. Nevertheless, some relationships did develop between companions of the same age and endured throughout life.

DEMOGRAPHY AND THE SPARTAN ECONOMY

By their conquests of Laconia and Messenia, the Spartans created a situation where they never constituted more than a small fraction—perhaps a twentieth—of the total population of their territory. Hence, as is often the case with ruling aristocracies, their numbers were never deemed to be sufficient. Furthermore, unlike other Greek states, at the very start the lack of trade and colonization limited the growth of Sparta's population, for it had no colonies to which it might sometime in the future export a population that could no longer be supported at home. Xenophobia also restricted Sparta's numbers. Unlike the Athenians, for example, at no time did Spartans marry foreigners, nor did they recruit large numbers of new citizens of non-Spartan origin, although the desperation occasioned by the long war with Athens during the fifth century known as the Peloponnesian War did move them to take some exceptional measures. In this emergency, they allowed some non-Spartiate boys living in Sparta to be trained for service in the Spartan army, freed some helots for military service, and appointed perioeci to some positions of command. Some of these practices continued after the end of the war and into the Hellenistic period when the population problem was even more acute.

Sparta's Shrinking Population

The Spartan lifestyle exacerbated the population decline. Sparta was the only Greek state in which male infanticide was institutionalized. Moreover, many deaths can be explained by the Spartan soldier's obligation to stand his ground and give his life for his country, rather than surrender. This ideal was reinforced by peer pressure, epitomized by statements attributed to Spartan women such as that of the mother who told her son as she handed him his shield to come home "either with this or on this." (Spartan soldiers who were not buried on the battlefield were carried home on their shields.)

The reduction in the number of Spartans was gradual. In addition to the high rate of infant and juvenile mortality found throughout the ancient world, the Spartan problem was aggravated by their unusual marriage practices. Women married only several years after they became fertile; opportunities for conjugal intercourse were limited; husbands were continuously absent at war or sleeping with their army groups when wives were in their peak childbearing years; and both sexes engaged in a certain amount of homosexual, nonprocreative sex. As if these obstacles to maintaining the population were not sufficient, some women also declined to bear children. The risks of maternity were considered equal to those soldiers faced on the battlefield: The only Spartans who earned the distinction of having their names inscribed on tombstones were those who had died in childbirth or in battle. Spartans, like other Greek women, probably had access to contraceptives including the use of herbs, douches of vinegar or water, and mechanical barriers made of wads of wool soaked in honey or olive oil. Control over fertility is often indicative of high status for women, and Aristotle may have been correct in contending that Spartan women controlled domestic matters, managing households that constituted a significant portion of the family's fortune.

Sparta's population problem was also accelerated at times by natural disaster, economic problems, and the emigration of men. There were nine thousand male Spartans in the Archaic period. In 479 there were eight thousand male citizens, five thousand of whom served at the battle of Plataea. There, according to Herodotus, each Spartan hoplite was accompanied by seven helots who served as light armed forces and performed the menial jobs. These figures are probably not exact, but they do give an idea of the proportion of Spartans to helots in the army. In 330 Aristotle reckoned the number of Spartans at one thousand. By 244 there were no more than seven hundred. By Roman times very few Spartans were left to perform their hoary rituals and tests of endurance for tourists. We have no exact information either on the absolute number of female Spartans or on their numbers relative to the number of males.

Helots and the Spartan System

The Spartan economic system was designed to enable citizens to devote all their time and energy to the defense and welfare of the polis. The state saw to it that they had everything they needed as measured by a standard of austerity, not luxury. Although the perioeci, who conducted business with the rest of the Greek world, used silver and gold coins, Spartans themselves were permitted to use only iron money: These flat bars or cakes made of iron had no value beyond the boundaries of Spartan territory. The Spartans used iron until the end of the fifth century, when there was a vast influx of gold and silver after their victory in the Peloponnesian War, but they did not mint their own coins until the Hellenistic period.

The goal for men was economic equality, which was, in reality, a minimum income for all that would allow them to follow the Spartan way of life. The Spartans referred to themselves as *homoioi* ("peers," or "men of equal status").

As we shall see later, however, economic equality was an illusory ideal. When Messenia was conquered, the territory was divided up into nine thousand equal kleroi. At birth, each boy was allocated a share of this land by the state, and a family of helots came with the land. The institution of helotry was inextricably tied up with the Spartan system, essential as it was to releasing Spartan men and women from the need to produce or purchase their food.

The owner of each **kleros** was entitled to receive a specified amount of produce annually from the helots who worked it. The helots' burden seems to have varied over the centuries. Tyrtaeus describes them as sharecroppers, forced to give their masters half their yield, but Plutarch mentions a fixed rent of seventy bushels of barley for each Spartan man and twelve for his wife, in addition to oil and wine. Although they were not free, helots were not the same as slaves elsewhere in Greece. They belonged to the state, not to individuals. They lived in stable family groups on a farm assigned to them, and could not be sold abroad. Aside from the obligation to provide sustenance for the owner of the plot of land, to serve as auxiliaries in the army, and to mourn at the death of kings and magistrates, the helots had no specific obligations to their masters. They were permitted to sell excess crops in the market and to accumulate some money in that way.

So that they should never forget that they were enslaved, the helots were subjected to an annual beating. They were also obliged to wear a primitive and humiliating costume that identified them immediately, including animal skins and a leather cap. Submitting to the rule of others but living in their own territory, the helots did not lose their desire for freedom. The service they performed in the Spartan army, moreover, provided them with useful knowledge in their ongoing struggle against their masters. In 464 some of them took advantage of the earthquake that had devastated Sparta and staged a rebellion at Ithome that lasted ten years. In 455 the Spartans agreed to let the rebels depart on condition that they should never return to the Peloponnesus. The Athenians settled many of them at Naupactus, on the northern side of the Corinthian Gulf. Finally, in 369, Messenia regained its independence with the aid of Thebes and other Boeotian enemies of Sparta.

The system of helotry distinguished Sparta sharply from other Greek states, making it the only polis with an economic system totally dependent on geographical and social distance between landowners and workers on the land. Despite the prevalence of slavery in the Greek world, nowhere else was the labor of the lowest class so essential to survival. Furthermore, although agriculture remained the basis of the domestic economy throughout the Greek world, other sources of gaining a livelihood were customarily developed; at Sparta alone among major states, agriculture remained the sole basis of the citizens' economy.

The Spartan system was a remarkably successful experiment in what is now called social engineering. To be sure, despite the ideology of equality among citizens that was associated with their polis, disparities of wealth did not disappear. Except for the members of the royal family and the tiny group elected to the Council of Elders, however, the role played by differential wealth in determining status and power was far smaller in Sparta than in other Greek poleis. The

Spartans called themselves the "Men of Equal Status" for good reason. Rich or poor, they all had survived the same judgment at birth, they had endured the same training, and they wore the same uniform and fought side by side with the same weapons in the phalanx.

SPARTAN GOVERNMENT

Like Sparta's social and educational system, its government was much admired by contemporaries. It consisted of monarchical, oligarchical, and democratic elements: These constituted the kind of system political theorists like Aristotle called a mixed constitution. Spartan conservatism made for a reluctance to abandon traditional institutions like monarchy and the council of elders when other Greek poleis had either abolished or redefined the functions of these institutions and had decreased the importance of hereditary power in government. The various organs of government and shared offices were designed to serve as checks and balances to one another, minimizing the danger that the government would take too rapid, radical action.

Dual Kingship

The executive office was divided between two families. Two kings (*basileis*) served as the head of government. The succession was hereditary. The two kings, who were both cooperative and competitive with one another, and who were equal in authority, served as a mutual check on the power of the monarchy. Sparta, moreover, was never without a leader, and thus avoided what the Greeks called "anarchy" (absence of leadership or of government).

The kings exercised military, religious, and judicial powers. One king served as commander-in-chief of the armed forces, and the other supervised domestic matters at home and took charge if his co-king was killed in action. The kings functioned as the chief priests and conducted all the public sacrifices. They were also expected to serve as moral exemplars. Thus, the courage and self-sacrifice of King Leonidas and his troops, who obeyed the command of the Spartans to fight at Thermopylae in 480 BC against all odds in the war against the Persians, became legendary, although many other Greeks fought bravely at the same battle.

Gerousia

The kings shared their judicial functions with the other members of the *gerousia*, the Council of Gerontes ("Elders"). In addition to the two kings, the gerousia was composed of twenty-eight men over the age of sixty who served for the rest of their lives. Election to the gerousia was the highest honor to which a Spartan could aspire. Candidates appeared in an order determined by lot. The winners were chosen by acclamation in the assembly. Those who received the loudest shouts were considered elected, a procedure Aristotle later criticized as "childish." No bill could be brought before the assembly until it had first been discussed by the gerousia, and the gerousia could decline to accept a decision of the assembly by summarily declaring an adjournment. It also served as a criminal court for cases of homicide, treason, and other serious offenses that carried the penalty of disenfranchisement, exile, or death.

Ephors

Every year the Spartans elected five ephors by acclamation from candidates over the age of thirty. The ephors ("overseers") supervised the kings and represented the principle of law, precious to the Spartans as it was to many Greeks. The ephors took a monthly oath to uphold the office of the kings as long as they behaved in accordance with the laws, and they shared some of the kings' executive powers; but they were also empowered to depose them. Ephors monitored the kings in Sparta, and two of them always accompanied a king who was on campaign. The ephors presided over the gerousia and assembly and dealt with foreign embassies. They also exercised judicial powers in civic matters and in cases involving perioeci.

One ephor was always "eponymous," that is, his name was used at Sparta to signify the year. For example, Thucydides dates a treaty of 421 as follows: "The treaty is effective from the 27th day of the month of Artemisium at Sparta, when Pleistolas is an ephor; and at Athens from the 25th day of the month of Elaphebolium, when Alcaeus is an archon" (5.19). As a check on the ephors' power, they served for only one year, could not be reelected, and were subject to an audit by their successors. Thus, they were both a democratic and an oligarchic constituent of government.

The ephors exercised total control over the education of the young and enforced the iron discipline of Sparta. They were in charge of the *krypteia* ("secret police"), a force designed to control the helots. This feature of government was unique to Sparta among Greek cities. Young men were sent out for a year to spy on the helots and were encouraged to kill any helots they caught, especially the best of them who might be most prone to rebel. The ephors declared war against the helots annually, thus making it possible for the Spartans to kill them without incurring the religious pollution that usually accompanied acts of homicide.

Assembly

In terms of its membership, the assembly was the most democratic organ of Spartan government, for it included all adult male citizens. It met once a month at full moon, outdoors. Unlike the Athenian assembly, however, the Spartan assembly did not debate; citizens listened to a proposal made by the gerousia and simply voted to accept or reject it, without discussion. The Spartan was trained to obey and to conform, not to take sides in public debate. Lycurgus was said to have outlawed rhetoric teachers. This ethos gave rise to the English word "laconic" (derived from Laconia), which is used to describe a spare style of speech or someone who talks very little.

The Mixed Constitution of Ancient Sparta

Since antiquity, many political theorists have admired Sparta's government, believing it to confirm the basic principle that the best guarantee of stability lies in a blend of monarchic, oligarchic, and democratic elements. Certainly Sparta had kings, and the ideology of economic equality among male citizens fostered an egalitarian spirit. In reality, however, the oligarchic element considerably outweighed the other two. Power lay predominantly with the gerousia. As time went by, moreover, the five ephors also gained increasing power over the kings and frequently took the lead in framing foreign policy. Even if we discount the 95 percent or so of disenfranchised residents of Laconia—perioikoi, helots, and Spartan women—the truth is that even within the subgroup of male citizens, participation in government was limited to a very small group of men, most of them rich.

THE PELOPONNESIAN LEAGUE

Until the Roman conquest of Greece, Sparta itself was never subject to the ongoing rule of non-Spartans. After the defeat of Argos in 546 BC, Sparta had become the most powerful state not only in the Peloponnesus, but in all Greece. With Peloponnesian states other than Messenia, Sparta adopted a policy of alliance, rather than conquest, and gradually assumed a position of leadership. Eventually, around 510–500, "Sparta and its allies," or "the **Peloponnesian League**" as historians today call the Spartan alliance, was organized. The League included all the states in the Peloponnesus except Argos and Achaea, as well as key poleis that lay outside the Peloponnesus, such as Thebes. The purpose of the League was mutual protection. Each state pledged to contribute forces in case of war and swore an oath "to have the same friends and enemies, and to follow the Spartans wherever they lead." The League was not an empire, but an alliance; no tribute was paid except in wartime, and Sparta did not dictate the policy of the League.

The government of the League was bicameral, consisting of the assembly of Spartans and the congress of allies in which each state had one vote. Only Sparta could convene a meeting of the League and only Spartans served as commanders of its armed forces. Sparta's own reputation for distinction in military matters along with the existence of the League made Sparta the natural leader of the Greeks in their war against the Persians. The League remained in existence until the 360s when Corinth and other member states were obliged to quit it after Sparta's defeat by Thebes.

HISTORICAL CHANGE IN SPARTA

Because there are no witnesses to the full operation of the Spartan community as described by Plutarch, and Xenophon states that the laws of Lycurgus were no longer enforced in his own time, we must admit the possibility that some features of the Lycurgan legislation were observed only briefly, or partially, or not at all. There are twentieth-century parallels for the failure of similar totalitarian dystopias or utopias. Modern historians follow the general model traced by Aristotle of drastic change over time in Spartan society, dating the "normalization," or loss of distinctiveness, to the later fifth century. Such a change may be observed in the public behavior of male Spartiates, but it is not at all clear that women's lives had been fundamentally altered, for, as Aristotle pointed out, women had never completely submitted to the Lycurgan system.

Some change, however, is plainly discernible. One area in which development is apparent is that of land tenure. Land was the most valuable commodity in the ancient world. Two systems of land tenure, a public one and a private one, existed in Sparta. When a man died, his kleros reverted to the state and then was allocated to another Spartan baby, who was not necessarily related to the previous owner. At the end of the fifth century or early in the fourth, the Lycurgan system regulating public property was abandoned. Thenceforth a man could give his kleros and his house to anyone he wished, or bequeath them by testament. This change undermined the ideal of economic equality and eventually led to the concentration of great wealth in the hands of a minority. This shift created an impoverished underclass who failed to meet the economic requirements for full citizenship, for they could not make the necessary contribution to a syssition. They were no longer "Men of Equal Status" but known as "Inferiors."

By the Classical period (if not earlier), in addition to the land designated for distribution as kleroi, some land was held as private property. Although women had probably been excluded from the distribution of kleroi, they owned a larger portion of the private land than women in any other Greek city. Land came into women's possession as dowry and inheritance. It seems likely that before the free bequest of land was introduced, daughters automatically inherited half as much as sons. Some families, of course, had daughters but no sons. Sparta was always plagued by a lack of men, for men were continually lost in battle, left Sparta for mercenary service, or failed to meet the census requirements for full citizenship. Moreover, although male infanticide was systematically practiced, it seems unlikely that female babies were eliminated in this way. Plutarch, who supplies details about the official elimination of male infants, says nothing about girls, even though his interest in the rearing of girls is noteworthy. If this inference is correct, then these factors probably created a substantial imbalance in the sex ratio. A woman could inherit all her father's land, and many women became extremely wealthy by this means. Thus Aristotle's statement that in his day women owned two-fifths of the land of Sparta is credible.

The Spartan Mirage

The admiration writers like Xenophon and Plutarch felt for Spartan society led them to exaggerate its monolithic nature, minimizing departures from ideals of equality and obscuring patterns of historical change. This perspective in turn made Sparta very attractive to subsequent thinkers for whom a static society seemed to offer the stability lacking in a more dynamic state (such as democratic Athens).

The fascination with Sparta in modern political thought also owes much to Plato. Already in antiquity Sparta served as "the other" vis-à-vis Athens and its democracy, as intellectuals unsympathetic to Athens exaggerated the differences between the two societies. In their writings, Sparta became a virtual utopia, a paradise of *eunomia*—a word meaning "governed by good laws." The most dramatic instance of this concept is probably found in the blueprint for the utopian state in Plato's *Republic,* where many features of this idealized Sparta appear. They are evident, for example, in Plato's description of the life of his philosopher-rulers, the "guardians." Central to both social systems are commonality and totalitarian control. Women and men of the top class are given the same education, including physical training. The private family, with its emphasis on women's monogamy and the transmission of property to legitimate male heirs, is eliminated among Plato's guardians. Sexual intercourse is guided by eugenic considerations. Female guardians do not have to perform domestic labor, for members of the lower classes perform the work usually accomplished by Greek women. Their only gender-related task is that of giving birth to children. Marriage is dispensed with, as the state educates all children. Private property and money are likewise outlawed to minimize the envy and class conflict that perpetually threatened to dissolve the fabric of Greek society.

Controversy about Sparta and its critics, both ancient and modern, continues to the present day. For the past 2,400 years, historians and philosophers have put forward views that vary radically, even though they are based on readings of precisely the same texts. Readers have widely differing reactions to the veritable mountain of anecdotes that has survived from antiquity embodying the underpinnings of the Spartan ethos. Many of these are collected in Plutarch's *Sayings of Spartan Women*. Plutarch reports that a Spartan mother burying her son received condolences from an old woman who commented on her bad luck. "No, by the heavens," the mother replied, "but rather good luck, for I bore him so that he could die for Sparta, and this is precisely what has happened." Another woman, seeing her son coming toward her after a battle and hearing from him that everyone else had died, picked up a tile and, hurling it at him, struck him dead, saying "And so they sent you to tell us the bad news?"

The notion of a people whose response to stimuli is the very opposite of what human nature would seem to dictate has exercised a hold on the human imagination. As late as the twentieth century, critics of Western capitalist society have idealized the Spartans as highly virtuous, patriotic people produced by a stable noncapitalistic society. In recent years, however, those who cherish individual freedom and social mobility have come to see in Sparta a forerunner of totalitarian regimes such as Nazi Germany. Furthermore, the blueprint for twentieth-century Communism had many affinities with the Spartan utopia. Even today, however, the old idealization of Sparta has reappeared in the works of some feminist theorists, who have noted that the lives of women in aristocratic Sparta appear to have been more enjoyable and in many ways preferable to those of women in democratic Athens.

Figure 4.6. Hilaire Germain Edgar Degas' painting, "Young Spartans Exercising" (1860). In this painting, Lycurgus stands among the mothers in the group of adults in back. Degas stated that his source for his interpretation was Plutarch. Thus the painting reveals the power of the utopian, naturalistic view of Sparta that was perpetuated in the modern era. Compare the costume of the girls in this painting to the dress on the Greek bronze statuette in Figure 4.5. London, The National Gallery.

Although Athens was no more a typical Greek polis than was Sparta, examining Athens and Sparta together is a useful way of understanding the ancient Greek view of life. It is to Athens that we now turn.

KEY TERMS

ephebe	krypteia	perioeci
ephors	Lacedaemon	Plutarch
gerousia	Laconia	syssition
helot	Lycurgus	Xenophon
homoioi	Messenia	
kleros	Peloponnesian League	

SUGGESTED READINGS

Cartledge, P. A. 2001. *Spartan Reflections*. Berkeley and Los Angeles: University of California Press. Important collection of essays dealing with various aspects of the political and social history of ancient Sparta and the "Spartan Mirage."

———. 2003. *The Spartans: The World of the Warrior-Heroes of Ancient Greece*. Woodstock, NY: The Overbrook Press. Lucid, up-to-date history of Sparta by the leading historian of the city.

Fitzhardinge, L. F. 1980. *The Spartans*. London: Thames and Hudson. Extensively illustrated cultural and social history of Sparta.

Kennell, Nigel M. 1995. *The Gymnasium of Virtue: Education and Culture in Ancient Sparta*. Chapel Hill: University of North Carolina Press. Readable revisionist discussion of the agoge (educational system), which Kennell argues was largely invented in the Hellenistic and Roman period.

Pomeroy, Sarah B. 2002. *Spartan Women*. New York: Oxford University Press. Clearly written, comprehensive account of the lives and images of Spartan women.

Powell, A., ed. 1989. *Classical Sparta. Techniques Behind Her Success*. Norman: University of Oklahoma Press. A collection of essays including Ephraim David, "Laughter in Spartan Society," and Stephen Hodkinson, "Inheritance, Marriage and Demography: Perspectives upon the Success and Decline of Classical Sparta."

Rawson, Elizabeth. 1969. *The Spartan Tradition in European Thought*. Oxford, UK: Oxford University Press. Reprinted in 1991 with a new introduction by Keith Thomas. The history of the idea of Sparta from Classical Greece through the Renaissance, Whig England, and Nazi Germany, with a short note on the United States.

CHAPTER FIVE

The Growth of Athens and the Persian Wars

During the Archaic period, numerous Greek city-states struggled with a variety of problems—factional quarrels between aristocratic families, tension between aristocrats and the people, and tyranny. Sparta found a unique solution to the Archaic crisis and so did Athens. By 500 BC the problems of Athens had been largely resolved. The last tyrant had been expelled, Athens had a democratic government, and aristocratic stasis was largely confined to competing for office and persuading the assembly. Because of their relative harmony, wealth, and great numbers, the Athenians had become the second most powerful Greek polis; and they were poised to play a major role in the great war that was about to begin. While the Greek city-states were evolving, the Persian Empire was growing into an ambitious power that would threaten to engulf the Hellenic world. A strong Athens would be vital to the defense of Greece against invasions by the Persian kings **Darius I** and **Xerxes**.

ATHENS FROM THE BRONZE AGE TO
THE EARLY ARCHAIC AGE

Literary evidence and physical remains show that during the Late Bronze Age, Athens was the largest and most important settlement on the Attic peninsula and a major Mycenaean palace center that exercised a loose control over the other fortified palace centers in the region. These remained, however, independent of the Athenian wanax. Archaeology also confirms the tradition that the upheavals at the end of the late thirteenth century BC spared Athens. Still, if the story about the Achaeans taking refuge at Athens is true, they would have found in Attica the same collapse of the centralized ruling structure, drastic depopulation, and dispersal into small village communities as in the regions from which they had fled.

The first sign of Athenian recovery from the postinvasion slump is the appearance of Protogeometric pottery around 1050 BC. Although reduced to a cluster of villages around the Acropolis, Athens continued without interruption as the central place of Attica. It is likely that by 900 BC, if not earlier, the basileus of Athens was preeminent within Attica. The appearance of rich ninth-century graves reveals significant growth in wealth and overseas trade during the later Dark Age. The population around Athens rose sharply during the eighth century, and new settlements appeared throughout Attica, perhaps through "internal colonization" from the plain of Athens.

Significantly, Athens did not colonize overseas during the late eighth century. The synoecism or "joining together" of the towns and villages of Attica into a political unity under the leadership of Athens was probably gradual, only being completed around the middle of the eighth century. The Athenians ascribed the unification to Theseus, whom myth linked with his companion, the Dorian hero Heracles. Theseus' exploits, such as defeating the Minotaur in Crete and the Amazons in Athens, were enshrined in Athenian art and literature. In making Theseus the founder of their polis and its democracy, the Athenians followed the common Greek practice of attributing important events of the preliterate period to some great figure from the legendary past.

More important than the details of the process of unification is the fact that after the Dark Age every settlement in Attica considered itself "Athenian," and

Figure 5.1. Detail of Attic red-figure cup by Epictetus, c. 510 BC, showing the Athenian hero Theseus killing the bull-headed Minotaur, who here wields a large stone. London, The British Museum.

none attempted to declare its independence as happened elsewhere, nor were there subordinate populations such as the Spartan helots or perioeci. The unification of Attica, however, created unique problems. Although all Athenian citizens could participate in the government of Athens, in reality people who lived in or near Athens would find it easier to vote than those who lived farther away. Thus, for example, a visit to Athens by a farmer who lived fifteen or twenty miles away would probably require three days. The importance of this fact for understanding Athenian history cannot be underestimated because until the outbreak of the Peloponnesian War in 431 BC, most people still lived in the countryside.

The early government of Athens was aristocratic. Probably during the later eighth century the chiefs of Attica replaced the paramount basileus with three civic officials called collectively archons—that is, "the leaders"—who divided the leadership roles among themselves. One of the archons, called the *basileus,* administered the cults of the polis and judged lawsuits pertaining to cult property and other religious matters. The *polemarch* (war archon) commanded the army and judged disputes involving noncitizens. The most prestigious office was that of the *archon,* who had overall supervision of public affairs, including presiding over the council and the assembly and judging nonreligious cases. He is known as the eponymous archon, because he gave his name to the year. Six judicial officials called *thesmothetai* ("layers down of the rules") were added later, making up the governing body of the "nine archons." The nine archons were elected annually from candidates drawn from the small circle of aristocratic families known as the Eupatrids ("people with good fathers").

The archons governed Athens in concert with the council that met on the hill (*pagos*) sacred to the war god Ares and was called for that reason the Council of the Areopagus. Because archons joined the council after the end of their term, sitting archons would probably think twice before flouting its wishes. Citizen males also participated in the assembly, but its precise role in the government and the part that the ordinary citizens played in it are unknown, although Aristotle claimed that it elected the archons (*Politics* 2.1274a 1–2 and 15–17).

Alongside these official state institutions were other forms of social organization that directed the lives of the citizens. In Attica, as in the rest of Greece, the basic social units—the individual households (*oikoi*)—were grouped into larger but poorly understood kin-like associations: tribes, phratries, and clans. Every citizen family belonged to one of four *phylai* ("tribes") and to another smaller group within their tribe, called a *phratry* ("brotherhood"). Although all the Ionian peoples had the same four tribes, they probably were not very ancient but were invented in the eighth century as the earliest poleis formed. It is possible that they served as political and military divisions—each tribe furnishing a contingent to the army. The phratry may originally have designated a "brotherhood of warriors," like the warrior bands led by Dark Age chieftains that we see in Homer. By the seventh century, however, the phratries were concerned with matters of family and of descent. Membership in a phratry was a means of proving citizenship, and in cases of unintentional homicide, the members of the victim's phratry were obligated to support his family, or, if the victim had no family, to pursue the case on his behalf. The "clans" (*genē*) were associations of aristocratic households dominated by a top oikos and claiming descent from a common ancestor. It was within this framework that the events of seventh- and sixth-century Athens unfolded.

The Conspiracy of Cylon

Only two events of Athenian history are known from the seventh century, both plainly connected with unrest of some kind. About 632 BC, an Olympic victor named **Cylon** took advantage of his marriage connection with Theagenes, the tyrant of nearby Megara, to seize the Acropolis and attempt to become tyrant of Athens, only to find himself and his supporters besieged by the Athenians. Cylon and his brother escaped, but his supporters, who had taken refuge at the altar of Athena, surrendered to the nine archons on condition that their lives would be spared. The conspirators even tied a thread to the statue of Athena, and descended while holding onto it, hoping the goddess would protect them. When the thread snapped, however, the archon Megacles and his supporters killed them. People believed that Megacles had committed sacrilege, and soon his family was exiled, including dead relatives whose bodies were exhumed and cast beyond the Attic frontier.

Although Cylon's coup failed, it played an interesting role in future Athenian history because of the prominent family to which Megacles belonged. The Alcmaeonid genos would contribute important politicians to Athens, including Cleisthenes and Pericles, two of the most prominent Athenian statesmen of the sixth and fifth centuries. Politically motivated demands for the expulsion of the "accursed" repeatedly sent shock waves through the body politic because people believed that the family's shared responsibility for its members' impious actions might call the wrath of the gods down on the state.

Draco and Early Athenian Law

More is known about the codification of Athenian law by a mysterious man named **Draco** around 620 BC. Because *drakōn* is Greek for "snake," and the Athenians worshiped a sacred snake on the Acropolis, some scholars have suggested that priests published the laws of "Draco" on the authority of the sacred snake. It is more likely, however, that Draco was a real person.

The best known of Draco's laws is that concerning homicide, which replaced the family and kin with the state as the arbiter of justice in cases of both intentional and unintentional killings. Before Draco's homicide law, bereaved family members were entitled and obliged to avenge the deaths of their slain relatives, unless the kin could be persuaded to accept compensation. Draco transformed such disputes into trials in which the next of kin, backed by his phratry, prosecuted the accused killer before magistrates who determined the appropriate penalty: death for murder or exile for unintentional homicide.

Little is known about Draco's other laws except that they were severe, stipulating death as the penalty even for minor offenses. The fourth-century Athenian orator Demades quipped that Draco's laws were written not in ink but in blood. What was significant about Draco's laws was their role in the process of developing the authority of the state at the expense of that of the family, and, it should be noted, of the magistrates also. The establishment of fixed principles of justice limited the magistrates' ability to shape their decisions in accord with their social and professional ties to particular litigants. The problems that were causing unrest in Athens, however, were both economic and political; purely legal reforms could not soothe the tensions that seemed to be inviting tyranny, such as enslavement for debt, which would soon become a principal grievance of the poor.

THE REFORMS OF SOLON

Solon's legislation in the 590s provides the best evidence for the nature of these problems. Solon tried to strengthen the fragile agricultural base of the Athenian economy by grafting onto it a thriving commerce. Because of the poor soil of Attica, the Athenians could not raise enough grain to feed their increasing population. Consequently, they obtained wheat from abroad by bartering crops suited to their land—olives, vines, figs, and barley. High-quality olive oil packaged in vases made from the excellent clay of Attica was their most significant export, much of it going to the Black Sea and Italy where it was prized by the Etruscans whose tombs contain numerous fine Attic vases. Athens even seized the strategic city of Sigeum in northwest Anatolia about 600 BC, allowing it to threaten ships entering the Hellespont. Besides oil, wine, and pottery, the Athenians had at their disposal silver produced in the mines at Laurium in southeast Attica.

Although the Athens of 600 had great potential for economic development, many poor sharecroppers were losing the struggle to survive. For a second time the Athenians turned to a respected individual to resolve the crisis. Early in the sixth century, perhaps in 594, they empowered Solon, an aristocratic poet with a reputation for wisdom, to draw up a new law code that would ease the sufferings of the poor and avoid a tyranny. The poor wanted the abolition of debts and the redistribution of land; what they got was the abolition of debt slavery. Over time, Solon's reforms mitigated the risk of dividing the Athenians into haves and have-nots by creating a sliding scale of privilege that contained something for everyone.

Solon defended his work in poetry, fragments of which still survive. Decrying both the selfishness of the rich and the revolutionary demands of the poor, he identified wealth as an unstable and problematic force in human affairs: "There are many bad rich men," he wrote, "while many good men are poor"; but, he went on, he would not exchange his virtue (*arete*) for the riches of the wealthy, "for virtue endures, while wealth belongs now to one man, now to another" (cited in Plutarch, *Life of Solon* 3). Although Solon urged justice for the people, he was also committed to defending the rights of the elite both to their land and to a preeminent role in government:

> The commons (*demos*) I have granted privilege enough,
> not lessening their estate nor giving more;
> the influential, who were envied for their wealth,

I have saved them from all mistreatment too.
I took my stand with strong shield covering both sides,
allowing neither unjust dominance.

(Solon fr. 5; West)

"In large things," Solon wrote about his endeavors, "it is hard to please everybody." His rueful lament that in trying to please everyone he pleased no one is ironic in view of the cult that developed after his death, when he would become the beloved "founding father" of Classical Athens. Democrats and antidemocrats alike claimed him as their ideological ancestor and invoked his support for their programs. Although the earliest surviving sources for Solon's reforms—aside from his own poems—were written centuries after his death, it is possible to reconstruct the outlines of his programs.

Solon's first act was to address the sufferings of the poor. These included both sharecroppers who were called *hektemoroi* ("sixth-parters"), perhaps because they paid a rent equal to a sixth of their produce to a wealthy landowner, and failed debtors, who had borrowed against their property and themselves and could not repay their debts. Hektemoroi were forced to pay; this was a form of "protection" money. Under the law, many members of both oppressed groups and their families became slaves of their debtors if they could not meet their obligations. Solon not only made it illegal for loans to be secured by anyone's property or person; he also freed those who had been enslaved for debt and canceled the obligations of the hektemoroi. This bold measure was known as the *seisachtheia*, the "shaking off of burdens," and for many generations was commemorated by a festival of the same name. Solon also redeemed and brought home Athenians who had been sold as slaves outside Attica. What happened to the former hectemors is unclear, but the fact that Athens became a land of free small farmers suggests that Solon let them keep the land occupied at the time of his reforms. None of this, however, should be construed as an attack on slavery per se. Solon had no problem with Athenians enslaving non-Athenians.

Solon's other economic measures were less dramatic but equally important. By revising Athenian weights and measures, he facilitated trade with other states. He also encouraged olive cultivation and prohibited the export of grain, because it was needed at home. To attract artisans from other regions, Solon offered them citizenship if they would settle permanently with their families. He was also credited with a law that sons who had not been taught a trade were not required to support their mothers and fathers in old age. He was even said to have empowered the Council of the Areopagus to inquire into every man's means of supporting himself and to punish those who could show none, a dramatic contrast to the Spartan ethos that soldiering was the only appropriate work for a citizen.

By establishing a constitution in which political privilege was allotted in accord with income, Solon also tried to deal with the grievances of the newly rich non-elite families who resented the Eupatrid monopoly on privilege. He revised the traditional system of property classes by adding a fourth class at the top. In the new system citizens were ranked according to agricultural wealth. The new class, the *pentakosiomedimnoi,* or "500-measure men," consisted of those whose estates produced at least 500 *medimnoi* ("bushels") of produce; any combination of oil, wine, or grain would do. Below them came the *hippeis* ("horsemen," as they were the men who could afford to keep a horse for the cavalry), whose income was between 300 and 499 medimnoi; followed by the *zeugitai,* men who could afford to own a team of oxen, with 200 to 299; and finally the *thetes*—some poor farmers and agricultural workers and some artisans—who produced less than 200 medimnoi.

Although the chief magistracies were limited to members of the first two classes, zeugitai could hold lower state offices and the thetes could join the others in the assembly (the *ekklēsia*), which was to meet regularly. Slaves and resident aliens called metics were excluded from the system, as were women, who formed about a third of the citizen body. Citizen men from all classes could serve in the *heliaia,* a pool of prospective jurors. These people would serve in courts set up to receive appeals from the judicial decisions of the archons and try the cases of magistrates whom someone wished to accuse of misconduct in office. Solon's most revolutionary contribution to the Athenian judicial system was his insistence that any male citizen—not just the victim or the victim's relatives—could bring an indictment if he believed a crime had been committed. Once the concern of families, justice was now the business of the community of male citizens as a whole.

Solon did not alter Draco's homicide laws, but he reduced the penalties for other crimes and decreed an amnesty for persons exiled for crimes other than homicide or attempted tyranny. It was probably this amnesty that allowed the Alcmaeonid family to return to Athens. Solon feared the concentration of land in the hands of a few dominant families. It was probably for this reason that he allowed childless men (like himself) to adopt an heir by means of a will, thereby abrogating the traditional rule that such property passed automatically to the nearest male kin.

Solon's laws regarding sex and marriage reflect the traditional Greek view that a state was a conglomeration of oikoi. Although some of these laws seem intended to extend governmental power to cover women's private lives, Solon's concerns about the excessive power of aristocratic families suggest that his more intrusive provisions, such as restrictions on women's dress, reflect his apprehension about conspicuous consumption by rich families rather than a desire to control women's activities. Several of Solon's policies, however, had a significant impact on women's lives. For example, the nearest male relative of a man who died without a son was required to marry the dead man's daughter and have sex with her at least three times a month to produce a male heir and thus keep the property in the family. A similar concern for maintaining the purity of family lines probably accounts for the fact that, although Solon had abolished debt slavery and had forbidden fathers as a rule to sell their children into slavery, he made an exception for a man who discovered his unmarried daughter was not a virgin.

Solon's legislation is remarkable for its creativity and scope. Solon had been given an unusual opportunity to think long and hard about the nature of a community. His laws established the principle that the Athenian citizen body as a whole would guide the Athenian state. Indeed, he virtually established the notion of citizenship itself. His law that neutrality was unacceptable in a time of civil strife demonstrates his determination that all male citizens take part in civic affairs, essentially defining a citizen as a person involved in public concerns. His laws also made clear that, although the regulation of women's behavior was essential to a well-ordered society, their role was limited to the private sphere; thus he excluded them effectively from the body politic.

Solon's laws were inscribed on wooden tablets called *axones* that were set up in the agora, where everyone could see them even though most could not read them. After the Athenians swore to keep his laws in effect for a hundred years and each archon had been compelled to swear that he would dedicate a gold statue at Delphi if ever he violated any of them, Solon left Attica, partly to see the world and partly to escape pressure to alter his legislation. Solon was neither a democrat nor a revolutionary. There is, nevertheless, some justice in the claim that he was the father of the democracy, for by abolishing the hectemor (sixth-part) system and debt slavery, Solon not only helped create the free peasantry that formed the basis of the democracy; he also established the distinction between freedom and slavery that was to be central to the Athenian concept of citizenship.

Pisistratus and His Sons

Solon's reforms eased social tensions in Attica. By intensifying the competition for political office, however, they probably indirectly fostered the civil strife that led to the tyranny of **Pisistratus**. The inhabitants of sixth-century Attica were loosely divided into three factions known as the Men of the Plain, the Men of the Coast, and the Men of the Hill. Historians still debate the composition of each group. The Men of the Plain were probably large landowners; the Men of the Coast were fishermen and craftsmen; and the poorer inhabitants of the Attic highlands made up the Men of the Hill—perhaps the city dwellers were in this last group as well.

Pisistratus' Seizure of Power

Around 560 BC, a distant relative of Solon from northern Attica named Pisistratus successfully carried out a coup. Pisistratus' backers included not only the Men of the Hill, but also some of the city dwellers. Herodotus tells how Pisistratus wounded himself and his mules and then appeared in the agora demanding a bodyguard to protect himself from his alleged enemies. Although Solon supposedly warned the Athenians against his kinsman's duplicity, the assembly voted Pisistratus a bodyguard, whereupon he seized the Acropolis and with it the reins of government.

After about five years, the parties of the plain and the coast united against Pisistratus and drove him out, but when Megacles, the leader of the coastal party, quarreled not only with the party of the plain but also with his own faction, he decided to ally with Pisistratus and agreed to reestablish him in Athens provided he married his daughter. A century later Herodotus marveled at the story that Pisistratus effected his return to Athens by dressing a tall beautiful woman in armor and putting out the rumor that Athena was escorting him to Athens, although "from the very earliest times the Greeks have been distinguished from the barbarians by their intelligence and freedom from simpleminded foolishness . . . " and "the Athenians . . . are said to be the foremost Greeks when it comes to brains" (*The Histories* 1.60).

Whatever the truth of the tale, Pisistratus' alliance with his father-in-law Megacles did not endure. Pisistratus already had two grown sons whose position he did not wish to undermine by fathering any children with Megacles' daughter,

Figure 5.2. Attic black-figure *hydria* (water jar) attributed to the Priam Painter, c. 520 BC, showing women using hydrias to get water at a fountain house that recalls those constructed by Pisistratus. Toledo, Toledo Museum of Art.

so, according to Herodotus, he had intercourse with his wife *ou kata nomon*— "in unconventional ways" (1.61). (Herodotus suggests that Megacles found out from the bride's mother, who had asked her some pointed questions.) Outraged, Megacles joined with Pisistratus' enemies, and they drove him out a second time.

During his exile, which lasted from about 555 to 546 BC, Pisistratus gathered a force of mercenary soldiers with wealth drawn from the gold and silver mines of Mount Pangaeus in northern Greece. Supported by Lygdamis of Naxos and the cavalry of Eretria, he landed at **Marathon** and defeated the opposition in battle. He then governed Athens for over ten years until he died of natural causes in 527. Pisistratus gave his tyranny legitimacy by maintaining Solon's system in force while manipulating the laws so that his friends and relatives were elected archons, as mercenaries held in check potential opponents, whose children he used as hostages. When the last of Pisistratus' sons was expelled in 510, the way lay open for the development of the democratic institutions that are associated with the city of Athens. Although it might seem that a tyranny would roll back Draco's and Solon's efforts to undermine the influence of powerful families, the reality was that after the fall of the Pisistratids, the development of democracy profited from the tyranny's equalizing effect: Under the rule of the tyrants, all Athenians—rich and poor—found themselves in surprisingly similar circumstances.

Pisistratus' Policies

Strengthening the economy was a major focus of Pisistratus' program. Like Solon, he was concerned about both agriculture and commerce. He offered land and loans to the needy. He encouraged the cultivation of the olive, and Athenian trade expanded greatly under his regime. During the first half of the sixth century, Athenian exports had begun appearing throughout the Mediterranean and Aegean, and it is difficult to believe that this explosion was not due at least in

Figure 5.3. This silver coin, worth four drachmas and thus known as a tetradrachm, was minted at Athens c. 520–510 BC. The obverse displays the portrait of Athena in an Attic helmet and the verso shows her attributes the owl and olive branch. On the right the first three letters of the word for "of the Athenians" appear. New York, American Numismatic Society.

part to Solon. Under Pisistratus, fine Attic pottery traveled still farther—to Ionia, Cyprus, and Syria in the east and as far west as Spain. Black-figure painting reached its apogee shortly after the middle of the century, and around 530, potters began to experiment with the more versatile red-figure style. Pisistratus or his sons also issued the first "owls"—silver coins stamped on the obverse with the image of Athena, and on the reverse her symbol, the owl—that quickly became the soundest currency in the Aegean.

The growth of commerce was accompanied by an ambitious foreign policy. Pisistratus installed his friend Lygdamis as tyrant at Naxos, conveniently making Naxos available as a residence for Pisistratus' hostages. Pisistratus also placed Sigeum under the control of one of his sons and established a foothold across the Hellespont in the Thracian Chersonese (the Gallipoli peninsula), by sending **Miltiades**, a member of the Philaid clan and a potential rival, to rule the Dolonci, a Thracian tribe that lived there.

In Athens, Pisistratus' building projects provided jobs to the poor while focusing attention on the city as the cultural center of Attica. Replacing the private wells guarded by aristocrats with public fountain houses not only meant construc-

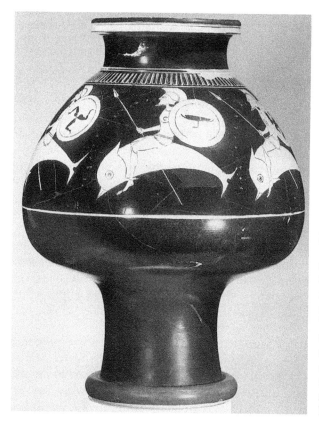

Figure 5.4. Attic red-figure *psyktēr* (wine cooler) attributed to Oltos, c. 520–510 BC, showing armed warriors riding on dolphins, probably represents the chorus of an early theatrical production. The vessel was made for use at a drinking party known as a symposion and therefore depicts a wine cup as the device on the central warrior's shield. New York, The Metropolitan Museum of Art.

tion jobs but also a shift from private to public patronage. With expanded opportunities for jobs and housing in the city, Athens' population grew, and those who lived in the urban area found it easier to vote. Pisistratus also rebuilt the temple of Athena on the Acropolis and began a temple to Olympian Zeus so large that it was completed only seven centuries later by the Roman emperor Hadrian.

Pisistratus' support of religion and the arts enhanced both his own reputation and that of the city of Athens. The worship of Dionysus flourished in Pisistratid Athens, and Dionysian scenes of drinking and unrestrained merrymaking were popular subjects of vase painting. He established two new festivals, the greater and lesser Dionysia, and instituted around 534 BC competition in tragic drama as part of the Dionysia. At the Dionysia, choirs of "satyrs" wearing goat skins honored Dionysus by conversing with their leader in a "goat song" or *tragōdia* that evolved into the Attic "tragedies" of the fifth century. Pisistratus also commissioned the first editions of Homer's *Iliad* and *Odyssey* and made Homeric recitations a regular part of the great Panathenaic festival, which was celebrated at Athens every four years. The Panathenaea culminated in a great procession carrying to Athena's temple the robe woven for her by Athenian girls. This was not a small piece of fabric like the cloak the Spartan girls wove for their small archaic wooden figure of Artemis, but a huge robe for a larger-than-life-size statue of Athena that was wheeled up to the Acropolis on a boat-shaped wagon like an unfurled sail on a ship. Ironically the procession up the Acropolis at the Panathenaea would serve as the occasion for the murder of Pisistratus' son Hipparchus in 514. (See Plate XIb.)

The Collapse of the Tyranny

Patronage of the arts became still more conspicuous after Pisistratus' death. Thucydides believed that Pisistratus' son **Hippias** ruled alone, although others including Aristotle claimed that Hippias' brother **Hipparchus** was co-tyrant. In any event, Hippias and Hipparchus adorned their court with celebrated writers—Simonides of Ceos, whose choral odes were famous; the love poet Anacreon of Teos; and Lasus of Hermione, known for composing novel "hissless hymns," that is, poems in which the sound "s" was never heard. Cultural prestige, however, could not keep the hereditary tyrants secure. In 514, Hipparchus, spurned by a young man named **Harmodius**, insulted Harmodius' sister by forbidding her to carry a basket in the Panathenaic procession. Outraged at the suggestion that his sister was not a virgin, Harmodius and his lover **Aristogiton** plotted to assassinate the tyrants at the procession. When one of the conspirators was observed chatting with Hippias, the others panicked and immediately killed Hipparchus. The results were devastating for Athens: The paranoid autocracy of Hippias replaced the benign government of two aristocrats.

Hippias' tyranny lasted another four years until 510, when he was driven into exile thanks to the efforts of the exiled **Alcmaeonids**. The key to their success was good relations with Delphi. Taking advantage of the Delphians' failure to rebuild the temple of Apollo, which had burned down, the Alcmaeonids subsidized its reconstruction, even providing a frontage of first-class Parian marble instead of ordinary stone. In return, the priests made sure that whenever the Spartans went to Delphi for advice about future projects, they always received the response: "First free Athens." Inasmuch as the Spartans enjoyed their reputation as the enemy of tyranny, they were receptive to this suggestion. In 510 King Cleomenes blockaded Hippias on the Acropolis. When Hippias' children were captured, the tyrant capitulated and departed with his family to Sigeum.

The Athenians understandably chose to remember the heroism of Harmodius and Aristogiton rather than the Spartan intervention, as illustrated, for example, by drinking songs like the following:

> I will carry my sword in a bough of myrtle
> the way Harmodius and Aristogiton did
> when they killed the tyrants
> and restored equal laws to Athens.

The Reforms of Cleisthenes

Predictably, renewed factional strife followed the exile of Hippias. An aristocrat named Isagoras was elected archon in 508 BC on a platform of disenfranchising persons given citizenship by the tyrants. His rival **Cleisthenes**, the leader of the Alcmaeonid family, opposed the plan and won popular support. Isagoras responded by using the old curse to force Cleisthenes into exile, but despite the support of the Spartan king Cleomenes, he failed in his plan to set up an oligarchy. Instead of capitulating, the indignant Athenians blockaded the Spartans on the Acropolis, forced the surrender of Cleomenes and Isagoras, and invited Cleisthenes and his followers back to Athens.

Recognizing the danger to the state posed by family rivalries, Cleisthenes carried in the assembly a package of far-reaching reforms intended to break the power of rich families (other than his own). His methods were ingenious. He transferred the civic functions of the four ancient Ionian tribes to ten new tribes established on a new basis. First he divided Attica into three broad geographical areas: the city, the coast, and the plain. Each area was subdivided into ten *trittyes*, or "thirds" composed of residential units called demes (villages or townships). As the demes (which had been in existence for a long time) varied in size—there were 139 in all—the number in each trittys also varied, but each tribe in the new system contained one trittys from each geographical area. Each of the ten new tribes—Erechtheis, Aigeis, Pandionis, Leontis, Akamantis, Oeneis, Kekropis, Hippothontis, Aiantis, and Antiochis—was named after a local hero and had its own officials and sanctuaries. The requirement that citizens identify themselves by their demotic, that is, the name of their deme, instead of their father's name, undermined family loyalty. Tradition was not so easily cast aside, however, so we still think of Pericles as the son of Xanthippus and the historian Thucydides as the son of Olorus.

The ten new tribes also formed the basis for the creation of a new council, the Council (*boulē*) of Five Hundred, with each tribe annually providing fifty members

Figure 5.5. The tyrannicides Harmodius and Aristogiton were commemorated in a lost bronze statue group of c. 477–476 BC that replaced an earlier group, which was taken to Susa during the Persian Wars. These Roman marble figures are a copy of the replacement group. Naples, National Museum.

Plate Ia. A diver carefully excavates amphoras, the standard transport containers from the Bronze Age well into the Roman Empire, from a ship that was wrecked before 1300 BC off the coast of modern Turkey near Uluburun. The Canaanite ship was on its way toward the Greek mainland with a cargo of copper and tin, the ingredients of bronze; on board were at least two Mycenaean passengers. See Chapter 1.

Plate Ib. At the same wreck, divers inspect some of the metal ingots that comprised most of the ship's cargo: ten tons of copper and one ton of tin.

Plate II. Gold-plated silver diadem from the "Treasure of Priam" excavated at Troy by Heinrich Schliemann and modeled by Mrs. Schliemann in Figure 1.1b in Chapter 1. Staatliche Museen Berlin: Museum für Vor- und Frühgeschichte. See Chapter 1.

Plate III. Idealized harbor-village scene from a seventeenth-century BC fresco that spans three walls of a room in a house excavated at Akrotiri on Santorini (ancient Thera), which was buried in volcanic ash ca. 1628 BC; the African flora and the fauna in the lower panel are a reflection of Minoan contact with Egypt. Athens, National Archaeological Museum. See Chapter 1.

Plate IV. Terra-cotta chest (c. 850 BC), covered by a lid with five model granaries, found in the same grave as the jewelry in Figure 2.3, and accompanied by two other freestanding granary models. The chest testifies to the agricultural wealth of the deceased woman and her family. Athens, Agora Museum. See Chapter 2.

Plate V. Laconian cup attributed to the Arcesilas Painter, c. 560 BC. On the interior of this drinking cup King Arcesilas II of Cyrene is depicted supervising workmen weighing and carrying bales of silphium, a plant used for medicine. The monkey atop the scales, the tame wildcat under the king's seat, and the lizard behind him are the Spartan vase painter's way of indicating the scene's exotic African location. This cup provides evidence of close commercial ties between the two poleis. Paris, Bibliothèque Nationale, Cabinet des Médailles.

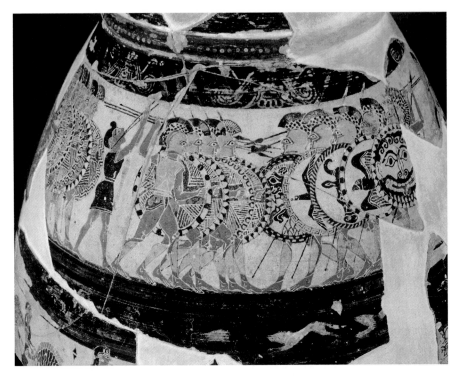

Plate VIa. Detail of Corinthian polychrome *olpe* (wine jug), known as the Chigi Vase, with a rare depiction of a battle between phalanxes of hoplites (c. 640 BC). Rome, National Etruscan Museum of the Villa Giulia. See Chapter 3.

Plate VIb. Statue of a warrior, mid-fifth century BC. This statue is one of a pair of remarkably well-preserved bronze statues of warriors—possibly from a victory monument—recovered from the sea bed near Riace in southern Italy. The statue is larger than life size, and the warrior is depicted wearing a diadem, symbolic of victory. The teeth and eyelashes are made of silver, the eyes of bone and glass, and the lips and nipples of red copper. Reggio, Regional Museum.

Plate VIIa. The Vix Crater (ca. 530 BC) is the largest extant archaic bronze crater (height 164 cm = 5′ 4 ½ ″; capacity ca. 1,200 liters = 317 gallons) and formed part of the grave goods of an elite Celtic woman buried at Vix in southern France. The crater, which was probably the product of a Laconian workshop, was made in sections for ease of transport. It most likely reached Vix as a diplomatic gift and not through trade. Châtillon-sur-Seine Museum.

Plate VIIb. Mature woman with head and shoulders covered by a mantle. Compare her attire with dress of unmarried Spartan girl shown in Chapter 4, Figure 4.5. Part of the lid of the Vix Crater.

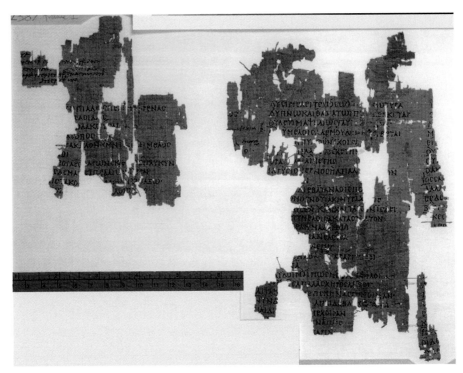

Plate VIII. Archaic poetry on Hellenistic papyrus. Alcman, *Partheneion PMG* 3.61–64. *Oxyrhynchus Papyrus* xxiv 2387. Late first century BC or early first century AD. These fragments of a papyrus roll containing poems by Alcman and works by other authors found in Oxyrhynchus, Egypt, illustrate the fragile nature of many of our texts from antiquity. The top line of the section on the right is *lusimelei te posōi takerōtera*. The first four lines of this text are reconstructed: "With limb-loosening desire and more meltingly than / sleep and death she gazes towards . . . / nor is she sweet in vain. / But Astymeloisa does not answer me." See Chapters 4 and 12.

Plate IX. Procession of life-size guards from the palace of Darius the Great, Susa, Iran; glazed brick, late sixth century BC. Bearded guards carrying bows, quivers, and spears, wearing earrings, gold bracelets, fillets, and patterned garments. The uniform but majestic style in which these warriors are portrayed may be compared with the individuals in Greek art. See Chapter 5. Berlin, Pergamon Museum.

Plate Xa. François Vase. This fine black figure volute crater of the mid-sixth century, inscribed with the names of the painter Clitias and the potter Ergotimus was exported from Athens to Italy and found in an Etruscan tomb. Horizontal friezes on both sides depict epic myths. Inscriptions give the names of the characters. The side shown here illustrates, from top to bottom, the Calydonian Boar Hunt, showing Meleager administering the death blow to the monstrous beast; the funeral games of Patroclus, companion of Achilles; gods attending the wedding procession of Peleus and Thetis, who became the parents of Achilles; Achilles chasing the Trojans Troilus and Polyxena at the fountain house; animals and sphinxes; and pygmies fighting cranes (foot). See Chapter 5. Florence, Museo Archaeologico.

Plates Xb. François Vase detail depicting Thetis. The clothing on this vase displays the intricate weaving produced by women. The skin of women is shown as white and the skin of men black. See Chapter 6.

Plate XIa. Attic red-figure calyx-krater (mixing bowl for wine and water), attributed to Euphronius, c. 515 BC. In this vase's depiction of a symposium (drinking party) men and youths reclining on couches are entertained with music by a hetaira (prostitute) who is playing the double pipes. Like most ancient pottery, this vase was broken when excavated. Sometimes restorers paint in the missing pieces, but sometimes, as in this piece, they simply add blank patches. Munich, Staatliche Antikensammlungen.

Plate XIb. The white ground cup, c. 450 BC, is a phiale from which a libation would be poured, perhaps onto a flaming altar like the one painted on it. It shows women led by a female flute player practicing a dance; the presence of the altar and the ribbons with which the women's hair is bound indicate that the women are participating in a religious ritual. Painter of London D 12. Boston, Museum of Fine Arts.

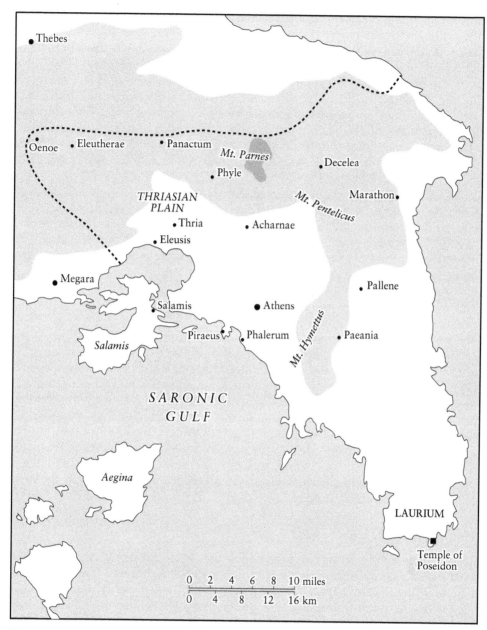

Figure 5.6. Attica.

chosen by lot. Recognizing the principle of proportional representation—an important advance in government—the fifty slots for the boule were distributed among the demes in accordance with the population of each. The use of the lot in determining the composition of each year's boule was a key democratic feature of the Cleisthenic system. The boule's chief functions were to prepare business for the ekklesia (the assembly) and to manage financial and foreign affairs. Because five hundred was an unwieldy number, each tribe represented the whole boule for a tenth of the year. During a tribe's period of service its members were called *prytaneis,* and the term "prytany" was used to designate a period of time covering the thirty-five or thirty-six days that each tribe's members performed their service. The chair and secretary each changed every day by lot. The army also was reorganized on the basis of the ten tribes, with each tribe electing its officers including a *stratēgos,* or chief general. Unlike archons, *stratēgoi* could be reelected repeatedly, so that in time the board of ten strategoi became the most prestigious executive body in Athens.

Because Cleisthenes was not granted extraordinary powers such as those with which Solon had been invested, his measures needed to be passed in the assembly. His reforms, consequently, were in themselves the product of democratic action. Around 500 BC, a meeting place for the ekklesia was carved out of the rock on the hill called the Pnyx, and from then on the assembly met there regularly and framed policy for the state.

THE RISE OF PERSIA

The political transformation of Greek poleis occurred at the same time as the emergence of the Persian Empire, the largest of all Ancient Near Eastern empires. The sources for Persian history are limited. Although the Persians developed a cuneiform-based alphabetic script to write their language, no Old Persian literature survives except for inscriptions primarily devoted to recording the building activities of the Persian kings. Persian history necessarily depends, therefore, on non-Persian sources: Babylonian, Aramaic, Hebrew, and especially Greek historians for whom the Persians, despite their achievements, were merely barbarians, that is, people who spoke "barbar, barbar," gibberish. Despite these limitations, historians working with archaeologists have succeeded in reconstructing the story of the rise of the Persian Empire.

Persia Before Darius

The Persians were an Indo-European people who had settled in southwestern Iran by the early first millennium BC. It was not the Persians, however, but the Medes, who built the first Iranian empire by joining with the Babylonians to overthrow the mighty Assyrian empire in 612 BC. In the mid-sixth century BC, **Cyrus II**, who governed Persia (ruled 559–530 BC), revolted, and made Media the first of the **satrapies** (provinces) of the Persian Empire. During his long reign Cyrus extended Persia to include all Western Asia, but it was his conquest in 546 of the Lydian king Croesus that brought the Greeks of Asia Minor into the empire and led ultimately to the confrontation between the Persians and the European Greeks that would redefine the course of Greek history. Events within the Persian Empire, however, delayed the confrontation for over half a century. First, Cyrus' son Cambyses

(530–522 BC) conquered Egypt; and then, Darius I (522–486 BC), the founder of the dynasty that ruled the empire until its conquest by Alexander the Great, seized power and reorganized the empire.

The Achievements of Darius

Cyrus was praised by Greek and Asian sources alike as a benevolent and talented ruler who avoided the Assyrian and Babylonian practice of deporting rebellious populations and supported local religions and cultures. Because Cyrus allowed the Jews to return from exile in Mesopotamia to Jerusalem and to rebuild their temple there and worship freely, the Old Testament records the declaration of the Hebrew prophet Isaiah to the Jews:

> Thus says the Lord to his anointed, to Cyrus,
> whose right hand I have grasped
> to subdue nations before him and strip kings of their robes,
> to open doors before him—and the gates shall not be closed:
> "I will go before you and level the mountains,
> I will break in pieces the doors of bronze and cut through the bars
> of iron,
> I will give you the treasures of darkness and riches hidden in secret
> places. . . . "
>
> (Isaiah 45:1–3 New Revised Standard Version)

Nevertheless, it was Darius I's reorganization of the empire that ensured its survival for almost two hundred years. He centralized the government and began the construction of the great ceremonial center of Persepolis. Building inscriptions and administrative documents record that Greeks were among the workforce of men and women drawn from all corners of the empire who built the royal buildings. Darius facilitated travel for commercial purposes in many ways, even building a canal linking the Nile and the Red Sea to the Indian Ocean and Persian Gulf. Darius was also the first Persian king to mint his own coins of silver and gold. The gold coins, Daric staters or "darics," celebrated the king's talent at archery, a skill highly prized by the Persians, who, Herodotus reported, learned three skills—to ride, to shoot straight, and to tell the truth. Finally, Darius divided the empire into twenty provinces or satrapies governed by royal appointees and paying an annual tribute to the king. Spies known as the "Eyes and Ears of the King" discouraged rebellions. Supreme political power was concentrated in the person of the king, who ruled as the designee of the Zoroastrian god of light and truth Ahuramazda and defended his subjects against the supporters of Ahriman, god of darkness and falsehood. In accordance with his exalted status, the king exercised absolute authority over his subjects, who prostrated themselves in obeisance before him and performed at his command forced labor and military service. (See Plate IX.) But unlike the Jews, who were grateful for their liberation, the Greeks pitied the subjects of the Persian king, considering them his slaves.

THE WARS BETWEEN GREECE AND PERSIA

About 512 BC Darius campaigned against the European Scyths and thus became the first Persian king to enter Europe. Although he failed to conquer Scythia, he subdued Thrace and reduced it to a satrapy. Darius' westward expeditions piqued his curiosity about the mainland Greeks, and a rebellion in his empire brought him into direct contact with them.

The Ionian Revolt

In 499 BC the Ionian Greeks revolted. Discontent in Ionia was considerable. Taxes had risen under Persian rule, and the Greeks resented the puppet tyrants the Persians had imposed. Violence might not have erupted, however, except for the ambitions of Aristagoras, the tyrant of Miletus. Hoping to add Naxos to his domain, Aristagoras had persuaded the Persians to join him in an unsuccessful effort to subdue the Cyclades islands and perhaps to invade mainland Greece. When the plan failed, Aristagoras, noticing the restlessness of the Ionians, decided to recoup his failing fortunes by uniting them in revolt.

Aristagoras resigned his tyranny and then set about overthrowing tyrants in the other Greek cities in Asia Minor. Most fell without bloodshed, but the tyrant of Mytilene was so unpopular that he was stoned to death. The Ionians showed their unity by issuing coinage on a common standard. Herodotus' account of Aristagoras' attempts to gain support from King Cleomenes sought to illustrate the Spartan character as most Greeks imagined it—cautious, conservative, and leery of foreign adventures; it also highlighted the assertiveness of Spartan women and the respect due them. Aristagoras, Herodotus reports, carried with him a bronze map of the world to show Cleomenes the wealthy peoples the Greeks would conquer if they chose to liberate the Ionians. Capitalizing on the Spartans' dislike of foreign customs, he suggested that they could easily defeat men who fought in trousers and wore peaked caps on their heads. But when Aristagoras told Cleomenes that the Great King lived three months' march from the sea, Cleomenes, Herodotus relates, "cut short the rest of what Aristagoras had to say about the journey and said: My dear Milesian guest, leave Sparta before sundown, because it doesn't matter how smoothly you make your case to the Spartans if what you want is to lead them away from the sea for three months" (*The Histories* 5.50). Not yet willing to abandon his quest, Aristagoras followed Cleomenes to his house, carrying with him the customary sign of supplication—an olive branch, covered with wool—and as he sat in Cleomenes' home as a suppliant, he noticed young Gorgo, who was eight or nine years old, standing by her father. He asked that Cleomenes send his daughter away, but

> Cleomenes told Aristagoras to say whatever he wanted and not to hold anything back on account of the child. Aristagoras began by promising nearly six hundred pounds of precious metals if only Cleomenes would do what he had asked. When Cleomenes turned

Figure 5.7. Detail of the Achaemenid relief from the Apadana at Persepolis (c. 500–480 BC) showing delegations bringing tribute to the Persian king, who received a wide variety of goods from the subjects of his empire as tribute. Berlin, Preussischer Kulturbesitz.

up his nose at this, Aristagoras kept increasing the amount of money until he was finally offering nearly thirty thousand pounds! Then the child cried out, "Father! If you don't get up and go away, this stranger will corrupt you!" Cleomenes was delighted with his child's advice and went into another room; Aristagoras left Sparta for good and never did get his chance to point out anything more about the road to the Great King on his map.

(*The Histories* 5.51)

The Athenians were more receptive, especially because they feared that the Persians might try to restore Hippias to power in Athens. As a result, they agreed to send twenty ships to aid the Ionians; the Eretrians to the north were willing to send five.

Six years after it began, the Ionian Revolt ended in a major naval defeat near Miletus in 494 BC. Greek morale had fallen; the tyrants Aristagoras had expelled were spreading pro-Persian propaganda; before the battle was over, the Samians and Lesbians had deserted. Miletus was defeated, its women and children were enslaved, and the men were relocated to land near the mouth of the Tigris River.

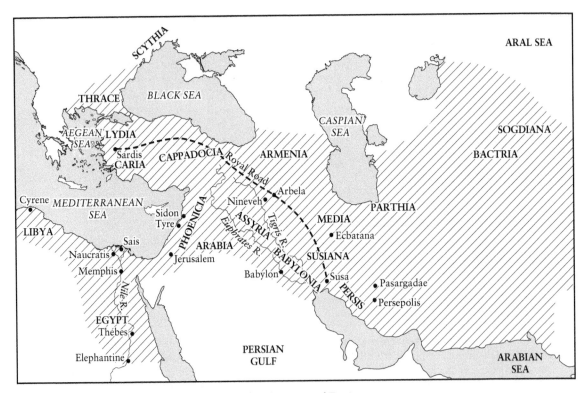

Figure 5.8. The Persian Empire in the reign of Darius.

In addition, early in the rebellion, much of Sardis, the capital of the satrapy of Lydia, was burned; whether accidentally or on purpose is unknown.

Darius would not forget the destruction of Sardis, nor would the Greeks forget the annihilation of Miletus. Home of the philosophers Thales, Anaximander, and Anaximenes, and the geographer Hecataeus (who had warned Aristagoras of Persia's overwhelming superiority), Miletus had been one of the richest and most cultured cities in the Greek world. When the poet Phrynichus produced a tragedy entitled *The Capture of Miletus,* the Athenians fined him one thousand drachmas for reminding them of their misfortune. Although the Athenians had withdrawn from the rebellion after the burning of Sardis, their outrage reveals their sympathy with Miletus in its final hour and a growing sense of identity among the Ionians.

Not surprisingly, they also feared that the mainland Greeks might suffer the fate of Miletus. In this situation, a rising politician named **Themistocles**, who had just been elected archon, persuaded the Athenians to convert the three rocky harbors of Piraeus into a fortified naval and commercial base. Because Themistocles, unlike most Athenian politicians, lacked strong family connections and the support of the leisured landowning class, he sought the backing of those who made their living by trade. Acutely sensitive to the Persian threat—Thucydides praised him for his ability to foresee what the future held (1.138)—Themistocles served Greece well at this critical time.

Darius' Invasion of Greece

The desire to avenge the burning of Sardis strengthened Darius' interest in Greece. In 492 BC an expedition led by his son-in-law Mardonius failed when the fleet was wrecked rounding the Chalcidic peninsula, although it did restore Persian prestige in northern Greece, conquering Thrace, Thasos, and Macedonia. Two years later Darius sent another expedition straight across the Aegean. Mindful of the fate of Miletus, many Greek cities offered earth and water, the proverbial tokens of submission that signaled recognition of the king's supremacy. On the mainland, Argos and Thebes went over to the Persians. Sparta and Athens, however, remained steadfast in their opposition.

Darius' primary goal was to punish Athens and Eretria for their role in the Ionian rebellion. In the summer of 490 his fleet arrived in Greece, commanded by his nephew Artaphernes and Datis, a Mede, who brought with them the aging former Athenian tyrant Hippias. Eretria quickly fell, its temples being burned in revenge for the sack of Sardis and its people exiled to central Asia, where the wandering prophet of the Roman Empire, Apollonius of Tyana, supposedly found their descendants still speaking their native Greek several centuries later. From Eretria, the Persians sailed to the old Pisistratid stronghold of Marathon in northern Attica.

The Athenian assembly immediately voted to dispatch their forces to Marathon, and a runner, Phidippides, was sent to Sparta, supposedly covering fully 140 miles by the next day. The Spartans, however, claimed that they could not march before the new moon because they were celebrating a festival of Apollo, the Carnea. As the Spartans were deeply religious and no cowards in war, their explanation was probably sincere.

The Battle of Marathon

The Athenians were outnumbered, perhaps by a factor of two to one. Although the Persian force included cavalry, archers, and skirmishing troops, the Athenian hoplites were more heavily armed. The most serious problem faced by the Athenians was disunity among the ten strategoi; some wanted to wait for the Spartan reinforcements and others thought delay risky. When the Athenians began to suspect, however, that the Persians were preparing to depart for the port at Phaleron, the general Miltiades (nephew of the Miltiades whom Pisistratus had dispatched to protect Athenian interests in the Chersonese) persuaded his colleagues to attack immediately. His stirring words appear in Herodotus' *Histories*:

> Callimachus, it is up to you, right now, to enslave Athens or to make it free, and to leave for all future generations of humanity a memorial to yourself such as not even Harmodius and Aristogeiton have left. *Right now,* Athens is in the most perilous moment of her history. We already know what she will suffer if she bows down to the Medes and is turned over to Hippias, but if this city survives, she can become the foremost city in all of Greece. Let me tell you just how this is possible, and how it is up to you—and only you—to determine the course of events. We ten generals are split right in two, with half saying fight and the other half not. If we don't fight now, I am afraid that a storm of civil strife will so shake the resolve of the Athenian people that they will go over to the Medes. But if we fight now, before the cracks can show in our society, and provided that the gods take no sides, why then we can survive this battle. All this depends on *you*. It hangs on your decision—*now*. If you vote with me, your fatherland will be free and your city will be first in all of Hellas, but if you choose the side of those who urge us not to fight, then the opposite of all the good I've spoken of will fall to you.
>
> (*The Histories* 6.109)

And so, early one morning in late September of 490, the Athenians and their Plataean allies attacked, shouting, covering the mile or so dividing them from the Persians at double speed despite their heavy hoplite armor. Knowing they were outnumbered, they concentrated their forces, even though it meant their wings would be dense and the center thin. The Persians, who were caught by surprise, broke under the attack of the determined hoplites fighting in defense of their freedom and fled in confusion to their ships.

Arriving too late to participate in the fighting, the Spartans visited the battlefield and surveyed the Persian corpses. Herodotus maintained that the Athenians lost 192 men, the Persians 6,400. The number of Greek dead is probably correct, for the names were inscribed on the battlefield; they included Callimachus. The dead were

Figure 5.9. The tumulus for the Athenian dead at Marathon. The stele to the left is a modern sign.

cremated where they had fallen, and a monument was subsequently erected on the site. Some Plataeans and some Athenian slaves also died, but their numbers are unknown. The playwright Aeschylus, who fought at Marathon, later mentioned only his service at Marathon in his epitaph, writing that "The glorious grove of

Marathon can tell of his valor—as can the long-haired Persian, who well remembers it." For the next two generations, the *Marathonomachoi*—the veterans of Marathon—enjoyed singular prestige in Athens as exemplars of traditional Athenian values in an increasingly luxurious and complex society. Not all Athenians, however, rejoiced in their victory. Herodotus reports that a shield signal was flashed from Athens after the battle urging the Persians to hurry to Athens. (Gossip ascribed this act of treachery to the Alcmaeonids, but Herodotus denied indignantly that the Alcmaeonids had been to blame.) For years accusations of Persian sympathies would dog aspiring Athenian politicians as a convenient device to damage a rival's reputation.

Athens After Marathon

Political leadership in Athens changed after the Battle of Marathon in a very specific manner. The need for capable military commanders resulted in a new method of selecting archons, who, as primarily judicial officials, now seemed less important than the strategoi. Beginning in 487 BC, therefore, archons were chosen by lot from candidates drawn from the demes as was the **Council of the Five Hundred**. As a result, ambitious men shifted their interest from the archonship to the *stratēgia* (generalship), leading ultimately to the decline in influence of the venerable Council of the Areopagus, which was composed of former archons.

Themistocles, who was hostile to the aristocratic ethos that granted special power and prestige to the Areopagites, may have inspired this reform, but he cannot have foreseen its long-term effects on Athenian politics. Selection by lot was a procedure associated with democracy in Greece that tended to discourage the machinations of special interest groups. It also ensured that a significant proportion of the men eligible for each office would participate in politics, and gave legitimacy to the process by enlisting the gods in the choice of officials. The Athenians were no fools, however. All would-be officeholders underwent an interrogation known as *dokimasia,* and the lot was not used to select strategoi, leading to the ten strategoi becoming the most prestigious of all Athenian officials.

At the same time, the Athenians first successfully employed one of Cleisthenes' most remarkable innovations, **ostracism**, a procedure thought to have been intended to prevent the emergence of a new tyrant. Every spring the Athenians had the option of voting to send one of their fellow citizens into exile for ten years. The process took

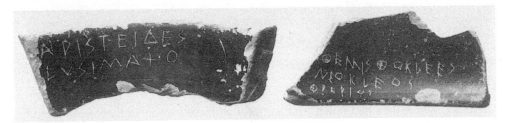

Figure 5.10. Numerous *ostraka* have been discovered in the Athenian agora. These bear the names of Artistides, son of Lysimachus, and Themistocles, son of Neocles, of the deme Phrearrhioi.

its name from the *ostraka*—broken pieces of pottery—on which voters scratched the name of the man they wanted to banish. Ostracized Athenians stood accused of no crime and remained citizens, but they had to live in exile for ten years simply because they had received a plurality of six thousand votes cast by their fellow citizens.

Inevitably historians have wondered if Cleisthenes really created this procedure, as the first man so exiled—a Peisistratid named Hipparchus—was not ostracized until 487. The answer may lie in the requirement for six thousand votes to be cast for an ostracism to be valid: so Hipparchus' ostracism may not have been the first attempted ostracism but merely the first successful one. In any event, it is probably no coincidence that the first man ostracized was related to former tyrant Hippias, and that all but one of the other men ostracized in the 480s—Themistocles' great rival Aristides—were members of the Alcmaeonid family that had been accused of trying to betray Athens to the Persians in 490.

Themistocles' role in the first three ostracisms is unclear, but his dispute with Aristides over how best to face a renewed Persian threat was the central issue in the ostracism of 482. Darius, in fact, began preparations for a new invasion of Greece soon after the Persian defeat at Marathon, but revolts in Babylon and Egypt and Darius' death in the fall of 486 delayed it for almost six years. Meanwhile, the Athenians had made a spectacular silver strike at Laurium in southeastern Attica that yielded over two tons in the first year. In the bitter debate over its use,

Figure 5.11. A trireme at sea. Working in England and Greece, twentieth-century scholars and naval architects reconstructed the Athenian trireme of the Classical period.

Aristides advocated sharing it among the citizens, whereas Themistocles argued for building two hundred **triremes** (light, fast, maneuverable warships with three banks of oars). They were allegedly to be used against Athens' old enemy, Aegina, but were really for defense against the Persians. The ostracism of 482 decided the issue; Aristides left Athens, and the fleet that would save Greece was built. It is difficult to imagine how history might have turned out had the vote in that ostracism been different.

The Invasion of Xerxes

Darius' son and successor, Xerxes (Cyrus' grandson on his mother's side), was at first ambivalent about carrying out the invasion, but by 484 BC he had made his decision, and the Greeks learned that ships were being built in large numbers throughout the ports of the extensive Persian Empire from Egypt to the Black Sea. Engineers and laborers were dispatched to the Hellespont, where they bridged the crossing with boats, and to northern Greece, where they cut a canal across Athos so that the shipwreck Mardonius had suffered in 492 could be avoided.

While the Athenians were still constructing warships, Xerxes' heralds arrived in Greece seeking earth and water, and many states, including Thessaly and Thebes, complied. At a congress held at Corinth in 481 BC, thirty-one states limited mainly to Athens and the Peloponnesian League formed an alliance that historians call the Hellenic League. Even Aegina and Athens reconciled in the crisis, and Aristides and the other exiles were recalled. Nevertheless, the fact remains that only a tiny minority of the more than a thousand poleis actively opposed Xerxes, and many fought for him.

Sparta was awarded supreme command on land and sea. After an unsuccessful attempt to find a defensible position in northern Greece, the Hellenic League decided to make a stand in central Greece, placing a land force at the pass of **Thermopylae** on the Malian Gulf while the fleet settled in at nearby Artemisium off northern Euboea. At the instigation of Themistocles, the Athenians probably voted to evacuate Attica and wait out the war on the island of **Salamis** and in nearby Troezen in the Peloponnesus. A third-century copy of the decree discovered at Troezen in 1959 probably preserves the substance of Themistocles' motion:

> The Gods
> Resolved by the Council and People
> Themistocles, son of Neocles, of Phrearrhioi, made the motion
>
> To entrust the city to Athena the Mistress of Athens and to all the other Gods to guard and to defend against the Barbarian on behalf of the land. The Athenians themselves and the foreigners who live in Athens are to send their children and women to safety in Troezen, their protector being Pittheus, the founding hero of the land. They are to send the old men and their movable possessions to safety on

Salamis. The treasurers and priestesses are to remain on the Acropolis guarding the property of the gods.

All the other Athenians and foreigners of military age are to embark on the 200 ships that are ready and defend against the Barbarian for the sake of their own freedom and that of the rest of the Greeks along with the Lacedaemonians, the Corinthians, the Aeginetans, and all others who wish to share the danger.

(Jameson 1960, adapted)

The odds facing the Hellenic League were great, so great that the Delphic oracle issued a stream of oracles discouraging resistance to the Persians. The Spartans were told that their only hope lay in the death of a king and the Athenians that salvation was to be found in the "wooden walls," which Themistocles argued was

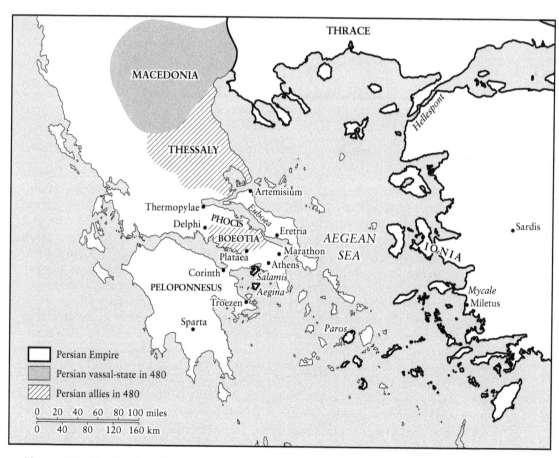

Figure 5.12. The Persian Wars.

the new navy. Although the oracle may partly explain King Leonidas' tenacity in holding Thermopylae, hard calculation also called for a land operation, however unpromising, to buy time for Greece while the fleet off Artemisium could cripple the Persian navy. As luck would have it, a storm fortuitously intervened so that even before the indecisive fighting at Artemisium, the Persians had lost many ships.

The Battle of Thermopylae

Leonidas marched into Thermopylae with about seven thousand men, a fairly small force. Local Phocian forces were assigned to defend a secret path over the mountains leading to the rear of the Greek forces. Unfortunately, a Greek traitor betrayed the secret and guided Xerxes' personal guard, the so-called Immortals, over it. On learning the Persians were at his rear, Leonidas dismissed the bulk of his forces, and with only the Thebans, Thespians, and three hundred Spartans and their helot attendants, Leonidas fiercely defended the pass, killing many "Immortals" including two brothers of Xerxes before being killed themselves. On Xerxes' orders, the body of Leonidas was decapitated and impaled. Throughout antiquity Greeks took inspiration from the epitaph composed for the Thermopylae dead attributed to Simonides:

> Go tell the Spartans, stranger passing by,
> That here, obeying their commands, we lie.

The Battle of Salamis

Their victory at Thermopylae opened the road to Athens and central Greece to the Persians. From their refuge on Salamis the Athenians soon saw the smoke of the burning Acropolis. While the Peloponnesians urged withdrawal of the fleet to the Peloponnesus, Themistocles, fearing that the Greeks might indeed pull back from the Isthmus, sent a messenger to Xerxes urging him to occupy the narrows and block the escape of the Greeks. Herodotus, who came from Halicarnassus in Ionia, took delight in telling how Xerxes' prudent adviser Artemisia, queen of Halicarnassus, in vain advised him against fighting a needless battle. Xerxes quickly learned the wisdom of Artemisia's advice as he watched from his throne the Persian fleet, unable to maneuver in the straits of Salamis, suffer a massive defeat, losing more than two hundred ships. Rather than confronting the foolishness of his decision to fight, Xerxes reacted to the defeat by furiously executing his Phoenician captains for alleged cowardice in the battle and retreated to Asia with the remainder of his fleet. Less than a year later, in the spring of 479, Xerxes' forces, led by Mardonius, were totally destroyed at Plataea by the largest Greek army ever mobilized. Almost at the same time the Greek fleet that had pursued the Persians eastward defeated their navy at the Battle of Mycale near Miletus, finally liberating the Ionians and ending the Persian threat to Greece forever.

The Persian Invasion Through Greek Eyes

Victors celebrate the history of their triumphs; the vanquished try to forget or trivialize them. Until recently, Greek historical sources and scholars who caricatured the Persian Empire as merely an "Oriental despotism" largely shaped our views of the Persian Empire. Modern historians have been overwhelmingly "Hellenocentric," following the lead of fifth-century Greek authors such as the playwright Aeschylus, who believed that Xerxes had incurred the wrath of the gods and was responsible for his own defeat and the death of many noble Persians because of his folly. In 472 BC Aeschylus produced a tragedy, *The Persians,* celebrating the Athenian role in the Persian defeat and the values for which they had fought—liberty as opposed to slavery, responsible democratic government as opposed to capricious autocracy and monarchy. It was the historian Herodotus, however, who gave definitive form to the Hellenocentric view of the Persian Wars. He highlighted in his *Histories* the unexpectedness of the Greek victory and sought its causes in the fundamental institutions of Greek and Persian society and government. Herodotus depicted Xerxes, in contrast to Cyrus, as an impious madman who was responsible for initiating the decline of Persia. Xerxes' chief character flaw, in Herodotus' view, was *hybris* ("arrogance"). Imagining himself to be on the same level as the gods, he dared to bridge the Hellespont, thereby setting in motion a process that led to his own defeat.

DOCUMENT 5.1

The Chorus from Aeschylus' *Persians* (472 BC)

In his tragedy about Salamis, Aeschylus stressed the differences between eastern despotism and Greek freedom. Here the chorus of Persian elders laments Persia's defeat by Greece:

> They throughout the Asian land
> no longer Persian laws obey,
> no longer lordly tribute yield,
> exacted by necessity;
> nor suffer rule as suppliants,
> to earth obeisance never make:
> Lost is the kingly power.—
> Nay, no longer is the tongue
> imprisoned kept, but loose are men,
> when loose the yoke of power's bound,
> to bawl their liberty.

(*The Persians* 584–593; Benardete)

Although Greek historical sources tend to depict Persian history as the gradual degeneration of the mighty empire established by Cyrus the Great, the Persians were not decisively defeated until their conquest by Alexander the Great (from 334–323 BC). They continued to play an influential role in Greek politics, both in civic disputes and in rivalries between Greek states, favoring now one side, now another. They were instrumental in the Spartan victory in the Peloponnesian War, and fourth-century Greek history cannot be understood without constant concern for Persian involvement in Greek affairs.

The Other War: Carthage and the Greek Cities of Sicily

In Herodotus' account, Athens, Sparta, and their few allies faced the might of Persia virtually alone. He emphasized their isolation by telling how they rebuffed the demand of **Gelon**, the powerful tyrant of Syracuse, for a share in the command of the Greek forces despite his offer of two hundred ships and more than twenty thousand troops. Their refusal was timely, however, because the Greek cities of Sicily faced a massive attack from the north African city of Carthage simultaneously with the Persian invasion of Greece.

The Sicilian cities had prospered from the beginning of Greek settlement of the island in the eighth century BC, gradually gaining control of the eastern half of the island and subduing or pushing into the interior its various native populations. They built some of the greatest temples and theatres in the Greek world, and their athletes competed in the Olympic games and had their exploits celebrated by the finest sculptors and poets of the Greek homeland. Political instability, however, accompanied prosperity. Whereas tyranny was declining in Aegean Greece, it flourished in Sicily, reaching a climax in the late sixth century, when Gelon, the tyrant of Gela, seized Syracuse and then brutally conquered most of the cities of Sicily, sometimes even transferring or selling into slavery whole populations to ensure his control.

Fearful they would suffer a similar fate, the cities of Messina and Selinus sought help from Carthage. Carthage responded in force, allegedly invading Sicily with an army of 300,000 men and a fleet of two hundred ships in 480 BC. The decisive battle took place at Himera and ended in a total Carthaginian defeat and the suicide of the Carthaginian commander, who jumped into the sacrificial fire when he learned of the Greek victory.

Gelon celebrated his victory by dedicating a huge golden tripod and a statue of Nike (Victory) to Apollo at Delphi. Gelon died in 478 BC, and his empire disintegrated soon after, but the significance of his victory at Himera lived on, ensuring the security of the Greeks of Sicily for the rest of the fifth century BC. Understandably, therefore, Greek legend maintained the Battle of Salamis and the Battle of Himera were fought on the same day.

The unanticipated success of the little city-states over Persia in the east and Carthage in the west had little impact on these great empires, but in Greece it would give birth to a civilization of extraordinary brilliance and originality. The unity the Persian Wars had sparked, however, would prove short-lived, and its fragility would place limits on how long Greek civilization could endure.

KEY TERMS

Alcmaeonids

Cleisthenes

Council of the Five Hundred

Cylon

Cyrus II

Darius I

Draco

Gelon

Harmodius and Aristogiton

hektemoroi

Hippias and Hipparchus

Marathon

Miltiades

ostracism

pentakosiomedimnoi

Pisistratus

Salamis

satrapies

Solon

Themistocles

Thermopylae

trireme

Xerxes

SUGGESTED READINGS

Brosius, Maria. 2006. *The Persians: An Introduction*. London: Routledge. Brief introduction to the Achaemenid Persians as well as the Parthians and Sasanians who succeeded them.

Cartledge, Paul. 2006. *Thermopylae: The Battle that Changed the World*. Woodstock, NY: Overlook Press. Brilliantly written analysis of the Battle of Thermopylae and its legacy from antiquity to the present.

Cawkwell, George. 2005. *The Greek Wars: The Failure of Persia*. Oxford, UK: Oxford University Press. A detailed study of the relations between Greece and Persia written from the perspective of Persia.

Dillon, Matthew. 2002. *Girls and Women in Classical Greek Religion*. London: Routledge. A comprehensive, well-organized, and readable survey of the roles of women of all statuses in public and private religion.

Green, Peter. 1996. *The Greco-Persian Wars*. Berkeley and Los Angeles: University of California Press (revised edition of *Xerxes at Salamis*). A dramatic account of Xerxes' invasion of Greece.

Hale, John R. 2010. *Lords of the Sea. The Epic Story of the Athenian Navy and the Birth of Democracy*. New York: Penguin. Lively history of Athenian naval power.

Kagan, Donald and Gregory F. Viggiano. 2013. *Men of Bronze: Hoplite Warfare in Ancient Greece*. Princeton: Princeton University Press. A collection of essays that confront the controversies concerning hoplite warfare and its relationship to the Greek polis.

Parker, Robert. 1996. *Athenian Religion: A History*. Oxford, UK: Clarendon Press. Detailed study of the development of Athenian religion in the context of Athenian political and social history.

Shapiro, H. A. 1994. *Myth Into Art: Poet and Painter in Classical Greece*. New York: Routledge. An analysis of the ways in which poets and painters tell the same myth, this book also is a guide to the understanding of Greek vase painting.

Strauss, Barry S. 2004. *The Battle of Salamis: The Naval Encounter that Saved Greece—and Western Civilization*. New York: Simon & Schuster. Readable military history including analysis of the texts and discussion of the cultural differences between Greeks and Persians.

CHAPTER SIX

The Rivalries of the Greek City-States and the Growth of Athenian Democracy

In the struggle to prevent a Persian takeover of Greece, a powerful sense of Hellenic identity was forged. Eager to avoid a third invasion, a number of Greek states entered into an alliance led by the Athenians, whose naval strength had been instrumental in winning the war. Tribute from this league enabled Athens to offer state pay for public service such as jury duty, thus expanding the number of men who could afford to participate in government. The fact that the lower-class citizens who rowed the triremes were becoming increasingly pivotal to the city's well-being also made it difficult for the rich and wellborn to maintain their monopoly on political power. Democratic reforms consequently reduced the advantage wealthy aristocrats enjoyed in politics, although nothing whatsoever was done to remove the civic disabilities of women or to abolish slavery. Indeed, Athens' imperial ventures probably increased the number of slaves in Attica, and the status of women seems to have declined with the growth of equality among citizen males.

During the decades that followed Xerxes' defeat, moreover, Athens became a major cultural center. Tourists came from all over Greece to watch the tragedies performed in honor of the god Dionysus, and the Athenians diverted some of the money they received for policing the seas to celebrate religious festivals and to erect magnificent public buildings such as the temple to Athena called the Parthenon; for the Greeks' deliverance from Persian autocracy, the gods received ample thanks. The tragedians **Aeschylus**, Euripides, and Sophocles were all born in Athens, as were the comic dramatist Aristophanes, the sculptor Phidias, and the historian **Thucydides**. Many Greek thinkers like the historian Herodotus and the philosopher Anaxagoras came from elsewhere to enjoy—and enhance—what Athens had to offer.

Athens was not the only site that could boast major cultural attractions. At Delphi, for example, donors grateful for deliverance from Persia dedicated splendid monuments and superb works of art. Olympia remained a vital religious center as well; the games were extended to five days, and after its completion in 456 BC visitors could admire the imposing temple of Zeus. Democracies similar to that evolving at Athens developed in a number of places, most prominently Syracuse in Sicily, and throughout the Greek world intellectuals could be found bringing new ideas to birth. While Socrates was asking questions about justice and the human community in Athens, on the island of Cos, Hippocrates was discussing medicine and the human body.

The Aftermath of the Persian Invasions and the Foundation of a New League

While the fleet of the Hellenic League was at Byzantium in 478 seeking to consolidate Greek power in the east, the Greeks began to complain bitterly about their commander **Pausanias**, regent for Leonidas' underage son Pleistarchus. He conducted himself, they alleged, like an eastern potentate, dressing like a Persian and fortifying his position with a bodyguard of Medes and Egyptians. Sparta's attempt to hold onto its position of primacy by sending out another commander was not successful, and the Athenians were offered the chance to lead a new maritime League, an opportunity they were all too happy to seize. In 477 BC, representatives from Athens and dozens of other states met at Delos and took oaths binding themselves into an organization designed to fight the Persians. Some members of the old Hellenic League joined; others did not. In exchange for annual contributions in ships or money, Athens agreed to lead the League in military operations against Persia and respect the internal autonomy of each polis in the alliance. Although policy was to be established by a League assembly, it would be executed by an Athenian high command that would also control the treasury. Thus from the beginning, power in the League was concentrated in Athenian hands. The small size of Greek states is reflected in the number of poleis who enrolled in the alliance—probably about 150. Whereas the goals of the Peloponnesian League had never been defined, those of what is called by modern historians the **Delian League** were fairly clear: containment of Persia, the gathering of booty as compensation for damages done to Greece during the war, and simple revenge.

In view of the personality problems that had brought down Pausanias (and with him Spartan naval leadership), it was particularly fortunate for the Athenians that they had at their disposal a man as famous for his probity and affability as Aristides. It was he who was charged with assessing each state's appropriate contribution to the League treasury. Some of the larger states such as Lesbos, Samos, Chios, Naxos, and Thasos chose to make their contributions in ships; most preferred to pay cash. Although records of the tribute paid in the League's

Figure 6.1. The bronze dedication from the Sanctuary of Apollo at Delphi known as the "serpent column," made after the Greek victory over the Persians in 479 BC, was moved by the Roman emperor Constantine to his new capital Constantinople (the former Byzantium and the modern Istanbul). It stands there today in a square known as the Hippodrome, the former site of a Roman racetrack.

first years are lacking, it is possible to track the history of payments beginning in 454 BC through the compendium that survives today called the *Athenian Tribute Lists,* which lists the one-sixtieth of each contribution that was dedicated to the goddess Athena Polias; these figures multiplied by sixty give the size of each state's contribution in a given year.

From Delian League to Athenian Empire

For over a quarter-century the League fought against Persia and, led by Miltiades' son **Cimon**, the Athenians and their allies expelled the Persians from Europe and made it impossible for them to establish naval bases in Ionia. In 476, Cimon set out with the League's navy for the northeast. The fortress of Eion on the Strymon River in Chalcidice was taken with little difficulty. The Athenians then moved against Scyros, a rocky island east of Euboea inhabited by pirates. Enslaving the pirates and their families, they established on the island the kind of colony that was known as a **cleruchy**. Unlike most Greek colonies, which were fully autonomous and independent of the mother city, cleruchies were in effect part of Athenian territory, and all their inhabitants (called cleruchs) retained their Athenian citizenship. Generally chosen by the government from among poor

Figure 6.2. Section of the Athenian Tribute List inscribed on a marble slab showing payments for 433–432 BC by the citizens of Mykonos, Andros, Siphnos, Syros, Styra, Eretria, Grynche, and Rheneia. Athens, Epigraphical Museum.

Athenians, each cleruch was granted a parcel of land (a *klēros*, hence the word "cleruch"). Cleruchies filled a double function: They provided an outlet for the disaffected and potentially contentious poor, and they operated as garrisons in the empire to discourage rebellion from Athens.

Shortly afterward, the Athenians and their allies sailed against Carystus in southwestern Euboea, compelling the city to join the Delian League; and when the island of Naxos decided to leave the League, the Athenians forcibly prevented its withdrawal and in fact confiscated its fleet, ordering the Naxians thenceforth to pay their tribute in money rather than ships. These two developments highlight the problematic nature of the Delian League. A strong case could be made—and was made—that because all Greek states benefited from the existence of the League, all should pay tribute and support its fleet. Against this argument, however, resentful poleis adduced their right to make their own determinations about the extent of the Persian peril. Because the League's existence was justified only by the need for continued protection of Greece from the Persians, moreover, the Athenians would have a problem if Cimon and his navy did too good a job of squelching any designs Persia might have on Greece. This is precisely what happened around 467 when the Persian forces were badly beaten by those of Cimon at the mouth of the Eurymedon River in southern Asia Minor. Cimon's success probably played a role in the revolt in 465 of the important island of Thasos, located just off Thrace. When the Thasians were finally overcome by Athenian might, they were compelled, like the Naxians, to yield their ships and switch to cash payments into the League treasury, an obligation that would be all the more onerous as the Athenians also confiscated the Thracian mines that had previously been in Thasian hands.

The Athenians' refusal to permit states to remain aloof from the League, combined with the gradual conversion of tribute payments from ships (which

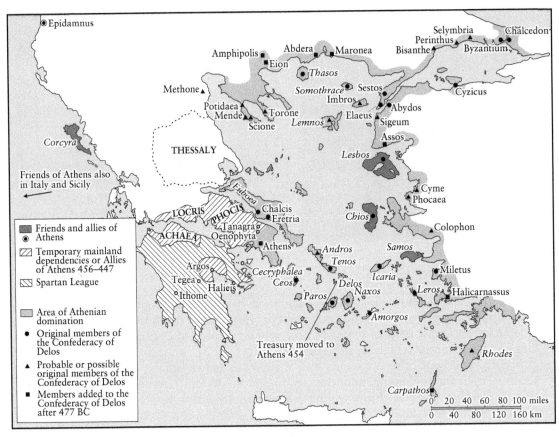

Figure 6.3. The Athenian Empire at its height.

had been commanded by admirals from their native poleis) to money, sent an increasingly clear message that Athens ruled the sea and was converting the naval alliance into an empire. Although Athenian leaders seem to have been largely of one mind about the merits of naval imperialism, however, they were divided about Athens' proper relationship to Sparta. These conflicts, moreover, were tied to disagreements about the further democratization of Athenian political life. Although sources for Athenian politics during these decades are sparse, some underlying fault lines are discernible: Themistocles encouraged competition with Sparta and the development of democracy, whereas Cimon favored Sparta and opposed any further democratization.

The forces in Athens favoring warm relations with Sparta and opposing the increasingly democratic trend in the government were strong. So was Themistocles' personality: His sharp tongue and quickness to claim credit for his achievements played into the hands of his enemies, and he was ostracized around

471 BC. In the 460s, the Athenians and the Spartans united against him, claiming that he and Pausanias were engaged in treasonable correspondence with the Persian king. Themistocles fled to Persia, and Pausanias was starved to death by the Spartans in a temple where he had sought asylum.

New Developments in Athens and Sparta

Having rid themselves of a keen and colorful politician in Themistocles, the Athenians were left with the genial and gentlemanly Cimon. Themistocles and Cimon were opposites in every way. Slow where Themistocles had been quick, and courteous where Themistocles had been insolent, Cimon was no intellectual, but he had a flair for generalship. Because of his military reputation, he continued to command a good deal of respect in the Athenian assembly even after the development of a calculating and determined coalition led by Ephialtes, whose purpose was to break with Sparta and further the growth of democracy.

For some years Ephialtes and his associates had been making attacks on individual members of the venerable and aristocratic Council of the Areopagus. Matters came to a head in 462, not long after Cimon's return from Thasos. Two years earlier, when an earthquake in Sparta killed thousands of people and destroyed most houses, the helots had seized the moment and revolted. Unable to dislodge the rebels from their stronghold on Mount Ithome, the Spartans appealed for aid to the cities with which they were still technically allied by the terms of the Hellenic League formed in 481 for the defense of Greece during the Persian wars.

The Fall of Cimon and the Reforms of Ephialtes

Sparta's request touched off a vigorous debate in the Athenian assembly. Cimon, it seems, defended the time-honored alliance between Athens and Sparta, imploring the Athenians "not to cripple Greece or deprive their own city of its yoke-fellow," whereas Ephialtes exhorted his fellow citizens to "let Sparta's pride be trampled in the dust" (Plutarch, *Life of Cimon* 16.8). Cimon carried the day, and he marched off to Sparta with four thousand hoplites. Something about the way the Athenian soldiers conducted themselves in Sparta, however, sparked panic in the conservative and fundamentally xenophobic people they had come to help. Alone among the allies, the Athenians were sent home. Their abrupt dismissal imperiled what harmony had been achieved among the Greek states. Athens now made an alliance with Sparta's enemy Argos; Cimon, moreover, was ostracized for his miscalculation, leaving an open highway for Ephialtes and his associates. If the Spartans were alarmed by the Athenians' innovative and forward-looking ways of construing the world, they did a bad job of squelching these. Cimon's ostracism marked the beginning in Athens of full-blown democracy, taking democracy in the Greek sense of diffusing political power throughout the male citizen body, with no votes for women, no citizenship for immigrants, and slaves in abundance. Ironically, moreover, the naval ascendancy that Cimon had done so much to create played a large role in fostering the democratic reforms he opposed. Cimon seems to have supported a moderate hoplite democracy: that is, government by those who could afford to provide their own weapons and armor. The success of his naval operations, however, underlined the increasing importance to the state of the men who rowed the triremes (some moderately poor, some indigent), a development that served to undermine the old-fashioned system associating power with property and contributed to its replacement by a more broadly based form of government.

Ephialtes was able to seize on the discrediting of Cimon's policies by passing some significant democratic reforms. Although the details remain obscure, we know in a general sense that he substantially diminished the power and prestige of the ancient Council of the Areopagus. (Time had already done some of Ephialtes' work for him: Because the Areopagus consisted of ex-archons, it had been growing less and less aristocratic with each year that had passed since 487, when the Athenians had begun selecting archons by lot.) At the instigation of Ephialtes, the assembly passed measures constricting the jurisdiction of this body, transferring many of its functions to the boule, the ecclesia, and the body of prospective jurors known as the *hēliaia*. Ephialtes was careful, however, to show respect for its venerable history and long traditions by leaving it with jurisdiction over homicide and some religious matters.

Shortly after the **Reforms of Ephialtes** were enacted, men who presumably disliked the turn the government was taking arranged for Ephialtes' assassination. Upon Ephialtes' death, the leadership of the loosely organized political group to which we give the somewhat misleading term "party" devolved on his dynamic associate **Pericles**, who remained the most prominent politician in Athens from roughly 461 to his death in 429.

The "First" (Undeclared) Peloponnesian War (460–445 bc)

Pericles took the lead in shaping Athenian policy throughout the decade during which Athens chose to wage war with both the Persian Empire and the Peloponnesian League. Hostilities with Persia survived Cimon's ostracism, and tensions with Sparta and its allies escalated. The period from 460 to 445 bc is sometimes called the **"First" Peloponnesian War**, an undeclared war between the Athenian and Spartan leagues that consisted of a series of battles often punctuated by considerable intervals of peace. (The famous Peloponnesian War, which was fought fairly steadily for twenty-seven years from 431 to 404, was really the second Peloponnesian War.)

Athens' Conflicts with Its Neighbors

Sitting between Corinth and Attica, the commercial state of Megara played an important role in the outbreak of both Peloponnesian wars. Around the time of Ephialtes' death it decided to bolt from the Peloponnesian League and ally itself with Athens to obtain protection from the designs of Corinth. Not surprisingly, the Corinthians were alarmed by the Athenians' possession of the Megarian port of Pegae on the Corinthian Gulf, from which it was easy to sail to the west. They became more agitated still at the upshot of the helot rebellion that had followed the earthquake in the Peloponnesus, for when the helots on Mount Ithome finally surrendered on condition that they be permitted to leave the Peloponnesus, the Athenians settled them at Naupactus near the mouth of the Gulf, on the northern shore. This bold action drove an additional wedge into the Corinthians' sphere of influence. With the two states locked in trade rivalry, moves that promised to expand the territory easily accessible to Athenian shipping were bound to spark hostility in Corinth, and it was predictable that the tension between Athens and Corinth would play a large role in determining the diplomatic relations of the Greek states.

In 459 BC, Corinth and Aegina combined against Athens. The Athenians not only repelled a Corinthian invasion of Megara but also built the so-called Long Walls, linking Athens to the port of Piraeus. This prudent strategy had the effect of making the whole town complex impossible to besiege by land, as supplies could always be brought in by sea. Around the same time they engaged Hippodamus of Miletus, the first Greek town planner, to design the port area, which he laid out in a grid pattern similar to that of his home state in Ionia.

The Spartans' decision to enter the war against Athens in 457 did more harm to them than to their designated enemy. Fighting the Athenians in Boeotia, what the Spartans chiefly accomplished was to draw Athens into Boeotian affairs. By 456, the Athenians had come to control the whole region with the exception of Thebes, and Athenian influence (or pressure) had made democratic governments the norm in the Boeotian poleis. West of Boeotia, Phocis and Locris joined the Delian League, as did the vanquished island of Aegina, and Athens also gained two states in the Peloponnesus itself, Troezen on the east coast and Achaea on the Corinthian Gulf.

Disaster in Egypt and the Transfer of the League Treasury to Athens

Athens' land empire now stood at its maximum extent. Determined to continue operations against Persia, Pericles persuaded the Athenians to send ships both to Cyprus, where they hoped to inflict damage on the Phoenician fleet, and to Egypt, which had rebelled from King Artaxerxes. The Egyptian campaign, however, ended in disaster; Thucydides reports losses of some two hundred Athenian and allied ships with their crews, a total of forty thousand men. It was at this juncture that the Athenians decided to proclaim their ongoing supremacy by transferring the League treasury from Delos, vulnerable to pirates and Persians alike, to Athens itself. Historians consequently have used 454 as a convenient date to stop referring to the Delian League and begin speaking of the Athenian Empire, although in reality the transformation had been going on for some time.

A Brief Hiatus: Athens at Peace with Persia and Sparta

Returning from his ten years' exile in 451, Cimon negotiated a truce of five years between Athens and Sparta and abandoned Athens' alliance with Argos. Argos in turn signed a thirty-year treaty with Sparta; the expiration of this treaty in 420, eleven years after the beginning of the (second) Peloponnesian War, would create a volatile situation in mainland Greece. When Cimon died campaigning in Cyprus in 450, the Athenians apparently made peace with Persia.

Peace with Sparta followed in 445 when the Athenian land empire collapsed virtually overnight as a revolt in Euboea was followed by the defection of Megara. After sixteen years of imperialism within mainland Greece, the Athenians had lost thousands of lives and had no more territory than they had possessed when fighting had begun. King Pleistoanax of Sparta invaded. Through delicate diplomacy and probably outright bribery as well, Pericles persuaded Pleistoanax to return home, but terror had been struck in the Athenians' hearts. Although in time Pericles himself subdued Euboea, Megara reverted to the Peloponnesian League and Athenian influence in Boeotia crashed to a close as Thebes assumed leadership of an antidemocratic Boeotian League.

The peace of 445 was optimistically named the **Thirty Years' Peace**, although it would not last even half that long. The key provisions of the peace were five: Neither state was to interfere with the allies of the other; neutrals were free to join either side; disagreements were to be settled by arbitration; no allies were permitted to switch sides; and each hegemon was free to use force to resolve conflicts within its own alliance.

PERICLES AND THE GROWTH OF ATHENIAN DEMOCRACY

The guiding spirit of Athenian imperialism was Pericles, who owed his position at Athens in part to his repeated election to the post of strategos and in part to the high regard in which the Athenians held him. Although he always served concurrently with nine other strategoi, none of the other generals exercised a parallel influence in the ecclesia.

The Athenian Assembly

The ecclesia met in the open air on the hill known as the Pnyx. In the early decades of the fifth century it convened only about a dozen times a year, but the number of meetings soon expanded, and in Pericles' time ten days rarely went by without at least one meeting. Rain or shine, assemblies that promised discussion of serious problems were likely to be attended by about six thousand—the quorum for certain important actions such as ostracism. This number was probably an eighth or so of all adult citizen males in Attica during Pericles' career, when the city's population was at its height. During the first half of the fifth century, boys with at least one Athenian parent would be enrolled in their demes as citizens at the age of eighteen, but in 451, for reasons that are uncertain, Pericles persuaded the Athenians to limit citizenship to those whose parents were both Athenians. Citizenship was important for girls as well as boys: Although Athenian women could not vote or hold offices, they were now the only women who could bear Athenian children.

The consequences of the **citizenship law of 451** were profound. Throughout Greece, the discouragement of marriage between citizens and aliens increased the jingoistic tendencies of the polis. The insistence that people marry citizens of their own state eliminated a powerful source of connectedness among poleis and fostered a sense of separateness that frequently led to war. Social problems were also created within the polis. Limited in their choice of marriage partners to Athenian women, married Athenian men frequently opened the door to domestic tensions by maintaining sexual relationships with the exotic "foreign" women they could not marry if they wanted their descendants to be citizens.

Those who attended the assembly might be lifelong advocates of certain policies and could well be followers of a popular politician, but they were not members of political parties as we know them today, for there was no such thing in Athens. Classical Greek even lacks a word for a political party; writers used expressions like "those around So-and-So" to identify political groups. Even among men who attended meetings of the assembly, the degree to which citizens chose to participate varied widely. As at gatherings of academic faculties today (or town meetings in New England), some never spoke, some spoke occasionally, but a core of engaged citizens spoke frequently. Some people spoke extemporaneously; others brought notes or even a text. Speakers had to be prepared for their remarks to be interrupted periodically by laughter, applause, or heckling. Once the debate was concluded—assembly meetings rarely went past early afternoon, for some time had to be reserved before supper for the daily meeting of the boule—voting was conducted by show of hands. Who attended the meetings of the assembly? Common sense would suggest that those who lived in the city were more likely to turn up than those who lived far away, and no doubt the walk in from distant villages discouraged some citizens, especially on rainy days. Nonetheless it seems that people did take the trouble to make the trip when vital matters (like whether or not to go to war) were slated for discussion.

Athenian Officials

Athens had no president or prime minister; the generals exercised power in politics only by virtue of the esteem in which they were held. Until Pericles' death, men who lacked military reputations did not generally become distinguished politicians. The converse tended to be true as well—military heroes expected to be rewarded with political careers. All this changed after Pericles' death, when politics and the military began to diverge as careers and it became less unusual for a man to be just a general or just a politician; concomitantly the government ceased to be dominated entirely by the scions of famous clans. Throughout Athenian history, however, wealth and lineage remained important factors, and generals continued to involve themselves in politics more than they do in many countries today.

The board of ten generals on which Pericles served was only one of many bodies the Athenians established. Including jobs entailed by the administration of the empire, there may have been as many as seven hundred official positions in Classical Athens, and most offices were held, like the strategia, by boards of several men, all serving one-year terms. Many, like the archons, were selected by lot. Most citizen males by the time they died had held some public office at one time or another, and a good number had held several. By diluting power in this way, Athenian voters believed they could inhibit the growth of an identifiable class of permanent officials (what we might call bureaucrats) with interests different from those of the populace at large.

The Judicial System and State Pay for State Service

By the time of Pericles, the Athenians had come to call their form of government *dēmokratia,* a government in which the *kratos* ("power") was in the hands of the *dēmos* ("the people"), by which they meant the male citizens in their capacity as voters in the assembly—and as jurors in the courts. The large size of Athenian juries—several hundred, occasionally as many as 1,501—facilitated the legal fiction that a decision of a jury was a decision of the demos, and consequently there could be no appeal from a verdict in an Athenian courtroom. The Athenians were a notoriously litigious people. In Aristophanes' *Clouds,* a lively comedy whose depiction of Socrates contributed substantially to the hostility against the philosopher, one of Socrates' pupils points out Athens on a map to the crotchety Strepsiades, but Strepsiades is not persuaded. "What's that you're saying?" he asks; "I'm not convinced, since I don't see any courts in session" (208).

To ensure that the privilege of serving on juries would be spread as widely throughout the citizen body as possible, not long after Ephialtes' death Pericles introduced a measure providing pay for jury service. It was a small amount, less than a day's wages for an average laborer, but not trivial, and no doubt this legislation bolstered Pericles' popularity at the polls. In time, Athenians came to be paid for serving on the boule and even for attending the assembly; for many years during the fifth century magistrates were also paid for their time. Today it seems natural to compensate people for the time spent serving the community, and state pay for state service is now the norm. Many Athenians, however—mostly affluent men who could afford to serve without remuneration—viewed this system as a discreditable attempt on the part of democratic politicians to buy popularity and votes. In the aristocratic value system, it was acceptable for Cimon to court popularity by inviting passersby to pick fruit from his orchards and by holding banquets for the hungry at his home, but it was manipulative and underhanded of Pericles to introduce measures in the assembly providing for compensation to those who served the state.

Despite a variety of constitutional reforms and creative innovations designed to maximize popular participation in civic life, rich Athenians continued to enjoy substantial prestige. Democratic politicians, moreover, cleverly harnessed the wealth of the elite into the service of the state by establishing a network of public services known as liturgies. These included major outlays such as maintaining a trireme and training its crew (the liturgy known as the trierarchy), leading and financing a delegation to a religious festival in another Greek state, paying and training a team of runners for the intertribal torch races at festivals within Athens, or offering a banquet to all members of one's tribe on the occasion of a religious festival. Some of the most elaborate (although not as expensive as the trierarchy, which remained the costliest liturgy) involved training choruses for performances at Attic festivals in honor of Athena or Dionysus. About a hundred civilian liturgies were performed each year. Everyone profited from this system. Those who lacked the means to offer such services benefited from the generosity of those who provided them, and the rich could reaffirm their status while performing vital military, cultural, religious, and civic functions for the community. A competitive element also fostered excellence, for prizes at contests went to the victorious choregist as well as to the successful poet.

LITERATURE AND ART

A word commonly attached to the art and literature of the earlier fifth century is "grandeur." During this vigorous era of transition, talented poets, painters, architects, and sculptors carried the traditions of the sixth century throughout the wider Greek world; and in Athens the defeat of Persia was marked by innovations in tragic drama (see Chapter 7) so striking as to constitute a new art form.

Lyric Poetry

Lyric poets were among the most distinguished writers of the fifth century. Simonides (c. 556–468 BC) is remembered chiefly as the unofficial poet laureate of the Persian wars. He was probably in Athens when the Persians invaded Greece, and his epitaphs for the war dead (such as the one cited in Chapter 5) became to Greek literature what the Declaration of Independence and the Gettysburg Address are to Americans (only easier to remember, because they were in verse).

Sicilian tyrants were well known for their interest in culture, and both Simonides and his nephew Bacchylides benefited from their patronage. Although both were famed for their success in the genre known as the epinician ode, that is, poems written *epi-nikē* ("upon [an athletic] victory"), the verdict of posterity went rather to **Pindar**. At the courts of Sicilian tyrants as well as elsewhere in Greece, Pindar enjoyed the favor of the rich and powerful. His worldview was diametrically opposed to that of democrats in Athens and elsewhere. Like Theognis, Pindar took it as axiomatic that merit was inherited. His many odes, rich in allusion and soaring in language, share a deeply held belief in an old-fashioned heroism—an excellence that takes as its starting point the assumption that men of worth spring from illustrious families that can trace their origins ultimately to divine ancestors. Writing numerous epinician odes, he was also disposed to associate physical prowess with all-around virtue. By connecting recent achievements with divine blood and tracing the ancestry of his subjects, he was able to elaborate his poems with powerful myths about gods and ancient heroes. His concern with the notion of excellence lent a lofty and inspirational quality to his verse.

DOCUMENT 6.1

Excerpt from Pindar's Sixth Nemean Ode

The occasion of this poem was the victory of Alcidamas of Aegina in the boys' wrestling contest at Nemea, perhaps in 465 BC. The poet recalls the Olympic victory of Alcidamas' grandfather and sings of the immortality conferred by poetry.

There is one race of men,
one race of gods.
Yet from one mother
we both take our breath.
The difference
is in the allotment
of all power,
for the one is nothing
while the bronze sky exists forever,
a sure abode.
And yet, somehow,
we resemble the immortals,
whether in greatness of mind
or nature, though we know not
to what measure
day by day and in the watches of the night
fate has written that we should run.
And now Alcidamas gives clear proof
that the power
born in the blood
is like
the fruit-bearing fields
that now, in alternation,
yield mankind
yearly sustenance from the ground
and now, again, resting
withhold their strength

. . .

treading in the footprints of his father's father,
Praxidamas—
for he, victorious at Olympia,
first brought the Aeacidae garlands from Alpheos;

> . . .
> come, Muse, direct
> upon this clan
> the glorious breath of song—
> for when men have passed out of our midst
> poems and legends
> convey their noble deeds. . . .
>
> (1–25 Nisetich)

The Visual Arts

Greek painters and sculptors shared a fascination with both the human and the divine. Throughout the decades of change and growth that mark the fifth century, the plastic arts reveal a powerful drive to organize the world in accord with harmony, balance, and proportion. During the fourth century, Plato, in the blueprint for the ideal society he described in his dialogue *The Republic,* would identify justice as the condition that is obtained when all parts of the soul and state are in balance. The connections Plato posited between beauty and truth underlay much of the Greek view of the world throughout the Classical period.

Greek painting and sculpture achieved what they did within the constraints posed by a variety of conventions. Bronze and marble, the customary materials for sculpture, were difficult to work with and did not lend themselves to naturalism. The two generations or so that followed the Persian wars mark a period of transition during which Greek artists begin to emancipate themselves from the formulas of the Archaic period. Some of the changes may have had to do with a rejection of eastern influences in the wake of the bitter conflict with Persia; the ties with the Near East that were so conspicuous in Archaic styles now seem more tenuous. The visual arts also become less static during these decades, and action becomes important. Conveying a strong sense of movement in a still medium is no small achievement. Some of the most outstanding artists of these decades managed despite the constraints of their craft to build a sense of anticipation and excitement.

To be sure, the tranquility of Archaic sculpture persists in some of the work of this period. It is evident, for example, in the bronze charioteer dedicated at Delphi in the 470s by Hiero's brother Polyzalus after his victory in the chariot races at the Pythian games. (See Plate XIV.) The eerie stillness of the body and the garment that falls from it in perfect folds show precisely the discipline and self-control that Pindar celebrated in the aristocrats who carried off prizes in these events.

A free-standing sculpture that conveys a dramatic sense of movement to come was the so-called *discobolus* ("discus thrower") of the Athenian sculptor Myron, who was known for his striking realism: Admirers commented that a bronze cow of his on the Acropolis could easily be mistaken for the real thing. Although the bronze discobolus Myron made around 460 does not survive, Roman copies enable us to appreciate the pent-up energy the athlete is about to unleash as he hurls his arm forward leaning into the throw. (See Figure 6. 4.)

The relief sculpture with which Greeks adorned their temples offered still greater opportunities for storytelling. One key example is the **temple of Zeus at Olympia**, completed between 470 and 456 BC just when the dramas of Aeschylus were defining the Attic stage. Excavations have brought to light remarkable sculptural groups on the portions of the temple known as the pediments—the elongated triangular spaces under the roof that sat atop the columns and cried out for decoration. In the temple of Zeus, each pediment extended for over eighty feet from left to right and rose in the center to a height of ten feet. The west pediment celebrated the triumph of order and civilization over the animal-like barbarism represented by the Centaurs, who in their characteristic drunkenness had sought to disrupt the wedding of the hero Peirithoos to Deidameia only to

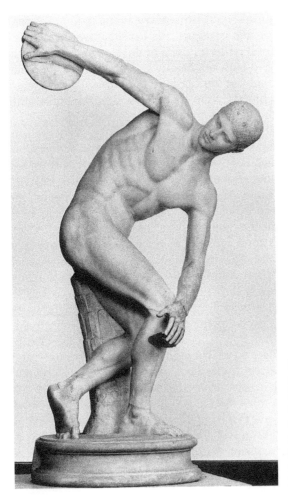

Figure 6.4. Roman copy of the *discobolus* (discus thrower) by Myron. A passage in the second-century AD author Lucian showed scholars that Myron's lost bronze statue was the model for Roman marble copies, for Lucian described the original work in detail. Rome, National Museum.

a

b

Figures 6.5a–b. The marble pedimental sculpture of the temple of Zeus at Olympia (c. 460 BC) represents scenes from Greek mythology. As these reconstructions show, (a) the east pediment tells the story of the chariot race between Pelops and Oenomaus, king of Pisa; (b) the west pediment depicts the melee that ensued when Peirithoos made the mistake of inviting the barbarous centaurs to his wedding. Olympia, Museum.

Figure 6.5c. This unusually naturalistic marble statue of an elderly seer is the third figure from the right in the reconstruction of the east pediment in Figure 6.4a. This male figure's half-reclining pose enables him to fit into the narrower space toward the side of the triangular pediment. Olympia, Museum.

find themselves worsted in the melee by Peirithoos and his friend Theseus. In the center of the relief stands a figure whom most scholars identify as Apollo upholding the principles of civility.

The east pediment portrayed a more complicated story—an episode in the life of Agamemnon's ancestor Pelops, who won his bride Hippodameia in a chariot race arranged by her father Oenomaus, an event associated with the beginning of the Olympic games. Numerous figures in the scene depicted on the temple have survived, including one of the most remarkable individuals depicted in relief sculpture, a pensive seer who even before the race has begun knows what is going to happen (Figure 6.5c). (Although the race was fixed, Pelops managed to defeat the duplicitous Oenomaus, who was killed, and marry Hippodameia.)

Grave stelae also provided an important venue for relief sculpture. Although most commemorated the deaths of men, women and girls were depicted on their

Figure 6.6. This marble grave relief depicting a young girl with her pet doves from Paros dates from the mid-fifth century when luxurious funerary monuments with figural images appear to have been forbidden in Athens. The relief's beautiful white Parian marble was originally colorfully painted, and some details rendered solely in paint, such as the girl's sandal straps and her doves' feathers, are now entirely lost. New York, The Metropolitan Museum of Art.

tombstones as well. One of the best-preserved funerary reliefs of the fifth century offers a portrayal of a little girl holding her pet doves. This poignant reflection of the dead child makes clear that for all their preoccupation with war and civic engagement, the Greeks could also feel private losses deeply.

Thousands of vases survive from the Classical period. Neither vases nor works of sculpture are easy to ascribe to any particular artist; by convention, painters are often known simply by the subject matter of their most memorable works or the places where they were or can be found (e.g., the Pan painter, the Berlin painter). Like sculpture, vase painting of the earlier fifth century was focused on the human figure, to which the curving surfaces of the vessels lent a sense of movement and grace. Even more than in drama, in which actors' faces were covered by masks, the possibilities of facial expression are limited by the medium, and character portrayal is weak; we are often given a clear sense of what the dramatis personae of the vase are experiencing at the moment in time the artist has chosen to capture, but little understanding of who they have been over their lifetimes or what their driving anxieties or concerns were. The figures on Greek vases are portrayed in action, not contemplation—they almost never appear to be posing for the artist—and we ask ourselves not only, "What are they thinking? What are they feeling?,"

Figure 6.7. Some vases depicted craftspeople at work, such as this Attic black-figure neck amphora showing shoes being made and a blacksmith forging. Boston, Museum of Fine Arts.

but also frequently, "What has just happened, and what will happen next?" As in the Archaic period, classical vases frequently took their subject matter from mythology (see Plate XIII, showing Orestes pursuing his mother Clytemnestra with his drawn sword).

Unlike sculpture, however, painting was as likely to treat mundane scenes of daily activities as it was to portray deeds of epic proportion. Vases have provided social historians with a wealth of information about how people spent their time at work and at play, showing women and men in a variety of activities: Shoemakers, blacksmiths, agricultural workers, and other laborers are portrayed going about their tasks (see Figure 6.7). We are indebted to vases for images of domestic space and the depictions of women from all social groups. Vases that were used at drinking parties for mixing and drinking wine frequently show prostitutes entertaining men. Some women are shown playing pipes, others are engaged in various stages of flirtation, and some scenes are frankly pornographic. Common prostitutes were often slaves. A woman of higher status who nevertheless mingled with men and received pay for her services was known as a *hetaira*. Such women were likely to be **metics** (discussed later in this chapter), either ex-slaves or freeborn, who—like male metics—gravitated to Athens because it was a commercial center. A few of these women, like Aspasia, the common-law wife of Pericles and the most famous hetaira of all, participated actively in the intellectual life of their male associates. In contrast, many paintings on vases used by respectable women depict wedding scenes, or women visiting tombs or sitting at home spinning wool or adorning themselves, often in the company of other women.

OIKOS AND POLIS

The Greek polis comprised *oikoi* ("families," "estates," or "households," each with a male head). The oikos was the primary unit of production, consumption, and reproduction. Citizens did not become members of the polis directly as individuals, as they do in most modern states; rather, they first had to be accepted as members of an oikos.

Demography and the Life Cycle

The average age at death in Classical Athens for adult females was about thirty-six years and for adult males forty-five years. An average woman bore about 4.3 children, perhaps 2.7 of whom survived infancy. Athenian men married at approximately the age of thirty and women around the age of fifteen. Women were often widowed as a consequence of war, and the age difference heightened the likelihood of widowhood overtaking a woman before old age; men also lost young wives in childbirth. Marriages could also be ended by divorce, which was not stigmatized unless some scandal was involved. Widowed and divorced people often remarried, and children of divorced parents generally lived with their fathers, to whose oikos they belonged.

Family Membership

When a baby was born in Attica the father decided whether to raise or expose it. He doubtless evaluated the newborn's health as well as the financial impact of raising another child. Most sons were raised, because male heirs were the normal means of perpetuating the lineage, and it was of great importance that families not die out so that the cults of the ancestors would continue. The offspring of a daughter were legally considered to belong to her husband's family, not her father's. As boys grew up, their labor was considered valuable. Moreover, they were expected to support their aged parents, bury them, and look after their tombs. Parents placed less value on girls, who lacked earning power and whose children would belong to a different family. Although the eldest child was normally raised regardless of its sex, some historians have conjectured that as many as 20 percent of newborn Athenian girls were abandoned in places like the local garbage dump. Slave dealers collected a few of the exposed infants and turned them over to wet nurses to be raised and sold as slaves. Most exposed infants, however, died, and exposure quickly became infanticide, without the stigma and pollution attaching to murder.

In Athens, after a baby boy was accepted as a member of his father's family, he needed to be approved by his father's quasi- or pseudo family: A boy inherited membership in his phratry ("brotherhood") and deme ("city ward or country village") from his father. The father introduced and enrolled his baby in his phratry and vouched for him as being his own and born of an Athenian mother.

Childhood

Throughout the Greek world, children's lives depended on their parents' circumstances much as they do today. Most children were breastfed either by their mothers or by someone else, but archaeologists have found some pottery feeding bottles. Poorer children—including slaves and helots—probably began helping to work the land at an early age. Children of both sexes also participated in the religious activities of the family, such as performing sacrifices of food or animals. Child exposure was practiced by all classes, and we can only guess at what impact it had on siblings when their mothers' pregnancies ended in the mysterious disappearance of the infant. The mild weather common in Greece made it possible to play outdoors most of the year, and references in literature describe a number of standard games. *Khytrinda* combined elements of monkey-in-the-middle and tag, and *posinda* was some sort of guessing game. Not surprisingly, social realities were reflected in some games: In *drapinda*, the child who is "it" has to get others who play the part of runaway slaves. Physical remains also tell us about children's lives. Archaeologists have found various bells and rattles, such as hollow animal forms with loose pebbles inside, that babies and toddlers could shake. Vases depict children with pet birds, dogs, rabbits, goats, and occasionally cats or monkeys (see Figure 6.8). Older boys kept hunting dogs. Swings

Figure 6.8. Attic red-figure *chous* (wine jug) of c. 425–420 BC depicts a little boy or toddler holding a cake for his pet bird. A toy roller leans on the wall behind him. Athenian children had their first taste of wine from jugs like this one at the *Anthesteria* festival celebrating the new wine, and they are often depicted on these jugs. Boston, Museum of Fine Arts.

and seesaws also appear on vases. Schooling was only for the rich, and mostly for the male rich; the rhythm of the school day and the school year did not define children's lives. In Sparta, of course, boys had the unusual experience of being packed off to military academy by age seven, and they had no summer vacations to look forward to.

Marriage

Marriage was the social institution that sustained the oikos, and its principal purpose was reproduction (see Figure 6.9). At the time of betrothal the bride's father or other guardian declared in the presence of witnesses, "I give you my daughter to sow for the purpose of producing legitimate children." After the bridegroom agreed, "I take her," he and his fiancée's father agreed to the size of her dowry. For

Figure 6.9. Detail of Attic red-figure *lebēs gamikos* (wedding bowl) attributed to the Washing Painter, c. 425–400 BC. A bride displays a baby boy, the hoped-for result of her marriage. A standing woman toward the right is holding a *loutrophoros*, a wedding vase used to transport water for the prenuptial bath. The flying Nike (winged victory) on the far right holds a vase for perfumed oil. Munich, Staatliche Antikensammlungen und Glyptothek.

respectable girls there was no alternative to marriage, and the obligation to dower each daughter doubtless was a prime motivator in female infanticide.

Before her marriage, it was customary for a girl to dedicate her dolls and other toys to Artemis to mark her transition to adulthood. Traditionally, an Athenian wedding took place at night, and the central event was the procession in which a chariot driven by the bridegroom carried the bride to the home of her future husband (see Figure 6.10). Torches lit the way, and relatives bearing gifts followed the couple on foot. Some gifts would also be brought the following day, when it was the custom of the bride's friends to visit her in her new residence, perhaps to cushion the blow of the radical break she was forced to make with her past.

Although there was a double standard for sexual conduct and husbands might have additional sexual partners of either gender, Greeks could be legally married to only one spouse at a time. Marriages between close relatives such as first cousins or uncle and niece were common. In a family with no son, or in which a son or sons had died childless (in war, for example), the obligation to perpetuate the oikos fell on the daughter, called an ***epikleros*** (someone "attached to the

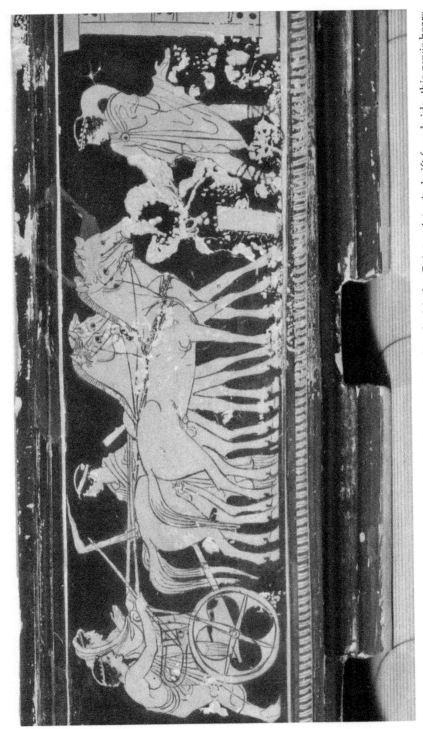

Figure 6.10. Attic red-figure *pyxis* (cosmetic box), c. 430 BC, attributed to the Marlay Painter. A typical gift for a bride, this pyxis bears appropriate subject matter for its intended owner: a wedding procession leaving the bride's house. The groom is shown mounting the chariot onto which he has lifted his bride, whose head is veiled. London, The British Museum.

estate," sometimes translated "heiress" for convenience, although she herself inherited nothing). The epikleros was required to marry the closest of her father's male relatives who was capable of procreation, usually her uncle or first cousin. If the two were married to other spouses, they had to divorce them. A son born of the union with the epikleros would be considered his grandfather's heir; and to encourage the production of heirs, the laws of Solon required men who married epikleroi to have sex with them at least three times a month. Men without any children at all would try to adopt a male relative so that their lineage would not die out.

The wife's dowry plus the husband's contribution constituted the economic foundation of the oikos at the start of a marriage. At Athens dowries consisted of cash and movable property. The husband provided the land and the house with most of its contents. The ideal, at least for those who farmed their own land, was to furnish most of the basic necessities of life for the family without needing to depend on purchasing supplies at the market. The division of labor was by gender: Women's work was indoors and men's outdoors. The husband brought into the house agricultural products such as fruit, grain, vegetables, and raw wool; and the wife and domestic slaves transformed these products into textiles and food ready for consumption (see Figure 6.11). Wives were also responsible for storing the household contents safely, so that there would always be enough to eat and wear, and even to sell if the family fell on hard times.

The fundamental division of domestic space was between men and women. Even in a small house with only two rooms, one upstairs and one on the ground floor, the upper room was the women's quarters and the lower room the men's.

Figure 6.11. Attic black-figure *lekythos* (oil jar) attributed to the Amasis Painter, c. 550–540 BC, showing women producing cloth. The woman at the left is spinning yarn, while two women weave cloth on a vertical loom at the center. New York, The Metropolitan Museum of Art.

Entertainment took place in the men's quarters, so a visitor to the Greek home would meet only male members of the family; when strangers were in the house, women and girls would withdraw to the secluded parts of the home and not even be mentioned by name. The females in the household, both free and slave, slept in the women's quarters. They also produced textiles there, although in warm weather they might move their looms into an interior courtyard and work outdoors, protected by the surrounding walls.

DOCUMENT 6.2

The customary division of labor in the oikos is spelled out in Xenophon's Socratic dialogue the Oeconomicus, *in which Socrates' friend Ischomachus explains to him how he taught his fourteen-year-old bride to manage the household.*

He told me he said to her: "Wife, the gods seem to have shown much discernment in yoking together female and male, as we call them, so that the couple might constitute a partnership that is most beneficial to each of them. . . ."

"Those who intend to obtain produce to bring into the shelter need someone to work at the outdoor jobs. For plowing, sowing, planting, and herding is all work that is performed outdoors, and it is from these that our essential provisions are obtained. As soon as these are brought into the shelter, then someone else is needed to look after them and to perform the work that requires shelters. The nursing of newborn children requires shelters, and so does the preparation of bread from grain, and likewise, making clothing out of wool. Because both the indoor and the outdoor tasks require work and concern," he said, "I think the god, from the very beginning, designed the nature of women for the indoor work and concerns and the nature of man for the outdoor work. . . .

For the woman it is more honorable to remain indoors than to be outside; for the man it is more disgraceful to remain indoors than to attend to business outside.

. . .

"And how did you arrange things for her, Ischomachus?"

"Well, I thought it was best to show her the possibilities of our house first. It is not elaborately decorated, Socrates, but the rooms are constructed in such a way that they will serve as the most convenient places to contain the things that will be kept in them. So the rooms themselves invited what was suitable for each of them. Thus the bedroom, because it was in the safest possible place, invited the most valuable bedding and furniture. The dry store rooms called for grain, the cool ones for wine, and the bright ones for those products and utensils which need light. I continued by showing her living rooms for the occupants, decorated so as to be cool in summer and warm in winter. I pointed out to her that the entire house has its facade facing south, so that it was obviously sunny in winter and shady in summer. I also showed her the women's quarters, separated from the men's quarters by a bolted door, so that nothing might be removed from them that should not be, and so that the slaves would not breed without our permission. For, generally, honest slaves become more loyal when they have produced children, but when bad ones mate, they become more troublesome."

(*Oeconomicus* 7.18, 20–22, 30, 9.2–5 Pomeroy)

The Greek Economy

Like women, slaves were a "muted group." Although they are ubiquitous in literature and the visual arts, their thoughts were not recorded, and few have left their mark on the historical record. We do know that the work of slaves did not always take place in the oikos. Large numbers of slaves were employed in the craft industries, some working for their owners and others rented out by them. Their jobs tended to be gender specific. Men worked in factories making swords, shields, furniture, pottery, and other items, whereas women often worked in textile-related industries. Inscriptions recording expenses incurred in construction on the Athenian Acropolis show that slaves were paid the same as free workers. Of course, the wages of slaves who were rented out were paid to their masters.

By no means were all craftspeople slaves; Aristotle in fact contended that most craftsmen were rich. Greeks whose social and economic status allowed them some choice, however, shunned work that made them subject to the commands of another person, and this included most craft fields. Such a life, they believed, was demeaning to a free male citizen. Unlike farming, to which a certain nobility was always attached, manual work performed indoors was despised by many wealthier Greeks and known by the name "banausic" labor, which means literally work performed over a hot furnace, and distinctions between skilled and unskilled labor were often ignored. It may be that the leisured classes disdained indoor work because of its connection with slaves and women. Litigants in Athenian courtrooms enjoyed making snide remarks about their opponents (or their opponents' relatives) ever having held any kind of job or even having run a business, and political theorists—who always came from the upper classes—contended often that strenuous indoor work should disqualify people from voting on the grounds that it damaged the mind as surely as it compromised the body. Most Greeks, however, had limited choices about how to support themselves and their families; and there is no reason to believe that those who worked for others or performed indoor manual labor were embarrassed about their professions. Tombstones frequently boasted of craft skills; surviving examples include epitaphs of a woodcutter and a miner. As elsewhere, the ideology of literate elites was at odds with the daily practice of ordinary people.

The disdain with which some Greeks regarded paid labor did not prevent a great deal of work from getting done or a good bit of money from being made.

Sometimes, however, revenue was the product of imperialism and other forms of exploitation. Without the tribute paid by subject allies it would have been difficult for the Athenians to initiate the system of state pay for state service and thus expand the proportion of citizens able to participate in the business of government. Democracy was not entirely dependent on empire; the Athenians lost their empire in 404 BC but continued to have democratic government for several generations until their conquest by Philip of Macedon in 338 (and democracy persisted even after that). But it certainly seems to have received its impetus from the surplus funds generated by imperial tribute. The splendid buildings with which the Athenians began adorning the Acropolis after relocating the treasury in Athens certainly owed their existence to imperial revenues: no empire, no Parthenon. In addition, the empire's maritime nature meant that it served as the organizing principle of Greek trade. The centrality of the Athenian Empire to commercial life became obvious in the late 430s when the Athenians banned Megarian merchants from trading in imperial ports, claiming they were simply making rules for their own sphere of influence as stipulated by the Thirty Years' Peace. The consequences of this move were fatal to Megarian trade, and outrage over this prohibition was one cause of the long Peloponnesian War of 431–404.

Agriculture and Trade

Before the nineteenth century AD, most people in the world made their living by agriculture, and fifth-century Greeks were no exception. "Most men," Aristotle wrote, "gain their livelihood from the land and its fruits" (*Politics* 1256a). Although some land was tilled by slaves or serfs (as in Laconia and Thessaly, for example), most free men, no matter how poor, were proud to farm their own land. Tragedy and comedy alike praised the farmer as the bulwark of the state. The works of the comic dramatist Aristophanes are filled with praise of the countryside and portray the farmer as the most solid of all solid citizens, honest and unpretentious. In his *Orestes*, Euripides offered a character sketch of the down-to-earth farmer: He was nothing much to look at, the playwright has his messenger say,

> But a real man;
> not the sort one sees loafing in the market
> or public places . . . but a small farmer,
> part of that class on which our country depends;
> an honest, decent, and god-fearing man,
> and anxious, in the name of common sense,
> to say his bit.
> (*Orestes*, 919–923 Arrowsmith)

It was trade that united the far-flung states that ringed the seas, and the routes over which material goods traveled also served as vital conduits for the exchange of ideas; but many of the commodities traded were the products of agriculture and animal husbandry. Most trade went by boat, land traffic being a slow and expensive business over rocky roads; the cost of carting heavy goods by land might well exceed the price of the goods themselves.

The diversity of natural resources in the ancient world made trade a necessity; no polis had everything, and some poleis had very little indeed. Athenian commerce, especially, was driven largely by the need for grain to feed a large population. Athens was by far the most populous of the Greek cities, with a population that normally varied between 200,000 and 300,000. Grain might come from north or south. One crucial source was the Black Sea region, which also provided hides, cattle, fish, hemp, wax, chestnuts, iron, timber, and slaves. For this the Athenians exchanged wine and oil, sometimes in decorated vases. These exports were themselves often resold elsewhere; the Phoenicians often sent Attic vases to Egypt, and a good deal of secondhand pottery from Athens has been discovered in Etruria in Italy. Italians also bought Attic pottery firsthand. Another key granary lay in Egypt, where Attic olive oil was also traded for papyrus, ivory, glasswork, slaves, and exotic animals. Carthage provided textiles; Etruria, fine bronze work and boots; Sicily, pigs, cheese, and grain; and Phoenicia, purple dye and dates. Corinth exported its own wares as well as serving as an intermediary between east and west, sending out tiles and metalwork. Already in the fifth century some silks from China made their way to Greece via Scythian intermediaries. Arabia exported perfumes and Persia carpets. Important sources of metals were identified early: Cyprus for copper, Spain for tin, Laconia as well as the Black Sea for iron, and Thasos and Mount Pangaeus in northern Greece for gold. All these goods flowed throughout the Greek world, but most of all they flowed into Piraeus.

Metics in Fifth-Century Athens

Many rich residents of Athens, however, did not own land, as it was illegal for them to do so without special dispensation. These were the resident aliens known as metics, and they played a key role in the economy. Craftspeople and entrepreneurs who had come from all over the Greek world to conduct business in Athens, metics accounted for a significant proportion of the Athenian population. They could not vote or hold office; neither could their children or their children's children. They lived in rented homes. But rented homes can be quite lovely, and metic families mingled comfortably with citizen families and suffered no social disabilities. A number of the characters in Plato's works were metics, and the most famous Platonic dialogue, *The Republic*, was set at the home of the wealthy metic Cephalus, whom Pericles had invited to Athens from Syracuse. Citizens, metics, and slaves often worked side by side, sometimes for the same pay; a list of workers at one construction site included eighty-six laborers whose status can be determined—twenty-four citizens, forty-two metics, and twenty slaves. In a crisis, metics could be drafted into the armed forces.

Many of Athens' most distinguished intellectuals were metics, including the philosopher Aristotle. Pericles' common-law wife Aspasia belonged to the metic class, and it was for this reason that he required a decree of the assembly to grant citizenship to their children. The inability of metic women to produce children who could enjoy Athenian citizenship played a large role in shaping the contours of Athenian society, creating two classes of women available as long-term partners to citizen men—metic mistresses and citizen wives. (In addition, a variety of prostitutes, both slave and free, were available for briefer encounters; and male owners enjoyed the privilege of sexual access to their slaves, both male and female.) Most metic women, of course, were housewives married to metic men. Slaves who were granted their freedom became metics rather than citizens. Metics lived in some other poleis, but almost nothing is known of their condition outside Athens.

The cultural achievements of sixth- and early fifth-century Greece were substantial, but the difficulties the city-states experienced in getting along with one another (and their aversion to uniting into a single political unit) would have a profound impact on the direction Greek civilization would take. The Thirty Years' Peace held a great deal of promise, but it was problematic in many ways. Dividing the Greek world openly into two spheres of influence—a Spartan land empire in mainland Greece and an Athenian naval one in the Aegean—was a dubious enterprise. From one standpoint, by drawing lines clearly, the agreement seemed to hold out the hope of peace; but it also fostered a potentially dangerous bipolarity. The notion of submitting disputes to arbitration was all very civilized in the abstract, but with every state of any reputation allied with one side or the other, just who was going to act as mediator? No treaty, moreover, could change the fact that Megara still sat uneasily on the Attic border or could diminish the commercial rivalry between Athens and Corinth. In 445 it was impossible to predict whether the peace would last.

Key Terms

Aeschylus	"First" Peloponnesian War	Reforms of Ephialtes
Cimon	Ischomachus	temple of Zeus at Olympia
citizenship law of 451	metics	Thirty Years' Peace
cleruchy	Pausanias	Thucydides
Delian League	Pericles	
epikleros	Pindar	

Suggested Readings

Cohen, David. 1991. *Law, Sexuality, and Society: The Enforcement of Morals in Classical Athens.* Cambridge, UK: Cambridge University Press. What the framing and application of law reveal about sexual values and practices.

Cohen, Edward E. 2002. *The Athenian Nation.* Princeton, NJ: Princeton University Press. An iconoclastic study of Athens that envisions it not as a descent group of male voters but as a broadly conceived nation in which many different groups had important roles to play.

Ehrenberg, Victor. 1973. *From Solon to Socrates*. 2nd ed. London: Methuen. This remains a sensitive and thoughtful study of the evolution of Greek culture during the sixth and fifth centuries.

Fantham, Elaine, Helene Foley, Natalie Kampen, Sarah B. Pomeroy, and H. A. Shapiro. 1994. *Women in the Classical World: Image and Text*. New York: Oxford University Press. An examination of the written and visual evidence for the lives of ancient women, placed within their historical and cultural context.

Hanson, Victor. 1989. *The Western Way of War: Infantry Battle in Classical Greece*. New York: Knopf. A gripping account of the experience of hoplite battle.

Jones, Nicholas F. 2008. *Politics and Society in Ancient Greece*. Westport: Praeger. Lucid introduction to the basic institutions of Greek society.

Just, Roger. 1989. *Women in Athenian Law and Life*. London: Routledge. A study of how Athenian men sought to define and locate women.

Ma, John, Nikolaos Papazarkadas, and Robert Parker, eds. 2009. *Interpreting the Athenian Empire*. London: Duckworth. A collection of recent essays drawing on archaeology, epigraphy, and the availability of documents in non-Greek languages that have made it possible to pose fresh questions about the empire that open the door to innovative approaches.

Meiggs, Russell. 1972. *The Athenian Empire*. Oxford, UK: Oxford University Press. A richly detailed examination of Athenian imperialism and the world that came under its sway.

Pollitt, Jerome J. 1972. *Art and Experience in Classical Greece*. Cambridge, UK: Cambridge University Press. A sensitive survey of Greek art that grounds it firmly in its historical context.

Pomeroy, Sarah B. 1998. *Families in Classical and Hellenistic Greece: Representations and Realities*. Oxford, UK: Clarendon Press. Comprehensive history of the family drawing on a wide range of sources including literary texts, inscriptions, papyri, and archaeological evidence.

Samons, Loren J., II. 2007. *The Cambridge Companion to the Age of Pericles*. Cambridge, UK: Cambridge University Press. Valuable collection of essays by leading scholars on major aspects of Periclean life and culture.

Starr, Chester G. 1990. *The Birth of Athenian Democracy: The Assembly in the Fifth Century B.C.* New York: Oxford University Press. Brief but illuminating analysis of the fundamental institution of the Athenian democracy.

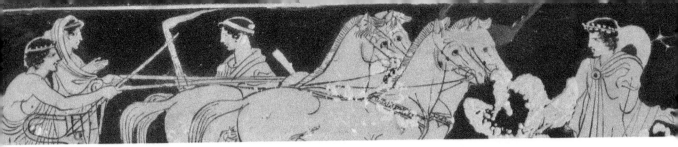

CHAPTER SEVEN

Greek Life and Culture in the Fifth Century

Avoiding war was particularly important when the Greeks had precious achievements to protect in so many areas. From Sicily to Anatolia, temples to the gods proclaimed the grandeur of Hellenic civilization. Greek ships sailed in all directions, enabling men and women hundreds of miles away to exchange their wares and profit from a wide variety of resources and skills. Novel experiments in government were in progress. The same diversity that fostered the dynamic creativity of the Greeks, however, also fragmented their world. The world of the polis, moreover, was in many ways a narrow one. Despite the growth of what the Greeks called democracy, ultimately each polis was grounded in the rule of elite, free, male citizens over everyone else; and the inability of the *poleis* to get along boded ill for the future of Greece. Inevitably, prospects for the future were clouded by intermittent suspicions that the peace between the Athens and Sparta might not endure.

GREECE AFTER THE THIRTY YEARS' PEACE

After the signing of the peace in 445 BC, many Greeks were optimistic. The fact that their optimism was misplaced makes it easy to view the years before the outbreak of the Peloponnesian War in 431 as only a prelude to hostilities. Although it is important to try to understand events in their historical context rather than assessing them in terms of their consequences, hindsight also has some value. Viewed from the perspective of the war that followed, certain events of the 440s and 430s take on particular significance.

During this period the Athenians showed a marked interest in the west and in the northeast. Athens had multiple motives for accepting Megara into its alliance

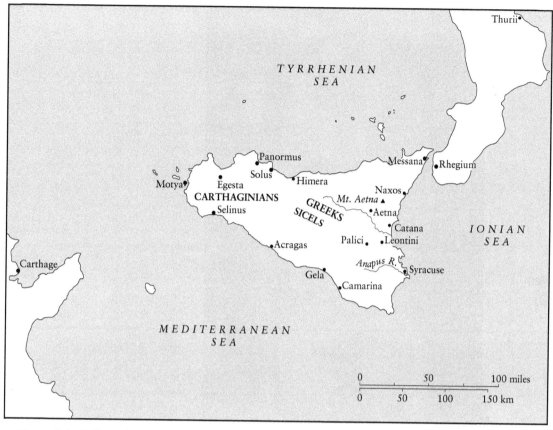

Figure 7.1. Sicily and southern Italy.

in 460, but access to the port of Pegae on the Corinthian Gulf was one factor, and the settlement of the Messenians at Naupactus several years later provided a convenient stopping place for ships heading west. In the 450s Athens had probably also contracted alliances with several Sicilian cities including Leontini, a city with a history of tense relations with Syracuse, a colony and ally of Athens' trade rival Corinth. Commerce with the western Greeks played a key role in the Athenian economy, and gradually the Greek cities of Sicily adopted Athenian currency.

That Athens had a growing interest in the rich lands to the west is confirmed by Pericles' decision to found a colony in southern Italy in 443. Thurii, however, was not an ordinary foundation, for the Athenians invited the other Greek states to share in founding a Panhellenic colony. Although the constitution of Thurii was democratic and the local coins were stamped with the head of Athena, the city adopted the laws of the lawgiver Zaleucus of Locri Epizephyrii in Italy, and when a disagreement later led the colonists to ask the Pythia to whom they belonged, the Delphic oracle claimed them for Apollo, not Athens. Whatever Pericles'

Figure 7.2. This idealized portrait of Pericles survives in a Roman copy of the head of a lost Greek bronze statue by Cresilas of c. 430–420 BC. Wearing a Greek helmet of Corinthian type pushed up atop his head, Pericles is depicted as the *strategos* or military leader of Athens. Berlin, Staatliche Museen.

intentions for Thurii may have been, the Attic element in the population declined greatly over time, and the Corinthians do not appear to have taken offense.

Athens' immediate interest, however, lay in the area around Thrace and the Black Sea region. From here the Athenians imported hides, dyes, and, more important, grain and the timber they needed for their fleet. Around 445 the Athenians founded the Thracian colony of Brea, and about a decade later Pericles led an Athenian squadron into the Black Sea.

Meanwhile, an alarming revolt broke out in the east. In 440, first Samos and then Byzantium rebelled, raising fears for the very survival of Athens' Aegean empire. Years later, according to Thucydides, some Greeks claimed that Samos "had almost managed to wrest from the Athenians their control of the sea" (8.76.4). When Samos' oligarchic government quarreled with the new democratic regime in neighboring Miletus, the Milesians together with some Samian exiles complained to Athens. One of three privileged allies (along with Lesbos and Chios) who contributed ships instead of paying tribute, Samos rebelled at Athens' order to submit the matter to arbitration, leading the Athenians to send forty ships to replace the oligarchy with a democracy.

Samos thereupon revolted from Athens with the aid of the satrap of Sardis. The subsequent revolt of Byzantium raised the specter of an empire-wide upheaval. The determined campaign that followed involved all ten of the Athenian strategoi and more than 200 ships—160 from Athens and 55 from the remaining allies in the navy, Lesbos and Chios. When Samos fell after a long siege, the Athenians dismantled the Samian navy and established a democracy. A heavy indemnity was imposed and hostages were taken. About the subjugation of Byzantium we know nothing, except that the Byzantines agreed to return to the empire.

At the same time, Athens kept a hand in the northeast, planting the colony of Amphipolis on a strategic point on the Strymon River by the border of Macedonia and Thrace in 437. In addition to protecting Athens' access to grain, timber, and minerals, Amphipolis helped the Athenians monitor activities in the recently organized kingdom of the Thracian Odrysians to the north and east as well as in Macedonia to the west. But the fact that the town drew much of its population from neighboring towns undermined its loyalty to Athens, and in 424 it surrendered to Sparta.

Virtually nothing is known about how Spartans viewed the world between the Thirty Years' Peace in 445 BC and their declaration of war on Athens in 432. Thucydides, however, remarks that the Corinthians claimed that they dissuaded the Spartans from attacking Athens at the time of the Samian rebellion: "We did not cast the deciding vote against you," they reported, "when Samos revolted from you, and when the Peloponnesians were evenly divided over whether to help them. We openly opposed it, saying that any city could punish its own allies" (1.40). If the story is true, then some members of the Peloponnesian League, including possibly Sparta, saw merit in attacking Athens in 440. Still, a war between Athens and Sparta was far from certain. Moreover, at the same time that the fate of peace hung in the balance, Greece experienced a remarkable burst of cultural creativity.

The Physical Space of the Polis: Athens in the Fifth Century

The Greek world was both one and many; although common features tied the city-states together, each polis was unique in culture. As so often is the case in attempts to recover the world of Classical Greece, however, the bulk of our knowledge about the development of the polis during the later decades of the fifth century comes from Athens. Even during the war, Athenian dramatists continued to produce masterpieces. Some of our best evidence about fifth-century Athens is physical, for the revenues of empire helped to adorn the imperial city with splendid buildings, many of which still impress visitors today.

The Acropolis

A hill was a distinct advantage to a city-state. Although most people today associate the word **acropolis** with the Acropolis of Athens, in fact it was a feature common to many poleis, which relied for protection on a fortified citadel from which one could see far into the distance. In Athens, the Acropolis was the spiritual focus of the polis. Because of its height and steeply sloped sides, this naturally fortified area had been the residence of early rulers and had always been home to the chief gods and legendary heroes of the Athenians. The sixth-century tyrant Pisistratus, like Pericles later, initiated an ambitious building project on the Acropolis, for he understood not only that such work would provide steady employment to the

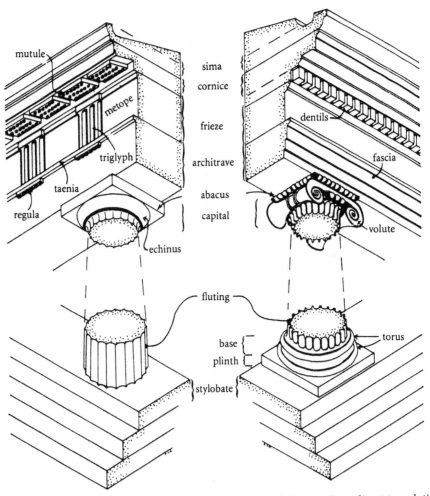

Figure 7.3. The Doric and Ionic orders. The Doric order (left) may be a direct translation into stone of building elements that were originally made of wood. The more complex capital of the Ionic order is a spiraled form known as a volute.

restless urban poor, but also that a beautiful city would create still more jobs, foster patriotism among all citizens, and attract wealthy, talented metics. It would be, as Pericles would later say in the pages of Thucydides, "the school of Greece." The Persian invasion of 480 BC destroyed the monuments and statues of Pisistratus' time. This rubble, in turn, was used as the foundation of the buildings constructed in Pericles' day on the Acropolis, largely financed by funds from the Delian League.

In the Classical period, the two principal architectural styles or orders were the **Doric** and **Ionic**. (The ornate Corinthian capital, invented in classical times, did not become popular until the Hellenistic period.) Both orders were used for the same building purposes, but they differed in details such as the shape of the columns and of their bases and capitals and in the features of the entablature, or structure that supported the roof. Architects strove to design buildings according to the principles of each order, rather than to invent new or highly individualized styles. Greek architects took from their work that special kind of satisfaction that comes from exercising creativity within the limits posed by an elaborate code of restraints. In this they resembled the tragedians.

The temple of Athena Parthenos ("the virgin") known as the **Parthenon** was a blend of Doric and Ionic elements. The rectangular structure with a ratio of eight columns on the front and back ends to seventeen on the sides was both aesthetically pleasing and appropriate to its commanding site on the acropolis.

Figure 7.4. This model of the Acropolis in the late fifth century BC shows the Panathenaic procession proceeding through the front gates (Propylaea), which are flanked on the right (south) by the temple of Athena Nike (Victory). The largest building is the Parthenon. The Erechtheum is on the left (north) of the Parthenon.

Greek architects knew that from a distance the eye would perceive straight vertical elements as thin in the middle and appearing to fall outward, and a horizontal foundation (stylobate) would appear to droop toward the center. As the Roman architect Vitruvius, who worked in the second half of the first century BC, explains, architects countered these illusions by subtle swelling (entasis) of the midportion of the columns, by tilting the columns and interior walls toward the interior lest they seem to be falling outward, and by increasing the height of the floor and steps toward the center. These refinements increase the impressions of solidity and height; some add strength to the building and are aesthetically pleasing to the viewer. The Parthenon was built of marble, but like other Doric temples, it preserves elements of earlier wooden construction, especially in the frieze where the triglyphs imitate the ends of three planks standing on their sides and follow the rule that all the corners of the frieze must end with a triglyph (see Figure 7.3).

Figure 7.5. Parthenon east frieze, slab V, a section of the continuous frieze running along the top of the exterior cella wall. It probably shows the presentation of the dress known as the *peplos* for the old olive-wood cult image of Athena at the Panathenaea. Other portions show a cavalcade of horsemen, religious officials, sacrificial animals, and the Olympian gods. The Parthenon sculptures in London are known as The Elgin Marbles. London, The British Museum.

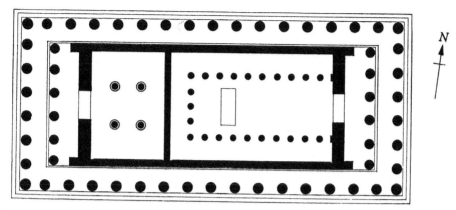

N

Figure 7.6. Plan of the Parthenon showing exterior colonnade and *cella* (main room) within. The cult statue of Athena was kept in the cella and the state treasury was stored in the back room.

Figure 7.7. The Parthenon, 447–432 BC, photographed in the twentieth century, seen from the southwest. In 1687, during the Ottoman Turkish occupation of Greece, ammunition stored in the building was ignited by Venetian bombardment, and the resulting explosion damaged the building and its sculptures.

Sculpture was an important feature of Greek architecture. The sculpture of the Parthenon depicted myths and history of Athena and Athens. The east pediment showed the birth of Athena and the west pediment illustrated the contest between Athena and Poseidon over primacy in Athens. A sculpted frieze running around the top of the exterior wall of the cella or "inner shrine" showed human figures, horses, sacrificial animals, and the twelve Olympian gods. Probably the array of human figures and animals depicts the procession at the Greater Panathenaic festival that was held every four years and the presentation of a new dress for the goddess by young girls who had helped to weave it.

The temple was not a place where worshipers congregated but rather the private home of a divinity whose image was placed inside and a storehouse for the cult's belongings. Thus, within the cella of the Parthenon was a tall figure of Athena constructed by fitting sheets of ivory and gold over a wooden scaffold. Locked in a back room were the goddess' possessions, among which were the

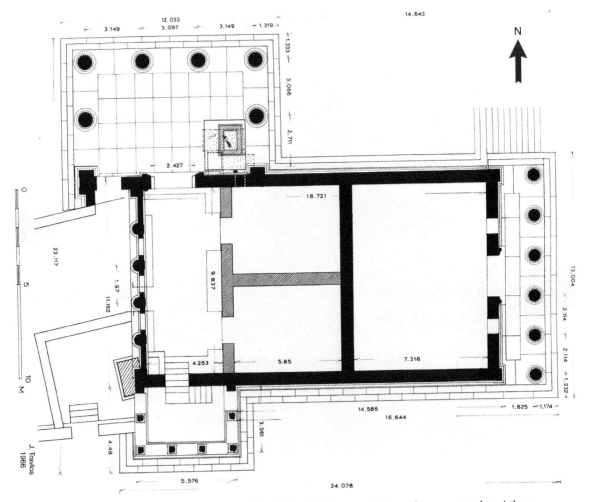

Figure 7.8. Plan of Erechtheum (421–406 BC). This graceful temple was sacred to Athena, Poseidon, and the legendary Athenian king Erechtheus. The complicated shape was the result of needing to skirt Athena's sacred olive tree and to enclose Poseidon's trident mark and perhaps the tomb of Erechtheus.

treasury of the city of Athens and, after the middle of the fifth century, that of the Delian League as well. In front of the Parthenon on the west stood a huge bronze statue of Athena Promachos ("Athena the Warrior who fights in the front"). The goddess was portrayed standing, with her left hand holding her shield and her right arm holding her spear. The statue was nearly thirty feet tall: sailors rounding Cape Sounion could see the welcome glint of sunlight off the tip of the spear. Like the statue inside the temple, it was the work of the sculptor Phidias. Viewed by his contemporaries as the greatest sculptor of gods, Phidias also created a huge gold

Figure 7.9. The Erechtheum, built 421–406 BC, photographed in the twentieth century: detail, showing the Porch of the Maidens (Caryatids), which faces the Parthenon. Since this photograph was taken, the statues were moved indoors to protect them from pollution and were replaced with copies.

and ivory statue of Zeus at Olympia that was considered to be one of the seven wonders of the ancient world.

In contrast to the Doric, which was massive, solid, and plain, the Ionic order gave a slender, graceful, ornate impression. The **Erechtheum**, a multiuse building sacred to Poseidon Erechtheus and Athena Polias, was purely Ionic. The building consisted of three Ionic porches. To support the roof, the south porch that faced the Parthenon employed six figures of maidens, called Caryatids (instead of columns). The building was begun in 421 BC, and because of the Peloponnesian War the decorations may never have been completed.

Many other buildings, temples, statues, and votive offerings adorned the Acropolis. Although little remains of these monuments nowadays except the bare marble framework of the major ones, in antiquity they were much more colorful:

Some of the architectural and sculptural features were painted red and blue and were covered with gold leaf. Below the Acropolis, dramas were staged in honor of the god Dionysus. Spectators sat in the open air in a semicircle on the bare hillside watching the performances that took place below in the orchestra ("dancing place").

The structures that comprised Pericles' building program confirmed most Athenians in their support for the empire, for without the tribute pouring in from subject states, such lavish public monuments would have been difficult to finance—indeed, nearly half of the annual revenues that flowed through the Athenian bureaucracy came from that tribute.

The part of a Greek city known as the *agora* was principally a center for secular human activity, but the gods, who were never excluded from human activities, also had their place there. The agora served as a market; as a meeting place for the exchange of goods and of news; and as a focus of social, political, and judicial activities. Daily life for women was ideally indoors and for men outdoors. Men who stayed indoors were suspected of being effeminate and antisocial, and women who ventured outdoors except for funerals and religious purposes were likely to have their chastity questioned. In the *Laws,* Plato noted that the greatest good in the polis is that the citizens be known to each other, as the men (certainly not the women) would be if they saw one another every day in the agora. Aristotle distinguished human beings from other living creatures by their use of speech (although, again, women were placed in a different category and are characterized as ideally silent). Speaking was essential for the activities that took place in the agora.

The Athenian agora was a large level space at the foot of the Acropolis on the road from the main city gate. The area was cluttered with public buildings of which the most easily identified is the round structure called the Tholos, which housed the boule, and where official weights and measures were stored. The agora was also the site of law courts, altars, shrines, statues, inscriptions, fountains, drains, and trophies of war. On the western border stood a Doric temple that was dedicated either to Hephaestus, the god of crafts, or to Theseus, a legendary hero and king of Athens. It has withstood the ravages of time far better than the Parthenon and is still in remarkably good condition. Roofed, multipurpose colonnades called stoas flanked the agora. Sandwiched between the permanent structures and within the stoas as well were shops, bankers' tables, booksellers, wholesale merchants, schools, and people buying and selling the necessities of life.

One important place in Athenian life was not a building: The hillside of the Pnyx where the assembly met towered above the city. Throughout the fifth century, citizens sat either on cushions or directly on the rocky ground that sloped from south to north, filling an area of 15,000 square feet. Around 400 BC the meeting place was evened out and enlarged, and benches seem to have been added. The adult male citizens of Attica gathered in all kinds of weather to listen to speeches and debates, to make motions, and to hold high officials to account. In voting (which was by show of hands), they not only took into consideration what they had heard on the Pnyx but also made use of all the information they had garnered in the agora.

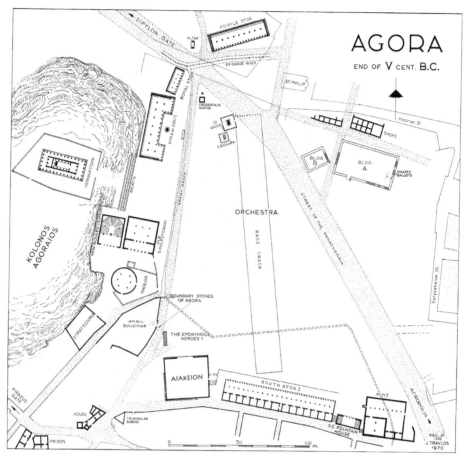

Figure 7.10. Plan of the agora in the Classical Period. Courtesy of American School of Classical Studies at Athens: Agora Excavations.

Rural Life in Attica

The growth of the urban center was not at the expense of rural areas. Public buildings were also located away from the city center. Gymnasiums and stadiums that required plenty of level space were often found in the suburbs, which were cooler and shadier and closer to plentiful supplies of water than could be found in central Athens. Cult centers and rural agoras, as well as fortresses and other structures for defense, were scattered throughout Attica. It was an easy walk, moreover, from city to country.

In the fifth century probably three-quarters of the citizens owned some rural property. Farming could be a part-time occupation and still produce enough food to provide sustenance for a family. Many people lived in villages, were loyal to their rural demes, and depended on their family farms. Except for the spaces set aside for public activities, Athens was neither a beautiful city nor a comfortable one, and many propertied citizens were happy to leave it to artisans, the urban poor, and metics, who were not permitted to own land in Attica. The city had merely grown up in the Archaic and Classical periods without conforming to a town plan. Streets were irregular and narrow, housing in the city center was flimsy, and sanitation was poor. These problems were exacerbated when the entire population withdrew inside the city walls during the Peloponnesian War.

INTELLECTUAL LIFE IN FIFTH-CENTURY GREECE

Looking at the vibrant civilization of Greece in the middle of the fifth century, it would have been hard for anyone alive at the time to believe the horrors that lay ahead. Magnificent temples to the gods dotted the landscape, decked out with friezes that celebrated human and divine accomplishment. Throughout the Greek cities people had begun to explore new ideas about the universe and humanity's place in it.

Speculating About the Natural World

Greeks of Hesiod's day had viewed the earliest state of the universe as a form-less void they called *chaos*. Out of chaos, they believed, the order of their own world had emerged—*kosmos*, a Greek word meaning both "order" and "beauty." Mythology served the important function of grounding the growth of cosmos from chaos in various actions taken by the gods. The great contribution of the sixth-century Greek thinkers of Ionia had lain in their determination to abandon this mythological and religious framework and attempt instead to explain the world by material processes alone.

In the archaic period, the Ionian rationalists had focused on the natural world rather than on the values of the human community. Their speculations, how-ever, raised inevitable questions about relations between gods and mortals, for the Ionians sought to enthrone human reason as the tool for understanding the universe and to replace divine plan (or caprice) with material forces. Anaxagoras from Asia Minor (c. 500–428 BC) was one of many intellectuals who were drawn to the glittering city of Athens. Anaxagoras viewed material objects as composed of infinitely divisible particles and conceived of their organization as the work of a force he called *nous* ("intellect"); from this came his nickname Nous ("the Brain"). The sun, he claimed, was not a deity but rather a white-hot stone a little larger than the Peloponnesus.

The workings of the universe also intrigued other fifth-century thinkers throughout the Greek world. Empedocles (c. 493–c. 433 BC), who lived in Sicily, pro-pounded a cosmogony based on the idea of four primary elements—earth, air, fire, and water. Physical substances, he argued, were produced when the twin forces of attraction and repulsion that he called "love" and "strife" acted on these elements, combining them in various proportions. Maintaining that these combinations were randomly produced, Empedocles conjectured that monstrous forms had probably been created early in history but had perished through their failure to adapt.

An alternative view of how the world is made was put forward by Leucippus and Democritus. Like Anaxagoras, Leucippus, who seems to have been active around the middle of the fifth century, believed that matter was created of tiny particles, and his ideas were further developed by his pupil Democritus from Abdera in Thrace (c. 460–370 BC). In their view, moreover, the tiny particles were *atoma* ("uncuttable"). Ironically, then, the word for "atom," which was split in the twentieth century with such devastating consequences, originally meant "that which cannot be divided." In addition to atoms, so the theory had it, there was "void"; falling through void, atoms collided in a variety of ways to form visible matter. What determined the manner of these collisions was a little uncertain—Leucippus insisted it was necessity and not chance, although other atomists disagreed—but the atomic theorists agreed on one thing: Whatever was active in shaping the form of matter was a natural force and not a divine being.

Although they certainly looked around them for models and paradigms, thinkers like Anaxagoras, Empedocles, Leucippus, and Democritus were essentially philosophers, not scientists. A mix of observation and systematic thinking, however, formed the basis of Greek medicine. Prayer probably remained the most common Greek response to illness in antiquity, but during the sixth century BC Greeks in Asia Minor began learning about anatomy from the observations Mesopotamians had made on animal entrails used in divination. By 500 BC, medical centers had been established on the island of Cos off the coast of Asia Minor and on the nearby peninsula of Cnidus. Some instruction also took place within the family; often the medical profession was passed down from father to son. Women were prohibited from practicing as doctors, but they frequently functioned as midwives.

Case studies formed the basis of the doctrines of **Hippocrates** of Cos (c. 460–c. 377 BC). The writings associated with Hippocrates' school included more than a hundred works composed over a long period, and there is no way to know which of these might have been written by Hippocrates himself. Greeks did not develop many cures for diseases. The principal contribution of the Hippocratics lay not in any specific discoveries about medicine but rather in their commitment to seeking rational explanations of natural phenomena. Epilepsy, for example, had been labeled "the sacred disease" by the Greeks; in their treatise *On the Sacred Disease*, the Hippocratics took a different view, claiming that this notion was put forward by charlatans who, "having no idea what to do and having nothing to offer the sick. . . . labelled the disease sacred in order to conceal their ignorance" (*On the Sacred Disease* 2). Another treatise, *Airs, Waters, Places*, examined the impact of climate on health, laying the foundations for epidemiology.

A large group of Hippocratic texts deals with gynecology. Along with the general devaluation of women in Greek culture, women's reticence about speaking to male physicians sometimes cut doctors off from information vital to understanding female reproductive processes. In the absence of real data concerning symptoms and sexual practices, where women were concerned, speculation often substituted for the careful observation on which the Hippocratics prided themselves:

If suffocation occurs suddenly, it will happen especially to women who do not have intercourse and to older women rather than to young ones, for their wombs are lighter. It usually occurs because of the following: when a woman is empty and works harder than in her previous experience, her womb, becoming heated from the hard work, turns because it is empty and light. There is, in fact, empty space for it to turn in because the belly is empty. Now when the womb turns, it hits the liver and they go together and strike against the abdomen—for the womb rushes and goes upwards towards the moisture, because it has been dried out by hard work, and the liver is, after all, moist. When the womb hits the liver, it produces sudden suffocation as it occupies the breathing passages around the belly.

(*Diseases of Women* 1.7 Hanson)

HISTORICAL AND DRAMATIC LITERATURE OF THE FIFTH CENTURY

In the verbal realm, the principal achievements of the Athenians during this period lay in history and in tragedy. Dozens of tragedians were active in fifth-century Athens, but only the works of **Aeschylus**, **Sophocles**, and **Euripides** have survived, and of these only a fraction of their output—seven each of Aeschylus and Sophocles, and nineteen of Euripides. History was the less common genre, but the two works that survived in their entirety—**Herodotus'** history of the Persian wars and **Thucydides'** history of the Peloponnesian War—enshrined in historical writing the model of the war monograph that has remained popular to this day.

Herodotus

Born in Halicarnassus in Ionia, Herodotus was heir to the traditions of Ionian rationalism and had a passionate curiosity about causes and origins. Why the Persians and the Greeks fought, what accounted for the Greek victory, how Darius came to rule Persia, where the Nile began, how the priestesses at Dodona came to be thought of as birds with human voices, where the Greeks got their gods—Herodotus used the Greek word *historia* ("inquiry") to describe his quest for understanding, and this word has given us our word for the investigation of the past: "history." In the opening sentence of his work he states that he has set forth the results of his inquiry "so that the actions of people shall not fade with time" and "so that the great and admirable monuments produced by both Greeks and barbarians shall not go unrenowned, and, among other things, to set forth the reasons why they waged war on each other" (*The Histories* 1.1).

Born probably shortly before Xerxes' invasion of Greece in 480, Herodotus was not old enough to remember the Persian wars, but he was able to interrogate his parents' generation about them. His interests were not confined to a particular series of historical events; like his somewhat younger contemporary Thucydides, he was fascinated by what history revealed about human nature and the way the world works. What he learned from his study of history was that power goes to people's heads, and that the mighty rarely meditate on their condition with sufficient judiciousness and reflection—that rulers hear what they want to hear, and rush headlong to their own destruction.

Herodotus' paradigm appears early in his history in his imaginative reconstruction of a conversation between Solon, the Athenian lawgiver, and Croesus, the fabulously wealthy king of Lydia. During his travels, Herodotus maintains, Solon came to Croesus' palace, where the king made a point of having attendants give Solon a tour that would highlight Croesus' prosperity. Afterward, Croesus asked Solon if there was anyone in the world who struck him as particularly fortunate. Feigning innocence of Croesus' purpose in asking this question, Solon named a little-known Greek man who had died fighting for his city and who was buried with honors leaving children behind him. When Croesus was dissatisfied with this response, Solon offered an alternative example. Two young Argives, he related, when their mother needed to attend a feast of Hera and the oxen had not yet returned from the field, yoked themselves to the family wagon and pulled it several miles to the temple. Amid the great words of praise lavished on the young men and on her for having such fine sons, their mother prayed to the goddess to bestow on her children whatever was best for humankind. Lying down to sleep in the temple, the youths never awoke, and the Argives dedicated statues to them at Delphi in commemoration of their excellence.

Resentful at not being named the most fortunate of men, Croesus spoke harshly to Solon, voicing his indignation at the notion that the Athenian should consider ordinary citizens more fortunate than a wealthy king like him. Solon in turn counseled him to think harder about what it means to be truly fortunate, cautioning him not to make facile judgments without waiting to see how things turn out in the end. "Now, you seem to me," he tells Croesus

> to be very rich and to be the monarch of many people, but I couldn't say anything about this question you keep asking me until I find out that you have ended your life well, because the rich man isn't any better off than the man who has enough for his everyday needs unless his luck stays with him and he keeps on having the best of everything until he dies happily. . . . You have to see how everything turns out, for god gives a glimpse of happiness to many people, and then tears them up by the very roots.

> (*The Histories* 1.32)

Croesus, however, does not listen. By carelessly misinterpreting a series of oracles, he loses his empire and comes to recognize Solon's wisdom.

It is not likely that Solon and Croesus really met. Solon's travels evidently preceded Croesus' accession to the throne around 560 BC. Herodotus has crafted this vignette to demonstrate the superiority of Greek over Persian ways of thinking—of the western dependence on the solid citizen over the eastern reverence for the powerful autocrat. Similar points are scored in Herodotus' characterization of the overconfident Xerxes. The implications of this are plain enough: For all their virtues, the Persians, like other eastern peoples, were dragged down by their habit of according immense power to a single individual, the king. Encouraging him in his childish self-confidence, they became slaves to someone who exaggerated his own importance not only vis-à-vis other mortals but, more dangerously still, in relation to the gods. In comparison, Greek civilization held all the promise that inhered in free institutions, in the rule of law, in respect for gods, and the acceptance of human limitations.

In this Herodotus was a typical Greek, but in other respects he sought to undermine assumptions he saw in the world around him—assumptions about the inferiority of non-Greek cultures and the low intellect of women. Greek men, in Herodotus' view, needed to think harder and longer about their place in the world. To assist them in this project, he included in his history many stories about the intelligence of clever queens (such as Queen Artemisia of his native Halicarnassus) and a detailed account of the accomplishments of the Egyptians, stressing the greater antiquity of Egyptian culture in relation to Greek and suggesting Egyptian origins for the Greek gods. For good reason Herodotus has been called not only the Father of History but also the Father of Anthropology. Indeed, some of the most memorable portions of his *Histories* are embedded in his accounts of non-Greek cultures—the Atlantes, who never dream; the Getae, who believe they are immortal; the Argippaeans, who are bald from birth; the Gyzantes, who eat monkeys; and the Callatian Indians, who eat the dead bodies of their parents. This distinctly un-Greek funerary practice appears in a dialogue that Herodotus sets at the court of Darius:

> During his reign, Darius called together the Greeks who were at his court and asked them how much money it would take to get them to eat the dead bodies of their fathers. They said they would not do it for any sum. Then he summoned a group of Indians known as the Callatiae, who eat the corpses of their parents. In the presence of the Greeks, and through a translator, he asked them how much money it would take for them to permit the burning of their parents on a funeral pyre. They gave a horrified gasp and demanded that he be silent.
>
> (*The Histories* 3.38)

To Herodotus the wide variety of customs in the world was a source of endless fascination.

Thucydides

Many intellectual currents of the fifth century flowed through Athens as Thucydides was growing up and while he composed his history. Careful observation, rational deduction, and a tragic view of the world can all be discerned in his work just as they can in that of Herodotus. Unlike Herodotus and the dramatic poets, however, his writing shows no interest in women. Whereas Herodotus, born a generation earlier, had conceived history as an interaction of divine and human forces, both vitally important, Thucydides saw the actions of people as pretty much exclusively responsible for how things turn out. Belonging to a later generation, moreover—and being an Athenian citizen—Thucydides had been exposed to a great deal of rhetoric in the assembly and perhaps the law courts as well; and speeches, both straightforward and manipulative, are prominent in his work.

Little is known concerning Thucydides' life. Because Thucydides served as a general in 424, however, he must have been at least thirty in that year, and historians conjecture he was born around 460. He came from an aristocratic family with kinship ties to some of Pericles' rivals, but had enormous admiration for Pericles. His opportunities for research took an unexpected turn when he was exiled after failing to keep the Spartans from taking Amphipolis. From then on, he was able to gather a great deal of information from non-Athenian sources but could no longer attend meetings of the Athenian assembly. He lived long enough to see Athens lose the war, just as Herodotus had lived long enough to see the Greeks squander their victory over Persia and become embroiled in internecine warfare.

Thucydides himself discusses his methodology at the outset of his history, stressing the lengths to which he went in his quest to determine the truth—and expressing impatience with those less committed to the search for knowledge. Most people, he complains, "expend very little effort on the search for truth, and prefer to turn to ready-made answers." His own approach will be different.

DOCUMENT 7.1

Thucydides explains his methodology in his history of the Peloponnesian War, contrasting himself with less reliable reporters—including, it seems, Herodotus, as well as rhetoricians given to virtuoso public displays.

One will not go wrong if he accepts the inferences I have drawn from the facts as I have related them, and not as they are sung by the poets—who embellish and exaggerate them—or as they are strung together by popular historians with a view to making them not more truthful, but more attractive to their audiences; and considering that we are dealing with ancient history, whose unverified events have, over the course of time, made their way into the incredible realms of mythology, one will find that my conclusions, derived as they are from the best available evidence, are accurate enough.

Even though people always think that the war they are fighting is the greatest there ever was, and then return to marveling at ancient wars once theirs has ended, it will be clear, after we examine the events themselves, that this war between Athens and Sparta actually was the greatest war there has ever been.

As to the statements the participants made, either when they were about to enter the war or after they were already in it, it has been difficult for me and for those who reported to me to remember exactly what was said. I have, therefore, written what I thought the speakers must have said given the situation they were in, while keeping as close as possible to the gist of what was actually said. As to the events of the war, I have not written them down as I heard them from just anybody, nor as I thought they must have occurred, but have consistently described what I myself saw or have been able to learn from others after going over each event in as much detail as possible. I have found this task to be extremely arduous, since those who were present at these actions gave varying reports on the same event, depending on their sympathies and their memories.

My narrative, perhaps, will seem less pleasing to some listeners because it lacks an element of fiction. Those, however, who want to see things clearly as they were and, given human nature, as they will one day be again, more or less, may find this book a useful basis for judgment. My work was composed not as a prizewinning exercise in elocution, to be heard and then forgotten, but as a work of permanent value.

(*The Peloponnesian War* 1.21–22)

Thucydides has often been described as the world's first scientific historian, and his work has been cited for its objectivity. This characterization rests on a misunderstanding of what the writing of history really involves. History is not a science, and it cannot be objective, because it entails humans writing about other humans. Every omission, every connection, requires judgment. There is no limit to the number of decisions that confront historians. Herodotus was more disposed to put everything in and let his readers sort it out, but one consequence of this decision is that he has been criticized for being less analytical than Thucydides.

The Birth of Tragedy

Drama played a central role in the spiritual and intellectual life of the polis. Wealthy citizens vied for honor and acclaim by undertaking the expense of training choruses, and during the festival of Dionysus in March actors and audience alike needed enormous stamina. Each dramatic poet presented three tragedies and one shorter ribald play called a satyr play in which the chorus dressed and behaved like the satyrs who were part of the cult of Dionysus. Groups of actors performed four dramas in a day, and spectators had not only to follow the intricate poetry of the choruses but also to turn up the next day and the day after that to compare the work of each playwright, to help determine who should receive the prize. A significant proportion of men—and probably women as well—attended the plays and no doubt continued among themselves a lively dialogue about the issues the dramas had raised. Even in eras of comparatively high literacy, ancient cultures remained oral to a considerable degree, and absorbing the complex imagery of Greek tragic choruses was not so difficult for people trained to listen and remember as it would be for most people today. Nonetheless, the popularity of performances that demanded serious intellectual work on the part of the audience tells us something about the richness of Greek culture. (Comedy will be discussed in Chapter 8.)

Female roles in drama were played by men. Masks facilitated the deception and also made it possible for one actor to play several parts. They were shaped at the mouth rather like megaphones and so made for good acoustics. To be sure, they discouraged the nuanced portrayal of personality. This was not, however, considered a great loss, for Greek tragedy was never intended to be naturalistic. Characters in Greek represented humankind in all its aspiration—and frailty. They are not easy to like or dislike, for they were not intended to be lifelike, flesh-and-blood individuals.

Nor was the material of tragedy anything one could call a slice of life. Tragedy was meant to be heroic and grand, far removed from the mundane. Plots were generally taken from the rich myths of the heroic age, but exceptions could be made for major events such as the Persian wars. (Even here, though, Aeschylus achieved a certain remoteness by setting the action of his *Persians* in faraway Asia, where people dressed exotically.) Formalities of several kinds limited the dramatist in his choice of material. No violence was permitted on stage, and all action had to take place within a twenty-four-hour period. Finally, the author had to contend with the challenge posed by the intricate meters of tragic verse.

Aeschylus

Aeschylus (525–456 BC) was the first of the famous tragedians of fifth-century Athens. He died in Sicily after a long life, during which he wrote around seventy plays. Only seven of these survive. After his death the Athenians paid homage to the greatness of his work by decreeing that the archon should grant a chorus to anyone who wanted to produce one of his plays. Already in the time of Pisistratus, Thespis had expanded the range of the choruses honoring Dionysus by adding an actor who could carry on a dialogue with the chorus; now Aeschylus added a second actor. This innovation made possible real conflict and moved tragedy beyond tableau into the realm of drama. At the same time, drama remained firmly grounded in poetry, and verse remained the vehicle for both tragedy and comedy throughout antiquity. (See Plate XVII.)

Aeschylus' greatest surviving achievement is the trilogy known as the **Oresteia**, which treats the supreme difficulty of understanding and obtaining a just social and religious order. Although the sets of four dramas that playwrights entered in the competition generally usually comprised three tragedies followed by a satyr play, these three tragedies did not need to treat the same theme, and frequently they didn't. In the case of the *Oresteia*, however, the three plays form one grand and complex drama, and this work is the only Attic trilogy that survives.

The *Oresteia*

The point of departure for the *Oresteia* was probably Ephialtes' curtailment of the powers of the Areopagite Council, for the trilogy culminates in precisely the sort of trial that remained within the Council's purview—a murder trial. It seems likely that Aeschylus supported the reforms and chose this august drama as a vehicle by which to reassure conservative Athenians that the trying of homicide cases, the privilege with which Ephialtes had conspicuously not tampered, was in fact the ancient mission of this venerable body. In this way he could draw attention away from the significant limitations that had been placed on its jurisdiction. The material with which Aeschylus chose to convey his message was the familiar tale of the cursed house of the ancient hero Pelops and his descendant Agamemnon, commander-in-chief of the legendary expedition against Troy.

The first play, *Agamemnon*, portrays the king's murder on his victorious return from the Trojan War by his faithless wife, Clytemnestra, and his cousin Aegisthus, who has become Clytemnestra's lover. Agamemnon's murder poses an agonizing dilemma for his children Orestes and Electra, for they are faced with a choice between killing their mother and allowing their father's death to go unavenged. Their pain and Orestes' eventual murder of Clytemnestra and Aegisthus form the subject matter of the second play, *The Libation Bearers*. (See Plate XIII.) As the play closes, Orestes finds himself pursued by the avenging earth goddesses known as the Furies. His suffering ends in the final play, *The Eumenides*. This play is set in Athens, where Orestes has taken refuge, hoping that a responsible government will afford him a fair trial. Athena's charge to the jury proclaims the glories of the Areopagus, the importance of justice, and the centrality of law.

Athena breaks the deadlocked jury's tie, and her grounds are revealing. Following Apollo's proclamation that it is the male and not the female who is the true parent, and bearing in mind her own birth (fully developed from the head of her father Zeus), she decides that the claims of the father trump those of the mother, justifying Clytemnestra's death. Now tamed, the Furies are given a new name, the Eumenides (Kindly Ones). Plainly Aeschylus conceives the creation of responsible government in Athens as the antithesis not only of tyranny but also of a disordered chaotic universe in which emotional and female forces of vengeance were paramount. The new world will be governed by orderly, rational institutions planned and staffed by men, with vengeance replaced by justice.

The choruses celebrated the awesome power of the gods while also exploring the nature of the human condition. "Sing sorrow, sorrow," the chorus chants toward the opening of his play *Agamemnon*, "but good win out in the end":

> Zeus: whatever he may be, if this name
> pleases him in invocation,
> thus I call upon him.
> I have pondered everything
> yet I cannot find a way,
> only Zeus, to cast this dead weight of ignorance
> finally from out my brain.
> . . .
> Zeus, who guided men to think,
> who has laid it down that wisdom
> comes alone through suffering.
> Still there drips in sleep against the heart
> grief of memory; against

our pleasure we are temperate.
From the gods who sit in grandeur
grace comes somehow violent.
        (*Agamemnon* 160–166, 176–183 Lattimore)

The genre established by Aeschylus would become one of the defining art forms of Greek civilization. Tragic drama, as it evolved throughout Aeschylus' career and in the hands of his successors Sophocles and Euripides, was in many ways the hallmark of Athenian greatness. Through Shakespeare and other great tragedians of Europe, this remarkable testament to the heroic struggle against human limitations forms an important part of a legacy that has endured to our own time.

Sophocles

Herodotus' warnings about the vicissitudes of fortune and the impossibility of judging a person's life until it is over are echoed in *Oedipus Tyrannus*, the most famous tragedy of antiquity. It was written by the poet Sophocles (c. 496–406 BC), author of over a hundred plays. Like Aeschylus and other tragic poets, Sophocles reworked the familiar plots of Greek mythology, with their emphasis on agonizing family discord, to express his view of the world.

Just after Herodotus' departure for Thurii, Sophocles produced the first of three surviving dramas about the unfortunate house of Oedipus, the legendary ruler of Thebes who was fated to kill his father and marry his mother. Although Sophocles' plays that deal with the family of Oedipus were not presented as a trilogy, we discuss them together following the chronological sequence of the myth.

In *Oedipus Tyrannus* we meet the hero, the highly intelligent and respected ruler of Thebes in the Heroic Age. Fated to kill his father and marry his mother, he slowly realizes as the action of the play unfolds that he has actually done precisely this. The consequences, of course, are devastating; Oedipus's wife/mother hangs herself and Oedipus gouges out his eyes. In this way Sophocles wrestled with some of the central questions of the human condition as Greeks saw it, such as the role of character in determining action and the power of fate and the gods.

Set in the playwright's own neighborhood in the Athenian suburb of Colonus, *Oedipus at Colonus* continues the family saga. The core of the play is yet another prophecy: The gods have decided that because of Oedipus' extraordinary suffering he will become a hero who will protect the land that gives him sanctuary. At the climax of the play, Oedipus disappears into the grove of the Eumenides and is transformed into a hero who will serve as Athens' protector.

In the *Antigone* we contemplate the painful tensions that arise in Oedipus' family after his death. One of his sons, Polynices, has died fighting to take the throne of Thebes from his brother. Polynices' sister Antigone wishes to fulfill her religious obligation and bury his body. But their uncle Creon, now king of Thebes, forbids anyone to take up this project on the grounds that Polynices was a traitor. Like many characters in Greek tragedy, Antigone now finds herself confronted with a painful choice. She must decide whether to honor her obligation to her brother and to the gods, which means facing death herself, or to obey the laws of the state and keep herself safe. She is headstrong and defiant; Creon is rigid and insensitive.

Although Sophocles is a conventional Athenian in his respect for the gods and their power to guide human life, in other regards he challenged conventional mores. Antigone's situation paralleled that of the Athenian girl known as an *epiklēros*, a girl with no surviving brothers, and it is hard to doubt that Sophocles' sympathies lie with the fatherless, brotherless girl who experiences all the helplessness that fell on Athenian women who lacked male protectors. Sophocles, as his other plays confirm, sympathized with the plight of Greek women. Creon, however, makes a good case for the importance of a law that makes no exceptions for family members, and as an Athenian democrat Sophocles certainly saw the need to uphold the rule of law. But is the decree of an autocrat really law, especially when the populace is on Antigone's side? Sophocles fully recognizes the complexity of the tortuous choices Antigone and Creon must make, and he sees in their confrontation proof of the wondrous complexity of humankind and the communities humans have struggled to develop.

DOCUMENT 7.2

The soaring poetry of the chorus celebrates the achievements of the human race in a memorable passage.

> Many the wonders but nothing walks stranger than man.
> This thing crosses the sea in the winter's storm,
> making his path through the roaring waves.
> And she, the greatest of gods, the earth—
> ageless she is, and unwearied—he wears her away
> as the plows go up and down from year to year
> and his mules turn up the soil.
> Gay nations of birds he snares and leads,
> wild beast tribes and the salty brood of the sea,
> with the twisted mesh of his nets, this clever man.
> He controls with craft the beasts of the open air,
> walkers on hills. The horse with his shaggy mane
> he holds and harnesses, yoked about the neck,
> and the strong bull of the mountain.
> Language, and thought like the wind
> and the feelings that make the town,
> he has taught himself, and shelter against the cold,
> refuge from rain. He can always help himself.
> He faces no future helpless. There's only death
> that he cannot find an escape from. He has contrived
> refuge from illnesses once beyond all cure.
> Clever beyond all dreams
> the inventive craft that he has,
> which may drive him one time or another to well or ill.
>
> (Sophocles *Antigone* 332–368 Wyckoff)

Figure 7.11. Lucanian calyx crater attributed to the Policoro painter. This vase, made in southern Italy and currently in the Cleveland Museum, dates from about 400 BC and offers a spectacular depiction of the last scene of Euripides' *Medea*. Here Medea is shown escaping in her chariot drawn by serpents; they are encircled by the rays of the sun god Helius. The desolate Jason stands below looking up on the left; on the right are the bodies of the murdered children and mourning them, their nurse and tutor.

Like Herodotus, Sophocles combined profound reverence for the gods with a compelling interest in the human dimension of life. In his plays, dialogue was expanded at the expense of the chorus; he also added a third actor where Aeschylus had used only two (not counting silent actors, who appeared on the stage but did not speak).

Euripides

In the spring of 431 Athenians and foreign visitors gathered in the theater of Dionysus to see Euripides' *Medea*. Plays by Euripides (c. 485–c. 406 BC) had been produced before, so the playwright was already known to the audience, but the subject matter for this drama was shocking. Although the plots of Greek tragedy derived from familiar myths, Euripides enjoyed innovation, and there is some reason to believe that the ending of the play came as a surprise to the spellbound onlookers.

In *Medea* Euripides used the tale of Jason, the celebrated leader of the Argonauts in their quest for the Golden Fleece, to undermine conventional views of what makes a hero. In his adventures Jason had acquired a wife—Medea, a sorceress from Colchis, at the far end of the Black Sea. He has such confidence in the excellence of the Greek way of life that even when he has decided to abandon Medea to marry a Corinthian princess, he boasts of the benefits he has conferred on her by rescuing her from a barbarian land and transplanting her to Greece. Predictably, these arguments do not sit well with a highly intelligent woman who has the advantage of a non-Greek perspective. The bitter laments of Medea enable the audience to see things differently as she details the constraints on her life as a woman in a Greek city:

We women are the most unfortunate creatures.
First, with an excess of wealth it is required
For us to buy a husband, and take for our bodies
A master; for not to take one is even worse.
And now the question is serious whether we take
A good or bad one; for there is no easy escape
For a woman, nor can she say no to her marriage.
(*Medea* 231–238 Warner)

Jason's shameful excuses for his actions, moreover, raise serious questions about a society that makes heroes of the kind of man who would rationalize his course of action on the grounds that his new marriage will give these children royal step-siblings. *Medea* was only one of the plays in which Euripides explored the dynamics of the conflict between reason and passion—reason, which could justify Jason in deserting the wife who had risked her life for him in her youth, and passion, which could move a mother to kill her offspring. Inevitably the agonizing conflict that marked plays like *Antigone* struck a particularly resonant chord with the audience in *Medea*, which was produced just as war was breaking out between two very different states with opposing views of the world.

CURRENTS IN GREEK THOUGHT AND EDUCATION

The convoluted arguments that help politicians who appear in Thucydides' narrative cloak ambition in fair-sounding words, and the verses in which Euripides' Jason defends his action as calculated to improve his children's lives, show the influence of the itinerant intellectuals who gravitated to Athens during the second half of the fifth century—the men who came to be known as the **sophists**, from the Greek word *sophistēs*, which means something like "practitioner of wisdom." Unlike the philosophers who sought to understand the world, the sophists contented themselves with teaching eager, paying pupils how to get by in it. Although their works do not survive except in fragments, it seems clear that they rejected facile assumptions concerning such topics as the connections between noble birth and true merit, the obligations owed to the gods, and the nature of law. Because of this, and because they enabled ambitious young men to speak effectively for or against any issue, they aroused suspicion in Athens.

Formal and Informal Education

The origins of the sophistic movement lie in the informal nature of Greek education, in its literary and aristocratic bias, and in its superficial nature. Since Homer's day, Greek children had learned primarily by watching the world around them and imitating respected elders. Few people in antiquity knew how to read, and most formal education involved listening and reciting from memory. Girls were rarely sent to school, and neither were most boys. The problem was not simply that poverty usually compelled children to stay home and work on the farm; the fact is that, with the exception of Sparta, Greek states did not provide public schooling. Parents of the upper classes, however, paid for their sons to be instructed in what was called *mousikē*, a subject that included the memorization of poetry. Because ancient poems were sung, mousike also involved learning to play the lyre. Beginning in the sixth century, more and more children also learned to read and write. Parents sometimes had daughters instructed in basic reading and writing skills in case they needed this knowledge to supervise household accounts or to manage temple properties if they became priestesses. Some instruction in math was also offered to children by private tutors and in schools, but not much was offered in the way of natural science or what we would call social studies. By the time boys progressed to the age at which adolescents today would enter college, moreover, they had ceased to be students and had become soldiers and citizens and their sisters were the mothers of two or three children.

Most education went on in less formal settings, however, and this sort of education would continue throughout life. In childhood, girls would absorb the norms of appropriate social behavior from their mothers and aunts, boys from their fathers and uncles. The upbringing of the two sexes was designed to cultivate different sets of skills for males and females. These differences were most pronounced in the upper classes, for poor children of both sexes were likely to learn farming and craft skills from parents. Among the elite, however, a sharp differentiation occurred in adolescence, for at this juncture girls married and reproduced. Their education in home management continued at the hands of their husband's older female relatives, and probably older slaves as well, who had considerable experience of child rearing. In addition, husbands sometimes took it upon themselves to give their wives vocational training in household management. In the *Oeconomicus*, written in the fourth century in the form of a Socratic dialogue, Xenophon describes how a husband, Ischomachus, trained his young wife to be a successful estate manager:

> [Socrates] said, "I would very much like you to tell me, Ischomachus, whether you yourself trained your wife to become the sort of woman that she ought to be, or whether she already knew how to carry out her duties when you took her as your wife from her father and mother."
>
> "What could she have known when I took her as my wife, Socrates? She was not yet fifteen when she came to me, and had spent her previous years under careful supervision so that she might see and hear and speak as little as possible. Don't you think it was adequate if she came to me knowing only how to take wool and produce a cloak, and had seen how spinning tasks are allocated to the slaves? And besides, she had been very well trained to control her appetites, Socrates," he said, "and I think that sort of training is most important for man and woman alike."
>
> (*Oeconomicus* 7.4–5 Pomeroy)

Whereas teenage girls might receive such instruction from their husbands, adolescent males were exposed to important influences of another kind. Books were expensive, and although literacy increased throughout the sixth and particularly the fifth century, learning still went on primarily in the interaction between two or more human beings, not in the interaction of a person with a written text. Relationships with somewhat older mentors formed a key element in the education of teenage boys. Just as younger teachers today often serve as role models for adolescents, so young men in Greece offered examples of manhood to those who were just developing into men. The one-on-one nature of these friendships, however—untrammeled by any need for a teacher to be evenhanded with an entire class of students—combined with different attitudes toward sexuality to produce a significantly different dynamic. As we have seen in Chapter 4, the bond between a Greek male teenager and his adult mentor was often profoundly erotic. What we know about these relationships is somewhat compromised by a reticence about sex in the written sources and by the need many Greeks felt to stress the intellectual and spiritual bond at the expense of the sexual one. In Plato's dialogue on love, the *Symposium,* the character Phaedrus praises this bond for its value in the moral improvement of both the individual and society as a whole. "I would maintain," he writes,

> The greatest benefit, to my mind, that a young man can come by in
> his youth is a virtuous lover, and a virtuous boyfriend is just as good
> for a lover too. Anyone who wants to live a good life needs to be
> guided throughout his life by something which love imparts more
> effectively than family ties can, or public office, or wealth, or anything
> else. What is this "something"? The ability to feel shame at disgraceful behavior and pride in good behavior, because without these qualities no individual or community could achieve anything great or fine.
> (*Symposium* 178C–D Waterfield)

The bond between the older lover (the *erastēs*) and the younger beloved (the *eromenos*) shored up the stability of society by encouraging each generation (or half generation) to imitate the one that had gone before.

Erotic bonds, of course, that had begun in school might also be strong between men of a similar age. Xenophon portrays Socrates describing the passion of Critobulus for Cleinias:

> This hot flame of his was kindled in the days when they used to go
> to school together. It was the discovery of this that caused his father
> to put him into my hands, in the hope that I might do him some
> good. And without question he is already much improved. For a
> while ago he was like those who look at the Gorgons—he would gaze
> at Cleinias with a fixed and stony stare and would never leave his
> presence. . . . It does look to me as if he had also kissed Cleinias; and
> there is nothing more terribly potent than this at kindling the fires of
> passion. For it is insatiable and holds out seductive hopes. For this

Figure 7.12. This red-figure drinking cup (ca. 475) depicts a mature bearded man fondling a barely adolescent boy who, in response, has his right hand behind the man's head perhaps preparing for a kiss. Oxford, The Ashmolean Museum.

reason I maintain that one who intends to possess the power of self-control must refrain from kissing those in the bloom of beauty.

(Xenophon, *Symposium* 4.23–24 Todd)

Finally, participation in the life of the city as a whole afforded an ongoing education to growing men, and to some extent to women as well, particularly those who served as priestesses. The poet Simonides put it well: *Polis andra didaskei* ("the polis teaches a man"). To some extent, women, particularly those who served as priestesses, and all women who attended state-sponsored festivals, benefited as well. (See Plate XIb.) Only in mature life, however—by attendance, for example, at tragic dramas and the thoughtful discussions that no doubt followed in private gatherings—did this education entail any real questioning of conventional wisdom. In general, the purpose of Greek education was a blend of indoctrination and socialization calculated to foster the perpetuation of traditional values.

All this changed when the sophists burst on the scene during the second half of the fifth century, sparking powerful tensions between the generations. Athens was a magnet for the philosophers and teachers of rhetoric who had sprung up throughout the Greek world as speculation about both the natural universe and the human community became increasingly popular among intellectuals. Democracy was grounded in skill at speaking and reasoning—in the ability to dissect and demolish the arguments of political opponents. The sophists offered to teach these skills. Sophists filled other needs as well, for they delighted in exploring tricky questions about the workings of the world. No common belief system marked the thinking of the various sophists, but they shared an enthusiasm for the kind of exercises in argumentation that are central to a great deal of higher education today.

The Sophists

Like the formal education that had gone before, the instruction offered by sophists benefited only a fairly small class of affluent students who could afford to pay. What the sophists had to offer, however, differed sharply from earlier education, for the sophists questioned conventional beliefs. One object of their explorations was the notion of *nomos*.

Herodotus had shown in his history the centrality of nomos to society. The Greek word meant both "law" and "custom"; there were state-sanctioned *nomoi* forbidding burglary, but there were also social nomoi regarding what to wear at your wedding and religious nomoi about how to worship Apollo. In a society that had existed for centuries without written law, only a blurry line divided a legal nomos and a conventional nomos based on tradition. The two, however, began to diverge the harder people thought about the problem. Herodotus' *Histories* demonstrated two different sides of nomos. On the one hand, the Greeks had fought the Persians to live by nomos rather than at the whim of a despot. On the other hand, the multiplicity of nomoi in different cultures reveals a diversity that suggests that local customs are the product of tradition rather than of abstract, unchanging principles of right and wrong. It was to demonstrate the force of nomos in society that Herodotus had told the tale of Darius' conversation with the Greeks and Callatian Indians about the proper disposal of the dead—cremation or consumption. Each society, he concluded, considers its own customs to be the best.

When this idea was assimilated to the speculations of the natural philosophers, an opposition evolved in many minds between the concept of *physis* ("nature"), and *nomos* ("convention"). The relationship between physis and nomos became central to Greek thought around Herodotus' time, for it carried powerful implications for the legitimacy of authority. If nomos was not the natural outgrowth of physis but actually existed in opposition to it, then the laws of the community were not necessarily to be obeyed, for they might have grown up randomly, endorsed by generations of unthinking traditionalists who had given no thought to their grounding in physis.

This concept of law varied conspicuously from the usual view that law ultimately came from the gods, and in fact the new ways of looking at the world had serious implications for relations between gods and mortals. One of the most renowned of the sophists who came to teach in Athens was Protagoras (c. 490–420 BC) of Abdera in Thrace, who moved to Athens around 450 and spent most of the rest of his life there. He is best known for two sayings with religious implications. "Each individual person is the measure of all things—of things that are, that they are, and of things that are not, that they are not." Nobody, in other words, can tell you what is real or true—no state official, no parent, and no god. Another contention was still more provocative: It is impossible to know, Protagoras is said to have observed, "whether the gods exist, or how they might look if they do. Numerous obstacles stand in the way, such as the shortness of life and the difficulty of the subject matter."

There was an answer, however, to the question, "Just what do these people teach, anyway?" That answer was rhetoric. Many Greeks believed there was no limit to the sophists' use of rhetoric. The anonymous treatise known as *Dissoi Logoi* (Double Arguments) reveals the moral relativism that many associated with sophists. Can sickness ever be good? Certainly, if you are a doctor. But what about death? Death is good for undertakers and gravediggers. The author goes on to enumerate the many examples of cultural difference found in Herodotus to demonstrate that no act is intrinsically good or bad. A mental universe in which nothing was purely good or patently evil was not one in which all Greeks wished to dwell.

For these reasons, the sophists drew to themselves a considerable amount of odium. They found themselves under attack not only in conversation but on the stage. In 423 Aristophanes produced the *Clouds,* in which the intellectuals of Athens—the "eggheads"—are derided as teaching a corrosive rhetoric that made a mockery of decent, sensible values. The man Aristophanes identifies as running the "think shop" was not, however, a sophist. Like some of Aristophanes' other characters, he was a real person, but not one who taught rhetoric or accepted fees. He was Socrates, and the disposition to identify him with the sophists contributed to his execution just after the end of the war that broke out between Athens and Sparta in 431.

The Breakdown of the Peace

The terms of the Thirty Years' Peace contained within them the seeds of war. Arbitration was meaningless when all the major states were lined up on one side or another; rules made in one sphere of influence might well have an impact on the other; and some states enjoyed an ambiguous status, with one foot in each camp. Although the Greek states had shown that they could overlook their differences in the face of a great threat such as that posed by the invasion of Xerxes, the polis was a prickly creature by nature, sensitive to perceived slights to its honor and threatened diminution of its rank. On all these fronts the peace was vulnerable, as the events that began in 435 in a remote corner of the Greek world were to prove.

A Provocative Alliance: Athens and Corcyra

In that year a civil war between the democrats and the oligarchs in the Corcyraean colony of **Epidamnus** moved the democrats to seek assistance from **Corcyra**. When their mother city turned them down for reasons we do not know, they were encouraged by Delphi to hand themselves over to their "grandmother" Corinth instead. Despite their own oligarchic leanings, the Corinthians welcomed the opportunity to make life hard for the Corcyraeans, with whom they had a long-standing feud, and agreed to assist the democrats. The Corinthians and Corcyraeans were soon fighting at sea.

This conflict set into motion a chain of events that had dramatic consequences for the Greek world. Needing an ally but unable to approach Sparta because of Corinth's membership in the Peloponnesian League, the Corcyraeans went to

Athens instead. An alliance between Corcyra and Athens would not violate the terms of the Thirty Years' Peace, as the treaty permitted neutrals to join either side. The Athenians were nervous about offending Corinth by such an alliance, but they were even more apprehensive about the prospect of Corinth defeating Corcyra in battle and obtaining for themselves Corcyra's substantial fleet. To gain those ships for Athens, therefore, they voted to make an alliance. They made a point of calling it a "defensive alliance" only, but this technicality fooled nobody; it was fairly clear that the Corinthians would indeed attack the Corcyraeans, and when they did, Athens would find itself at war with Corinth, one of the most powerful members of the Peloponnesian League.

This is precisely what happened. In the late summer of 433 a Peloponnesian fleet of 150 ships, 90 of them Corinthian, attacked the Corcyraeans. With Athenian help, the Corcyraeans were ultimately victorious, and the Corinthians were furious. Prospects for peace between Athens and Sparta were receding.

The Problem of Potidaea

With chances of war now greatly increased, Athens issued problematic decrees against two members of the Peloponnesian League. The city of **Potidaea** on the Chalcidic peninsula was both a Corinthian colony and a member of the Athenian alliance. In the tense political climate, Potidaea's anomalous situation inevitably attracted Athens' attention, especially in view of the exceptionally close relations between Corinth and Potidaea, which even took its annual magistrates from Corinth. (Corinth's markedly contrasting relationships with its two colonies Corcyra and Potidaea are an important reminder of the many different possibilities for metropolis/colony ties.) During the winter of 433–432, the Athenians ordered the Potidaeans to dismiss their Corinthian magistrates, reject any future officials from Corinth, tear down their seaward defenses, and give hostages as security. When Potidaea refused these demands, Athens found itself involved in an expensive two-year-long siege in which Potidaea was aided by Corinth and the Macedonian king Perdiccas, whom the Athenians had alienated by supporting two rival claimants to his throne.

The Athenian Decree Against Megara

Around the same time, the Athenians took action against Megara. Because Thucydides considered the **Megarian decree** only a pretext and not a major cause of the war, much is unclear about this third crisis. The Athenians apparently accused the Megarians of harboring escaped slaves and of cultivating some sacred and undefined land that lay between Eleusis in Attica and Megara. They passed a decree against Megara, probably in 432, excluding Megarian merchants from all ports of the Athenian empire. This decree enabled the Athenians to inflict considerable harm on a member of the Peloponnesian League without technically infringing the terms of the Thirty Years' Peace, as there were few significant Greek ports outside the Athenian empire.

Even more than the other actions taken by the Athenian assembly during the 430s, the sanctions against Megara and the refusal to revoke them are associated with the name of Pericles. The plays of Aristophanes and Plutarch's biography of Pericles make it plain that some people considered the friction with Megara pivotal in bringing on the war and blamed Pericles for the outbreak of hostilities. Scattered references in Thucydides confirm this. In the autumn of 432 BC the Corinthians denounced the Athenians before the Spartan assembly. Although the Spartan king Archidamus urged caution, the Spartans voted that the Athenians had violated the Thirty Years' Peace. They then summoned delegates from the Peloponnesian League who duly voted to go to war with Athens.

Last-Ditch Attempts to Avert War

Hostilities did not immediately follow, but rather several months of diplomacy in which each side tried to portray the other as responsible for the impending war. Thus, the Spartans insisted that peace could be preserved if Athens would only "free the Greeks" (in other words, abandon their empire), expel any "cursed" Alcmaeonids in the city (Pericles was an Alcmaeonid on his mother's side), and rescind the Megarian decree; the Athenians demanded that the Spartans purify "the curse of the goddess of the Bronze House," a reference to the impieties involved in the death by starvation decades earlier of Pausanias, who had taken refuge in Athena's temple. In the end, after several months of fruitless negotiations, the impatient Thebans forced ambivalent Sparta's hand by attacking Athens' ally Plataea. Because Plataea enjoyed a special position in Greece as the site of a great victory against Persia in 479, this assault was considered particularly heinous. Afterward nobody could question that the Peloponnesians and the Athenians were at war.

RESOURCES FOR WAR

Thus ended the period of a half-century between the Persian and Peloponnesian wars to which Thucydides gave the name the Pentacontaetia ("the Fifty Years"; actually forty-seven years). In the jockeying for position that went on during the months leading up to the Theban attack on Plataea, the Spartans seem to have come out ahead. Although it was they who had declared war, the Greek world was inclined to see imperialist Athens as the aggressor. When war broke out, Thucydides writes

> Popular opinion favored the Spartans by far, especially since they had proclaimed that they were going to liberate Greece. Everywhere, city and citizen alike were eager, if at all possible, to join with them in word and deed, and everyone felt that any plan would come to a standstill if he himself could not take part in it. That is how angry most people were at Athens—some because they wanted to rid themselves of Athenian rule, and others because they were frightened lest they fall under that rule.
>
> (*The Peloponnesian War* 2.8)

Figure 7.13. Alliances at the outset of the Peloponnesian War.

ODRYSIAN KINGDOM

THRACE

Abdera
Neapolis
Maronea
Thasos
Thasos
Aenus
Samothrace
Cardia
Imbros
Sestos
Abydus
Sigeum
Troy
Lemnos
Tenedos
Antandrus
Methymna
Lesbos
Mytilene
Scyros
AEGEAN
SEA
Cyme
Phocaea
Chios
Erythrae
Clazomenae
Teos
Colophon
Notium
Carystus
Ephesus
Andros
Samos
Tenos
Priene
Myconos
Miletus
Delos
Iāsus
Paros
Halicarnassus
Siphnos
Caunus
Naxos
Cos
Cos
Melos
Cnidus
Thera
Ialysus
Rhodes
Camirus
Rhodes
Lindus

Selymbria
Byzantium
Perinthus
Chalcedon
PROPONTIS
Dascylium
Cyzicus
Lampsacus

PHRYGIA

Adramyttium
MYSIA

LYDIA
Sardis

CARIA

The belligerents differed not only in temperament but also in the nature of their military strengths. The Athenians had far greater financial resources than the Peloponnesians and a superior navy that included more than four hundred Athenian and allied ships. Accordingly, Athens hoped to conduct as much of the war as possible at sea, and the Spartans would focus on the land. The Athenians were fighting essentially a defensive war, the goal of which was to preserve the empire the Spartans sought to destroy. For Athens a stalemate would amount to victory. Sparta needed something more.

KEY TERMS

acropolis

Aeschylus

agora

Corcyra

Doric order

Epidamnus

Erechtheum

Euripides

Herodotus

Hippocrates

Ionic order

Megarian decree

mousikē

nomos

Oeconomicus

Oresteia

Parthenon

physis

Potidaea

sophist

Sophocles

Thucydides

SUGGESTED READINGS

Beard, Mary. 2003. *The Parthenon*. Cambridge, MA: Harvard University Press. The history of the building from temple to medieval cathedral to mosque and armory, the transfer of the Elgin Marbles to Britain, and the twentieth-century building restoration.

Boedeker, Deborah and Kurt Raaflaub, eds. 1998. *Democracy, Empire and the Arts in Fifth-Century Athens*. Cambridge, MA: Harvard University Press. Collection of essays dealing with the relationship between empire and cultural achievements.

Camp, John M. 2001. *The Archaeology of Athens*. New Haven, CT: Yale University Press. A thorough discussion of this important subject by a scholar who spent many years in Athens.

Foley, Helene P. 2001. *Female Acts in Greek Tragedy*. Princeton and Oxford: Princeton University Press. Nine essays dealing with the apparent contradiction between the depiction of tragic heroines and the actual role and status of Athenian women, with particular attention to women as moral agents.

Guthrie, W. K. C. 1971. *The Sophists*. Cambridge, UK: Cambridge University Press. A brilliant study of the issues regarding the sophistic movement, excerpted from the author's six-volume *History of Greek Philosophy*.

Harris, William V. 1989. *Ancient Literacy*. Cambridge, MA: Harvard University Press. A survey of the evidence for literacy and the lack of it in ancient Greece and Rome.

Hurwit, Jeffrey M. 1999. *The Athenian Acropolis: History, Mythology, and Archaeology from the Neolithic Era to the Present*. New York: Cambridge University Press. An eminently readable history of the most famous hill in the Greek world.

Jones, Nicholas F. 2004. *Rural Athens Under the Democracy*. Philadelphia: University of Pennsylvania Press. A study of settlement patterns, rural homes, deme centers, rural festivals; and the habits and religion of country dwellers, their image in literature, and their relationship to urban dwellers.

Kagan, Donald. 1969. *The Outbreak of the Peloponnesian War*. Ithaca, NY: Cornell University Press. The first installment in Kagan's monumental four-volume history of the war.

Marincola, John. 2006. *The Greek Historians*. Cambridge, UK: Cambridge University Press. A highly readable survey of recent work on Herodotus and Thucydides as well as a study of their themes, sources, and narrative methods.

Neils, Jennifer, ed. 2005. *The Parthenon. From Antiquity to the Present*. Cambridge, UK: Cambridge University Press. Detailed essays analyzing the artistic and architectural features of the Parthenon as well as its place in Athenian history.

Roberts, Jennifer T. 2011. *Herodotus: A Very Short Introduction*. Oxford, UK: Oxford University Press. A concise introduction to Herodotus's thinking about Greeks, Persians, and the many other peoples in the world he knew.

Vlastos, Gregory. 1991. *Socrates: Ironist and Moral Philosopher*. Ithaca, NY: Cornell University Press. An attempt to capture the essence of the philosopher, by one of the foremost students of the Socratic dialogues.

CHAPTER EIGHT

The Peloponnesian War

We think today of war as a government initiative forced on young men and women who may or may not be eager to fight. Things were very different in Sparta and Athens, where it was the common soldiers meeting in assembly as voters who took the decision to go to war. Because Greek states were small and men were liable for service through middle age, citizens were not voting to send a group of unfamiliar youths to fight: They were voting to go themselves, along with their sons and brothers, to do the killing and the dying. What they signed on for amounted, they knew, to spearing, stabbing, and trampling other soldiers, to ramming ships and sinking them. They might throw enemies into pits or be thrown into pits themselves. They might annihilate entire cities, killing the men and enslaving the women and children, or they might be annihilated themselves. They might go to their deaths in a hail of arrows, or find themselves flailing around in the water as enemies speared them like fish—or held their heads under water until they could no longer breathe, or sank their ships and left them to drown in choppy waters. Death by drowning was particularly frightening to Greeks, as the souls of men who had not been buried were unable to find a resting place in Hades and would wander forever. All this the Athenians knew, as did the Spartans and their allies, when they voted to begin the Peloponnesian War. Yet a majority on each side thought that the honor and security gained in war would be worth it. (As is always the case in history, a minority thought no such thing but was outvoted.) In the end, with tens of thousands dead, neither side really gained anything.

When war broke out between Athens and Sparta, few Greeks foresaw that it would be different from any war they had ever experienced or even imagined.

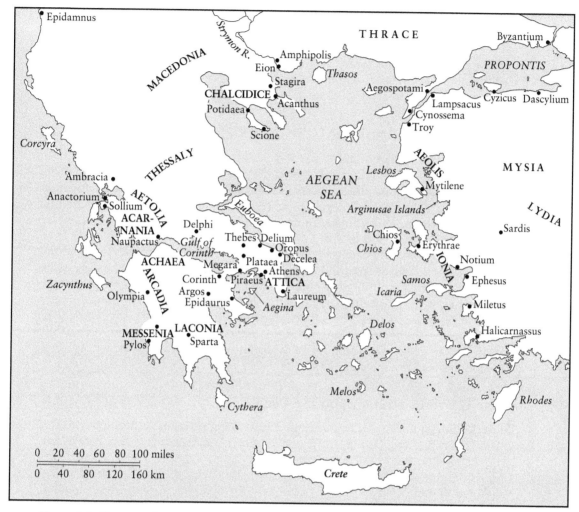

Figure 8.1. Theaters of operation during the Peloponnesian War.

The twenty-seven-year conflict cost thousands upon thousands of lives and proved a stern teacher. It enhanced many of the worst features of Greek society—competitiveness, jingoism, lack of compassion, and gross disregard for human life. At the same time, a number of extraordinary thinkers sought to focus attention on the problems people face in their attempts to live together: The writings of Thucydides, Sophocles, and Euripides showed vigor and spirit throughout the war years, and the comic dramatist **Aristophanes** continued to produce plays of irrepressible wit through three decades of fighting and for a generation afterward. The Peloponnesian War would alter the world the Greeks knew in many respects. Comfortable assumptions about the citizen-fighter and women's role in the polis would break down, and conventional morality and piety would face many challenges. Much, however, would stay the same—the polis as a political unit, the primacy of agriculture, the rivalries of the city-states, and the worship of the Olympian gods. The trauma occasioned by the war and its aftermath was also strikingly fertile, for the war supplied the impetus for many of the social, political, and intellectual changes we identify with the fourth century and the period after the death of Alexander in 323 BC that we call the Hellenistic Age.

THE ARCHIDAMIAN WAR (431–421 BC)

To many Greeks alive at the time, the decade of fighting that stretched from 431 to 421 seemed like a discrete entity in itself, and in fact this war has been given its own name—the Archidamian War, after the Spartan king and commander Archidamus. We owe the concept of a single Peloponnesian War extending from 431 to 404 to Thucydides. Another historian might have seen a continuous war extending from 460 to 404, or three wars—one from 460 to 446, one from 431 to 421, and another beginning somewhere between 418 and 415 and continuing to 404. Students of historiography (the writing of history) use the expression "colligation," that is, "tying together," to describe the way historians "create" an event or a process by linking together separate events in such a way that they form a coherent whole. Joining what others might construe differently, Thucydides, the earliest and most important source for this period, has by colligation successfully enshrined in history the concept of what is today commonly known as "the" Peloponnesian War, the war of 431–404.

The Periclean Strategy and the Plague

Pericles devised an ingenious strategy for winning a war he conceived as essentially defensive, and it is a measure of his influence and eloquence that he was able to persuade his fellow Athenians to do something so conspicuously at odds with human nature. Harassing Peloponnesian territory with their navy, the Athenians declined to participate in hoplite battle with the Spartans. At Pericles' instigation, the Athenian farmers abandoned their land, taking with them what few household goods could be loaded on wagons, and huddled with the city dwellers inside the Long Walls that linked Athens to Piraeus. These walls, Pericles rightly perceived, made Athens in essence an island. Food and other necessary goods would continue to be imported by ship from throughout the empire. The enemy, Pericles calculated, would tire of ravaging the land when nobody came out to fight. Seeing that the superior training and numbers of their infantry would do them no good, they would soon sue for peace. The Spartans, meanwhile, conjectured that the Athenians would grow restive cooped up in the overcrowded city throughout the campaigning season and, seeing their land being ravaged, would be unable to tolerate the frustration. They foresaw one of two consequences: Either the Athenians would seek peace or they would overrule Pericles and come out to fight a losing battle. In judging that the enemy would give up after a couple of years, both sides miscalculated badly, but there was nothing intrinsically foolish in their thinking.

It was with reluctance and apprehension that the Athenians abandoned their homes and the familiar temples nearby, and when the farmers arrived in Athens only a few were able to find shelter with friends or relatives. Most had to seek out empty space in the city or bunk down in temples and shrines. Some wound up spending the summer campaigning season in the towers along the walls.

Although the first year of the war saw few casualties, by tradition the Athenians held a public funeral for those who had been killed, and Pericles was chosen to offer the eulogy. How closely the stirring paean to Athens that appears in Thucydides' history approximates what Pericles actually said is unclear. We have no other versions of this speech. It could represent Thucydides' accurate recollection of what was said, or a faulty recollection, or a composition of his own. In any case, the speech we have focuses not on the dead themselves but on the city of Athens and the way of life it represents—a way of life that is defined as the antithesis of everything Spartan.

It would be a mistake, Pericles suggested, to think that an easygoing polis such as Athens, with its love of words, of ideas, and of beauty, could not compete successfully in war with a highly regulated, militarized society like Sparta, where words are despised as a hindrance to action, people have little choice about how they live their lives, and anxious secrecy is the order of the day. "We love nobility without ostentation," Pericles says,

Figure 8.2. Attic red-figure *stamnos* (storage jar) attributed to the Achilles Painter (c. 450–440 BC). An armed warrior, departing for battle, takes leave of family members. London, The British Museum.

and we have a virile love of knowledge. Furthermore, wealth is for
us something to use, not something to brag about. And as to poverty,
there is no shame in admitting to it—the real shame is in not taking
action to escape from it. Finally, while there are those who manage
both the city and their own private affairs, there are others who,
though wrapped up in their work, nevertheless have a thorough
knowledge of public affairs. For we are the only people who regard
a man who takes no interest in politics to be leading not a quiet life
but a useless one. We are also the only ones who either make governmental decisions or at least frame the issues correctly, because we
do not think that action is hampered by public discourse, but by not
learning enough in advance, through discourse, about what action we
need to take.

***

To sum up, I tell you that this city, taken all in all, is the school of
Greece, and as far as I am concerned, any man among us will exhibit
a more fully developed personality than men elsewhere and will be
able to take care of himself more gracefully and with the quickest
of wit.

(The Peloponnesian War 2.40–41)

Pericles' concluding charge to the women of Athens sat oddly on the lips of
a man who lived with a female companion far more visible and renowned than
many of his fellow politicians:

And since I must also make some mention of womanly virtue to those
who will now be widows, I will define it in this brief admonition:
your greatest fame consists in being no worse than your natures, and
in having the least possible reputation among males for good or ill.

(The Peloponnesian War 2.45)

This is certainly striking advice in a society as loquacious as the one Thucydides
depicts in Athens. It is posited on a notion of woman as in every way the opposite
of political man, in whose mind reputation counted for practically everything.

The next year brought a horrific surprise: a ghastly plague that attacked the
population of Athens. Its origin is unknown, as is its precise nature; speculation
has ranged from smallpox and measles to the Ebola virus, anthrax, and toxic
shock syndrome. Recently, however, scientists managed to isolate bacterial DNA
from dental pulp in a mass grave of this date, and their analysis suggests that the
disease was an earlier form of modern typhoid fever. Whatever it was, it spread
with deadly speed in the crowded, unsanitary environment of a city packed to
capacity and beyond. Probably about a third of the populace died. Thucydides,
who himself fell ill but recovered, took pains to record everything he could about

the course and symptoms of the illness so that it would be possible for readers to recognize the disorder should it ever reappear: He reports the oral bleeding, the bad breath, the painful vomiting, the burning skin, the insomnia, the memory loss, and the often fatal diarrhea and goes on to describe the way in which people reacted to the disease. A nihilistic lawlessness began to characterize life in the city:

> Fear of the gods? The laws of man? No one held back, concluding
> that as to the gods, it made no difference whether people worshiped
> or not since they saw that all alike were dying; and as to breaking the
> law, no one expected to live long enough to go to court and pay his
> penalty. The far more terrible verdict that had already been delivered
> against them was hanging over their heads—so it was only natural to
> enjoy life a little before it came down.
>
> (The Peloponnesian War 2.53)

Demoralized by the plague and frustrated by being forbidden to march out and offer battle, some Athenians tried to open negotiations for peace with the Spartans, ignoring Pericles' cautions against this and in fact voting to depose him from the strategia (bringing forward some charge against him, as was common in Athens when politicians had ceased to please their constituency). Nothing much happened when Pericles was out of office except the long-awaited surrender of Potidaea. Finding that other leaders conducted the war no better, the Athenians returned Pericles to office at the next elections. Then he caught the plague and died.

Cleon and Diodotus: The Revolt of Mytilene (428–427 BC)

The 420s saw a change in the character of Athenian government. Although no formal distinctions divided rich from poor or separated social classes, until the war Athenians had felt most comfortable with political power in the hands of men from old, wealthy families—men like Cimon and Pericles. Now this ceased to be true. Richer men still had the advantage in politics, but many had died in the plague, allowing men whose fathers and grandfathers had made money in business to compete successfully with those whose families had been living off their landholdings for generations. New words, moreover, crept into discussions of Athenian politics: *dēmagōgos* and its relative *dēmagōgia*, which first appears in the surviving literature in Aristophanes' *Knights*, produced in 424 BC. Literally a "leader of the people"—surely there is nothing wrong in that—the word demagogos came to signal a calculating politician who manipulated the voters for his own ends rather than letting himself be guided by patriotism and principle: hence our English word "demagogue."

The most prominent of the demagogues was **Cleon** (d. 422 BC), who first appears in the pages of Thucydides in a dramatic debate that took place in 427. The year before, several cities on the island of Lesbos had revolted from the Athenian empire under the leadership of the largest of them, **Mytilene**. The promised Spartan aid never materialized, and when the Mytileneans surrendered, the Athenians initially voted to put all the men in Mytilene to death and to sell the women and children into slavery, dispatching a boat to bring the news to the general in command on the island. The next day, however, some people at least had second thoughts, and a debate ensued. Cleon shows a cocky self-assurance in the dismissive way he addresses his audience: "I, for my part," he begins, "have often noticed before that democracies cannot rule over others, but I see it especially now in these regrets of yours about Mytilene. . . ." (Thuc. 3.37). Deriding the Athenians for their openness and flexibility, he advocates a policy of harsh consistency. Bad laws that stay the same, he insists, are better than good ones that change. His studied anti-intellectualism contrasts pointedly with the praise of deliberation and debate in Pericles' funeral oration delivered three years earlier. Yet in other respects Cleon, for all his crassness, is plainly Pericles' heir. "You don't understand," he says, "that you hold your empire as a tyranny and that your subjects are schemers who are governed unwillingly" (Thuc. 3.37). Compare Pericles in his last speech: "You hold your empire like a tyranny by now. Taking it is thought to have been criminal; letting it go would be extremely dangerous" (Thuc. 2.63).

Diodotus, who is otherwise unknown, spoke against proceeding with the original plan, making a marvelous argument grounded in human psychology. Deterrence, he contended, was not as effective as commonly believed, because people who undertake risky ventures do so in the expectation that they will succeed, not fail. Furthermore, he argued, there was no merit in killing people even when they had surrendered, for to do so removed any incentive for surrender in future rebellions. He then made a key observation about the dynamics of the empire. "So far," he maintained,

> the populace in all of the cities is well-inclined toward you. Either they do not join in rebellion with the oligarchs, or, if they are forced to do so, they quickly turn against them. Thus, when you go to war you have the populace of the city you are attacking on your side.
> (*The Peloponnesian War* 3.47)

Although some might debate the accuracy of Diodotus' contention, it certainly makes us think twice about Thucydides' claim that the Athenian empire was universally detested in the subject cities.

Diodotus won the day, and a second boat was sent out to overtake the first. It must have been a dramatic moment when the second boat arrived just as the death sentence was being announced. Instead of putting all the men to death and enslaving all the women and children, the Athenians executed the ringleaders of the revolt. Still, these amounted to more than a thousand men, a significant proportion of the adult male population in a state the size of Mytilene.

The War Continues

The tendency to keep land in the family constricted social mobility in Greece, limiting opportunities for improving one's lot in life. As Thucydides points out, the war raging throughout Greece intensified the long-standing tensions between the aristocrats, who considered a lavish lifestyle to be their birthright, and the ordinary citizens struggling to make a living, for the former could expect help from Sparta and the latter from Athens. The result was *stasis* ("civil strife") more frequent and ferocious than ever before. Thucydides vividly describes the agony that ensued when the democratic party in **Corcyra** gained the upper hand and, as allies of the demos, the Athenians under their admiral Eurymedon made no move to curtail the butchery. To avoid death at the hands of the democrats, some oligarchic partisans

> hanged themselves from trees. Others killed themselves in any way they could. Eurymedon remained at Corcyra for seven days with his sixty ships, during which the Corcyraeans ceaselessly slaughtered those among them whom they thought to be enemies. . . . One saw every imaginable kind of death, and everything that is likely to take place in situations like this did, in fact, take place—and even more. For example, fathers killed their sons; people were dragged from the temples and slaughtered in front of them; some were even walled up in the temple of Dionysus and left to die.
> (*The Peloponnesian War* 3.81)

War, Thucydides concluded, is a violent teacher.

Two years after the bloody episode at Corcyra, the Athenians initiated a project that, although it would not determine the final outcome of the war, nonetheless had dramatic short-term effects. Stuck at **Pylos** in the western Peloponnesus because of bad weather, the Athenian strategos Demosthenes (not to be confused with the famous fourth-century orator by the same name) decided to build a fort there. The legendary home of Nestor, this promontory combined with the narrow island of **Sphacteria** to enclose a body of water known today as the Bay of Navarino.

Fearing that Sphacteria might fall into Athenian hands, the Spartans positioned 420 hoplites on the island. When the Athenians succeeded in marooning them on the island, the Spartan government panicked and sent envoys to Athens to plead for an armistice: So limited was the number of Spartans that their government was willing to do anything to get those hoplites back—even make a peace that took no account of their allies' interests. On the advice of Cleon, however, the Athenians turned the Spartan ambassadors away.

The Spartans, then, remained on Sphacteria, and when Cleon made disparaging remarks about the failure of Athens' generals to capture them, he took for his particular target the respected strategos **Nicias**. An immensely wealthy and notoriously pious man, Nicias had impressed many Athenians by the vast sums he spent on religious festivals, and his base of support lay with Athens' richer and more conservative voters—the sort of men who despised Cleon. Pointing his finger at Nicias, Thucydides reports, Cleon "said scornfully that if the generals

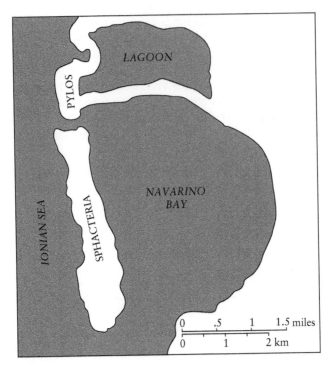

Figure 8.3. Pylos and Sphacteria. The Athenians achieved a great coup by marooning hundreds of Spartan soldiers on the island of Sphacteria, which lies off the west coast of the Peloponnesus.

Figure 8.4a. This bronze shield found in the Athenian agora bears an inscription identifying it as booty the Athenians took from the Spartans at Pylos in 435–424 BC. Athens, Agora Museum.

Figure 8.4b. Line drawing of the shield in Figure 8.4a showing the inscription.

were real men they could easily set out with an armada and capture the troops on the island. If he were in command, he continued, that was what he would do" (Thuc. 4.27). Nicias promptly suggested that Cleon himself be given a special commission to go to Pylos and get hold of the stranded hoplites. Against the expectation of upper-class Athenians, the inexperienced Cleon worked well with Demosthenes, and to the astonishment of Greeks of all social classes, the Spartan soldiers surrendered rather than fight to the death. As 128 of the Peloponnesians had been killed in the fighting, the Athenians now had 292 bargaining chips with which to negotiate an end to the war. Seeing their position strengthened by the possession of hostages, the Athenians resolved to keep fighting rather than to make peace. This was probably a mistake, for any peace that Sparta made to regain its men was likely to alienate its allies and foster the disintegration of the Peloponnesian League.

The presence of Spartan hostages at Athens put an end to the annual invasions of Attica, but the war did not end, for in 424 the Spartans discovered in Brasidas what they had previously lacked, at least since the loss of Archidamus around 427: a charismatic general. As talented an orator as he was a strategist, Brasidas, by his campaigns up north in Chalcidice, very nearly won the war for Sparta, just as Demosthenes and Cleon had nearly won it for Athens at Pylos.

Brasidas and Chalcidice (424–422 BC)

Athens' hold on Chalcidice had always been fragile, and when some Chalcidic towns requested Spartan aid and were joined in their appeal by Athens' on-again, off-again ally Perdiccas of Macedonia, the Spartans promptly dispatched Brasidas. Once in Chalcidice, Brasidas persuaded the towns of Acanthus, Stagirus, and Argilus to revolt from Athens.

Although Brasidas had accomplished much for Sparta, the greatest prize lay ahead. Gaining possession of Amphipolis would require a little more effort, but this cherished Athenian stronghold was Brasidas' principal target, and in fact he brought it over to the Spartan side in less than twenty-four hours. Horrified by this loss, the Athenians banished one of their generals who had been nearby at Thasos when the catastrophe occurred: the historian Thucydides. The events of that snowy December night in the north played a large role in determining just what form Thucydides' history of the war, already begun earlier, would take. Just as they cut off the opportunity for hearing speeches delivered in the assembly and for picking up the latest scuttlebutt in the agora, they also ensured that Thucydides, freed from civic responsibilities and perhaps more trusted by foreigners now that he was on the outs with the home government, would have more reliable non-Athenian sources. Thucydides seems to know a great deal about Brasidas' thinking, for example; perhaps the two men got to know each other.

The following spring (423) the Athenians and the Spartans signed a year's armistice. When the armistice expired in 422, however, Cleon, now a regularly elected general, met Brasidas in battle at Amphipolis. Greek generals fought in the front lines, and in the fighting both Cleon and Brasidas were killed.

The Peace of Nicias (421 BC)

The door to peace was opened by the deaths of the men Aristophanes called the pestles who were grinding down the mortar of war. Athens and Sparta had both had enough. Agriculture in Attica had been horribly disrupted and with it the trade between city and countryside that was the foundation of polis life, and the Athenians were unsettled by the patent unrest throughout their sphere of influence in the north. Sparta was nervous about continuing its war with Athens when the Spartan-Argive truce of thirty years was on the verge of expiring. A number of Spartan soldiers had died in captivity in Athens, and the Spartans were extremely eager to recover the survivors. Both sides were disturbed by the degree to which they had been compelled to hire mercenaries to keep the war going; it seemed like a bad precedent, and it was also costly. The other key players on the diplomatic scene, however—Corinth, Megara, and Boeotia—had somewhat less to gain from peace in general (although they had also experienced devastation during the war), and nothing to gain from the particular peace on which the Athenians and Spartans agreed. In fact, they refused to sign it. The highly problematic agreement known as the Peace of Nicias (named for the principal Athenian negotiator, Cleon's old rival) was essentially a victory for Athens.

The terms of the peace were to be observed for fifty years. Athens was to keep the empire with which it had entered the war; the treaty contained the expression "the Athenians and their allies." Sparta was to return Amphipolis, and Athens would abandon Pylos and the island of Cythera and release all prisoners of war. Although at tremendous cost in money and human lives, the Athenian war goal had been met: The Spartans had failed to destroy the empire. Without even trying, the Athenians had done much to weaken the Peloponnesian League. After a grueling war of ten years, Sparta had suffered loss of life and prestige. Now it was about to lose its allies as well, and disaffection among them placed the new peace in serious jeopardy.

Angry that no substantial damage had been done to the Athenian empire and that two cities on the west coast, Sollium and Anactorium, remained in Athenian hands, Corinth refused to sign the peace. Megara would not sign an agreement that allowed the Athenians to retain its port Nisaea—as the Spartans should have foreseen. The Boeotians, furious at the order to relinquish the border fortress of Panactum to the Athenians, not only declined to sign the treaty but demolished Panactum sooner than give it back. The Amphipolitans refused to return to the Athenian empire and even began revering Brasidas rather than the Athenian Hagnon as their founder; in retaliation, the Athenians held on to Pylos. The chance for a productive alliance between the two most powerful states in Greece was lost, and Thucydides viewed the Peace of Nicias as a false peace, a troubled interlude before the resumption of hostilities.

THE RISE OF COMEDY

Spartan sources for attitudes toward the war are lacking, but comic drama supplies considerable evidence for the Athenians' feelings. Although comedy may have begun in the sixth century in Athens and to the west (in Megara and even

Figure 8.5a. Attic red-figure *chous* (wine jug) attributed to the Nicias Painter, c. 410 BC. Old Comedy and its costumes appear to be reflected on this vase, which depicts Nike (Victory) driving Heracles in a chariot pulled by centaurs preceded by a comic actor carrying two torches. Paris, The Louvre.

Figure 8.5b. Other side of the same vase, showing that the centaurs are preceded by a comic actor carrying two torches. Paris, The Louvre.

Syracuse), and the first victory accorded to a comic poet at the City Dionysia was recorded in 486 BC, it was only during the Peloponnesian War that the genre we know as Old Comedy erupted on the Athenian stage. (The name distinguishes it from New Comedy, which began in the late fourth century.) Comic dramas were produced twice a year in Athens, both times in competitions among several dramatists at festivals of the god Dionysus. The only complete plays that survive, however, were written by the comic genius Aristophanes (c. 450–385 BC).

Unlike the tragedians, Aristophanes did not take his plots from mythology; rather, his story lines were firmly grounded in the culture and politics of his day. Everything he saw around him was grist for his mill—pretentious teachers, overactive law courts, pompous aristocrats from the horsy set, and self-interested politicians whom he blamed for the chaos and misery of life in Athens during the Peloponnesian War. Not even the illustrious Pericles was spared. In the *Acharnians* he was pilloried for starting the war because some Megarians stole two of his mistress Aspasia's prostitutes! Like many Athenians, Aristophanes dreamed of an earlier day when role models were provided by the "men of Marathon" rather than by silver-tongued sophists, and a number of his plots involved protagonists who felt just as he did. Typical was the madcap scheme hatched in *The Birds* in which two alienated Athenians take refuge up in "Cloudcuckooland" in the sky, plot out a utopian society, and, with the aid of their newfound feathered friends, come to rule the world in accord with their own principles. Naturally the chorus sported beaks for the occasion; in *The Wasps*, which parodied the courts, chorus members representing jurors were outfitted with suitably phallic "stings." As in tragedy, all parts in comedy were played by men, so that in the *Ecclesiazusae* (*Congresswomen*), where women disguised themselves as men to take over the assembly, what the audience really saw was men disguised as women dressing up as . . . men.

Obscene and boisterous, Aristophanes' plays also manifest a tender love of the countryside, a nostalgia for a simpler time, and a sober commitment to peace. Although Aristophanes' comic genius was unique, his values must have been congenial to the community; the decision whether to grant a chorus for training lay with the city magistrates, and of course prizes were awarded by citizen judges.

The *Peace* of Aristophanes

In 421, with an end to the war in sight, Aristophanes wrote his *Peace*; by the time it was presented, the treaty was close to becoming a reality. Here, parodying a lost play by Euripides, Aristophanes shows his protagonist Trygaeus riding on a huge dung beetle to the house of Zeus (accomplished on stage by beam and pulley) to inquire why Zeus is destroying Greece by war. There he learns from Hermes that the gods have been alienated by the two sides' childish squabbling. The audience cannot have been entirely comfortable with Hermes' evenhanded allotment of blame. The gods, he says,

> were frequently for peace.
> But you guys wanted war. Laconians,
> when once they got a little piece of luck,

would say, "By God, those Atticans will pay!"
Or if it seemed that luck was on your side,
and then the Spartans came about a peace,
at once you'd cry: "We're being taken in!
Athena! Zeus! we can't agree to this!
If we hang on to Pylos, they'll come back. . . ."
                                          (*Peace* 211–219)

He then explains that War has imprisoned Peace in a cave and, having obtained a
huge mortar in which to grind down all the Greek cities, has sent his slave Tumult
in search of pestles. Tumult, however, has learned that Athens and Sparta have
recently lost their pestles—Cleon and Brasidas. Perhaps, then, there is some hope
of setting Peace free.

   Trygaeus finally persuades Hermes to help him orchestrate the rescue of Peace.
This is no mean task, as it is difficult to get all the Greeks to pull together on the
necessary ropes even with divine assistance, but in time their efforts are successful. The blessings Peace will bring are celebrated in terms that reflect the concerns
of the Athenian farmers in the audience:

Trygaeus: Fellow farmers! Stop and listen! Can you hear these
                wondrous words?
            No more spears, men, no more javelins, no more fighting
                with our swords!
            We've got peace with all its gifts now, we can trade in all
                that arming
            For a happy, happy song as we march home to do some
                farming.
Chorus: What a day, not just for farmers but for anyone
                worthwhile:
            What a yearned-for, hoped-for vision! See how joyously I
                smile
            As I think about how soon I'll see the vines upon my land;
                And the fig-trees that I planted as a youth with my own
                hand!
                                          (*Peace* 551–558)

Between Peace and War

The peace so joyously anticipated by Aristophanes was not long lasting; events
were to prove that the thousands who had died in the Archidamian War had given
their lives for nothing. Although the Athenians and Spartans who desired peace
wanted it very badly indeed, they had to contend with formidable counter-
vailing forces.

   As a rule, it is dangerous to accord too large a role to high-profile individuals
in shaping the course of history. At times, however, a particular person does seem

to bear an extraordinary share of the responsibility for the way things turn out. Such was the case with the flashy Athenian aristocrat **Alcibiades**. Strategos for the first time in 420, Alcibiades had little prospect of making a name for himself in a tranquil world. His future glory was contingent on the disintegration of the fragile peace. To Alcibiades, even more than to the average Greek aristocrat, a life without glory was barely worth the name.

Alcibiades, Renegade Aristocrat

Alcibiades had been three when his father died, and he was raised in the home of his relative Pericles. Handsome, witty, athletic, charming, and sensuous, he was eagerly courted by lovers of both sexes; and his rakish personality and flamboyant lifestyle were notorious.

Alcibiades never did like rules. His passions included his teacher Socrates, the breeding and racing of horses, and indeed competition in all its forms, on and off the track. His wealthy family had connections abroad, and despite his relationship to Pericles, his grandfather had been the Spartan *proxenos* at Athens—the man charged with representing Spartan interests in his home state. To the family connections that were his by birth, he added a marriage connection; his wife Hipparete belonged to one of the most wealthy and prominent families in Athens.

At first it appeared that Alcibiades' interest in reactivating the war would come to nothing. Although Elis and Mantinea joined the alliance Athens had formed with Argos, Sparta managed to defeat the new grouping in battle, scoring a decisive victory in Mantinea in 418 BC, and also succeeded in mending fences with its disaffected allies Boeotia and Corinth, thus in effect restoring the Peloponnesian League. Meanwhile tensions ran high among the various would-be leaders in Athens. An ostracism might have decided the rivalry of Alcibiades and Nicias, the hawk and the dove, but the two men seem to have panicked and mobilized their supporters to turn on a third man, Hyperbolus, instead.

The fact that ostracism was in reality something of an honor is underlined by Plutarch's claim that it was Hyperbolus' unworthiness that sparked this decision; a contemporary comic poet apparently quipped, "The man, indeed, deserved the fate, but not the fate the man." At this distance, it is impossible to determine whether the Athenians' distress at the outcome of the ostracism resulted from Hyperbolus' political insignificance or his social origins; those who had been ostracized earlier in the century came from aristocratic families. In any event, the Athenians now seem to have abandoned ostracism and turned to a different strategy for ensuring democratic control of government, making use of the *graphē paranomōn* ("indictment for illegal proposals") to punish politicians who brought forward proposals in conflict with existing laws. Like ostracism, however, this procedure was often used politically—a development that is not surprising, as without a written constitution or bill of rights, only a highly subjective judgment could determine what new laws were and were not in harmony with the old.

The Destruction of Melos (416 BC)

The years that followed were marked by conflict in Athens and chaos in the Peloponnesus. A disturbing Athenian naval expedition stands out from this troubled time, memorialized in some of the most frequently read pages in Thucydides. In 416, probably at the instigation of Alcibiades, the Athenians dispatched ships to the little island of **Melos**, which was allied with neither Athens nor Sparta, and ordered it to join the Delian League. Hope of Spartan assistance moved the Melians to turn Athens down. Spartan aid did not materialize, and as punishment for their recalcitrance, the Athenians decided to kill all the Melian men and sell all the women and children into slavery—all of them. The ambivalence that had led them to limit their punishment of the Mytilenaeans to "ringleaders" in 427 was now a thing of the past. The episode plainly made a deep impression on Thucydides, who chose to include in his history a chilling rendition of the conversation between the Melians and the Athenians—the only sustained dialogue in his work. Melos was a tiny island in a remote locale. How did Thucydides know what was said there in such detail? He didn't. The set piece known as the "Melian Dialogue" shows us Thucydides experimenting with an art form closer to drama than to history. There he showed the Athenians articulating the philosophy that has become known by the German word *Realpolitik*, or political realism:

> Given what we believe about the gods and know about men, we think that both are always forced by the law of nature to dominate everyone they can. We didn't lay down this law, it was there—and we weren't the first to make use of it. We took it as it was and acted on it, and we will bequeath it as a living thing to future generations, knowing full well that if you or anyone else had the same power as we, you would do the same thing.
>
> (*The Peloponnesian War* 5.105)

To treat an enemy the way the Athenians treated the Melians was not unheard of in Greece; this is precisely what the Athenians had done to the inhabitants of rebellious Scione in 421. But the Melians had not been enemies of Athens, and what the Athenians did to them tarnished their reputation into the next century and beyond.

The year after the massacre (415 BC), Euripides confronted the Athenians with his anguished *Trojan Women*. No one could seriously doubt that this exquisitely painful drama, ostensibly set in Troy in the aftermath of the city's fall, was designed to illustrate the dreadfulness of war in general and the current war in particular. "Toddlers," sang the men in the chorus dressed as women,

> in terror pressed against their mothers' skirts
> as soldiers burst from ambush, poised to strike.
> Pallas Athena's work, this killing was.
> The altars of the gods ran red with blood

and desolation reigned in every bed—
the murdered men a glory to the Greeks,
the women taken to breed Argive sons,
and only sorrow left for fallen Troy.

(555–565)

The specter of the enslavement of the wives and sisters and daughters of the Trojan heroes and the execution of the young Astyanax, Hector's son, thrown to his death from the city walls, was all too evocative of recent developments: Many of those sitting in the audience had themselves done the killing at Melos. It also proved prophetic of events yet to come.

The Invasion of Sicily (415–413 bc)

While a small number of men met daily to practice singing the unsettling choruses in Euripides' sobering drama, many more busied themselves preparing for the largest military expedition in Athens' history. Pericles had warned the Athenians that attempts to expand their empire would undermine their chances of winning the war, but Pericles was long dead and his strategy had died with him. In the winter of 416–415, temptation had appeared to the Athenian assembly in the form of ambassadors from the Sicilian city of **Egesta**, an old ally now at odds with its neighbor Selinus. In a war with Egesta, Selinus could count on the backing of Syracuse, the most powerful city in Sicily—and a Corinthian colony. Athenian involvement in Sicily, therefore, could mean renewed war with the Peloponnesian League, but it could also lead to great wealth and an expanded sphere of influence.

When Alcibiades advocated full support for Egesta and Nicias argued with equal passion against involvement in Sicily, a huge undertaking, the Athenians resolved on a peculiar compromise. Alcibiades would indeed be sent west with a large force, but he would be accompanied by two other strategoi—Lamachus, an experienced general, and Nicias himself, whose presence they hoped would serve as a check on Alcibiades' rashness. Everyone alike, Thucydides wrote,

> fell madly in love with the expedition: the older men because they thought that it would either conquer Sicily or return unharmed, given its great strength; the elite of military age because they longed to see far away places and broaden their minds, and because they were confident that they would come home safely; the rank and file of soldiers because they thought that they would make money right away and also acquire an empire where they could collect soldiers' pay forever.
>
> (*The Peloponnesian War* 6. 24)

As in Sparta when the war was first being contemplated, those who were against the invasion were intimidated by the majority and held their tongues for fear of being thought unpatriotic.

The idea that Nicias' prudence would counter Alcibiades' impulsive nature was singularly wrongheaded. Shortly before the expedition was to sail, moreover, a bizarre nocturnal escapade in Athens sparked a scandal of extraordinary proportions that spilled over from religion to politics. Outside Athenian homes and temples stood religious images known as herms—stone pillars adorned with the face and erect phallus of the god Hermes. They were meant to bring good luck and protection from danger. One morning not long before the expedition was to set sail, the Athenians awoke to find that nearly all these herms had been defaced—or rather dephallused.

Cultural differences make it hard for us fully to understand why Athenians reacted to this sacrilegious prank with utter terror and became convinced that a plot was afoot to overthrow the government, but this is exactly what happened. Although many were punished and indeed a number put to death, responsibility for the project has never been determined. It may have been the work of one or more of the organizations known as *hetaireiai*. Drinking clubs composed of upper-class young men, often with oligarchic leanings, hetaireiai involved themselves in

Figure 8.6. This fragmentary fifth-century herm found in the excavations of the Athenian agora may have been one of those mutilated in 415–414 before the Athenians sailed for Sicily. Athens, Agora Museum.

a variety of social and political activities. To democrats, they seemed sinister and potentially treasonous.

Not surprisingly, fingers were pointed at Alcibiades, precisely the sort of irreverent individual who would set his drinking companions on such an enterprise whether they belonged to a hetaireia or not. Fuel was added to the flames by accusations that Alcibiades had staged a burlesque mocking the mystery rites celebrated at Eleusis, violating their secrecy by parodying them in front of the uninitiated. Because he had solid support among the adventurous sailors bound for Sicily, Alcibiades wisely demanded that he be tried at once, before the fleet left. Instead, his opponents waited to bring charges until the expedition had sailed.

The fleet the Athenians dispatched for Sicily was entirely out of proportion to the size or importance of its intended objective. It consisted of 134 triremes with 130 supply boats, a total of more than 25,000 men. Dozens of merchant vessels decided to accompany the navy, hoping for profits. Both citizens and foreigners crowded the shore gazing with astonishment at the armada, which Thucydides says was the most expensive any Greek city had launched until that day. Throughout the fleet libations were offered to the gods from cups of silver and gold, and the crowd on shore joined in the prayers. Of the many who sailed for Sicily, however, few returned. The Athenians received less support from the cities of Sicily and southern Italy than they had expected, and even the eager Egestans turned out not to have the resources they had claimed. Envoys dispatched to Egesta, it proved, had been duped into believing the city was rich when in fact it was poor. Thucydides tells how the various Egestans received the crews of the Athenian ships in their homes, rounding up as many gold and silver cups as they could find in town and in the neighboring cities and presenting them at parties as if they belonged to the host:

> They all used the same goblets, for the most part, and they showed so much of it everywhere that it absolutely awed the Athenian crewmen, who, when they returned to Athens, spread the news about the great wealth they had seen. Those who had been deceived in turn misled others, and they were all held responsible by the troops when word got out that Egesta did not have any money.
>
> (*The Peloponnesian War* 6.46)

Just about everything that could have gone wrong with the Sicilian enterprise did. Lamachus died fighting. Alcibiades was recalled to stand trial, and on the journey managed to jump ship and defect to Sparta. When in the winter of 415–414 envoys from Syracuse and Corinth came to seek Spartan aid for the Sicilian campaign, Alcibiades warned the Spartans that the Athenians were planning to conquer Sicily and Italy, attack Carthage, and then go after the Peloponnesus. The dispatch of a Spartan general to Sicily, he suggested, might be necessary if the Spartans wanted to prevent an Athenian takeover of the entire Greek world.

Nicias and Lamachus had occupied the plateau known as Epipolae west of Syracuse and had begun building a north–south wall with the idea in mind of blockading the city. Now in sole command, Nicias successfully moved the Athenian fleet into Syracuse's harbor, creating a real possibility of blockading the city, but the Spartans were determined to prevent the Athenians from conquering Sicily and had sent a talented commander, Gylippus, to see what he could do.

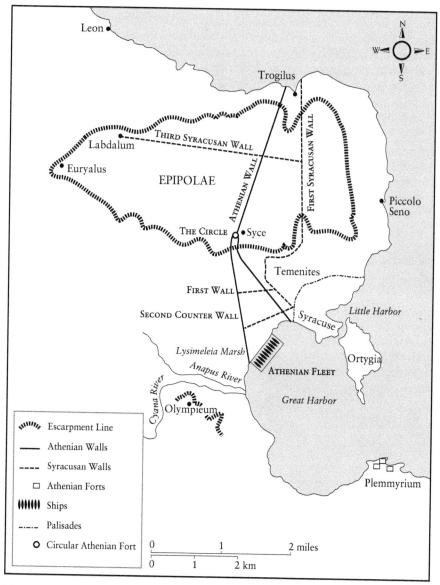

Figure 8.7. Diagram of Syracuse and Epipolae.

The arrival of Gylippus with reinforcements changed the situation dramatically. Gylippus scaled the Epipolae heights via a pass that the Athenians had carelessly left unguarded—the same pass they themselves had used a few months before. The Syracusans, moreover, built a counter wall that destroyed Athenian chances for a blockade.

Convinced the situation was hopeless, Nicias tried to dissuade the Athenians from continuing their efforts in Sicily by a long letter to the assembly maintaining that only a force as large as the original expedition could have any chance of success. To his horror, the Athenians sent Demosthenes out at the head of the proposed reinforcements. When he arrived with the second fleet and promptly suffered a serious reverse on the Epipolae heights, Demosthenes advocated withdrawal. Once more, however, religious anxiety intruded into the secular sphere. When everything was ready for the Athenians' departure, Thucydides related,

> and just as they were about to sail, there was an eclipse of the moon, which happened to be full. The event made most of the Athenians feel uneasy, and they urged their generals to stay; and Nicias, who was too inclined to believe in the interpretation of omens and that sort of thing, refused even to discuss a move until after they had stayed for "three times nine days," as their seers decreed. This was the reason the Athenians stayed on after all their delays!
>
> *(The Peloponnesian War 7.50)*

On learning that the Athenians had been planning to leave, the Syracusans attacked the Athenian fleet and blocked the exit from the harbor. A fierce battle ensued, with some two hundred ships rammed together in a tight space. The din made it impossible to hear the calls of the coxswains.

Unable to make their escape by sea, the Athenians resolved to depart over land, abandoning their sick and wounded. About forty thousand men set out on the dismal trek, the Syracusans hot on their heels. Nicias and Demosthenes became separated; the Syracusans caught up first with Demosthenes, who surrendered in the hope of saving his soldiers' lives. The Syracusans then overtook Nicias' army.

DOCUMENT 8.1

Thucydides is at his narrative best in portraying the final collapse of the Athenian effort in Sicily.

The Athenians pushed on to the Assinarus River, all the while being devastated by the spears, arrows and stones coming from everywhere and by the hordes of cavalry and other troops. They thought that if they could just get across the river, things would be a little easier for them. They were desperate to stop the pain, to drink some water. When they got to the river, they broke ranks and ran into it, every man struggling to make the brutal crossing first as the enemy bore down. Driven to cross all together, they fell onto one another and trampled each other down. Some were killed immediately by their own spears; others got tangled up in their equipment and with each other and sank into the river. Syracusans positioned on the other bank, which was steep, hurled down spears at the Athenians, most of whom were jumbled together ravenously drinking from the nearly dry riverbed. The Peloponnesians went down into the river after them and did most of the killing there; and though it quickly became fouled, the Athenians nonetheless fought among themselves to gulp the muddy water clotted with blood.

Finally, with dead bodies heaped atop each other in the riverbed, and the army decimated, some in the river and others—such as got across—by the cavalry, Nicias surrendered himself to Gylippus, trusting him more than the Syracusans. He told Gylippus and the Spartans to do with him what they wanted, but to stop slaughtering his men. After this, Gylippus ordered his troops to take prisoners, whereupon the surviving men were brought in alive, except for the large number who had been hidden by individual Syracusan soldiers. They also sent a search party out after the three hundred who had broken through the sentries by night and captured them. . . . A large number, of course, were killed, for there was a great slaughter at the river, greater than any which occurred in the whole war.

(*The Peloponnesian War* 7.84–85)

The Athenians had lost tens of thousands of men and accomplished nothing. For them, the outcome of the campaign was so horrific that they at first refused to believe the appalling news. Plutarch claims that word of the disaster first reached Athens by way of a hapless man who had reported it matter-of-factly to a barber in Piraeus as if it were common knowledge: The agitated barber promptly ran the five miles to Athens, where he repeated the tale. He was in the very process of being tortured as a troublemaker when messengers arrived to confirm the astonishing story. As Thucydides was later to write, "All was lost. Ships. Men. Everything" (7.87).

THE WAR IN THE AEGEAN AND THE OLIGARCHIC COUP AT ATHENS (413–411 BC)

The Greek world was as stunned by the Athenians' defeat at Syracuse as it had been by their victory at Marathon. The myth of naval superiority that had held the Delian League together was shattered. Athens' fighting force was vastly smaller than it had been in 431. Money was in short supply; previously one trierarch had been appointed for each ship, but soon after the disaster in Sicily the Athenians introduced the syntrierarchy, allowing two men to share the expense. For Athenian subjects, suddenly revolt became not merely an option but a powerful temptation. Alcibiades cruised the seas on Sparta's behalf, fomenting rebellion wherever he could. Meanwhile in Attica, some twenty thousand slaves deserted to the Spartan king Agis, who at Alcibiades' instigation had established himself in a fort at Decelea in northeast Attica. The disappearance of the slaves from the mines prevented the continued working of the silver veins, and the strength of the encampment at Decelea interfered gravely with Athenian agriculture. Now the Spartans could ravage Attica all year, killing farm animals as they went and keeping Athens in a perpetual state of siege. Seeing success well within their grasp, the invigorated Spartans set about building a new naval force of a hundred triremes and began negotiating for Persian support.

Incredibly, it took Sparta eight years to bring Athens to its knees—eight years during which the Athenians, crippled by devastating losses in Sicily, survived the loss of the huge island of Euboea off the Attic coast and an oligarchic coup in the city. The history of these eight years was crowded with shifting alliances, plots and counterplots, murders and lies. Within Athens, lines between democrats and oligarchs blurred as key players in the political arena moved back and forth between the parties, and a new creature appeared, the "moderate"—a politician whose motives for keeping one foot in each camp were often impossible to determine: Sincere patriotism became increasingly difficult to distinguish from unprincipled timeserving. The Spartans were divided as to how seemly it might be to barter the Ionians' freedom in exchange for Persian gold, and the Persians could not decide which side, if any, to support. Through it all, Alcibiades remained a wild card, cagily shifting position to suit the rapidly altering international situation. The fortunes of battle swung wildly back and forth. In 413 Athens seemed to be finished; by 410 the Spartans sued for peace. Athens won a stunning victory in 406 only to lose the war by 404.

Civil Strife in Athens

For nearly a century after the clash between Cleisthenes and Isagoras, Athens had been free from the danger of civil war. Unrest erupted, however, when men of oligarchic inclinations played on the Athenians' anxieties about the failure of their democratic leaders to prosecute the war more successfully, particularly in Sicily. The machinations of Alcibiades provided a catalyst for a more substantial change in the government. Having worn out his welcome in Sparta—whether because of his alleged affair with the wife of King Agis or for some other reason—he had begun to plot a return to Athens. The entry of Persia into the equation provided the springboard he needed. In the years that followed the Athenian defeat in Sicily, Persian policy toward Greece was determined not primarily by the king, Darius II, but by the coastal satraps—Pharnabazus (the satrap of Dascylium) in the north, and **Tissaphernes** (the satrap of Sardis) in the south.

Tissaphernes in particular had a lively interest in Greek affairs, and indeed in Greek culture as a whole. At first he leaned toward Sparta, and in fact negotiated a series of treaties with Sparta in which the Spartans, uncomfortably but unmistakably, agreed to sell out the freedom of the Greek cities of Ionia in exchange for Persian gold. Thus died the Spartans' claim to be the liberators of Greece. Not long afterward, however, Alcibiades persuaded Tissaphernes that it might be better for Persia to let Athens and Sparta wear each other down. When Tissaphernes' support for the Spartan cause began to waver, Alcibiades sent word to Athens that he had it in his power to bring the Persians into the war on the Athenian side—but that their support would be contingent on replacing the democracy with an oligarchy. His support, of course, would be contingent on his recall.

That Alcibiades really believed he could persuade Tissaphernes to pour money into the Athenian treasury is unlikely, although not impossible. He couldn't, but by the time it became clear that the Persian support he had promised was illusory, the wheels had been set in motion for a change in government and Alcibiades' return. It is an index of how deeply the long war had shaken the Athenians that in 411, the assembly, some members intimidated and others just demoralized, voted itself out of existence and placed the safety of the state in the hands of a new, provisional **Council of Four Hundred**, which, it was understood, would soon give way to a larger body of five thousand. Despite the way the war had undermined confidence in the democratic government, this vote was made possible only by the absence of the fleet, based now at Samos; for sailors, who were generally poor men, could be counted on to oppose any reforms that had the effect of limiting the franchise to property owners.

Experiments in Oligarchy

Neither of the reformers' notions was entirely new. Solon was believed by many people to have created a council of four hundred, and the five thousand were thought to correspond to the hoplite class. Sailors were right to be alarmed by such projects. What was really at issue here was the disenfranchisement of the lowest class in the Solonic census, the thetes. The notion of "hoplite democracy" had been Cimon's ideal, and he was not alone. From this moment many Athenians of antidemocratic tendencies began to make use of a new watchword, "the ancestral constitution," that is, a democracy limited to landowners, which they insisted was more traditionally Athenian than the upstart democracy that included the poor men who served as rowers in the fleet. This issue, which had seemed to be settled nearly a century before with Cleisthenes' victory over Isagoras, was now once again on the floor.

Carrying arms and flanked by an additional 120 men, the Four Hundred also entered the Bouleuterion where the council met, paid the councilors the balance of what was owing to them, and dismissed them. There were now two Athenian governments—the oligarchy of the Four Hundred in the city and the democratic fleet stationed at Samos, which functioned as the assembly.

The belief that Athens' foreign affairs would do better under oligarchic guidance suffered serious setbacks when the peace with Sparta failed to materialize— and Euboea successfully revolted from the Athenian empire. The hoplites whom the Four Hundred had set to fortifying the promontory of Eetionia at Piraeus mutinied, and the Five Thousand were promptly installed. They then recalled Athens' exiles, including Alcibiades, and governed Athens for eight months, from September 411 to June 410. Not a great deal is known about their government, but they seem to have limited the franchise to the hoplite class (cutting out the thetes who manned the triremes). Thucydides, who was frequently impatient with democracy, praised the government of the Five Thousand as a laudable blending of democratic and oligarchic elements.

The vigor the Athenians showed in rebuilding their fleet and carrying on the war despite acute domestic conflict was remarkable. After a victory at Cynossema, the Athenians, led by Alcibiades, scored a still more striking one at Cyzicus, where the Spartans lost their admiral-in-chief, Mindarus. The battle is memorable for the "laconic" dispatch the Athenians intercepted on its way to Sparta afterward: "Ships lost; Mindarus dead; men starving; can't figure out what to do." (It is also memorable as the first major encounter of the war not described by Thucydides: Thucydides' account breaks off shortly after Cynossema. From this point on, the principal sources are Xenophon and Diodorus.) The victories in the east had been won by the cooperation of the Five Thousand in Athens and the fleet at Samos, and in June the democracy was formally restored at Athens. A number of the leaders of the Five Thousand remained powerful under the democracy. Among these was Hagnon's son Theramenes, who seemed to find a place for himself in any group. Animosity and suspicion were not entirely gone, however, and as one of its first official acts the restored democracy administered a loyalty oath, requiring each citizen to swear: "I will do my best to kill by word and by deed, by my vote and by my hand, anyone who overthrows the Athenian democracy, holds office under an undemocratic regime, or seeks to establish a tyranny either for himself or for someone else. If anyone else kills such a person, I will consider him clean in the eyes of gods and spirits" (Andocides, *On the Mysteries* 97). The Spartans sought peace from the restored democracy, but only on the basis of the status quo. That the Athenians had regained their confidence is indicated by their refusal.

THE LAST YEARS OF WAR (407–404 BC)

In 407, however, the union of two powerful men dramatically altered the situation in the Aegean. Alcibiades was not the only Greek with charm. An enthusiastic friendship sprang up between Cyrus, son of the Persian king, and **Lysander**, the ambitious chief admiral of the Spartan navy. Ultimately, their alliance spelled doom for Athens.

That same year, Alcibiades, having raised a hundred talents for Athens by looting the coast of Caria, decided it might finally be safe to return home. Once more, however, his ascendancy in his native polis was remarkably brief. Within a matter of months, the Athenians lost twenty-two ships to Lysander at a naval engagement off Notium, where Alcibiades had left his personal pilot Antiochus in charge with orders to under no circumstances engage the Spartans. Antiochus, a friend of Alcibiades, probably had no business in a position of such authority, but the strength of the Athenian reaction attests to the continuing agitation of Alcibiades' enemies. Alcibiades' career at Athens was finished. It is certain that he was not reelected to the strategia, and it is likely that he was actually deposed before his term was out. Rumors circulated that he had fortified a castle in the Gallipoli peninsula as a refuge in case of emergency. Now that the emergency had materialized, he promptly withdrew to this very fortress. He never saw Athens again.

That spring the Athenians offered freedom to slaves who would join the navy that was about to set out for the area of Lesbos. There they scored an impressive victory in a huge naval battle off the Arginusae islands, sinking fully seventy-five Peloponnesian ships. Some twenty thousand Greeks lost their lives. The aftermath of the **Battle of Arginusae** witnessed a bizarre frenzy of self-destruction. Although the Athenian commanders were heartened by their victory, they knew that their admiral Conon and his fleet were blockaded at Mytilene. While the Athenian strategoi were debating whether to set about retrieving the sailors in the water or sail to Mytilene to rescue Conon's force, a sudden storm came up that made rescue impossible. When news of the casualties reached Athens, people began anxiously to cast blame on one another. The generals blamed the trierarchs and the trierarchs blamed the generals. Whether the men in the water were dead or alive is uncertain, but for Greeks the recovery even of bodies was important because the souls of those left unburied would wander eternally in Hades, unable to find a resting place. The eight generals in command were summoned home for trial, and six chose to return. In violation of customary procedure—and over the protests of the philosopher Socrates, whose turn it happened to be to chair the assembly meeting for that day—the generals were tried on a single slate, condemned, and executed. Ironically, after the death of his legitimate sons, Pericles had implored the Athenians to confer citizenship on his sons by Aspasia, and Pericles the Younger was among the generals put to death.

The Final Battle

Again, the Spartans offered peace on the basis of the status quo (although they were willing to evacuate Decelea); again the Athenians declined. Time, however, was running out, as was the pool of talented commanders—and money. The next major battle would be Athens' last stand. Late in the summer of 405 BC, Lysander, making good use of the subsidies he had obtained from his friend Cyrus, established a base in the city of Lampsacus in the Hellespont. In August the Athenian admirals Conon and Philocles stationed their fleet across the channel at **Aegospotami**. Alcibiades, seeing that the Athenians' position was highly vulnerable, descended from his fortress and advised them to move, but they disregarded his cautions. Attacking one day when the Athenians were peculiarly off their guard, with at least some crewmen ashore foraging for provisions, the Spartans captured 171 ships, and their infantry overwhelmed the Athenian camp. Understandably, the Athenians' carelessness gave rise to rumors of treachery. Only a handful of Athenian vessels escaped, one of them the official state trireme the *Paralus*, and another commanded by Conon. Remembering the fate of the victors of Arginusae, Conon took refuge in Cyprus and did not return to Athens until he had engineered a victory over the Spartans at Cnidus in 394, ten years after the end of the war.

Lysander then called a meeting of the allies to solicit their thoughts about the proper treatment of the prisoners. In the discussion, Xenophon reports, speakers brought up both the many deeds the Athenians had already done that were contrary to custom and law, and the many resolutions they had passed in their Assembly concerning how they would treat their enemies if they had won the battle—in particular, the vote to cut off the right hands of those they captured. It was also noted that the Athenians, when they had captured a Corinthian and an Andrian trireme, had thrown all the men on those ships overboard. (Philocles was the Athenian general who had sent these men to their deaths.) Many other accusations were made against the Athenians, and it was finally decided to kill all those of the prisoners who were Athenians, with the exception of Adeimantos, who alone had attacked the decree in the Assembly about the cutting off of hands. He was, however, charged by some with betraying the ships. Philocles, who had thrown overboard the Corinthians and the Andrians, was first asked by Lysander what he thought he deserved for having begun uncustomary and illegal actions against the Greeks, and then had his throat cut.

(*Hellenika* 2.1.31–32 Marincola)

The Spartan victory at Aegospotami had cut off Athens from its principal source of grain; to make sure there would be no slipups, Lysander also decreed death as the penalty for anyone caught bringing grain to Athens. Lysander knew that the war was now over, and the Athenians would know it soon enough, for the *Paralus* was en route to Piraeus with the dismal tidings. The ship arrived at night, and as the news was reported, Xenophon relates, "a cry arose in the Piraeus and ran up through the Long Walls and into the city itself as one man imparted the calamitous news to the next. As a result, no one slept that night as they mourned not only for the men destroyed but even more for themselves" (*Hellenika* 2.2.1 Marincola). Late in the fall Lysander sailed victorious for Piraeus. Along the way he accepted the surrender of Athens' former allies and replaced their democracies with oligarchic governments beholden to Sparta. He also ensured still further stress on the Athenians' dwindling food supply by encouraging Athenian garrisons to return home. Samos persisted in its loyalty to Athens, in recognition of which the Athenians uncharacteristically granted the Samians citizenship. Agis, whose occupation of Decelea had played its desired part in the starvation of the city, moved down to the walls of Athens, where he was joined by Pausanias, his co-king. Miserable and terrified, Xenophon wrote, the Athenians were at a loss for what to do, and they saw no future for themselves but to suffer "the same evils that they themselves had unjustly inflicted on the citizens of smaller states. They had done these things not for the sake of avenging wrongs but simply to display their arrogance, for the only offense of these states was that they had allied themselves with the Spartans" (2.2.10).

In the end, Athens was spared. Not surprisingly, the Thebans, Corinthians, and other Spartan allies advocated doing to Athens precisely what had been done to Melos—killing all the adult men and selling all the women and children into slavery. The Spartans declined, pleading Athens' noble service to Greece during the Persian wars. The brutality of Lysander's temperament makes it more likely that the real motive was fear of the power vacuum into which Corinth—or more likely Thebes—could be counted on to rush.

Early in the spring the Athenians agreed to a treaty negotiated by Theramenes on the Spartans' terms: Athens would not only become Sparta's ally but also would agree to the destruction of the Long Walls and of the fortifications of Piraeus and would surrender all but a dozen ships. Exiles would also be recalled; these were largely men of oligarchic sympathies. The walls were pulled down, Xenophon says, to the merry accompaniment of flutes, for people believed that "that day would be the beginning of freedom for all of Greece" (2.2.23 Marincola). The Spartans' actions, however, presaged ill for freedom. The willingness to sell out the Ionians to Persia and the establishment of pro-Spartan oligarchies in cities formerly in the Athenian empire were bad signs, and worse was to come.

KEY TERMS

Aegospotami

Alcibiades

Aristophanes

Battle of Arginusae

Cleon

Corcyra

Council of Four Hundred

Egesta

Lysander

Melos

Mytilene

Nicias

Pylos

Sphacteria

Syracuse

Tissaphernes

SUGGESTED READINGS

Cawkwell, George. 1997. *Thucydides and the Peloponnesian War*. London: Routledge. An erudite but highly readable analysis of Thucydides' work that offers original and controversial insights into his account of the war.

Connor, W. Robert. 1992. *The New Politicians of Fifth Century Athens*. Indianapolis, IN: Hackett. A thoughtful examination of the changing dynamics of Athenian political life in the fifth century.

Ehrenberg, Victor. 1974. *The People of Aristophanes*. New York: Barnes & Noble. A study of the sociology and economics of the Athenian state based on a close examination of data in Aristophanes' comedies.

Green, Peter. 1970. *Armada from Athens*. London: Hodder and Stoughton. A spirited account of the Athenian invasion of Sicily by a distinguished ancient historian.

Greenwood, Emily. 2006. *Thucydides and the Shaping of History*. London: Duckworth. An examination of how Thucydides arranged his history so as to impress his view of the war on his readers.

Hanson, Victor Davis. 2005. *A War Like No Other: How the Athenians and Spartans Fought the Peloponnesian War*. New York: Random House. A real page-turner that brings the devastating war alive before the reader's eyes.

Hornblower, Simon. 1986. *Thucydides*. Baltimore: Johns Hopkins University Press. A penetrating study of the "historian's historian."

Kagan, Donald. 2003. *The Peloponnesian War*. New York: Viking Press. A close analysis of the war's military and diplomatic history that condenses the research of the author's four-volume history of the war previously published by Cornell University Press.

Lendon, J. E. 2010. *Song of Wrath: The Peloponnesian War Begins*. New York: Basic Books. An impassioned account of the war's origins and first ten years that grounds the conflict in fundamental Greek principles of vengeance, honor, and status rather than any objective cost–benefit calculus.

Meiggs, Russell. 1972. *The Athenian Empire*. Oxford, UK: Oxford University Press. A history of Athens' relationship with its allies from the inception of the Delian League to the end of the Peloponnesian War, with chapters on the judgments made on the empire in both the fifth and fourth centuries and a chart recording tribute payments for the years 453 to 420.

Pritchard, David, ed. 2012. *War, Democracy, and Culture in Classical Athens*. Cambridge, UK: Cambridge University Press. A collection of essays by classicists, ancient historians, political scientists, and archaeologists that offer new perspectives on the connections between democracy and warfare.

Rhodes, P. J. 2011. *Alcibiades: Athenian Playboy, General and Traitor*. Barnsley, UK: Pen and Sword Military. A lively, readable account of this controversial Athenian by a prominent scholar.

Segal, Erich, ed. 1996. *Oxford Readings in Aristophanes*. Oxford, UK: Oxford University Press. An anthology of important recent essays on Aristophanes dealing with topics such as Attic comedy's relationship to contemporary politics, the interaction of comedy and tragedy, and Aristophanes' approach to gender.

Strauss, Barry. 1993. *Fathers and Sons in Athens: Ideology and Society in the Era of the Peloponnesian War*. Princeton, NJ: Princeton University Press. A sensitive analysis of Athenian society during the last decades of the fifth century that grounds conflict in intergenerational tension.

Tritle, Lawrence A. 2009. *A New History of the Peloponnesian War*. Boston: Wiley-Blackwell. A poignant history of the war that places it in its cultural context, exploring the experience of soldiers and civilians alike.

CHAPTER NINE

The Fourth Century: Changing Ideas, Continuing Warfare

There was nothing inevitable about the Spartans' ultimate victory in the war. Darius II died in 404. Had the Athenians not been so careless at Aegospotami—or had they not been betrayed—the withdrawal of Persian support that would probably have attended on the king's death would seriously have compromised the Spartans' chances of winning. On the other hand, the long war taught Sparta a vital lesson about the centrality of naval power. When Sparta became a naval power, the Athenians lost an important advantage, lost the war, and lost their empire.

The economic consequences of the war were grave. Commerce by land and sea was disrupted; cities like Corinth were hard hit. Agriculture suffered in most of Greece (although not, presumably, in Sparta, where helots continued to till the land); the redoubled labor of women and slaves was not sufficient to compensate for the deaths of farmers or their long campaigns away from home. A good deal of territory was ravaged, and livestock and farming implements were destroyed, as were growing vines and olive trees. Some erstwhile farmers were driven to take service as mercenary soldiers, an increasingly popular profession. The historian Xenophon has left us a spellbinding autobiographical account called the Anabasis of the adventures of 10,000 mercenaries hired by the Persian prince Cyrus to help him overthrow his brother King Artaxerxes II. Stranded in the heart of the Persian empire by the death of Cyrus and the failure of his revolt, the huge Greek army regrouped under Xenophon's leadership and struggled through the rugged snow capped mountains of Armenia to the Black Sea and ultimately home. Meanwhile back in the cities of Greece, as usually happens in wartime, many women were forced to work outside the home, and the loss of thousands upon thousands of soldiers and sailors left many women without husbands. New patterns of labor within the oikos developed as well, as free women were more likely to work at home producing goods not only for in-house consumption but for sale as well.

In Athens, at least fifty thousand people had probably died of the plague, many of them before they could reproduce. War casualties seem to have included at least five thousand hoplite soldiers and twelve thousand sailors (including some three thousand executed by Lysander after Aegospotami). The number of adult male citizens in 403 was probably half what it had been in 431. Some cities, like Melos, had been virtually annihilated. In Sparta, absolute numbers dropped less sharply, but the various classes began to redefine themselves, as the ranks of commanders as well as soldiers were swelled not only by distinguished *mothakes* (children of Spartiate fathers and helot mothers) like Lysander, but also by helot fighters rewarded with freedom known as *neodamodeis* ("new citizens").

The use of mercenaries and the periodic emergency enfranchisement of helots and slaves—there were one thousand neodamodeis in Sparta by 421 and probably at least fifteen hundred by the end of the war—blurred the lines that had traditionally divided citizens from noncitizens and eroded the concept of the citizen-soldier and the citizen-sailor; and the frequency of bloody civil strife eroded the concept of the polis itself. At the same time, however, the shattering of faith fostered a questioning spirit that opened the door to the reflections of **Socrates**, Xenophon, and **Plato**. The Peloponnesian War transformed the Greek world, but it did not destroy it.

Oligarchy at Athens: The Thirty Tyrants

Sparta's behavior throughout the Aegean soon put to rest any lingering notions that its decision to spare Athens arose from a policy of generosity. In states formerly allied to Athens, Lysander set up "decarchies," boards of ten pro-Spartan officials designed to ensure oligarchic government and loyalty to Sparta. For Athens itself, plainly ten men would not suffice; there he forced the assembly to ratify a board of thirty. Athenian citizens, these thirty were sympathetic to Sparta and willing to sacrifice democratic principles, but they were not all committed oligarchs; they included, for example, the moderate Theramenes. The most prominent of those who came to be known as the **Thirty Tyrants**, however, left no doubt as to his political convictions. The oligarch Critias was a chilling figure—a pupil of Socrates; a relative of Plato; a brilliant intellectual; a passionate antidemocrat; a longtime admirer of the Spartan constitution; and, as events were to show, a man who would order murders by the hundreds without a qualm. Banished after the fall of the Four Hundred, to which he had belonged, Critias was now back with a vengeance. The Thirty, according to the author of the *Athenian Constitution*, "refrained from harming none of the citizens, but put to death those who were outstanding with respect to wealth or birth or reputation, wishing to free themselves from that source of danger—and also wanting to plunder their estates; and by the end of a short interval of time they had done away with no less than fifteen hundred" (*Ath. Pol.* 35.4). They also fortified their position with seven hundred Spartan soldiers and a Spartan garrison commander similar to those Sparta had established in states throughout the Aegean that it had "liberated" from Athenian hegemony.

Not all the victims of the Thirty were citizens who could possibly have been perceived as political enemies; many were wealthy metics whose wealth the Thirty coveted. Inevitably the Thirty were apprehensive about the possibility of a resistance movement, and they suspected, with some justice, that such a movement might be spearheaded by Theramenes, who had made clear his alarm at the bloodbath. Summoned to the boule for a "trial" at which young oligarchs with concealed weapons had been stationed by prearrangement, Theramenes defended moderate government so convincingly that many listeners were persuaded. The reward for his eloquence was death. Critias promptly announced that Theramenes was not entitled to a trial after all and had him dragged to prison from the altar at which he had taken refuge. Forced to drink hemlock, the poison used soon afterward to execute Socrates, Theramenes went out in style and not without irony, toasting Critias' health with his last drops.

Ultimately the Thirty were undone by their own excesses. Although Sparta had forbidden neighboring states to receive Athenian refugees, the murderous conduct of the Thirty had alienated many Greeks from Sparta, and neither Thebes nor Megara was disposed to turn the refugees away. It was in Thebes that Athenians under their leader Thrasybulus mounted an attempt to retake the city for the democrats. In the fighting, Critias was killed.

Because they expected Spartan aid, the oligarchs at Athens rejected Thrasybulus' call for peace and union between the two camps. As it happened, however, the murderous arrogance of Lysander and his associates was making many powerful men at Sparta nervous, including the kings Agis and Pausanias. Marching into Attica, Pausanias took the lead and masterminded not only the reconciliation of the various Athenian parties but also the eclipse (albeit temporary) of Lysander. Under his aegis, the Athenians agreed on the first recorded amnesty in history, truly a remarkable development in view of the bitterness in the city over the blood that had been shed. The amnesty declared that only the Thirty and their chief officers could be brought to justice for crimes committed before 403; all others were compelled to renounce the many bitter grievances that had accumulated. In September, Thrasybulus led his men unopposed to the Acropolis, where they sacrificed to Athena for the salvation of the city and their own safe return. The work of reestablishing democratic Athens then began.

THE TRIAL OF SOCRATES (399 BC)

The Athenians came remarkably close to respecting the terms of the amnesty on which they had agreed. Nonetheless, decades of war followed by months of terror under the Thirty had taken a heavy toll, and there was no lack of people eager to assign blame for Athens' problems. The colorful Socrates had annoyed jealous parents whose young sons had lionized him, and although the Athenians were averse to breaking the amnesty law, some were open to

Figure 9.1. This Roman copy reflects the head of a Greek portrait statue of Socrates from the third quarter of the fourth century BC that may have been created by the sculptor Lysippus. It depends on an earlier fourth-century portrait type that depicted the philosopher with the ugly face of a satyr and a bald head. Paris, The Louvre.

bending it. Three Athenians—Anytus, Meletus, and Lycon—decided that they had had enough of this eccentric old philosopher who haunted the public spaces of Athens confuting the careless in argument. Socrates (470–399 BC) had been quick to identify the drawbacks of democracy, and he had also been the teacher of (at least) two men who in different ways had harmed Athens: Alcibiades and Critias. The amnesty prevented his accusers from charging Socrates with inciting his pupils to treason, so instead they brought a rather odd three-pronged accusation: Socrates, they claimed, did not believe in the gods of the state; he taught new gods; and he corrupted the young. This sort of charge was unusual at Athens, but Greek states had no constitutional principles separating church and state or safeguards for protecting freedom of expression.

Because Socrates never wrote anything, we are dependent for our conception of him on the dialogues of his admirers Plato and Xenophon. Plato's pupil Aristotle observed about Socrates that the two things one could be certain of attributing to him were inductive reasoning and universal definition. We can be sure of a few other things. Socrates, an Athenian citizen, performed conventional civic services in Athens, fighting as a hoplite at Potidaea, Delium, and Amphipolis in the Peloponnesian War and serving as chair of the assembly on the day of the Arginusae trial in 406. His avocation was discussing interesting philosophical questions with young men, questions that focused on the best way for humans to think and live; at least in his mature years, he was not particularly excited by natural science. He believed that the best way to develop ideas was in the give and take of conversation, and that the best way to educate people was to ask them a series of questions leading in a particular direction (now named for him, "the Socratic method"). However painful it might be to find oneself the object of injustice, he was firmly convinced that doing wrong oneself was the only real misfortune that could befall a person. He had a keen wit and an engaging personality, and pupils flocked to him eagerly, even though he had nothing that could be called a school. He was not a sophist; he became poor through his refusal to charge fees, and his goal was to inculcate moral excellence, which he viewed as the particular excellence of a human being. Like the sophists, however, he used clever arguments and subjected conventional notions to rational analysis; and like them he disrupted the customary bond that placed education in the context of the family, wounding Athenian parents whose sons preferred his company to theirs—and who gave his ideas greater credence. Whom, Socrates asks Meletus in Xenophon's rendition of his defense speech, do I corrupt? "By god," Meletus replies, "I know some—those you've persuaded to obey you rather than their parents" (Xenophon, *Apology of Socrates* 20). It is not surprising, therefore, that he was mistaken for a sophist, or that the sophists' shady reputation should have rubbed off on him. He was parodied in Aristophanes' *Clouds*, which showed him carried across the sky in a crane in an unorthodox educational establishment known as a "think shop."

He also spoke sharply about democracy. Whether it is fair to say that he opposed it and would have liked to see a different regime instituted at Athens is another question. Socrates enjoyed puncturing illusions, and had he lived under a monarchy or an oligarchy, those would probably have been the governments he spent his time undermining. But if anything can safely be gathered from Plato's dialogues, then Socrates was troubled by the notion of amateur government in which anyone's opinion counted for as much as the next man's and in which a volatile assembly was swayed this way and that by rhetorical displays. Most people, he pointed out, aren't terribly thoughtful or analytical; so why should "most people," that is, the majority, make the life and death decisions that affect the polis?

This is a question any advocate of democracy must ask, and Socrates' insistence on asking it need not be taken as implying that he wanted decisions made by a minority. Combined with his association with Alcibiades and Critias, however, his pointed remarks about the foibles of democracy seemed downright unpatriotic, and he could easily enough be cast as a purveyor of dangerous ideas.

By Athenian custom, Socrates' trial took only one day. It is intolerably painful for most readers of Plato's *Apology of Socrates* to believe that the words written down by Plato were not actually spoken at Socrates' trial. Perhaps they were, and perhaps they weren't; Xenophon's account of Socrates' speech, also called the *Apology*, is less inspiring and much shorter. (The Greek word *apologia* does not connote "apologizing" in the modern sense but rather means a refutation.) Plato's rendition contains the famous dictum that "the unexamined life is not worth living" and constitutes an extraordinarily moving paean to intellectual freedom and the life of the mind. Shunning the strategy that he identifies as standard procedure in an Athenian courtroom—weeping, pleading, parading his children in front of the jury—Socrates, according to Plato, took the position that the best defense was a strong offense. Using the question-and-answer method for which he was famous and that had apparently gotten him into trouble, he demolished his accusers by demonstrating the inconsistencies in their allegations and then went on to explain in poignant detail the great service provided to the state by his relentless probing. His service to the state, he argues, is precious and irreplaceable. It is, literally, a godsend:

> Know that if you kill me, I being such a man as I say I am, you will not injure me so much as yourselves; for neither Meletus nor Anytus could injure me; that would be impossible, for I believe it is not the gods' will that a better man be injured by a worse. . . . . . .For if you put me to death, you will not easily find another, who, to use a rather absurd figure, attaches himself to the city as a gadfly to a horse, which, though large and well bred, is sluggish on account of his size and needs to be aroused by stinging. I think the god fastened me upon the city in some such capacity, and I go about arousing, and urging and reproaching each one of you, constantly alighting upon you everywhere the whole day long. Such another is not likely to come to you, gentlemen; but if you take my advice, you will spare me. But you, perhaps, might be angry, like people awakened from a nap, and might slap me, as Anytus advises, and easily kill me; then you would pass the rest of your lives in slumber, unless the god, in his care for you, should send someone else to sting you.
>
> (*Apology* 30C–31A Fowler, adapted)

Socrates persuaded nearly half the jury of 501 Athenian citizens; he seems to have lost his case by about thirty votes. Meletus, the principal accuser, had proposed the penalty of death. Athenian procedure called for convicted defendants to recommend an alternative penalty, and it seems clear that Socrates' accusers expected him to propose exile—and would have been quite content to see him leave town. He did no such thing, suggesting first that he receive Athens' highest honors as a reward for his benefactions or, alternatively, a small (but not trivial) fine. Xenophon ascribed this provocative strategy to Socrates' wish to end a satisfying life before the sad realities of old age overtook him; it is also possible that Socrates was testing the jury to see if they understood who he really was and what he really provided to Athens. A number of those who had wanted him acquitted had a change of heart and voted for the death penalty. Socrates was then executed by one of the customary Athenian methods, being ordered to down a poisonous draft of hemlock.

At his trial, if we are to believe Plato, Socrates prophesied that the Athenians would bring great odium on themselves for killing him. He was right. Throughout subsequent history, the execution of Socrates is the most serious charge that has been brought by the critics of Athenian democracy. Socrates' death also made a deep impression on his brightest disciples, young aristocrats like Xenophon and Plato. Xenophon's works were very popular in ancient Rome and during the Renaissance. The dialogues Plato began soon after his teacher's death in which Socrates served as a mouthpiece for his own thinking became the foundation of Western philosophy. In this way the strains occasioned by the Peloponnesian War played a dramatic role in the history of ideas, as an enormous explosion of creativity burst forth in the very city that had gone down to defeat.

The Fourth Century: Changing Ideas, Continuing Warfare

Already in the fifth century BC, Greek thinkers had begun to ask the key questions about the human community that would be explored in new ways in the fourth. What was the purpose of civic life? Were the laws of the polis in accord with nature or in conflict with it? Why were some people free and others not? Were the souls of men and women the same or different? Should Greeks war with other Greeks and enslave them when victorious? To these questions others came to be added. Did the autonomous city-state provide the best way of life? Was warfare worth the sacrifices it entailed? A smaller group debated larger questions—the nature of justice, of piety, of courage, of love. New genres took the place of the old as the search for meaning in life moved forward on different paths: Whereas the painful issues of human existence had been explored during the fifth century in tragedy and history, fourth-century thinkers developed the philosophical dialogue and prose treatise.

While some Greeks were subjecting their traditional values to scrutiny, others perpetuated the squabbles of the fifth century. In many poleis the economic problems arising from the war exacerbated class tensions and sparked bloody civil conflict. The eager involvement of Persia heightened an already chaotic situation. When an extraordinary individual arose to the north in the form of Philip of Macedon, the inability of the Greeks to work together productively had dramatic consequences, and the autonomous polis ceased to be the defining political institution of the Greek world.

The long years of fighting at the end of the fifth century had harmed the economy of many Greek states sufficiently to create a desire for both booty and revenge. The postwar poleis, moreover, showed remarkable resilience; and within less than ten years, the economy had rebounded sufficiently for people to contemplate new undertakings. The hostility of the Greek states soon found a focus, and that focus was Sparta. In 395 Sparta's old allies Corinth and Thebes were so bitter that they actually combined with Athens to attack their old hegemon; neither polis had gotten anything out of the war, and Sparta's proclivity for interfering with domestic governments caused considerable alarm. The war that ensued was known as the **Corinthian War**, as much of the fighting took place in the area of the isthmus. The first consequence of this futile war was the death of Lysander. Soon afterward, the Persian navy, commanded by the satrap Pharnabazus and the Athenian admiral Conon, defeated the Spartans decisively at Cnidus (394 BC) in southwest Asia Minor. When Conon returned victorious to Athens, he joined his fellow citizens in rebuilding the Long Walls, assisted by a large infusion of Persian funds.

In fighting this pointless war, the Greeks deployed not only hoplites and sailors but also a wide variety of lightly armed troops including archers, slingers, and javelin throwers. A particularly useful brand of javelin thrower was the man known as the **peltast**, named for the small, round wicker shield he carried, the Thracian *peltē*. Enjoying a mobility impossible for the more heavily armed hoplites, these troops could be used to forage for supplies, to seize and defend passes, to ambush enemy soldiers, and to ravage hostile territory. They also played key roles in what were basically hoplite confrontations, for harassment at a distance by javelin-throwing peltasts made it difficult for the heavily armed enemy hoplites to retreat. A hardy band of peltasts backing up a hoplite force could easily turn the tide of battle.

As time passed, the Persian king **Artaxerxes** decided his money would be better spent backing the Spartans to keep Athens in check. The combination was too much to fight against, and Athens and its allies were compelled to accept a humiliating peace, the text of which appears in Xenophon's *Hellenica*:

> King Artaxerxes believes it to be just that the cities in Asia should be his, as also the islands Klazomenai and Cyprus, but that the rest of the Greek cities, both small and large, should be autonomous, except for Lemnos, Imbros, and Skyros, which should, as of old, belong to the Athenians. Whichever of the two parties does not accept this peace, I will wage war on them by land and by sea, with ships and money, taking with me those who accept my views.
> (*Hellenika* 5.1.31 Marincola)

The guarantor of the peace was to be Persia's ally Sparta—most ironic in view of the fact that Sparta was getting a well-deserved reputation for meddling in the internal affairs of other states. In the guise of enforcing autonomy, Sparta promptly set about using force to dismantle a variety of existing arrangements. Mantinea, composed of five villages, was compelled to tear down its fortifications and dissolve itself into the five original communities. The Boeotian League was dissolved, and in 382 the Spartans occupied the Theban acropolis and installed a pro-Spartan government. The Spartan government then executed the head of the pro-Athenian faction at Thebes on the grounds of conspiring with Persia. Sparta's record of collaboration with Persia made this turn of events particularly scandalous.

Sparta, Athens, and Thebes

Spartan control of Thebes was short-lived; in 379 Theban democrats staged a coup and, with Athenian assistance, killed the oligarchs and expelled the Spartan garrison. Not long afterward, the Athenians allied with the Thebans for

Figure 9.2a. This beautiful monument, dating to 394 BC, commemorates the death of Dexileus, a cavalryman who died fighting in the Corinthian War, although the relief depicts him as victorious. Athens, Ceramicus, Oberländer Museum.

Figure 9.2b. Today, on the south side of the so-called Street of the Tombs in the Ceramicus cemetery, a cast stands in the original location of the monument of Dexileus.

mutual protection against Sparta. They also moved forward with their plans to establish a new naval confederacy known as the **Second Athenian League**. The establishment of the League was commemorated in a decree that proclaimed that all allies "will remain independent and autonomous, enjoying the form of government they wish, admitting no garrisons or magistrates and paying no tribute." League policy was to be controlled by two bodies of equal weight, the Athenian assembly (*ekklēsia*) and the assembly of the allies (*synedrion*). Although no tribute was specified, a system of *syntaxeis* ("contributions") was set up to finance League operations. Periodic defaults make clear the ambivalence of some League members, but the fact that about half the League's more than seventy members were former members of the Delian League certainly needs to be thrown in with the other evidence concerning the popularity of Athens' earlier experiment in league leadership.

From this point on, the history of Greece involves a dizzying sequence of shifting alliances marked by two notable military victories and outside interventions on the part of eastern potentates such as Mausolus of Caria, technically a Persian satrap but de facto an independent ruler who operated from Halicarnassus (the hometown of Herodotus), where he engaged Greek sculptors to construct the huge tomb for him that has given us our English word **mausoleum**. Mausolus saw the Athenian League as a serious obstacle to his ambitions, and he was quick to encourage any unrest he could detect; it was after receiving promises of Carian backing that Rhodes, Cos, and Chios revolted from Athens.

In mainland Greece, the Spartans and the Thebans met twice on the battlefield, with dramatic results on both occasions. In the 370s Thebes was stronger than ever, led by two intimate friends, **Epaminondas** and **Pelopidas**. Both had been involved in the liberation of Thebes from the Spartans in 379. Pelopidas excelled primarily in generalship, Epaminondas in charismatic political leadership. On the plain of Leuctra, Epaminondas packed his left wing (normally the weaker side of a Greek formation) fully fifty shields deep. He also advanced in an oblique line so as to hold back the center and right wing while overpowering the enemy with the left at the point where he could expect the Spartan king Cleombrotus to be. The cutting edge of the Theban line was provided by the elite corps known as the **Sacred Band**, 150 pairs of select hoplites. Plato was probably thinking of the Sacred Band when he wrote that "in view of their mutual emulation and their fear of dishonoring themselves in front of one another, there could be no better organization for a state or an army than for it to consist entirely of pairs of lovers. A handful of such men, moreover, fighting at each other's sides, could defeat practically the entire world" (*Symposium* 178–179). The Sacred Band and the novel tactics of Epaminondas carried the day, killing nearly half the Spartans present including their king Cleombrotus. The remainder of the Spartan army withdrew, the legend of Spartan supremacy in hoplite warfare forever shattered.

When the Spartans' weakness became apparent to their allies, democratic revolutions broke out in many cities, and a league was formed consisting of Mantinea, Tegea, and the communities of southern and central Arcadia. Arriving in the Peloponnesus to give support to the league, Epaminondas' army was unable to

Figure 9.3. These remains of the walls built by Conon and other Athenians after the Battle of Cnidus in 394 BC are still visible in Piraeus.

take the city of Sparta, but it ravaged Laconia—and succeeded in the liberation of Messenia. Helots were now to be citizens, and the new capital of Messene was founded on Mount Ithome. Epaminondas also founded a new capital for the Arcadian League, Megalopolis. This new foundation became the meeting place for the Council of Fifty that represented the communities of the league in proportion to their population, and of the Assembly of the Ten Thousand, open to all citizens. This development indicated a growing interest in experimenting with thoroughly amicable federations, a new phenomenon in Greece.

Within a few years and with comparatively little loss of life, Thebes under Epaminondas and Pelopidas managed to accomplish what generations of Athenians could not. Sparta was finished as an international power. This did not mean, however, that the Thebans achieved their goals. Pelopidas was killed fighting in Thessaly. Epaminondas' support in the Peloponnesus began to wane, and a number of Arcadian communities allied with Sparta—and Athens—against Thebes. Epaminondas met the alliance on the plain of Mantinea in 362 BC. Deploying the same strategy as at Leuctra and outnumbering the enemy

Figure 9.4. Hypothetical reconstruction of the Mausoleum. Its construction was overseen by Mausolus' widow, Artemisia, after his death (c. 350 BC).

by some ten thousand men, the Thebans were victorious. But Epaminondas himself was killed and with his dying breath counseled his countrymen to make peace.

For all his personal magnetism, Epaminondas seemed to have had no plan for Greece beyond replacing Athenian and Spartan imperialism with Theban imperialism. Ultimately Thebes gained nothing for itself, or for Greece, by its decade of military ascendancy. Although the liberation of Messenia offers great satisfaction to the enemies of slavery in all times and places, by knocking out Sparta as a military power Epaminondas performed a great service to Philip of Macedon, the future conqueror of Greece, something for which not all Greeks would ultimately be grateful. Philip was also the beneficiary of the agitation of Mausolus of Caria, who did much to foment disaffection in the Second Athenian League. Beginning in the mid-350s several key states broke away from the confederation. The sanitized Delian League had not endured more than a generation.

DOCUMENT 9.1

A democratic decree at Eretria, c. 340 BC

Athens was the most powerful democracy in Greece, but there were many other democracies in the Greek world, and a democratic assembly, depending on the power of the council, was able to pass nearly any legislation it wished. Sometimes assembly action could prove imprudent and expensive. One modest example of a democratic assembly decreeing itself into economic difficulties is found at Eretria. In 341, the Eretrians had thrown out the democrat-turned-tyrant Cleitarchus (installed with the support of Philip of Macedon, discussed in Chapter 10) and made an alliance with Athens. When their most prominent festival, the Artemisia, was to be celebrated in 340, the demos passed a decree that would make that year's celebration especially spectacular and, apparently, especially inclusive. This example of a sacred law reveals much more than how a festival was to be executed. It begins in typical fashion, indicating that this decree is the work of the council and the demos.

Gods. Execestus son of Diodorus proposed: in order that we may celebrate the Artemisia as magnificently as possible and that as many people as possible may sacrifice, resolved by the council and the people. The city is to arrange a competition in music with a budget of 1,000 drachmas to the Moderator and Guardian [Artemis] and provide lambs there for five days before the Artemisia, two of them being choice animals.

We see that there is a clear democratic emphasis on the inclusion of as many citizens as possible; the very fact that the demos has made changes to this traditional festival is an assertion of the new political reality of the democracy at Eretria. Later there is a list of the prizes to be awarded:

Prizes are to be given in the following way: to the rhapsode 120 (drachmas), to the second 50, to the third 20; to the boy singer to the pipes 50, to the second 30, to the third 20; to the adult lyre-player 110, to the second 70, to the third 55; to the singer accompanying himself on the lyre 200, to the second 150, to the third 100; to the singer of parodies 50, to the second 10.

A quick check reveals that the prizes in the inscription add up to 1,035 drachmas—already over budget! In addition:

Maintenance is to be granted to the competitors who are present of a drachma a day for each of them, beginning not more than three days before the pre-competition event and continuing until the competition takes place.

The number of competitors is not indicated, perhaps not even known, so this is possibly an expense that will be quite burdensome; it certainly adds to the budget overage. Finally,

Anyone who wants is to sell whatever he wants in the sanctuary, without tax and not paying any duty, and neither are the temple overseers to exact any tax from the sellers.

As was often the case, this religious observance will be exempt from the collection of all taxes. One may be left to wonder where else in the process of the worship of Artemis would the assembly be putting pressure on the savings of the Eretrians!

(nos. 73.1–8, 15–21, 21–24, 32–34, Rhodes and Osborne 2003, adapted)

Law and Democracy in Athens

Whatever its successes or failures abroad, Athens had retained its domestic stability and continued to practice democracy at home interrupted by only two very brief experiments in oligarchy in the later fifth century, each occasioned by the strains of the long war and one of them imposed directly by a foreign power. A key building block of the democracy was the people's courts known as **dicasteries** (*dikastēria*). Athenian society was notoriously litigious, and in the hands of unscrupulous politicians, court cases often became tools of factional strife. Trials of impeached officials—strategoi in particular—were frequently of a political nature, for impeachment at Athens was often used as a forum for a debate on foreign policy. Because decrees proposed in the assembly could be challenged by the graphe paranomon ("indictment for illegal proposals"), it can be argued that in fourth-century Athens the dicasteries rather than the ecclesia were the ultimate arbiters of policy. In the absence of a supreme court or a body of jurisconsults, dicasteries were also the arbiters of law. Courts were also used, of course, in the adjudication of private lawsuits and criminal cases with no political ramifications.

The Functioning of Dicasteries

All male citizens over the age of thirty were eligible to serve on dicasteries, and dicasts (jurors) were chosen each year by lot from those who volunteered. As we saw in Chapter 6, to ensure that the composition of the courts would reflect the voters of Athens, Pericles had instituted pay for jury service. The three obols a day, or half the average wage of a laborer, doubtless attracted the poor, who could not earn three obols another way, as well as comfortably retired older men who enjoyed the opportunity to sit with their fellow citizens in situations that often offered spellbinding entertainment. The number of dicasts allocated to a given case varied usually from 201 to 501 (odd numbers prevented a tie), although a larger body might be used for high-profile trials of a political nature; and some important political trials were held in the assembly itself. Large juries were designed in part to involve large numbers of citizens in decision making, in part to discourage bribery. Further obstacles to bribery included an elaborate mechanism to select juries by lot and the custom of choosing them at the last possible moment before the trial. Small plaques, each inscribed with a dicast's name, were inserted into a *klērotērion*, an allotment device that distributed the names haphazardly among the daily juries. Voting was by secret ballot. Each dicast was given two pebbles or bronze discs, one of which had a hole punched through it; a herald would proclaim that "the pebble with the hole is a vote for the prosecutor, and the whole pebble a vote for the defendant." To cast his vote the dicast would throw the one he wanted to be counted into a copper receptacle and discard the other pebble into the wooden one.

As the case of Socrates reveals, the dicasts also determined the penalty. Precedents were not binding, so each jury was sovereign and its decision final. There could be no appeal to a higher court, for an Athenian dicastery was both the highest court and the people. Consequently, dicasts functioned as judges as well as jurors.

Conduct of Cases

The conduct of cases differed from that in modern Western courts in that the Greeks relied heavily on the testimony of witnesses not only as to the facts but also as to the character of the defendant. It was customary for witnesses to testify to the virtues of the accused and the public services he had performed—or to the calamities his family would experience if he were convicted. Rules of time were stringently observed; minutes were measured out by a *klepsydra*, or water clock. Rules of evidence, however, were few, and defendants themselves were not discouraged from speechifying about their past services to the polis or from parading their vulnerable children before the jury. Even after the advent of writing, Greeks remained somewhat suspicious of texts, and jurors usually trusted the testimony given by witnesses under oath more than written evidence; they understood that a document such as a will could be forged. Slaves were often the only witnesses, for they were ubiquitous and often obliged to assist their owners in illicit activities. Theoretically, the testimony of slaves was admissible only if it had been given under torture, but we are uncertain how often such torture was actually inflicted. Following a guilty verdict, prosecutor and defendant proposed alternate penalties, as in the case of Socrates, and the jury decided between the two. The principle of self-help also meant that in private, or civil, cases, the prosecutor had to execute the judgment himself. When the orator Demosthenes succeeded in convincing a jury that his guardians had dissipated the fortune his father had left, it was his own responsibility to try to collect the missing funds and property.

Prosecutors and defendants understandably sought to present their cases as effectively as possible. One way to do so was to hire a professional speechwriter trained in the new art of rhetoric to write their speeches. A good example is a speech written in 419 for a man known to us only as the Chorus trainer, who was tried for murder when one of the boys in the chorus he had agreed to prepare for a festival died unexpectedly. We know about this case from a speech written on behalf of the Chorus trainer by Antiphon, an oligarchic politician who was eventually put to death by the democracy (after a speech at his trial that Thucydides pronounced the best he had ever heard. Thucydides must have read it, not heard it, because he was in exile at the time.)

The Choregus, as he was known in Greek, had accepted the liturgy of preparing a chorus of boys to perform at the festival of the Thargelia. He had incurred the hostility of some of his fellow Athenians, however, by trying to impeach a government official who, in conjunction with three private citizens, was embezzling from the state. The case was to be heard in late April. Just a few days before the court date, however, a certain Diodotus, one of the boys in the chorus, was given some kind of special drink to improve his voice. It did not in fact improve his voice. Instead, it killed him.

The news of Diodotus' demise was music to the ears of four men about to be tried on the Choregus' accusation, and they pressured the boy's brother Philocrates to lose no time in entering a charge of homicide against the Choregus. That way he would be precluded from appearing in public places until his case had been tried.

Figure 9.5. This surviving fragment of a kleroterion, or allotment device that assigned jurors to dicasteries, enables us to envision the way it must have functioned. Athens, Agora Museum.

Figure 9.6. Modern model of a klepsydra or water clock. In this device, which was used to time speeches in the law courts, water drained from the upper vessel to the lower one. It took several minutes for a vessel to empty. Ten vessels were allocated for cases involving large sums of money.

So much for the impeachment. Unfortunately, the four had overlooked certain fine points of Athenian law that prescribed a three-month inquiry preceding the trial, an inquiry that had to be conducted by the Archon Basileus, who was going to be leaving his office in only two months. Consequently the Archon Basileus refused to become involved in the case.

The trial of the embezzlers, then, proceeded, and at it they were convicted and heavily fined. Philocrates, brother of the dead Diodotus, apologized to the Choregus (for trying to have him convicted of murder!), and somehow the two men reconciled. A month later, however, the Choregus became a member of the Council of 500, to which by Athenian law he had been selected by lot. No sooner did he take office than it came to his attention that not only were no fewer than three boards of financial officers involved in further embezzlement, but that a number of private citizens were also profiting from the malfeasance—including Philocrates.

Once again, the Choregus brought charges of impeachment, and once again the embezzlers were convicted, but not before Philocrates had lodged a retaliatory charge of homicide against the Choregus. On this occasion the accusation was made in time, and the Choregus was brought to trial in November. The verdict in the case is unknown.

Crime and Punishment

Controlling crime was a very different affair in classical Athens from what it is in modern cities. There was for all practical purposes no law enforcement agency. The Scythian archers the state engaged as "police" were in fact used primarily for crowd control. If you were hauled into court and charged with a crime, it was because one of your fellow citizens had dragged you there.

Athenian ideas about what penalties were called for by various crimes also differed from those of most people today. Abandoning a helpless newborn to its fate was not a crime at all but rather an acceptable means of family planning or avoiding embarrassment. Killing a slave was illegal, but if the slave you killed was your own, there was nobody who had the legal standing to take you to court because the slave's relatives would not be citizens; ritual purification would probably be called for to purge you of blood guilt, but nothing beyond that. Whipping and torture were acceptable punishments for slaves but not for citizens, at least not after the fifth century. Citizen defendants were sometimes slapped with manageable fines, but it was not unusual for Athenian juries to vote for exile, the confiscation of property, the termination of civic rights (such as making proposals in the assembly), truly crippling fines, or death. Crimes that would be considered misdemeanors today could be punishable by death in Athens; we read of a man executed for stealing clothes. Surviving texts claim that the death penalty was mandated in a wide variety of cases ranging from citing a nonexistent law to failing to inscribe the name of a man in debt to the state on the official list. Socrates was put to death for his teachings in 399, Menon the miller was executed for keeping a free boy in his mill, and one Euthymachus was executed for putting a free girl from the town of Olynthus in northern Greece in a brothel. These last two cases illustrate the Athenians' determination to uphold the distinction between slave and free: Menon and Euthymachus had treated free people as one would treat a slave. Although many Athenians were in fact executed, self-imposed exile was considered entirely acceptable; and indeed, after the first speeches had been delivered at a homicide trial, the accused was free to leave town rather than wait to see how the trial turned out. Even the decision not to turn up for one's court date in the first place was honored, and extradition was not generally practiced.

In a society that relied to a considerable extent on self-help, unofficial executions were not unusual; a man who caught you in his house at night, or in a compromising situation in his house with his wife at any hour of the day, was entitled to kill you on the spot. The Athenians saw no point in paying people to build and oversee large jails, so imprisonment was not a common punishment. People who spent time in jail did so only if they were unable to post bail prior to their trial, if they were unable to pay a fine levied against them, or if they had been condemned to death and there was some unusual reason not to execute immediately.

The officials in charge of executions were known simply as the Eleven. Like most other Athenian officials, they were chosen by lot. The methods used to execute criminals varied over the course of Athenian history. There is some evidence that prior to the fourth century those destined for execution may have been hurled into a pit known as the *barathron*, but it may be that the barathron was used simply as a depository for the bodies of the executed. At some point a gruesome means of execution known as *apotympanismos* came into use. We are not certain exactly how this worked, but it was highly unpleasant, guaranteeing a prolonged and wretched death. It involved wooden boards and iron collars. It was similar, in other words, to crucifixion, but without the nails. This nicety is probably due to the Athenians' aversion to shedding the blood of their fellow citizens. In wartime, enemies, even civilians, were regularly killed by the sword, but the blood of fellow citizens was considered to be polluting. Archaeologists have found a mass grave near Athens containing seventeen skeletons with iron collars around the necks, wrists, and ankles and attached to pieces of wood. Probably such people had been sentenced to death by apotympanismos. Finally, hemlock came to be used, as in the case of Socrates, although apotympanismos may well have remained in use as well. It is widely recognized that the peaceful death portrayed by Plato in his dialogue *Crito* is a literary fiction designed to maximize Socrates' dignity: Although death by hemlock was not as degrading as death by apotympanismos, it does not, as Plato implied, simply create a chilly numbness followed by a peaceful passing. Hemlock causes miserable convulsions before death finally comes.

Murder and the Courts

The earliest known laws in Athens and those that remained unchanged for the longest time concerned homicide. Because the Greeks believed that murder offended the gods, there were religious sanctions against homicide, and anyone who killed another person outside of wartime was considered polluted. At the same time a pressing religious and social obligation lay on the male next of kin to avenge a death by killing the perpetrator, even if an act of homicide had been involuntary, say, as the result of a hunting accident. In accordance with basic principles of vendettas that operate across many societies, therefore, one homicide could evolve into an unending series of retaliations. The Athenians claimed to have founded the first law court in the world when Agamemnon's son Orestes came to Athens from Argos seeking absolution for the murder of his mother, whom he had killed to avenge his slain father. The Bronze Age myth that Aeschylus had fleshed out in his *Oresteia* had offered the playwright an opportunity to explain how law had come to replace family feud in just such a case. The court of the Areopagus in Athens adjudicated the case, marking the historic transfer of jurisdiction from the family to the state.

A personal element, however, remained, for accusations of homicide had to be brought by family members. Thus, although the murder of a slave by his or her master might be illegal, prosecution was unlikely in the absence of a citizen relative who could bring charges. Throughout Athenian history, self-help remained a central principle in law. (It also extended to helping friends and relations in a wide variety of instances. Citizens were expected to show both friendship and civic-mindedness by bringing cases on behalf of others who were wronged, such as orphans or girls of marriageable age without dowries.)

Besides the Areopagus there were four additional venues for murder trials. The court of the Palladion was used for unpremeditated killings, the Delphinion for justifiable ones (i.e., homicides committed in self-defense or by a man who discovered someone in the very act of having intercourse with his wife, mother, sister, or daughter). The Prytaneion handled cases of unidentified murderers and cases in which an animal or an object such as a falling roof tile had caused a death. Finally, those who were already sentenced to exile for homicide and were on trial for an additional murder had to plead their cases on a boat off the coast of Phreatto to avoid polluting the land of Attica.

The Athenian Democracy in the Fourth Century

The survival of so many speeches and inscriptions from the fourth century enables us to see Athenian democracy in action more vividly in this period than was possible for the fifth century. In some ways the democracy changed after the restoration of 403, particularly in the constitution of various ad hoc boards of *nomothetai* ("creators of laws") to approve and review legislation. The fundamental principles, however, remained the same. All free adult males had a theoretically equal right to participate in government regardless of differential prestige and economic standing. Women and slaves were excluded, and it was difficult for resident aliens or their children to become citizens. Only men with two citizen parents could vote. Wealth and illustrious ancestry were distinct advantages in seeking public office or pleading your case in court. Boasting of your services to the state was a good strategy if you needed to defend yourself in court. Although Solon's four classes were never formally abolished, it is clear that at least by the middle of the fourth century, public offices were open to men of all groups. Many thetes and zeugitai were selected for offices chosen by lot, such as service on the boule. Thus participation in government was widely diffused throughout the community of citizen males.

Jokes in Aristophanes' plays reveal a change in the dynamics of assembly attendance. The *Acharnians* (425 BC) alludes to the habit of roping citizens in with a cord covered with red paint that would smear the clothes of the recalcitrant; but when male actors playing women dressed as men pack the assembly in the *Ecclesiazusae* (392 BC) until a quorum is reached, the real men of Athens complain that they arrived too late to get their pay. The carrot replaced the stick shortly before 400, when a small salary was instituted for attendance at the assembly. By Aristotle's time, it had gone from one obol to a drachma (six obols) for an ordinary assembly and a drachma and a half for the *kyria ekklēsia*, that is, the principal assembly of a prytany. At the level of assembly attendance, then, the government of the fourth century was somewhat more democratic than the fifth, for a higher number could afford to take time away from work, although it remained the case that attending meetings was easier for those who lived close by and those who worked for themselves. Another democratic element was the large number of political issues ultimately decided in the courts, as when an official or citizen was charged with proposing an unconstitutional law via a *graphē paranomon*.

As in the courts, where even criminal cases depended on volunteer prosecutors to set them in motion, the voluntary principle played a key role in the assembly. In the absence of organized political parties, concerned citizens took it on themselves to initiate legislation. No well-defined group of officeholders saw itself—or was seen by others—as clearly marked off from the rest of the populace. By "politicians," people simply meant those who most enjoyed making proposals in the assembly and giving speeches in their support. The importance of oratory and debate to the functioning of the democratic system is attested to in the Greek word that comes closest to our word "politician": *rhētōr*. Because rhetores shared common interests and habits, no doubt people were comfortable identifying a particular citizen they might see walking down the street as "one of the rhetores," but it is important to remember that there was no official "board of rhetores" to which such men belonged. Today it would be peculiar to identify someone who did not hold public office as a politician, but the Athenians saw nothing strange about it. It was precisely because of the power private citizens could gain through skillful oratory that the Athenians made sure to have the graphe paranomon on the books to ensure the accountability even of those who took part in public affairs without holding office. Those convicted of proposing something illegal were generally fined; three convictions deprived a citizen of the right to make further proposals.

THE FOURTH-CENTURY POLIS

Although the bulk of our evidence comes from Athens, most Greeks, of course, lived in other city-states. In the fourth century as in the fifth, some Greek poleis were governed by democracies, others by oligarchies that varied in their narrowness. As had always been the case in Greece, uneven distribution of wealth fostered ever-present tensions that threatened constantly to erupt and disturb the tenuous concord that united citizens, and changes of constitution were frequent. Although warfare remained a fact of life, many people had come to question its efficacy in improving their situations. Whereas some poorer citizens continued to welcome war for the pay it offered to rowers in the fleet, those who had land or commerce to protect were hesitant. The ideal of the citizen-soldier was wearing thin, and an increasing share of the fighting was conducted by mercenaries from outside. Agriculture remained the basis of the economy, but the devastation of the land during the Peloponnesian War had fostered a drift to the cities. By throwing people together, this development heightened the awareness of economic inequality and sharpened class bitterness. Plato and his pupil Aristotle both took it for granted that a polis consisted in reality of two cities, one of the many poor and one of the few rich. The division of citizens into haves and have-nots that had always marked Greek states was exacerbated in the fourth century by the increased poverty of the have-nots, bringing latent tensions to the surface.

Stasis

When civil strife erupted, bloodshed was common, and religious pieties were often ignored. In 392, Corinthian democrats violated the sanctity of temples by murdering oligarchs who had taken refuge there. Diodorus reports revolutions in Argos, Corinth, Sicyon, and Phlius; and Xenophon recorded serious tensions in Tegea, Phlius, Sicyon, Pellene, and Elis. Diodorus, who shared the antidemocratic orientation of most ancient writers, took a certain satisfaction in relating the torture and murder of the elite by Argive democrats in 371, when class tensions erupted with violence exceptional even by Greek standards. After the execution of twelve hundred influential men, Diodorus contends,

> the populace did not spare the demagogues themselves. Because of the magnitude of the calamity, the demagogues were afraid that some unforeseen turn of fortune might overtake them and therefore desisted from their accusation, whereas the mob, now thinking that they had been left in the lurch by them, were angry at this and put to death all the demagogues. So these men received the punishment which fitted their crimes as if some divinity were visiting its just resentment upon them, and the people, eased of their mad rage, were restored to their senses.
>
> (*Library of History* 15.58.4 Sherman, adapted)

Beginning late in the fifth century, Greek intellectuals had begun calling for *homonoia* ("concord") among citizens, but the frequency with which the appeal was made reveals the discordant reality: In fact the slogan caught on during the contentious days of the Peloponnesian War. In praising the rule of law, Socrates had insisted in the pages of Xenophon's *Memorabilia* that throughout Greece homonoia was advocated by the "best men" (the aristoi). Aristotle, however, took a darker and more realistic view. In some states of his own day, he wrote in the *Politics*, the oligarchs in charge take an oath to be hostile to the demos and "plot whatever evil possible against the people" (1310a).

Not all poleis were constantly torn apart by stasis and debilitated by interpolis wars. Because the principal cause of internal weakness and vulnerability to outside attack was the frustrations of the poor, prosperity might act as a powerful deterrent. Megara with its brisk woolen trade flourished throughout the fourth century, and civil strife was rare. The progress of the economy was facilitated by peace with other poleis: The alliance between Corinth and Athens during the Corinthian War eliminated Megara's pivotal position in interpolis diplomacy, and the Megarians seem to have preserved their neutrality throughout that war. Megarian woolens found eager markets throughout Greece. Sheep grazed in abundance, and large numbers of slaves, probably mostly female, turned out well-made and inexpensive garments. The private homes of Megara were known for their elegance, and a variety of monuments decorated the city. The Athenian sculptor Praxiteles (370–329 BC) produced numerous statues of the gods for the sanctuaries of Artemis and Apollo and the temple of Aphrodite. Scopas, who contributed to the Mausoleum in Caria, also worked in Megara. Exactly what kind of government fourth-century Megara enjoyed is uncertain—Plato praised it but did not describe it—but it seems at least to have been fairly stable. Megara was not, however, entirely immune to the endemic stasis of the fourth century, for Diodorus reports an abortive uprising in the 370s.

Marginalized Workers in the Economy

The economy of each polis was different, but throughout Greece prestige attached to some kinds of work more than to others. Because social prejudices favored self-sufficiency through farming, or making money by selling the produce of one's land, free citizens tended to avoid involvement in commerce and banking, turning over these activities to metics and slaves. Such workers became important in the fourth century and often made considerable fortunes, for one phenomenon that distinguished the polis of the fourth century from that of the fifth was the rise of banking.

Bank owners trusted slaves to manage the daily operations of banks independently and even to travel with large sums of cash. Such slaves were highly skilled, usually literate, and very valuable. A slave who managed a bank could be completely responsible for his master's property. Therefore, a master might write a will freeing his bank manager on condition that he marry his widow and manage his bank in behalf of his minor children. Manumitted slaves became metics. Some of these metics, including a certain Pasio and Phormio, were among the wealthiest Athenians of the fourth century. In gratitude for their generous benefactions to the state, Athens rewarded them and their descendants with citizenship, making it possible for them to own land in Attica. Thus slaves in banking might experience rapid social mobility.

The stigma that attached to working for someone else was greater for women than for men; few women chose to work for wages outside the home unless compelled to do so by poverty. In the fourth century as in the fifth, however, some poor women worked outside their homes. Slave women were sometimes rented out by their owners; and former slaves, metics, and even citizen women in difficult financial circumstances worked at a variety of jobs. Some hired themselves out as nurses for other women's children, some sold goods in the marketplace, and older women often served as hired mourners at funerals. Although unacceptable for citizen women, prostitution was probably the work done most frequently by women outside the home. Some were put to work when they were still children. In Corinth, Nicarete, a former slave, purchased young girls from slaveholders and trained them for their work:

> Nicarete, who was the freedwoman of Charisius of Elis and the wife of his cook Hippias, bought seven girls when they were small children. She was an astute judge of natural beauty in little girls and furthermore she understood how to bring them up and train them skillfully, for she made this her profession and got her livelihood from the girls. She used to address them as daughters, implying that they were free women, so that she might extract the largest fees from those who wished to get close to them. When she had reaped the profit of the youthful prime of each, she sold all seven of them: Anteia, Stratola, Aristocleia, Metaneira, Phila, Isthmias, and this **Neaera** here . . . . . .
>   Neaera . . . . . . was working with her body, although she was still very young, for she had not yet reached puberty.
>   (*Pseudo-Demosthenes* 59.18–20 Murray)

Neaera's further adventures are also detailed in this speech, which is included in the corpus of Demosthenes although it was written by someone else. Two of Neaera's clients purchased her from Nicarete to be their slave. But when these men were about to marry, they offered Neaera the opportunity to buy her freedom. Neaera borrowed her purchase price from former clients, and repaid them from her earnings as a free prostitute. Her attempt at social mobility was quashed, however, when she moved to Athens, married a certain Stephanus, and pretended to be an Athenian citizen. Apollodorus, the son of the former slave Pasion and an enemy of Stephanus (who had brought against him one indictment for an illegal proposal and another for murder), brought her to trial for false assumption of citizen rights. He also charged Stephanus with living with a non-Athenian woman as though she were his wife, and with giving Neaera's daughter in marriage to an Athenian citizen as being his own daughter born from a citizen woman. Although the speech written for Apollodorus makes fascinating reading, Neaera's fate remains uncertain: The outcome of the trial is unknown.

PHILOSOPHY AND THE POLIS

The changing political situation in the Greek world helped shape Greek thought in each new generation, and the problems of the fourth-century polis were no exception. Philosophy evolved with the polis and survived it when Philip of Macedon brought the freedom of the independent city-states to an end in 338 BC. The Greek word *philosophos* means "a lover of wisdom," and for many years before Plato and Aristotle founded their famous schools in Athens, Greek thinkers had taken delight in searching for the underlying principles that shaped the cosmos and determined the life humans made in it. Democritus contended that he would "rather find the explanation for a single phenomenon than gain the kingdom of Persia." The truly prosperous man, Empedocles said, is one who enjoys the riches of a divine intelligence. Philosophers came in many shapes. Thinkers like Thales and Anaximander focused on the natural world. Others like Herodotus and Thucydides used the writing of history as a vehicle for their ideas about the human condition, and still others expressed them through dramas as did Aeschylus, Sophocles, and Euripides. In time, Xenophon and Plato would write dialogues and Aristotle treatises. These innovative thinkers explored the areas that still make up philosophy today—ethics, logic, epistemology (the philosophy of knowledge), metaphysics (the science of being), aesthetics, theology, philosophy of science, and social and political theory.

It was in the realm of social and political theory that philosophy was most closely tied to the polis. Because most surviving texts of political theory were composed in democratic Athens, one might imagine that they praised democracy. In fact, the opposite is true: The principal texts of Greek political theory were the work of intellectuals who were intensely critical of democratic government. Indeed, modern political scientists have observed that political theory—literally, "looking at the city-state"—was invented to show why democracy could not possibly work. It is the workings of democracy itself that reveal the ideology behind it.

Democracy and Political Theory

The anonymous satirist we call the Old Oligarch had portrayed Athenian democracy as a beautifully efficient way of guaranteeing the suppression of one class by another, but no surviving text treats the dynamics of democracy in a positive way. Reconstructing the theory behind democracy from written texts requires assembling patches from a variety of sources that engage the issue only obliquely. Thucydides' version of Pericles' funeral oration gives us a sense of what the Athenians at any rate prized in their government. At Athens, Pericles says, worth is assessed in terms of ability, not wealth or class. Athenians consider remaining aloof from politics a vice, not a virtue. They view debate as an aid to constructive action, not a hindrance.

Just as Thucydides, who was not particularly sympathetic to democracy, included Pericles' speech in his history, so Plato, one of democracy's sharpest critics, included a statement of democratic ideology in his dialogue *Protagoras*. There the famous sophist tells a quaint myth in support of his thesis that all people possess the rudiments of civic-mindedness. In earliest times, Protagoras says, people were unable to live together constructively in cities because of their lack of *politikē technē*, the skill of forming and managing a polis. Seeing this and fearing the destruction of the species, Zeus sent Hermes to bring *aidōs* ("shame") and *dikē* ("justice") to mortals. When Hermes asked Zeus whether these should be distributed to a select few, as was the case with the arts of medicine and other techniques, or to everyone, Zeus ordered him to give some to everybody, as "cities cannot be formed if only a few share in these skills as they do in the other arts" (322D). It is for this reason, Protagoras says, that when the Athenians come together to make decisions that require the sense of justice on which political wisdom depends, "they take advice from everybody, since it is held that for states to exist everyone must partake of this excellence" (322E–323E).

Further clues are provided in the dozens of orations surviving from the fourth century, which praise freedom of speech, liberty, equality before the law, and the rule of law. Our best clue to the theory of democracy, however, is its practice. The Athenian democracy itself reveals what most men in Athens believed about government: They believed in a democracy of male citizens that required active participation on the part of these citizens, guaranteed by frequent rotation in office, and they believed that the average free man was qualified to make political decisions, as evidenced by the use of the lot and the taking of important decisions in the assembly by majority vote. They believed in trial by jury, and they feared the corruption that inhered in small groups more than the mob psychology that threatened large ones. They believed that the people had the right to call its officials to account with regularity and on the slightest pretext. They believed that the stability of the state was so crucial that it was reasonable to exile a man for ten years under the system known as ostracism even if he had done nothing to break the law. They believed in slavery and patriarchy. They believed that the control of women's sexuality was essential to the smooth functioning of the community and that the sequestration of women and girls was a good step in this direction. We know all this not because they wrote it down, but because of how they chose to run their government and live their lives.

We know also that Greeks who did not live under democratic governments believed in the rule of law, which appears as a persistent leitmotiv in the literature of the fifth and fourth centuries. Its prominence begins with the efforts of Herodotus and Aeschylus to define and celebrate what it means to be Greek; for them, living under law played a key role in shaping that identity, and Herodotus stressed the Spartans' reverence for law. Euripides, however, connected law with democracy in his *Suppliants*, where he defined Athens even under Theseus as a place where

> Our city is not subject to one man.
> No, it is free, for here the people rule.
> (404–406)

Under a tyranny, one man governs, keeping the law in his private hands, and there is no equality:

> But when the laws are written down, the weak
> Enjoy the same protection as the rich.
> (434–435)

Although many Athenians identified their democratic constitution with the rule of law, Greek intellectuals sometimes saw things differently. Plato frequently identified democracy with tyranny, and his pupil Aristotle complained that the decrees of a democratic assembly were no different from the edicts of the tyrant.

Plato

It is certainly a tribute to Athenian democracy that it produced its own most astute critics. An aristocrat from one of Athens' most distinguished families and a relative of the oligarch Critias, Plato became a disciple of Socrates and was profoundly shaken by his death. The loss of his mentor, however, only heightened his creative powers. Over his lifetime, Plato composed numerous dialogues, in most of which the principal part is played by a character he identifies as Socrates. What is beauty? What is piety? What is justice? What is love? These questions were explored in Plato's Socratic dialogues. As Plato's thinking evolved with the passing of time, this "Socrates" had less and less in common with the historical Socrates and came to serve as a vehicle for Plato's own ideas.

Chief among these was the **theory of Forms**. Plato's belief in Forms was connected to his passion for definitions, for both depend on a conviction that seemingly disparate acts and items can nonetheless be classified in categories—that beautiful objects and acts and ideas, for example, all have something in common. In Plato's view, they all partake of the ideal Form of beauty. A beautiful sunset might seem different from a beautiful mathematical proof or a beautiful young athlete, but in fact what ties them together is more enduring than what sets them apart.

The relationship of appearance to reality in Plato's worldview can perhaps be best grasped in the context of mathematics. A ring or a princely diadem or the perimeter of a hoplite shield might seem to the casual observer to be circles, but they are not circles in the same sense that the locus of all points in a given plane equidistant from a given point is a circle. They only look like circles; if you were to put them under a magnifying glass, you would see that they were not circles at all, merely objects vaguely circular in appearance precisely because they bring to mind the Form of the circle. Only the circle depicted in the mathematical definition is a circle. Some people might say that these concrete objects are real circles and the geometrical concept is imaginary, but Plato was not one of these people. For Plato, only the concept is real. The tangible objects are debased copies, feeble imitations of the ideal Form. Plato, in other words, was an idealist and a dualist. He believed in an opposition between the physical world of appearances, which are deceptive, and the intellectual universe of ideas, which represent reality. The first is tawdry and serves only to distract people from ultimate truth; the second is noble, and to contemplate it ennobling.

In many ways Plato was a revolutionary. The close connection between appearance and reality was fundamental to Greek civilization. If you are rich and handsome, most of his contemporaries believed, then probably you are also good; if you are poor and ugly, presumably you are bad as well. If everyone admires you, then all is right with the world; if you are despised, then you have no reason to go on. For most Greek men, reputation, power, and material success were central to happiness. Like Socrates before him, who preferred being right to being alive,

Plato identified values that were more important than being well liked or envied. In his dialogue on government and education, *The Republic*, he raised a key question about justice. Let us say, he proposed, that you had a magic ring that would make you invisible. Would you practice justice, or would you take the opportunity to grab as much power and wealth as you could, practicing injustice in the happy expectation of getting away with it?

As usual, Plato does not appear in this dialogue. His brothers Glaucon and Adeimantus, however, do; and they are quick to point out the customary Greek view that only convention, nomos, holds people back from committing injustice. The behavior that the man-made nomoi of punishment and disgrace discourage, however, is encouraged by physis, the natural instinct that urges people to take whatever they can get away with taking. This was the drive that Thucydides' Athenians at Melos had identified as the customary engine of human conduct: People, they had argued, "are always forced by the law of nature to dominate everyone they can" (Thuc. 5.105). This sort of thing, Glaucon and Adeimantus say, is what the average person believes. It is up to Socrates to show that justice is in fact good for people.

This is a large task, and Socrates decides to shift gears and explore justice in the state to discover justice in the individual writ large: The state will serve as a model for the study of the soul. In the course of this exploration, he spins out threads that are even more revolutionary. The subject of the dialogue becomes an ideal state of Plato's imagining. It is a state divided into three classes, corresponding to Plato's conception of the tripartite nature of the soul. At the top are the guardians, who represent reason. Their supreme rationality, inculcated by years of education, qualifies them to govern. After them come the auxiliaries, who are characterized by a spirited temperament that suits them for the duties of soldiers. Last come the majority, who correspond to desire in the soul: They are not especially bright or brave and live only to satisfy their own material yearnings and to perform the menial tasks the state requires for subsistence.

The education and lives of the guardians soon become the focus of Plato's attention. They will study for many years, approaching the understanding of the Forms by applying themselves to mathematics. Surprisingly, the guardians will be of both genders, and Plato advocates a unisex education for them.

DOCUMENT 9.2

Socrates on the guardians

Although on the whole, Socrates argues, women are inferior to men in all skills besides weaving and cooking, nonetheless there will always be individual women who are more skilled than individual men. When Glaucon agrees, Socrates launches into his plan for having guardians of both sexes (although he always speaks of guardians and their wives, never guardians and their husbands).

SOC.   To conclude, then, there is no occupation concerned with the management of social affairs which belongs either to woman or to man, as such. Natural gifts are to be found here and there in both creatures alike; and every occupation is open to both, so far as their natures are concerned, though woman is for all purposes the weaker.

GLAU.   Certainly.

SOC.   Is that a reason for making over all occupations to men only?

GLAU.   Of course not.

SOC.   No, because one woman may have a natural gift for medicine or for music, another may not.

GLAU.   Surely.

SOC.   Is it not also true that a woman may, or may not, be warlike or athletic?

GLAU.   I think so.

SOC.   And again, one may love knowledge, another hate it; one may be high-spirited, another spiritless?

GLAU.   True again.

SOC.   It follows that one woman will be fitted by nature to be a Guardian, another will not; because these were the qualities for which we selected our men Guardians. So for the purpose of keeping watch over the commonwealth, woman has the same nature as man, save in so far as she is weaker.

GLAU.   So it appears.

SOC.   It follows that women of this type must be selected to share the life and duties of Guardians with men of the same type, since they are competent and of a like nature, and the same natures must be allowed the same pursuits.

GLAU.   Yes.

SOC.   We come round, then, to our former position, that there is nothing contrary to nature in giving our Guardians' wives the same training for mind and body. The practice we proposed to establish was not impossible or visionary, since it was in accordance with nature. Rather, the contrary practice which now prevails turns out to be unnatural.

GLAU.   So it appears.

SOC.   Well, we set out to inquire whether the plan we proposed was feasible and also the best. That it is feasible is now agreed; we must next settle whether it is the best.

GLAU.   Obviously.

SOC.   Now, for the purpose of producing a woman fit to be a Guardian, we shall not have one education for men and another for women, precisely because the nature to be taken in hand is the same.

GLAU.   True.

(The Republic 455 Cornford)

The guardians' lives will be unusual in many respects. The acquisitive principle that guides most people's activities will be alien to them, for Plato envisions a communistic regime within the guardian class; private property, although it exists for the other two classes, will be abolished for the top group. Nor will they have spouses in the conventional sense of the word. In short, they will have no oikoi—something that makes them eminently un-Athenian. They will not live in households, but the guardians must reproduce to perpetuate the system. An elaborate mathematical scheme will dictate temporary couplings. (Plato was deeply influenced by the Pythagoreans, and he found in mathematics not only the embodiment of perfect abstraction but elements of mysticism as well.) Once born of these short-term "marriages," however, children will be mixed in with all the other children conceived around the same time and raised in common nurseries. Thus, no parent will know his or her own child and vice versa.

Like other utopias, Plato's is designed to demonstrate the shortcomings of real states. Whether he ever planned or even wished to see his Republic established is uncertain. What is clear is his dislike of the existing governments in Greece, and particularly of democracy. Tyranny and oligarchy are easiest to dismiss; nobody should have to live by the whims of a power-hungry autocrat, and money is no measure of merit. Democracy is harder to dispose of, but living under a government he did not like galvanized Plato into a vehement attack on a system he categorized as "an agreeable form of anarchy" marked by "an equality of a peculiar kind for equals and unequals alike" (558C Cornford). The debunking of the so-called equality of democracy was common to the thinking of fourth-century intellectuals. Aristotle and Isocrates shared Plato's preference for what they labeled "proportional" or "geometric" equality. It was the ratio between merit and privilege, they argued, that should remain constant. Such a system was far more equitable, they believed, than the "arithmetic" equality of democracy that accorded equal privilege to people of unequal merit. For Plato, giving equal political power to all alike was no different from giving all students the same grade regardless of their performance on papers and exams.

Good government, Plato concluded, will never come into being until philosophers and rulers are one and the same. Hoping to realize this goal in an immediate and concrete manner, he accepted an invitation to travel to Sicily, where he sought to educate the tyrant of Syracuse Dionysius II in philosophy; but Dionysius was already a mature adult, and the experiment was a complete failure. Closer to home, Plato founded a school in Athens that he called the **Academy** because of its location by the groves of the ancient Greek hero Academus. There men and a few women studied for years to achieve an enlightenment that, in Plato's view, would qualify them to participate in government—but that he acknowledged would in fact drive a wedge between them and their unenlightened fellow citizens. Former students at the Academy included not only many famous philosophers, astronomers, mathematicians, and even scientists, but also politicians such as Plato's friend Dion, who overthrew Dionysius II, and Demetrius of Phaleron, the future tyrant of Athens. The presence of scientists at the Academy is a testimony to its breadth, for Plato himself was not drawn to science. How could he be, when he believed that only the eternal mattered—that the forms were the ultimate and only reality? Science deals with change and with motion. Like Parmenides, Plato conceived reality as unchanging and unchangeable. Without a mechanism for explaining change, Plato's idealist philosophy was antithetical to science.

Aristotle

It was Plato's star pupil **Aristotle** who founded the great institution of scientific learning at Athens, the **Lyceum**. His father had been a court physician in Macedon, and he had been trained in scientific observation from his youth. He was never happier than in the meticulous observation and classification of species. Scholars in all disciplines, but especially perhaps biologists, will recognize the delight he took in connecting the particular to the general, and in observing nature at work in all its perfection: Even of the animals that are not attractive to the senses, he wrote, "the craftsmanship of nature provides extraordinary pleasures to those who are able to recognize the causes in things and who have a natural inclination to philosophy" (*On the Parts of Animals* 645a9–10). Certainly Aristotle thrived in the constantly changing world of nature, whereas Plato was happiest contemplating the eternal truths of mathematics. For Aristotle, the dynamic power of change accounted for a great deal of the excitement of mental life. And not only this: It was movement toward a particular end—teleology, from the Greek *telos* meaning "end" or "goal"—that he saw as the guiding force behind life. A prime mover, he argued, shaped the universe in accord with his ends. Only the prime mover was not itself moved. Loosely speaking, the prime mover was what most people would call God. Aristotle's philosophy was very popular in Europe during the Middle Ages, when Thomas Aquinas (AD 1225–1274) adapted it to Christian theology.

Aristotle was a less eccentric person than Plato. Although he came from the Ionian city of Stagiros in northern Greece and hence did not belong in Athens the same way the blue-blooded Plato did, he was more firmly grounded in the customary relations of Greek society than Plato, who apparently never married or had children. He lived with two successive women, his wife Pythias and then, after Pythias' death, his concubine Herpyllis; he had a daughter and a son. After Plato's death in 347, when Aristotle had studied at the Academy for nearly twenty years, he left Athens and took up residence in Assos in Asia Minor. Several years later he returned to Macedon, where Philip had summoned him to serve as tutor to the young prince Alexander. It was on his return to Athens in 335 that he established the Lyceum. He and his students conversed there while strolling through the colonnaded walks (*peripatoi,* which gave his followers the name "peripatetics" by which they are still known today). When he was accused of impiety in the burst of anti-Macedonian feeling that erupted after news of Alexander's death arrived in Athens, Aristotle left Attica. Looking back somberly at the trial of Socrates, he observed that he did not want the Athenians to sin a second time against philosophy. He died the following year, in 322.

That Aristotle loved science while Plato loved mathematics reveals a profound difference between the two men and their ways of engaging with the world of ideas. Live things excited Aristotle and inspired in him the desire to categorize them. The same urge would lead him to classify all the political arrangements familiar in his day in his famous work of political theory, the *Politics*. Where Plato had used reason as virtually his only tool in the quest for understanding, Aristotle placed tremendous importance on observation. His stay in northwest Asia Minor and the adjacent islands was particularly rewarding to him because of the opportunity it afforded him to study the lagoon of Pyrrha on Lesbos, which teemed with life. Although reason was not his only tool, he was the founder of the discipline of logic. To Aristotle we owe the articulation of the fundamental principle of the syllogism, a now familiar form of reasoning that consists of a major premise, a minor premise, and a conclusion. For example, if all cats are mammals and Sneaky is a cat, then Sneaky must be a mammal; because Athens is in Attica and the Parthenon is in Athens, then the Parthenon must be in Attica.

Whereas Plato had developed a framework for discussing politics so theoretical that scholars are often puzzled as to what real states he might have had in mind, Aristotle approached the question of the human community by amassing and analyzing a tremendous amount of data. In this project he was assisted by his students at the Lyceum, where 158 essays on constitutions of various poleis were drawn up. That all these have disappeared except for *The Athenian Constitution* is an incalculable loss to the study of Greek history. Aristotle was fascinated by issues surrounding government. His principal work of political theory is his *Politics*, which remained a cherished handbook throughout the medieval, Renaissance, and early modern periods.

In his conception of the universe at large, Aristotle differed with Plato on a key point—the theory of Forms. To Aristotle, as to the average person, Forms had no existence separate from matter. In addition, Aristotle was troubled by his belief that Plato had failed, like Parmenides, to account for change. Aristotle also rejected the broad level of generalization at which Plato operated. In their views of the human community, however, the two men were quite similar. Both saw the polis as more than a practical arrangement for the exchange of goods and mutual protection; for them, human existence and the existence of the polis were coterminous. (The lack of a state structure would make a fully human existence impossible, but a structure larger than the polis seemed unimaginable. Aristotle identified the largest possible size for the state at ten thousand citizens, the number who could be addressed by a speaker at one time.) Aristotle is famous for having said "man is a political animal." What he actually said is that people are animals whose nature it is to live in a polis. Only in a polis could individuals realize their social natures and grow through the sharing of ideas. This growth, however, was limited to a few people of intellectual gifts who belonged to a social class that guaranteed them leisure for contemplation. Powerful obstacles prevented the poor from participating in politics—especially the nonfarming poor, who did "banausic" labor, arduous jobs that compromised the mind along with the body. The best state, he concludes, will not make common laborers citizens, for citizens must have adequate property to ensure sufficient leisure for goodness and political activity. So much for democracy.

Both the Athenian aristocrat and Athens' most famous metic, then, were intensely class conscious. Aristotle's political philosophy, however, differed from Plato's in two key respects. First, Aristotle believed in collective wisdom: A mass of people who are individually unwise, he argues, may surpass the wisdom of the few best men, just as potluck dinners may prove to be tastier than those hosted by a single individual. The masses, he claims, can be perfectly good judges of music and poetry, because "some appreciate one thing, some another, and taken together they appreciate everything" (*Politics* 1281b). For this reason, he is open to a compromise similar to that of Solon. Poor people in his ideal state would be allowed to choose officials and hold them to account, but not to hold office. Second, Aristotle had such a powerful belief in natural hierarchies—free over slave, Greek over non-Greek, adult over child, male over female—that he recurred with some frequency to this theme of the inferiority of women to men.

Unlike Plato, whose utopia entailed a unisex education aimed at producing guardian men and women who would govern together, Aristotle was a staunch supporter of patriarchy, which he believed had a solid basis in women's biological inadequacy. Women, he maintained, had colder bodies than men. For this reason, although they were able to provide matter for embryos, only men could provide the soul. In the womb, embryos that stopped short of full development for lack of heat became female. Thus women were literally half-baked. From this came the inferior strength he identified in a variety of species. The female, he contended, "is, so to speak, a deformed male" (*Generation of Animals* 737a). At times, as was the case with the Hippocratics, Aristotle's powers of observation deserted him when the subject was women. The twentieth-century philosopher Bertrand Russell quipped that Aristotle would not have claimed that women had fewer teeth than men if he had allowed his wife to open her mouth.

For all their differences, Plato and Aristotle shared a passionate conviction that the goal of philosophy was to enable selected people to pursue enlightenment in a republic of virtuous citizens. The state for them meant the polis, and it was central to the good life. Their thinking contrasts strikingly with that of most moderns, who are more likely to see the state as designed to guarantee individuals the freedom to pursue their private goals, particularly their economic ones. Although Plato and Aristotle were both intensely critical of democracy, they shared with the Athenian democrats an eminently Greek belief in the active nature of the polis. So far from an artificial institution whose chief goal was to redistribute goods and prevent crime, the polis was conceived by its residents as a force for the moral and spiritual improvement of its citizens. For this force to operate properly, citizens had to engage eagerly in political life; participation was a duty, not a right. The problems of the fourth century, however, raised serious questions about whether the polis as traditionally conceived was adequate to serve people's needs.

The great texts of Greek political theory continue to be read today. The insights they afforded, however, seem to have had little real-life application in their own day. Plato's students never did take over Athenian government, and Aristotle's influence on his pupil Alexander was limited. Identifying those who are likely to govern best is always a challenge; and it contributes little to point out the

Plate XIIa. Marble statue of a female figure (c. 530 BC) from the Athenian Acropolis traditionally called the "Peplos kore." Athens, Acropolis Museum.

Plate XIIb. Reconstruction of the statue in Plate XIIa as a depiction of Artemis, the goddess of the hunt. Numerous still-preserved traces of red color on the Acropolis statue reveal that it was originally brightly polychromed and suggest that the goddess's garment might have been decorated with animal friezes.

Plate XIII. Orestes pursues Clytemnestra with his sword drawn. She tries to dissuade him, reminding him of the breast he nursed as a baby. Red-figure vase from Metaponto, 420–410 B.C. The VRoma Project (www.vroma.org). See Chapter 7.

Plate XIV. This bronze charioteer was dedicated in the sanctuary of Apollo at Delphi in the 470s BC by Polyzalus the tyrant of Gela, Sicily, after one of his victories in the chariot races at the Pythian games. The statue, which originally stood in the car of a bronze four-horse chariot, has survived because an earthquake cast it into an ancient drain. The charioteer's colorful inset eyes with bronze eyelashes have been preserved. His teeth and the inlaid design on his headband are made of silver. Delphi, Museum. See Chapter 6.

Plate XV. Temple of Apollo at Delphi. The temple of Apollo, whose remains are visible today on the slopes of Mt. Parnassus, dates from the fourth century BC. Two earlier temples on the same site were destroyed. The temple at this Panhellenic sanctuary was surrounded by thirty-eight Doric columns of Corinthian limestone, six along the front and back and fifteen along each side, and was a little over half the size of the Parthenon at Athens. Considered the center of the earth and widely consulted throughout antiquity on all matters from marriage to warfare, the oracle at Delphi was abolished in 393 AD by the emperor Theodosius when he made Christianity the official religion of the eastern Roman Empire. Photo: Eliot Porter, 1970. See Chapters 5 and 6.

Plate XVI. Praxiteles (c. 400–330 BC), Aphrodite of Cnidus. Roman copy after Greek original (c. 350–30 BC) with later restoration, known as the Colonna Venus. The female nude began to be depicted in Greek art in the mid-fourth century, mostly portraying Aphrodite preparing to bathe. Here she modestly holds one hand in front of her. With this statue, which was famous for its beauty, Praxiteles established the canonical proportions of the female nude in sculpture. Vatican, Vatican Museum.

Plate XVII. The Theatre at Epidaurus was built in the fourth century BC; to its initial 34 rows of seats, the Romans later added 21 more rows, to increase the capacity to 15,000 spectators. The theatre is famous for its symmetry and its acoustics—still today tour guides strike matches on the *skene* (stage) that can be heard by tourists seated throughout the auditorium, even as far back as the camera that took this shot! The fourth century witnessed the revival of the works of the great fifth-century tragedians; Euripides was especially popular after his death (in 406).

Plate XVIII. The Derveni Crater, c. 330 BC. This extraordinary bronze krater, which is over two feet high, is decorated with elaborate repoussé reliefs, silver inlays, and separately cast elements that depict Dionysiac themes. It must originally have served as a mixing bowl for wine and water in a noble home at Pella, but was found near Thessaloniki reused as a funerary urn. An inscription on the rim identifies the owner as Asteiounios, son of Anaxagoras, from Larissa in Thessaly, probably a Greek in Macedonian service. This vessel exemplifies the adoption of Greek material culture by the Macedonian nobility. See Chapter 10. Thessaloniki, Thessaloniki Museum.

Plate XIX. Gold double Daric medallion minted by Alexander the Great. The double Daric was a Persian coin denomination weighing 16.5 g. Obverse: Head of Alexander the Great wearing elephant scalp headdress and horns of Ammon. Reverse: Image of an Indian elephant with monograms AB and X symbolizing Alexander's victory over Porus at the Hydaspes River. This medallion is in mint condition because it was part of a treasure hoard. See Chapter 11. Private collection. Photograph courtesy of Osmond Bopearachchi. O Bopearachchi and P. Flandrin, *Le Portrait d' Alexander le Grand: Histoire d'une découverte pour l'humanité* (Monaco: Éditions du Rocher, 2005).

Plate XXa. Royal tomb at Aegae, modern Vergina, late fourth century BC. The simple architectural façade masks a Macedonian barrel-vaulted tomb that contained the never-looted burial of a teenage male believed by some scholars to be Alexander IV, son of Alexander the Great, who would have been buried by Cassander to help legitimize his seizure of power in Macedon. See Chapter 12.

Plate XXb. This silver *hydria* was discovered in the Macedonian tomb in Plate XXa, encircled by a gold wreath of oak leaves, holding a teenage male's cremated remains. Sealed with a lid and cut horizontally into two sections, this vase was designed to serve as a funerary urn. See Chapter 10. Vergina, Vergina Museum.

Plate XXI. This late Hellenistic mosaic, the Alexander Mosaic from Pompeii, is believed to be a copy of a late-fourth-century BC painting depicting the Battle of Issus by Philoxenus of Eretria for King Cassander of Macedon. Alexander, on horseback toward the left, confronts Darius III, in a chariot on the right. Surprisingly, the focus of attention in this dynamic composition is not Alexander but the Persian king, who is sympathetically depicted as concerned for the welfare of his soldiers instead of fleeing the charge of the Macedonian king. See Chapter 11. Naples, National Archaeological Museum.

Plate XXII. Hellenistic terracotta depicting two women engaged in intimate conversation. Made at Myrina, late second century BC. Height 20 cm. London, The British Museum (Cat. No. C 529).

Plate XXIII. Basalt statue of Cleopatra VII, Egypt, in Egyptian royal regalia. The queen is portrayed holding a double cornucopia (horn of plenty) with her left arm, illustrating her admiration for her great predecessor Arsinoë II, who was often similarly depicted (see Figure 12.9). See Chapter 12 and Epilogue. St. Petersburg, State Hermitage Museum.

imprudence of according sovereign power to a power-hungry tyrant, a clique of rich men, or an angry mob. It is precisely because wealth and birth have historically been the criteria for inclusion in the elite that democracy has become a popular alternative to oligarchy. It is one thing to advocate an aristocracy of intellect and another to design practical machinery for establishing one. It was a central tenet of Greek intellectuals that most people lacked capacity for growth. Plato and Aristotle worked on the assumption that the secret to reforming government was in nurturing the tiny minority that had this capacity. Their goal was basically to design a constitution that minimized the power prudence must accord to the mindless masses who might otherwise rise up and slaughter their betters.

The fourth century BC witnessed an explosion of creative energy in many areas: Philosophy, biology, political theory, mathematics, and military science all made significant advances. Where all this fertility was leading is unclear. Solid foundations were established for intellectual traditions that lived and grew for centuries; many of them still flourish in altered—or unaltered—forms. The knowledge generated did not, however, offer salvation to Greece. The increasing specialization of the fourth century led to a division between generals and politicians that resulted in more professional military skills. Consequently, generals in the fourth century were better than those of the fifth. Their weapons and machinery were more versatile and sophisticated.

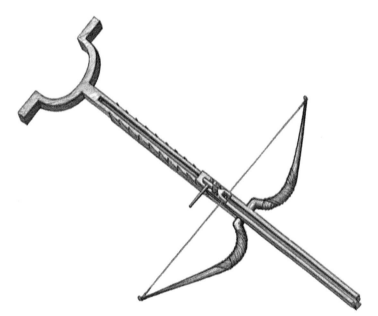

Figure 9.7. A modern reconstruction of the huge composite bow known as the *gastraphetes* that came into being in the time of Dionysius I, one of many military innovations deployed by the creative and ambitious ruler of Syracuse. From John Warry, *Warfare in the Classical World, An Illustrated Encyclopedia* (paperback) (Norman, OK: University of Oklahoma Press, 1995), p. 78.

In Sicily lived the most remarkable military innovator of his day, Dionysius I (not to be confused with Dionysius II, whom Plato later tried to educate), who had set himself up as de facto tyrant of Syracuse in 405. His advances were conspicuous in the arena of siege warfare. Greek sieges normally ended when hunger forced surrender. Dionysius, however, anticipated Alexander the Great in his ability to take cities by storm, making use of the new device known as the gastraphetes or "bellyshooter" (because of the way its operator used his stomach to activate it). (See Fig. 9.7.) In essence a huge composite bow, the gastraphetes was cocked by a soldier who rested his stomach in a groove and pushed the instrument to maximum extension by pressing forward on it. This device could hurl a projectile about 250 yards. Along with wheeled six-story siege towers with flying bridges, the gastraphetes seems to have been used to good effect in Dionysius' siege of Motya, a Carthaginian stronghold on the west coast of Sicily that he destroyed in 397. (Greek inhabitants who had remained loyal to Carthage were crucified.) With the addition of artillery to light and heavy infantry and cavalry, Dionysius' army was the most complex in organization and equipment of any fighting force in Greece down to his time.

DOCUMENT 9.3

Diodorus of Sicily, who often spoke harshly of Dionysius, nonetheless admired his energy and determination. He recounted in his Library of History the eagerness with which workmen tried to make the best contributions to the war effort. His account also stressed the force of Dionysius' personality.

After collecting many skilled workmen, he divided them into groups in accordance with their skills, and appointed over them the most conspicuous citizens, offering great bounties to any who created a supply of arms. As for the armor, he distributed among them models of each kind, because he had gathered his mercenaries from many nations; for he was eager to have every one of his soldiers armed with the weapons of his people, conceiving that by such armor his army would, for this very reason, cause great consternation, and that in battle all of his soldiers would fight to best effect in armor to which they were accustomed. And since the Syracusans enthusiastically supported the policy of Dionysius, it came to pass that rivalry rose high to manufacture the arms. . . .

In fact the catapult was invented at this time in Syracuse, since the ablest skilled workmen had been gathered from everywhere into one place. The high wages as well as the numerous prizes offered the workmen who were judged to be the best stimulated their zeal. And over and above these factors, Dionysius circulated daily among the workers, conversed with them in kindly fashion, and rewarded the most zealous with gifts and invited them to his table. Consequently the workmen brought unsurpassable devotion to the devising of many missiles and engines of war that were strange and capable of rendering great service. He also began the constructions of quadriremes and quinqueremes, being the first of the construction of such ships. . . . With so many arms and ships under construction at one place the beholder was filled with utter wonder at the sight.

(*Library of History* 14. 41.4-43.1 Sherman)

New ways of thinking also led to specialized monographs like Xenophon's treatises on the art of horsemanship and the skills necessary for a successful cavalry commander, and the *Siegecraft* of the author known as Aeneas Tacticus. No good, however, came of these improvements. Greeks simply expanded the repertoire of available methods for killing.

The inhabitants of mid-fourth-century Greece had no particular reason to believe that the world they knew was about to change. Though intellectuals like Plato and Aristotle subjected democracy to harsh criticism and frequent stasis threatened the stability of numerous states other than Athens and Sparta, few people suspected that the Greek political landscape of the future would differ radically from that of the past: Why doubt that autonomous poleis would continue to group and regroup in shifting alliances as they had done since the origin of the polis itself? Even Plato and Aristotle conceived of the unit of the city-state as a permanent fixture in political life. Although the bustling city in fact remained the core of Hellenic civilization for centuries to come, however, new developments in Macedon bode ill for Greek independence. The next chapter chronicles the rise of a remarkable man who would change the face of the Greek world.

KEY TERMS

Academy	Lyceum	*The Republic*
Aristotle	mausoleum	Sacred Band
Artaxerxes	Neaera	Second Athenian League
Corinthian War	Pelopidas	Socrates
dicasteries	peltast	theory of Forms
Epaminondas	Plato	Thirty Tyrants

SUGGESTED READINGS

Allen, Danielle S. 2000. *The World of Prometheus: The Politics of Punishing in Democratic Athens*. Princeton, NJ: Princeton University Press. A subtle analysis of Athens' values as a polis grounded in a study of attitudes toward punishment.

Balot, Ryan K. 2006. *Greek Political Thought (Ancient Cultures)*. Boston: Wiley-Blackwell. A wide-ranging history of Greek political thought that explores what the works of Greek political philosophers might mean for modern readers.

Bryant, Joseph. 1996. *Moral Codes and Social Structure in Ancient Greece*. Albany: State University of New York Press. The connection between values and social organization from the Archaic period through the Hellenistic Age.

Cartledge, Paul. 1987. *Agesilaos and the Crisis of Sparta. Baltimore*: Johns Hopkins University Press. A close study of fourth-century Sparta with a focus on the compelling figure of the king Agesilaos.

Edmondson, Jonathan and Virginia Hunter. 2000. *Law and Social Status in Classical Athens*. Oxford, UK: Oxford University Press. A fascinating collection of essays focusing on the ways in which Athenian law defined and sustained the different social statuses of citizens, metics, and slaves, treating topics such as prostitution, torture, and methods of execution.

Hansen, Mogens H. 1991. *The Athenian Democracy in the Age of Demosthenes*. Oxford, UK: Basil Blackwell. An engaging analytical study of Athenian democracy that is crammed with useful facts.

———. 1991. *The Trial of Socrates from the Athenian Point of View*. Copenhagen, Denmark: The Royal Danish Academy of Sciences and Letters. Discussion of the sources, a reconstruction of the trial, and an investigation of the political background of the prosecution.

Lee, John W. I. 2008. *A Greek Army on the March: Soldiers and Survival in Xenophon's Anabasis*. Cambridge and New York: Cambridge University Press. A detailed examination of life in a Greek mercenary army, dealing with topics including the ethnic and socio-economic relations among the soldiers, sanitation, and medical care.

Low, Polly. 2009. *Interstate Relations in Classical Greece: Morality and Power (Cambridge Classical Studies)*. Cambridge, UK: Cambridge University Press. A sophisticated exploration of the complex network of customs, expectations, and beliefs that under-girded all areas of interstate behavior in the fifth and fourth centuries BC.

Ober, Josiah. 1989. *Mass and Elite in Democratic Athens: Rhetoric, Ideology, and the Power of the People*. Princeton, NJ: Princeton University Press. A sociopolitical study of fourth-century Athens that uses the findings of modern social scientists to shed light on the ideology of the democracy as revealed in the work of the orators.

Rhodes, P. J. and Robin Osborne. 2003. *Greek Historical Inscriptions 404-323 BC*. Oxford, UK: Oxford University Press. Collection of 102 inscriptions from the Greek world: laws, decrees, regulations, treaties and alliances, honors, contracts. All are translated into English.

Todd, S. C. 1993. *The Shape of Athenian Law*. Oxford, UK: Oxford University Press. A detailed and analytical study of Athenian law dealing with both procedure and substance.

Trevett, Jeremy. 1992. *Apollodoros the Son of Pasion*. Oxford, UK: The Clarendon Press. Biography of an influential Athenian, who was the son of a former slave.

Tritle, Lawrence, ed. 1997. *The Greek World in the Fourth Century: From the Fall of the Athenian Empire to the Successors of Alexander*. London: Routledge. A collection of essays on the problems of the fourth century, including chapters on Thebes, the Greeks of Asia Minor, and the states of western Greece.

Wilson, Emily. 2007. *The Death of Socrates*. Cambridge, MA: Harvard University Press. Interesting study of accounts of the trial of Socrates from antiquity to the present.

Wood, Ellen Meiksins. 1988. *Peasant-Citizen and Slave: The Foundations of Athenian Democracy*. London: Verso. The relationship between agrarian labor and democracy in Classical Athens.

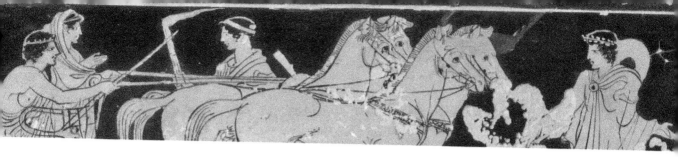

CHAPTER TEN

Philip II and the Rise of Macedon

I t is one of the paradoxes of ancient history that the Greek poleis maintained their independence as long as they did. Their tiny size and fractiousness made their escape from Persian conquest appear miraculous even in antiquity. The return of the threat of foreign conquest in the fourth century was not surprising, but the source of the threat was not the mighty Persian Empire but the hitherto insignificant kingdom of **Macedon**.

The success of Macedon in conquering the Greek states was due partly to the political divisions and economic strains that hindered the development of a consistent policy in Athens and partly to the mutual mistrust that prevented the formation of an effective united front by the leading poleis—Athens, Sparta, and Thebes. Credit, however, must also be given to the unique military and diplomatic gifts of **Philip II,** who became king of Macedon in 359 BC.

EARLY MACEDON

Herodotus claimed that Perdiccas, the first king of Macedon, was promised the land illuminated by the sun as his kingdom. The reality was different. For most of early Macedonian history, the kings of Macedon ruled a chronically unstable kingdom that was a state only in name. Sandwiched between **Thessaly** on the south, **Thrace** and the Chalcidian League on the east, Paeonia on the north, and Illyria and Epirus on the west, Macedonian kings struggled constantly to maintain their independence while striving to assert their preeminence over the local dynasts, who ruled the various regions that made up the kingdom of Macedon.

Figure 10.1. Philip II (359–336 BC). Miniature ivory bust of Philip II, probably part of the decoration of a bed. The closed right eye reflects the wound Philip received during the siege of Methone in 355/4 BC. Late fourth-century BC. Vergina, Greece.

Macedonia's geography made their struggle more difficult. Macedonia consisted of two distinct geographical regions: Lower Macedonia, the great alluvial plain created by the Haliacmon and Axius rivers during their course to the Gulf of Therma, and Upper Macedonia, the horseshoe of rugged uplands and mountains that stretched northwestward toward Illyria and Epirus. Lower Macedonia formed the heart of the kingdom of Macedon and supported a large agricultural population. Its mountainous hinterlands not only held extensive forests and rich mineral deposits but also sheltered various tribes who jealously guarded their freedom from the control of the lowland Macedonian kings. Uniting these two regions was the essential precondition for the growth and expansion of Macedonian power.

MACEDONIAN SOCIETY AND KINGSHIP

Were the Macedonians Greek? This question is the most contentious issue in Macedonian historiography. Conflicting claims to the territory of ancient Macedonia have made the question of the "Greekness" of the ancient Macedonians a burning issue. Modern nationalists may be confident of their answers, but contemporary ideology has little relevance to antiquity. Recent epigraphic discoveries suggest that "Macedonian" was a dialect of northwest Greek. It is clear, however, that in antiquity neither Macedonians nor Greeks considered the Macedonians to be Greek. Except for the ruling Argead house, which was believed to be of Argive origin, Greeks viewed the Macedonians as barbarians like their Thracian and Illyrian neighbors.

More important, although Macedonian kings encouraged the **Hellenization** of the Macedonian nobility, Macedonian and Greek culture had little in common. Cities were the core of what was most distinctive in Greek civilization, but prior to Philip's reign, city life in Macedonia was limited to a few Greek colonies on the coast of the Gulf of Therma and dynastic centers such as Aegae and Pella. Most Macedonians were farmers or seminomadic pastoralists living in scattered villages and owing allegiance to Macedonian aristocrats. Other differences divided the two cultures as well, such as the polygamy of the Macedonian kings and the Macedonians' love of unmixed wine and their preference for tumulus burial instead of simple cremation or interment. Indeed, the lifestyle of the Macedonian nobility had more in common with that of Homeric heroes than with that of Classical Greeks. War and hunting were central to the life of a Macedonian noble. Before being recognized as an adult, a young man had to spear a boar without the aid of a net and kill an enemy. Feuds resulting from heavy drinking, competition for preference at the royal court, and rivalries over the favors of young men and women were common.

The monarchy was the central institution of Macedonian society. Like Louis XIV of France, a Macedonian *basileus* ("king") was an autocrat who could well say "I am the state." Theories that maintain that royal power was limited by an army assembly have been shown to be groundless. The army might acclaim a new king and witness trials of nobles, but the king made all appointments and grants of land and privilege, and only he responded to petitions. Treaties and alliances were made with him personally, and foreign allies pledged their support to him and his family. The king could even choose which of his sons would be his successor.

Macedonian kings were autocrats but they were not all-powerful. Greek political theorists often equated monarchy and tyranny because of the supreme importance of the ruler's personality in the public and private spheres. This was especially true of Macedon, where the kings spent their lives in the midst of their *hetairoi* ("companions")—Macedonian nobles who formed their personal entourage. These nobles provided the kings with their advisers and the members of their bodyguard and served in an elite cavalry unit commanded by the king. As a result, Macedonian kings sat on insecure thrones. Only two predecessors of Philip II died natural deaths; the rest died in battle or fell victim to conspiracies.

The Predecessors of Philip II

Philip II was the beneficiary of almost two centuries of patient state-building by his Argead predecessors. The process began in the late sixth-century BC with an alliance between Amyntas I and Persia. The Macedonians were loyal allies, even

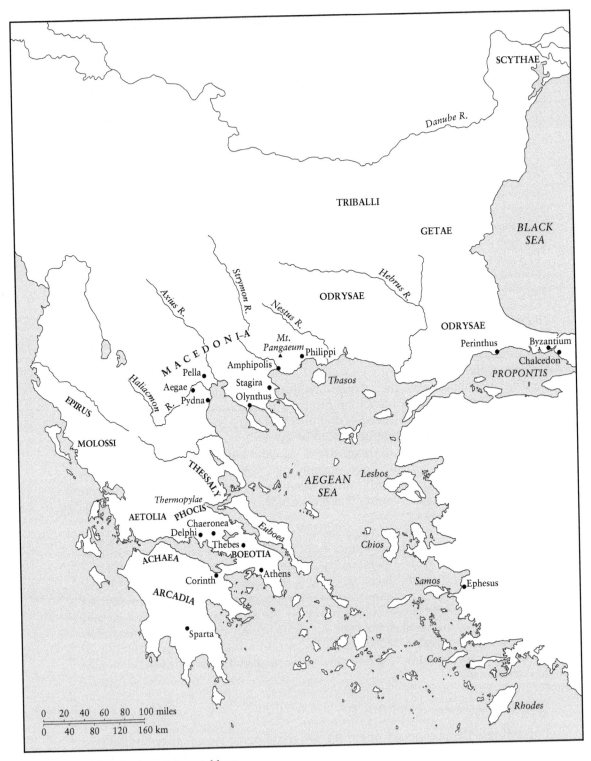

Figure 10.2. Macedonia and its neighbors.

supporting the Persian invasion of Greece in 480 BC. Not surprisingly, Amyntas' successor, Alexander I, encouraged the spread of stories after the Persian defeat testifying to his covert support of the Greek cause during the invasion.

Persian rule brought Macedon great advantages by shielding the kingdom from attack by its neighbors. After the Greek victory, Amyntas' fifth-century BC successors—Alexander I, Perdiccas II, and Archelaus—extended their territory northwestward into Upper Macedon and eastward to the rich silver mines beyond the Axius River, making the kingdom the strongest power in the region. Macedon's growing power and resources attracted the attention of Athens and other Greek cities. Macedonian grain fed many of Athens' allies and subjects, and Macedonian timber was critical to Athens' fleet. For their part, the Macedonian kings used their wealth to win recognition as Greeks and Hellenize the royal court. Alexander I may have competed in the Olympic games; and Archelaus supported Greek artists and writers, such as the Athenian tragedian Euripides, who wrote two tragedies at Archelaus' court: the lost *Archelaus*, celebrating his host's alleged Argive ancestry, and the *Bacchae*, offering a terrifying evocation of the power of Dionysus. By the reign of Philip II, the Macedonian court was the principal cultural center in Macedon and the focus of the social life of the Macedonian aristocracy. Growing Macedonian power, however, threatened Athenian interests in the north Aegean, prompting Athens to support Macedon's Thracian neighbors and various pretenders to the Macedonian throne.

When Philip II came to power in 359, Macedon was faced by the most severe crisis in its history. Chronic instability had left the kingdom vulnerable to threats from both Greek and non-Greek enemies. Philip's own brother, Perdiccas III, had been killed in battle in 360 BC by the **Illyrians** together with four thousand Macedonian troops and much of the Macedonian aristocracy. Surrounded by enemies and beset by dynastic rivalries, the kingdom seemed on the verge of collapse.

THE REIGN OF PHILIP II

Philip II was born about 382 BC, the last son of Amyntas III and his Illyrian wife Eurydice. Plutarch says that Eurydice learned to read to educate her children, but Philip's education ended abruptly with the defeat of his brother Alexander II and his own exile as a hostage in Thebes from 369 to 367 BC. His exile was not all loss. Philip's stay in Thebes soon after its victory at Leuctra gave him invaluable insight into contemporary Greek politics and military tactics.

Philip returned to Macedon in 367 as the kingdom descended into chaos. Three kings ruled Macedon during the next seven years. Political instability also provided Philip with an unexpected opportunity, because the crisis following Perdiccas' death demanded a ruler capable of taking decisive action. That ruler could only be Philip, as he was the sole surviving adult Argead. Not surprisingly, Philip quickly supplanted his infant nephew Amyntas as king of Macedon.

When Philip took power in 360, Macedon was threatened by foreign enemies and rival claimants to the throne supported by the Thracian King Seuthes II and the Athenians. In the next two years the situation changed dramatically. After

a

b

Figure 10.3a. Silver tetradrachm of Philip II. Obverse: Head of Zeus. Reverse: Mounted Macedonian king—probably Philip II—wearing Macedonian hat and cape. Oxford, The Ashmolean Museum.

Figure 10.3b. Silver tetradrachm of Philip II (359–336 BC). Obverse: Head of Zeus. Reverse: Jockey commemorating the victory of Philip's horse at Olympia in 356 BC. Oxford, The Ashmolean Museum.

neutralizing the Thracians and Athenians through astute diplomacy, Philip quickly defeated both the Paeonians and Illyrians and regained control of western and northwestern Macedonia. Philip's brilliant diplomacy paved the way for his decisive military victories over the Paeonians and Illyrians in 358 and set the pattern for the rest of his reign.

Success followed success during the remainder of the decade. Alliance with the Molossians in Epirus secured Macedon's western frontier and freed Philip to turn eastward and seize the Greek cities on the coasts of Macedon and the gold mines of Mount Pangaeus that financed his plans for the rest of his reign. In less than a decade, Philip had freed Macedon from the enemies that had threatened its survival since the sixth century. At the same time, far-reaching reforms gave the kingdom unprecedented military strength and political cohesion.

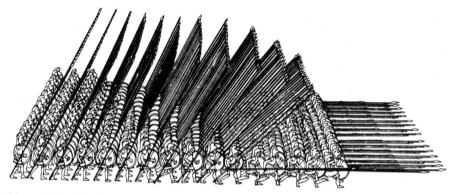

Figure 10.4. The Macedonian phalanx.

Figure 10.5. Macedonian infantry *sarissa* (modern reconstruction). Photograph used by permission of Professor W. Heckel.

The Reforms of Philip II

Philip II's reign coincided with a revolution in military tactics and weaponry that ended the Greek hoplite's dominance of the battlefield. By introducing these innovations to Macedon, Philip transformed it into the preeminent military power in southeastern Europe. His most important military reform was the reorganization of the Macedonian infantry. Philip created a new **phalanx** to replace the old undisciplined militia that had served Macedonian kings so poorly in the past. The six companies of the new phalanx were recruited from each of Macedon's traditional territorial divisions, but they were equipped with new weapons and assigned a new role in battle. Each member of the phalanx wore a metal helmet and carried a small shield and a short sword. His principal weapon, however, was a *sarissa*, an enormous pike that could be as much as eighteen feet long, allowing the soldier to strike a blow before his enemies could close and use their shorter weapons. The presence of the phalanx in a battle forced Philip's enemies to modify their tactics to cope with it and allow the companion cavalry to deal a decisive blow to an enemy force already confused by the phalanx and the elite guard units protecting its flanks.

Philip also strengthened the bonds between the army and the king by sharing its hardships and dangers, as his loss of an eye and other wounds attested. He conferred a new title on the common soldiers, *pezhetairoi* ("foot companions"), suggesting that they, too, like the nobles, were the king's personal companions. The rage of Alexander's soldiers at Opis in 324 at the thought of sharing this status with Persians revealed the strength of the bond Philip had forged with them. The bond between the king and the Macedonian nobility also changed. Perdiccas III's disastrous defeat had decimated the Macedonian nobility and enabled Philip to replenish the **royal companions** with Greeks and non-Greeks who flocked to Macedon in search of opportunity and wealth. (See Plate XVIII.) Members of the old nobility also benefited, receiving commands in Philip's new model army. Their sons became **royal pages**, personally serving the king and providing Philip with future officers, and also serving as hostages for the loyalty of their families.

Theopompus, the historian of Philip's reign, sarcastically characterized his new companions as men more suited to be "courtesans" than "courtiers." Still, they were loyal to Philip, and he rewarded them with land and treasure gained by his victories. Projects such as the draining of marshland in Lower Macedonia and the foundation of colonies such as Philippi further strengthened royal power and resources. As a result, Philip possessed what no previous Macedonian king had ever had before: a loyal base of support for his policies.

Philip Becomes a Force in Greece

Philip's predecessors had tried to avert the danger posed by a united Thessaly by supporting Larisa against Pherae and its Theban allies. Philip followed the lead of his predecessors, also intervening in Thessaly following the conclusion of an alliance between **Phocis** and Macedon's old enemy Pherae.

Phocis had emerged in the mid-350s as a major power in central and northern Greece, and the alliance of Pherae and Phocis alarmed both Larisa and Thebes, forcing them to seek Philip's aid. Philip initially underestimated the threat posed by the alliance of Pherae and Phocis. Although Philip suffered two severe defeats at the hands of Phocis in 353—the most serious of his entire reign—he crushed them a year later at the Battle of the Crocus Field. This battle transformed Philip's position in Greece. After occupying Pherae and exiling its tyrant, Philip was appointed by the Thessalian League *archōn* ("commander-in-chief") of Thessaly, uniting Thessaly and Macedon and virtually doubling the military forces at his disposal. It also allowed Philip to expand his influence deep into central Greece.

While Philip was busy in Thessaly, central Greece was convulsed by the Third Sacred War. The war originated in Thebes' attempt to humiliate Phocis by having the Delphic Amphictyony severely fine the Phocians in 357 for cultivating sacred land. Phocis' response was unexpected. Long Thebes' main rival in central Greece, Phocis had grudgingly recognized Theban suzerainty at the Battle of Leuctra. In 357, the Phocians made a desperate effort to regain their independence. Instead of submitting to Theban blackmail, they seized Delphi and used Apollo's treasures to recruit mercenaries. Athenian and Spartan hostility frustrated Thebes' attempt to avenge the sacrilege, allowing Phocis to subdue much of central Greece.

Conflicts with Thrace and Olynthus delayed Philip's intervention until 347. Although Macedonian power tipped the scales against Phocis, Philip sought to prevent Thebes from profiting from his victory by secretly negotiating surrender terms with Phocis. Facing the traditional penalty for such sacrilege—execution of all adult males—the Phocians accepted the relatively mild terms offered by Philip and surrendered in the summer of 346. Phocis' cities were broken up into their constituent villages, and the Phocians agreed to repay Delphi at a rate of sixty talents per year. Finally, Philip gained Phocis' votes in the Delphic Amphictyony, thus giving him a voting majority on the Amphictyonic Council. All Greece learned the full extent of Philip's new influence in Delphic affairs a year later when he presided over the Pythian games. Philip's triumph in the Sacred War also temporarily calmed relations between Macedon and Athens.

Philip, Athens, and the Peace of Philocrates

Tense relations between Athens and Philip dated to the beginning of his reign when he bought Athenian neutrality by promising to restore Amphipolis and then not only seized it but also captured Pydna, Methone, and Potidaea, thereby eliminating Athens' principal allies in the north Aegean. Athens delayed responding to Philip's actions for almost a decade. This was largely the result of the economic devastation caused by the Peloponnesian War, which limited Athens' ability to pursue a wide-ranging foreign policy in the early fourth century. Athenian power was further constrained in the 350s by the defection of several key allies from the Second Athenian League and by an important political innovation: the establishment of the **Theoric Fund**.

Eubulus (c. 405–c. 335 BC), Athens' leading politician, persuaded the Athenians to pass a law assigning all fiscal surpluses to the Theoric Fund, which funded public benefits such as repairing roads and fortifications and religious participation, including distributions to Athenian citizens at religious festivals; it was named after the "theatrical" performances that were part of these celebrations. The orator Demades rightly called the Theoric Fund "the glue of the democracy," as it reduced tension between the rich and the poor. It also, however, encouraged a pacifist foreign policy in two ways: by lessening the poor's need for the pay they received for rowing in the fleet and by increasing their concern that surplus funds would be redirected to military expenditures and their benefits reduced should war break out.

Eubulus' cautious financial policies had dramatic results. Athenian revenues rose from 130 talents to 400, enabling Athens to construct new triremes and to improve the docks and fortifications. The Laurium silver mines were reopened and foreigners were encouraged to settle in Attica and become metics. Only the threat of Macedonian military intervention in central Greece in the late 350s prompted the prosperous Athenians to finally take strong action.

With a Macedonian invasion of Attica seemingly imminent, the Athenians dispatched an expeditionary force in 352 to occupy Thermopylae, to block the Macedonian advance. The motion was made by a close associate of Eubulus. In a crisis, Athens' security overrode any scruples Eubulus and his supporters may have had about dipping into the Theoric Fund. Otherwise, however, Athens failed utterly to hinder the Macedonian king's growing influence in northern and central Greece. Athens' actions in the early 340s were similarly ineffective. When Olynthus tried to shift alliances from Macedon to Athens, Philip turned on his former ally. Athens' ineffective response to Olynthus' appeals for help in 348 allowed Philip to capture the city, raze it, enslave its citizens, and dismantle the Chalcidic League, Macedon's only potential Greek rival in the north Aegean.

Although Athens' restraint as Philip's power grew was prudent, its inability to regain Amphipolis or aid its allies was humiliating. Some Athenian politicians reacted by demanding a more aggressive Athenian policy toward Macedon. The most prominent of these politicians was the orator **Demosthenes**. Demosthenes' fame was such that the Roman statesman Cicero called his speeches against Mark Antony "Philippics" after Demosthenes' speeches against Philip. Originally a supporter of Eubulus, by 351 Demosthenes had become disenchanted with Eubulus' policies and begun to forge a new political identity. In the *First Philippic*, Demosthenes revealed his new views, attacking Philip and urging the Athenians to prepare for war by building a strong navy. Although Demosthenes continued to advocate resistance to Philip, even he recognized that the fall of Olynthus, Philip's triumph in the Sacred War, and the defection of Euboea made peace imperative if Athens was to avoid total disaster.

The Athenian politician Philocrates negotiated peace with Philip in the summer of 346. Negotiating the treaty and securing its approval by the Athenian assembly was a contentious process. Because the Peace of Philocrates quickly

Figure 10.6. Polyeuctus' posthumous bronze portrait statue of Demosthenes, erected in the Athenian agora in 280 BC, is reflected in this Roman marble copy. It shows the orator as gaunt, worried, and thoughtful. Vatican City, Vatican Museum.

collapsed amidst bitter recriminations, the details of its negotiation remain unclear but not its significance. Faced with the alternatives of fighting Macedon or accepting Philip's terms, Athens chose the latter. Athens abandoned its claim to Amphipolis, accepted the exclusion of its Phocian and Thracian allies from the treaty, and agreed that the city and the Second Athenian League would become allies of Philip and his descendants. Athens' inability to prevent the growth of Macedonian power and influence in Greece was clear to all.

The Aftermath of the Peace of Philocrates

The Peace of Philocrates ratified Philip's supremacy in northern and central Greece. His diplomatic triumph was, however, short-lived. As the likelihood of war with Macedon receded, support for the treaty dissipated. Philip's treatment of Phocis also cast doubt on the credibility of the treaty's negotiators, who had promised that the Phocians would suffer no harm. When Philip also gained Phocis' two votes on the Amphictyonic Council, the Athenians and Spartans angrily refused to send deputations to the Pythian games.

While Philip's critics in Athens steadily undermined the Peace of Philocrates and its supporters, Philip's proposals to strengthen the peace were rebuffed. Athens again demanded that he return Amphipolis. Philocrates, the architect of the peace, was indicted for bribery and fled into exile. Demosthenes, who had helped negotiate the treaty, unsuccessfully impeached his fellow envoy Aeschines to protect himself. Only Philip's need for peace in Greece during his Thracian campaign in 342 prevented him from taking strong action against Athens. He finally declared war in 340, when Athens joined Persia to frustrate his siege of the Hellespontine city of Perinthus. Athens responded with its own declaration of war.

The actual outbreak of hostilities was delayed for another year. First, Philip unsuccessfully besieged Byzantium; then he campaigned against the Scythians, who ruled the hinterlands of modern Romania's Black Sea coast and threatened Macedonian control of Thrace. Nevertheless, he still gave Athens a sharp reminder of the potential consequences of war with Macedon by capturing the entire Black Sea grain fleet in 340 BC, thereby threatening Athens with starvation.

Figure 10.7. This monument in the shape of a lion marks the graves of 254 Thebans buried at the site of the Battle of Chaeronea.

Philip's long-awaited opportunity to strike directly at Athens came in 339 when he accepted the Delphic Amphictyony's invitation to lead a sacred war against the city of Amphissa, near Delphi. By the end of the year the Macedonian army was in Phocis, within easy striking distance of Athens. Almost a decade later, Demosthenes proudly reminded the Athenians that only he had dared address the assembly when they learned of Philip's presence in Phocis.

> At dawn the next day the Prytaneis called the Council to the Chamber, and citizens moved into the Assembly. . . . The Council appeared, announced the news they had received, and brought forward their informant to repeat it. The herald then voiced the question "Who desires to speak?" No one moved. The question was repeated several times without a man standing up, though all the strategoi were there, all the orators, and the voice of Athens called for a word to save her. . . . I came forward and addressed the Assembly.
>
> (Demosthenes, *On the Crown 169–172* Saunders)

The Athenians' despair was understandable. Few Peloponnesian cities had heeded Demosthenes' appeal to join in resisting Philip, so when battle was finally joined in late summer 338 at Chaeronea in Boeotia, Philip faced only the levies of Athens, Thebes, and the Boeotian League and a handful of Peloponnesian units. A monumental stone lion still gazes over the plain of Chaeronea, marking the site of this pivotal battle in world history. Little is known about the battle itself beyond two facts: Greek casualties were heavy, and the decisive blow was struck by the companion cavalry led by Philip's eighteen-year-old son and heir, Alexander. A thousand Athenians were killed and another two thousand captured; the Thebans' cherished Sacred Band was annihilated. Philip's triumph was complete. After Chaeronea, resistance to Philip's authority in Greece would have been futile. All that remained to be determined was the form Macedonian domination of Greece would take.

PHILIP'S PLANS FOR GREECE

Philip's immediate concern after his victory at Chaeronea was how to deal with his two principal enemies. The Thebans were treated with exemplary harshness. As Thebes had a long record of collaboration with Persia and was Macedon's chief rival for power in Greece, Philip set out to break the city's power. Theban and other Boeotian prisoners were released only after payment of a heavy ransom. Thebes' political leaders were either executed or exiled. A Macedonian garrison was installed on the Cadmea, the city's acropolis. Finally, Thebes was stripped of its traditional position of leadership in the Boeotian League.

Philip's treatment of Athens was dramatically different. Capturing the city would require a difficult siege, and its fleet could threaten his projected Persian campaign. Consequently, Athens escaped significant punishment despite its leading role in the war. Athenian prisoners were returned without ransom, and the Athenian dead were escorted back to the city by an honor guard led by Alexander and Antipater, Philip's most trusted general. Nor did Philip object when Demosthenes, his most implacable opponent, delivered the funeral oration over the dead of Chaeronea.

Philip's actions were well received. Many Greeks welcomed the humiliation of Thebes, whose arbitrary behavior since the Battle of Leuctra had bred widespread resentment. Athens, for its part, showered the city's former enemies with honors, making Antipater and Alexander Athenian citizens and establishing a cult in Philip's honor in one of the city's gymnasia. Athenian suspicion of Philip, of course, did not disappear: A law passed in 337 promised severe penalties for conspirators against the democracy. Officially, however, relations were friendly. Antipater and Alexander were not the only Macedonian subjects to benefit from the thaw in relations between Philip and Athens. As was mentioned in the previous chapter, one person who took advantage of the new political climate was the philosopher **Aristotle**, a close friend of Antipater and the former tutor of Alexander. Aristotle returned to Athens in 335 and stayed until 322, when anti-Macedonian sentiment forced him to flee to Euboea, where he died. Philip's conciliatory policy toward Athens, however, had a more practical goal—winning Athens' acquiescence in his plans for Greece—and it succeeded. Not only did Athens offer no further resistance to Macedonian preeminence in Greece, but the Athenians also agreed to send representatives to the general meeting of Greek states at Corinth that Philip called in the summer of 337 BC.

The Corinthian League

Representatives of all the major Greek states except Sparta met at Corinth to learn Philip's plans. The centerpiece of the new order was an alliance, referred to by historians as the **Corinthian League**, but which Philip called simply "the Greeks." Its stated goals were two: to maintain a common peace in Greece and to avenge the Persian aggression against the Greeks. The alliance council (*synedrion*) was empowered to pass decrees binding on member states, to arbitrate disputes between them, and to try individuals accused of treason. Member states also received pledges of mutual nonaggression and support against attack or internal subversion. Not surprisingly, the delegates approved Philip's proposals and appointed him *hēgemōn* ("leader") of the alliance and commander of the war against Persia.

DOCUMENT 10.1

Oath of Members of the League of Corinth (338–337 BC)
Fragment of an Athenian inscription recording the oath sworn by the Athenians when they ratified the treaty establishing the League of Corinth.

Oath. I swear by Zeus, Earth, Sun, Poseidon, Athena, Ares, and all the gods and goddesses. I will abide by the peace, and I will not break the agreements with Philip the Macedonian, nor will I take up arms with hostile intent against any one of those who abide by the oaths either by land or by sea. I will not seize in war by any device or stratagem any city or fort or harbor belonging to those who share the peace. Nor will I suppress the kingdom of Philip or of his descendants or the constitutions in force among any of those [who share the peace], when they swore the oaths concerning the peace. I will not commit any act that contravenes the agreements nor will I permit any other to do so. If any one breaks the agreements, I will assist those who have been wronged in accordance with their requests. I will fight against those who break the common peace just as the common council and the leader (*hēgemōn*) decide. . . .

(*Inscriptiones Graecae* 2.236)

Although the primary purpose of the League of Corinth was to legitimize Philip's domination of Greece, it also reflected important trends in contemporary Greek thought. Ever since the end of the Peloponnesian War, Greek politicians and thinkers had tried to end the chronic political and social unrest that plagued Greece. Plato, as described in the previous chapter, offered in the *Republic* and the *Laws* utopian visions of ideal cities free of stasis. More pragmatic thinkers denounced wars between Greeks as civil wars, insisting that wars against barbarians were inherently just or even desirable as a way of reducing internal tensions in Greece. These ideas were embodied in the so-called common peaces, such as the King's Peace and its successors, that were characteristic of fourth-century Greek diplomacy.

The most prominent just-war theorist was the Athenian educator **Isocrates**. Isocrates was almost one hundred years old when the **Battle of Chaeronea** was waged. Throughout his long career as a speechwriter and teacher of rhetoric, he had argued that the solution to Greece's problems was conquering a portion of the Persian Empire to which economically deprived and potentially dangerous segments of Greek society then could emigrate. Isocrates had appealed unsuccessfully to various Greek rulers, including the Spartan king Agesilaus and the tyrants Dionysius I of Syracuse and Alexander of Pherae, to lead a united Greece in a crusade against Persia, so Philip must have seemed his last chance to see his dream realized. Unfortunately, we do not know how Philip reacted to Isocrates' letter urging him to lead such a crusade after his victory at Chaeronea; but by uniting in the League of Corinth the ideas of a "common peace" and a crusade against Persia, Philip was exploiting ideas that had been circulating in Greece.

The Death of Philip II

Philip's planned invasion of the Persian Empire was well timed. The 330s were a time of severe crisis for Persia. The power of the able but ruthless king Artaxerxes III

Figure 10.8. Theater at the Macedonian capital, Aegae, modern Vergina.

(358–338 BC) rivaled that of the founders of the empire. He had ended the satrapal rebellions that had disrupted the reign of his father Artaxerxes II (405–359 BC), reestablished Persian authority in Phoenicia and Asia Minor, and even reconquered Egypt. Philip's enemies such as Demosthenes appealed to Persia for assistance against Macedon, but in vain, as Artaxerxes III had been assassinated in 338 BC, precipitating a dynastic crisis that lasted for almost two years.

Philip exploited the chaos within the Persian Empire by sending an expeditionary force commanded by his trusted general Parmenion across the Hellespont in early 336 BC. The Macedonian army's march south along the Anatolian coast incited revolts in various Greek cities against their pro-Persian tyrants. At Eresus on Lesbos, the new government established a cult to Zeus Philippios, and the Ephesians placed a statue of Philip in the temple of Artemis. Parmenion's success augured well for the invasion Philip intended the next year. Fate, however, intervened.

Philip was assassinated at Aegae in summer 336 by **Pausanias**, a member of his own bodyguard. Philip's assassination climaxed a political crisis that had begun with his seventh marriage in 338. For most of his reign, Philip's queen had been his fourth wife, the Epirote princess **Olympias**, the mother of his designated heir, Alexander. Philip's other marriages had served diplomatic ends without threatening Olympias' position at court. His seventh marriage, however, was different, as Philip married a young Macedonian woman named **Cleopatra**, thereby allying himself for the first time with a powerful Macedonian noble family.

Whatever Philip's reasons for his marriage to Cleopatra—ancient writers explained it as a disastrous infatuation with a younger woman—its consequences quickly became evident. In short order both Olympias and Alexander fell from favor and fled into exile, amidst talk that Philip intended to supplant his son with a "Macedonian" heir. The threat to Alexander's position, however, proved short-lived; Cleopatra bore Philip a daughter he named Europa. The child's name bore witness to Philip's pride in his accomplishments, but a woman could not succeed to the Macedonian throne. Without a son to replace Alexander, Philip had to reconcile with him. A mutual friend, Demaratus of Corinth, effected the rapprochement. Although Olympias remained in exile in Epirus, Alexander returned to Pella and resumed his place at court. The crisis over the succession had ended, it seemed, without serious consequences.

Indirectly, however, Philip's ill-advised marriage to Cleopatra proved his undoing. Philip became embroiled in the enmities of her family, and one of them involved his assassin, Pausanias. According to Aristotle, Pausanias killed Philip because the king had ignored extreme abuse of him by Cleopatra's uncle Attalus. Pausanias had been raped by Attalus' servants to avenge the death of a young relative of Attalus, whom Pausanias had slandered because Philip had preferred the latter as his lover. Unwilling to offend Cleopatra's family, Philip tried to palliate Pausanias' grievance by promoting him to the coveted rank of royal bodyguard. The wedding of Philip's daughter Cleopatra at Aegae gave Pausanias an opportunity for revenge. As Philip led a splendid procession into the theater, Pausanias rushed forward and stabbed the king to death before the startled eyes of the guests from all over the Macedonian empire. So ended the reign of the most controversial of all Macedonian kings.

Since antiquity, historians have had difficulty assessing Philip and his achievements. Polybius was bewildered by Theopompus' observation that "Europe had never produced a man like Philip," which seemed contradicted by his lurid catalogue of Philip's "crimes and follies," including his unbridled sexuality and drunkenness, his betrayal of his friends and allies, and his destruction of Greek cities. The problem, of course, was perspective. The second-century BC historian Polybius found it difficult to sympathize with Theopompus' Greek view of Philip as a foreign, malignant force in Greek affairs and not as the founder of Macedonian greatness.

Both points of view have merit. Philip's influence on Greek affairs undeniably was largely negative. The destruction of cities such as Amphipolis, Methone, Stagira, and Olynthus is well documented. Philip was, however, first and foremost king of Macedon, and his primary concern was the welfare of Macedon, not Greece. In that regard he succeeded. During the twenty-four years of his reign, Philip transformed Macedon from a kingdom on the verge of dissolution to a unified state, ruling an empire that extended from the Danube to southern Greece. Whether his plans to extend Macedonian power into Asia were as grandiose as those carried out later by Alexander cannot be known. Nevertheless, it is clear that without Philip's legacy of a united, powerful Macedon, the achievements of Alexander and his successors would have been impossible.

KEY TERMS

Aristotle	Illyrians	Phocis
Battle of Chaeronea	Isocrates	royal companions
Cleopatra	Macedon	royal pages
Corinthian League	Olympias	Theopompus
Demosthenes	Pausanias	Theoric Fund
Eubulus	phalanx	Thessaly
Hellenization	Philip II	Thrace

SUGGESTED READINGS

Adcock, F. E. 1957. The *Greek and Macedonian Art of War*. Berkeley and Los Angeles: University of California Press. Clearly written introduction to Greek and Macedonian ideas of war.

Andronicos, Manolis. 1984. *Vergina: The Royal Tombs*. Trans. Louise Turner. Athens: Ekdotike Athenon. Beautifully illustrated account of the discovery of the Macedonian royal cemetery at Vergina.

Borza, Eugene N. 1990. *In the Shadow of Olympus: The Emergence of Macedon*. Princeton, NJ: Princeton University Press. Insightful history of the kingdom of Macedon from its origin to the reign of Philip II.

Carney, Elizabeth Donnelly. 2000. *Women and Monarchy in Macedonia*. Norman: University of Oklahoma Press. Pioneering study of the political significance of royal women in Macedonia.

———. 2006. *Olympias: Mother of Alexander the Great*. New York: Routledge. Lucidly written and insightful biography of the mother of Alexander the Great.

——— and Daniel Ogden, eds. 2010. *Philip II and Alexander the Great: Father and Son, Lives and Alternatives*. New York: Oxford University Press. Articles by leading scholars assessing various aspects of the relationship between Philip II and his son.

Sealey, Raphael. 1993. *Demosthenes and His Time: A Study in Defeat*. New York: Oxford University Press. Important revisionist biography of the Athenian statesman.

Worthington, Ian. 2008. *Philip II of Macedonia*. New Haven: Yale University Press. Vigorously written, detailed biography of Philip II.

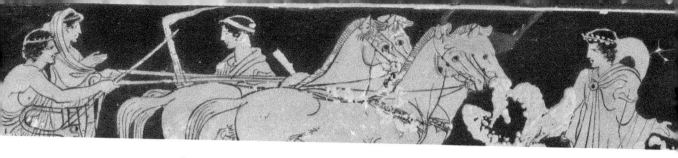

CHAPTER ELEVEN

Alexander the Great

Alexander the Great changed the world the Greeks knew forever, and the effects of his conquests reverberate to this day. News of recent events in Iran, Iraq, and Afghanistan echoes the names of places he passed through, destroyed, built, and changed and by which he, in turn, was changed. Alexander's death in 323 BC marked the end of the Classical period. Yet, rarely has an epoch-making reign begun in such uncertainty as that of Alexander.

Philip II had transformed Macedon into the leading military power in the region, controlling an empire that stretched from the Danube River to central Greece, but his assassination on the eve of his projected invasion of Asia threatened all of his achievements with ruin. Alexander III was only twenty years old at the time of his father's death in the summer of 336 BC. Omens were later said to have forecast his rule. His mother, Olympias, even claimed to have dreamed that lightning struck her womb. Although Philip had offspring from several of his wives, Alexander was treated as his father's heir throughout Philip's reign and carefully groomed for his future role. A series of Greek tutors, including Aristotle, provided him with an education in Greek literature and culture. From them Alexander gained his lifelong love of Homer and his determination to equal or exceed the exploits of his legendary ancestors, Heracles and Achilles.

Alexander also had practical training in kingship, governing Macedon in Philip's absence and suppressing a Thracian rebellion. He even commanded the companion (*hetairoi*) cavalry in the decisive Battle of Chaeronea in 338 BC. Nevertheless, Alexander's succession was not assured. Olympias and his closest friends and advisers were in exile, and there were rumors implicating Olympias and him in Philip's assassination. There was also talk of other possible successors, including

Figure 11.1. Idealized portrait head of Alexander from Pergamum (ca. 175–150 BC). The tilt of the head, beardlessness, and lion-like hair style were characteristic features of Alexander's personal image. Istanbul, Archaeological Museum 1138 (cat. 538).

the former king (*basileus*), Amyntas IV. **Antipater**, Philip's most senior commander, saved the succession for Alexander, however, by quickly presenting Alexander to the Macedonian troops at Aegae for the traditional acclamation as king.

CONSOLIDATING POWER

Alexander's personal role was never more important than in the critical first year of his reign. Philip's senior commanders urged the young king to proceed cautiously, consolidating his base in Macedon and conciliating Macedon's northern subjects and allies, even at the risk of losing influence in Greece. Not for the last time Alexander rejected the advice of the Macedonian old guard in favor of decisive action.

Greece first claimed Alexander's attention. Immediately after Philip's funeral, Alexander made a sudden and dramatic appearance there, forcing anti-Macedonian politicians at Athens and Thebes to abandon plans to exploit the confusion after Philip's assassination to free Greece. Alexander was confirmed quickly in Philip's former positions as *archōn* of Thessaly and *hēgemōn* of the Corinthian League, and Greek support for the war against Persia was reaffirmed. After returning from Greece, Alexander campaigned in the spring of 335 against the Thracians and Illyrians, thereby making clear that Philip's death would bring no easing of the Macedonian yoke.

Alexander's campaign extended as far north as the Danube. Only sketchy accounts of the course of events survive, but it is clear that his main target was the Triballi, who had humiliated Philip in 339 after his victory over the Scythians. The Triballi's attempt to hold a key pass against Alexander failed, thanks to the discipline of his Macedonian troops, who cleared a path for the wagons their enemies sent careening down the mountain in the hope of breaking their line. Triballian resistance quickly collapsed, allowing Alexander to launch an amphibious assault on an island where the Triballi had placed their women and children for safety. The other Thracian tribes submitted after a dramatic raid across the Danube into the territory of the Getae. He also concluded a treaty of friendship with a group of Gauls, the vanguard of a migration that would greatly affect southeastern Europe and Anatolia in the early Hellenistic period. Alexander completed his first major campaign by inflicting a severe defeat on his father's old enemy, the Illyrian king Cleitus. Although he received the first of his many battle wounds during the campaign, the Illyrian threat to Macedon's western frontier that had loomed over so many of his predecessors was at an end.

Alexander's long absence in the north sparked rumors of his death in Greece. Hope was mother to the fact. Demosthenes even introduced a supposed eyewitness of Alexander's death to the Athenian assembly. The Thebans revolted, besieging the city's Macedonian garrison on the Cadmea, the acropolis of Thebes, and inviting other Greek states to join them in the struggle for freedom. Forced marches by Alexander, however, brought the Macedonian army to Thebes before the rebellion could spread, persuading Athens and Sparta to withhold their support. When the Thebans nonetheless spurned his demand for surrender, the city was stormed and sacked. Alexander ordered that Thebes' Boeotian neighbors decide the city's fate; and they, ever resentful of Thebes' past efforts to subdue them, decided that the city should be destroyed and the remaining Thebans sold into slavery. Alexander carried out the decree, sparing from destruction only Thebes' temples and the descendants and house of its illustrious poet, Pindar.

Greeks long remembered the destruction of Thebes as one of the great atrocities of their history. Alexander himself was said later to have given special consideration to personal requests by individual Thebans. For the moment, however, his calculated use of terror achieved its purpose of discouraging resistance to Macedonian rule in Greece. For the second time in a little over a year, the Corinthian League acknowledged Alexander as its hegemon and affirmed its support for his policies. Alexander, for his part, moderated the severity of his demands on the Greeks, abandoning his call for the surrender of anti-Macedonian leaders at Athens and elsewhere in Greece.

Similar ruthlessness was employed in Macedon. As Alexander won popularity among his subjects with measures such as freeing Macedonians from all personal obligations except military service, he quickly eliminated potential rivals. The full extent of the purge is obscured by the sources' concentration on Olympias' brutal murder of Philip II's last wife Cleopatra and her daughter Europa. Fortunately, a spectacular archaeological discovery has illuminated these events.

At the modern village of Vergina, the site of the ancient Macedonian capital of Aegae, archaeologists discovered in 1981, under a tumulus approximately the size of a football field, three royal tombs. Tomb 1 was a chamber tomb that had been looted in antiquity but still contained the remains of an adult male, a young female, and an infant. The other two tombs—Tombs 2 and 3—were unlooted barrel-vaulted structures filled with grave goods as spectacular as those discovered by Schliemann at Mycenae a century earlier. Tomb 2 also contained the cremated remains of a middle-aged male and a young woman, and Tomb 3 held the remains of a teenage boy, almost certainly Alexander IV, the son of Alexander the Great. (See Plates XXa-b.) Scholars are divided over whether Philip II and Cleopatra were buried in Tomb 1 or Tomb 2, but in either case the fact remains that as one of the first acts of his reign, Alexander buried Cleopatra with full royal honors, probably in the hope of neutralizing the effects of her murder by Olympias. Once Alexander's hold on the throne was secure, however, he dropped all pretence of reconciliation and took decisive action against his enemies. The male members of Cleopatra's family were executed. Amyntas IV, Alexander's sole legitimate rival for the throne, who had survived Philip II's reign, also was sacrificed to the new king's need for security. Their surviving supporters fled to their only possible refuge, Persia, leaving Alexander as the unchallenged ruler of Macedon.

Invasion of Asia

With Macedon secure, Alexander invaded Asia in the spring of 334 BC. His army was fully 37,000 strong: its core was the 12,000 Macedonian phalanx troops, supplemented by 3,000 hypaspists ("royal guards") and 1,800 companion cavalry. It also included special light-armed units from Illyria and Thrace and almost 9,000 allied Greek infantry and cavalry. A fleet of almost 200 Greek ships supported his troops and maintained his communications with Europe.

Alexander's first actions in Asia were bold, even theatrical. He was the first Macedonian to land on Asian soil, leaping ashore and casting his spear into the land to claim all that he conquered as territory won by the spear. He then went to the traditional site of Troy, where he sacrificed to Athena, asked pardon of the legendary Trojan king Priam for invading Asia, and paid homage to his alleged ancestor Achilles.

The symbolism suited the leader of the Greek crusade, but serious problems lay behind all the bravado. Alexander had been compelled to leave almost half his Macedonian troops with Antipater to control Greece and Macedon. In Asia, everything won by Philip in 336 had been lost except for the bridgehead at Abydus. Worse yet, Alexander had sufficient funds for only a brief campaign, and his friends did not control the government and army. In Macedon, Antipater governed as his regent. Moreover, Alexander's second-in-command in Asia was **Parmenion**, a friend of Antipater and a former ally of Cleopatra's family, whose relatives held key commands in the army's critical cavalry units. Alexander needed a quick victory to achieve the goals of his campaign and to liberate him from the control of the Macedonian aristocrats who had made him king. Fortunately, the Persians proved to be "convenient enemies."

The vast extent of the Persian Empire slowed mobilization of its main forces to confront threats on its frontiers, forcing satraps to rely on their garrison troops to cope with invasions. Satraps normally employed a defensive strategy that would deny the enemy use of local resources until the **Great King** could mobilize and bring the empire's main forces to bear on the invader. The Anatolian satraps, who were unwilling to risk the losses in revenue and the destruction of royal lands that such a strategy would entail, chose a bolder course, deciding to confront Alexander directly in battle in the hope of killing him.

The strategy almost worked. The Persians met Alexander at the River Granicus, the modern Biga Çayı, in northwest Anatolia. The details of the battle itself are disputed, but it is clear that the Persians nearly succeeded in killing Alexander, who stood out clearly in the flamboyant "armor of Achilles" that he had taken from the temple of Athena at Troy. Only the daring action of Cleitus the Black, the brother of Alexander's nurse, saved the king from certain death: At a crucial moment Cleitus sliced off the arm of a Persian noble who was about to deal a fatal blow to an already dazed Alexander.

Because the Persians had staked everything on killing Alexander, the failure of their plan brought disaster. Their army was totally destroyed. The fate of the Greek mercenaries who formed the core of the Persian army was particularly harsh. Alexander ordered all but two thousand of them to be slaughtered as traitors to the Greek cause. The survivors were sent to Macedonia to work in chains. Alexander boldly announced his victory to the Greek world by sending to Athens three hundred suits of Persian armor as a dedication to Athena with the inscription "From Alexander, the son of Philip, and the Greeks, except the Spartans." His barbed reference to the Spartans highlighted their refusal to join the League of Corinth and share in the Panhellenic crusade against Persia.

Alexander's victory at the **Battle of Granicus** changed the character of the war, depriving the Persians of their ability to mount an effective defense in Anatolia while fomenting rebellion in Greece. Although the Phoenician fleet freely cruised the Aegean, the Greeks as a whole refused to commit themselves to the Persian cause. Alexander's forces, meanwhile, swept south along the west coast of Anatolia. In quick succession the satrapies of Lydia, Caria, and Lycia fell. By the spring of 333, Alexander had reached Gordium, the capital of the ancient kingdom of Phrygia, near modern Ancyra in central Anatolia. In less than a year, Isocrates' once seemingly impossible dream of severing Anatolia from the Persian Empire had been realized.

Alexander's rapid conquest of Anatolia exposed the contradiction in his dual position as hegemon of the League of Corinth and king of Macedon. As hegemon he was required to respect the commitments he and Philip had made to the League of Corinth. Consequently, he punished captured Greek mercenaries and turned deposed pro-Persian tyrants over to the league council for trial. As king of Macedon, however, he dealt with conquered territory as he saw fit, and increasingly his interests as king overrode his obligations to the League and his concern for Greek opinion.

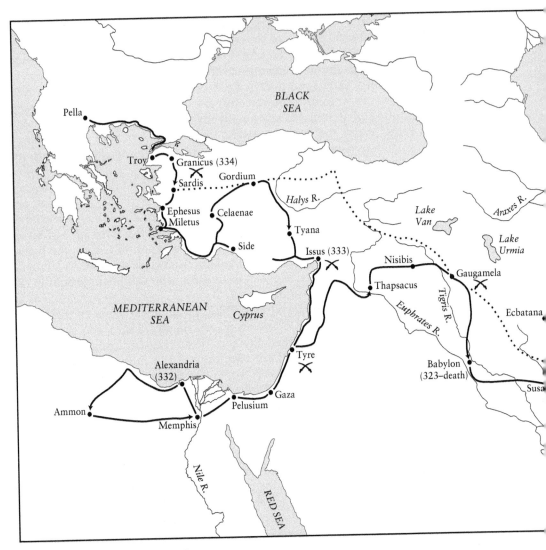

Figure 11.2. Alexander's campaign.

Greek Reaction

Alexander made his supremacy clear immediately after his victory at the Granicus. Greek and non-Greek cities that surrendered were ordered to obey their new Macedonian satrap and to pay the same tribute they had paid to the Persians. When it became clear that his previous severity had only stiffened the resolve of Greek mercenaries in Persian service to fight, he eased the terms for their surrender. Similarly, he encouraged democratic factions in the Greek cities of Asia when they offered their support to the Macedonian forces. The newly

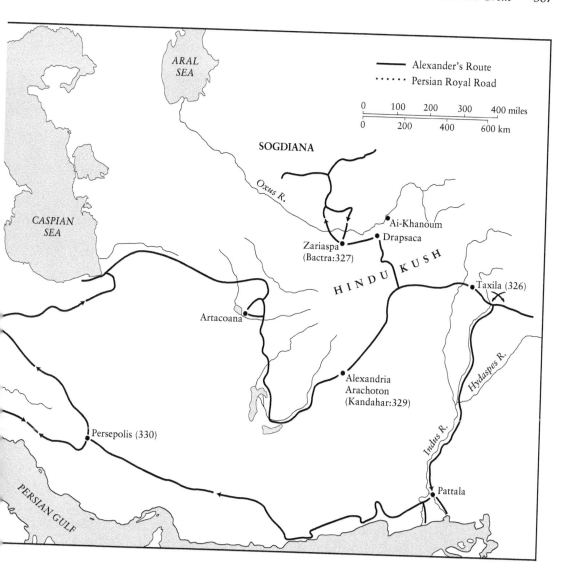

"liberated" cities, however, found that freedom had limits. They no longer paid "tribute" to the Persians, but they now made financial "contributions" to the Macedonians and were severely punished if they objected. Inscriptions from Chios and other Asian cities also document Alexander's readiness to intervene in the internal affairs of cities.

Alexander's relationship with his new non-Greek subjects was similar. Although his first Asian satraps were Macedonians, he soon began to court local support. In Caria, he entrusted the civil administration of the area to Queen Ada, who ruled as a widow like her predecessor Artemisia, who had commanded her own ships at the Battle of Salamis. Ada showed her affection and gratitude by adopting Alexander as her son and heir. Control of military affairs, however, remained in the hands of a Macedonian garrison commander responsible to Alexander. Still, the policy was clear. Non-Greek leaders who recognized Alexander could expect royal favor and promotion.

Although Isocrates had dreamed of a new greater Greece in Anatolia, the true situation was more accurately reflected in the symbolism of Alexander's dramatic severing of the **"Gordian knot."** According to a famous legend, rule over Asia was promised to whoever loosed the complex knot that connected the wagon pole to the wagon the first Midas had ridden when he became king of Phrygia. While he was at Gordium, Alexander fulfilled the prophecy by slashing through the knot with his sword, allowing no doubt that a new king had arisen in Asia.

A severe fever that brought Alexander to the brink of death delayed the departure of the Macedonian army from Anatolia until the summer of 333. His brush with death revealed his unique importance to the expedition. Without an heir, Alexander was indispensable. Only he held the army together and gave its actions force and direction. The army's dependence on Alexander would only increase as its march carried it farther and farther away from Macedon.

After his illness, Alexander made a characteristically bold decision. Instead of seeking to confront the forces of **Darius III** directly in Mesopotamia, Alexander moved south along the coast toward Egypt. Behind this decision lay a risky calculation. Having disbanded his own Greek fleet, Alexander hoped to end Persian naval operations in the Aegean by depriving the Persian fleet of its bases.

The strategy was daring and almost resulted in catastrophe. Alexander marched south along the coast during the late summer and fall of 333. At the same time, Darius III led the Persian Empire's main forces northwestward from Babylon, hoping to trap Alexander in Anatolia. On learning Alexander was advancing toward Syria, Darius followed at his rear, thereby severing Alexander's communications with Anatolia and his Macedonian base. Darius, however, failed to exploit his advantage by allowing Alexander to choose to confront the Persian army at Issus in Cilicia in a narrow coastal plain. Prevented from fully deploying his forces, Darius was unable to benefit from the Persians' numerical superiority.

Callisthenes, Aristotle's nephew and the campaign's official historian, treated the **Battle of Issus** as a Homeric contest between Alexander and Darius III in which victory resulted from a cavalry charge led by Alexander on the center of the Persian line. Darius was forced to abandon his army and flee. A famous painting of the late fourth century BC brilliantly depicted this moment; a mosaic copy of this painting was discovered at Pompeii and is now preserved in the Naples Museum. (See Plate XXI.) The flight of Darius turned the defeat of the Persian army into a fearful rout. Years later, Ptolemy I recounted in his history of Alexander how his units had crossed streams on the piled-up bodies of dead Persian soldiers.

Alexander's victory at Issus was a turning point in his campaign. The main Persian forces had been destroyed and Darius III had fled in disgrace. The royal treasure stored at Damascus quickly fell into Alexander's hands and ended the financial problems that had threatened his plans since their inception. Alexander had even captured Darius' family, including his mother, wife, daughters, and son and heir to the Persian throne.

Alexander had not merely defeated the Great King: He had humiliated him. This humiliation continued, as Alexander summarily rejected Darius' written offer of friendship and alliance in exchange for his family's return. He also accorded the Persian royal family the protection and public deference to which their former station entitled them but that they had lost when Darius deserted them. The symbolism was clear and unambiguous: Henceforth Alexander was the arbiter of the fate of the Achaemenids. The Greeks also understood the significance of Alexander's victory. After Issus, all hope of Persian aid against Macedonian rule had to be abandoned. Not surprisingly, the rest of Greece remained passive when Antipater crushed a Spartan rebellion in 331 BC.

Figure 11.3. The Alexander Sarcophagus (c. 310 BC). Found in the royal necropolis at Sidon, this huge sarcophagus contained the remains of Abdalonymus, whom Alexander appointed king of Sidon and one of his companions after the Battle of Issus. The side illustrated depicts Macedonians and persons in Persian dress participating in a royal hunt. Many traces of the original colors are preserved. Istanbul, Archaeological Museum.

From Issus to Egypt: Conquest of the Eastern Mediterranean (332–331 bc)

While Darius fled eastward, Alexander resumed his march toward Egypt. Most of the Syrian and Phoenician coastal cities surrendered, successfully concluding Alexander's plan to defeat the Persian fleet by depriving it of its bases. The situation is less clear with regard to the interior of Syria and Palestine, but the surrender of the Samaritans in northern Judaea suggests that the peoples of these areas also quickly came to terms with Alexander.

Only Tyre and Gaza resisted Alexander, and his response was characteristically vigorous. When the Tyrians rejected Alexander's request to enter the city and sacrifice to his ancestor Heracles in the guise of their chief god Melqart, he besieged the city for almost eight months. After being captured in August 332, Tyre also suffered the same brutal fate as Thebes: slaughter of most of the male population and sale of the surviving women and children. The decision by Gaza's Persian governor, a eunuch named Batis, to maintain his loyalty to Darius resulted in a similar fate for his city two months later. The fall of Gaza gave Alexander the greatest prize of the first phase of his Asian adventure: Egypt.

Alexander in Egypt

Alexander's stay in Egypt dramatically altered his view of himself and his public image, but the conquest of Egypt itself was anticlimactic, as the last Persian satrap of Egypt surrendered his satrapy without a fight.

Unlike most of the other peoples of the ancient Near East, the Egyptians had never accepted Persian rule. Severe Persian repression had followed Egyptian rebellions during the fifth and fourth centuries bc. Not surprisingly, therefore, the Egyptians welcomed Alexander's army during its march to the ancient capital

Figure 11.4. Alexander being the son of Ammon became an accepted part of the popular tradition concerning Alexander in late antiquity as illustrated by this contorniate (bronze medallion) showing Olympias (identified as Queen Olympias) feeding Ammon in the form of a snake. Macedon, c. 4th century AD. London, The British Museum.

of Memphis, where he held Greek-style games and sacrificed to Zeus. At the same time, Alexander also carefully avoided the errors of his Persian predecessors, publicly honoring the Apis bull, the living incarnation of Ptah, chief god of Memphis, and other Egyptian deities. Alexander doubtless accomplished much during the six months he spent in Egypt, but the sources concentrate on only two episodes: his consultation of the oracle of **Zeus-Ammon** and the establishment of **Alexandria**, the first city he founded.

The oracle of Zeus-Ammon, about three hundred miles west of the Nile in the oasis of Siwah, was one of the three principal oracles patronized by the Greeks. The report of Alexander's visit to Siwah was a tale of miracle and romance. Unseasonable rains provided water; and sacred animals, such as snakes or crows, served as guides. Unfortunately, Alexander revealed neither his motives for consulting the oracle nor its reply to him. Ancient and modern historians have proposed widely differing explanations for his visit, suggesting that he desired to duplicate his legendary ancestor Heracles' visit to the oracle; or to surpass the Persian king Cambyses, who had failed to conquer the oasis; or to obtain divine approval for the new city of Alexandria.

All the ancient accounts agree, however, that the decisive moment of his visit was when the chief priest of the oracle greeted him as "Son of Ammon." Through the process historians call syncretism ("the unification of religious beliefs"), Greeks equated Ammon with Zeus. The Greeks, therefore, understood that the priest had recognized Alexander as a son of Zeus. Whether or not the priest was merely according Alexander the welcome traditionally granted a king of Egypt, Alexander clearly took it as a divine sign that Olympias rightly claimed that there had been something more than mortal about his birth.

Alexander had probably selected the site for his new city during his trip to Siwah, but the actual foundation of Alexandria occurred after his return from the oracle in April 331. Strong Homeric associations influenced his choice of the site: Just offshore was the island of Pharos made famous by the *Odyssey*. It was also ideal for a great commercial center, with Pharos creating a sheltered anchorage and Lake Canopus linking it to the Nile and the interior of Egypt. Understandably, the sources depict Alexandria as destined for greatness, telling how birds consumed the sacred flour with which Alexander was marking its boundaries, thereby indicating that the city would nourish people from all over the world.

Founding Alexandria was Alexander's last major act in Egypt. It is difficult to assess the full significance of Alexander's conduct, but his actions in Egypt as a whole indicate continuity between his policies there and those he followed in the territories conquered earlier in the campaign. This is particularly clear with regard to Alexandria, which was founded as a Greek polis with citizenship limited to Greeks and Macedonians. Alexander's organization of Egypt itself likewise followed the model he had used in Anatolia. Thus, although he did not appoint a single satrap for the entire country, Alexander retained much of the Persian organization of Egypt, including the requirement that Egyptians pay tribute. Both Egyptians and Greeks exercised only civil authority. Military power remained in the hands of Macedonian officers.

Figure 11.5. Representation of Alexander as Pharaoh before Ammon-Ra and Khonsu-Thoth in the Bark shrine at Luxor temple at Thebes, c. 330–325 BC.

Only in one area was there significant change, but that area was the most important of all: Alexander's self-image. The revelation of his divine parentage at Siwah struck a responsive chord in Alexander. It confirmed his sense of his own uniqueness and heightened his personal identification with his heroic ancestors Heracles and Achilles. Henceforth, his unshakable belief in his connection to his divine father Ammon would be the linchpin of his personality. His belief in his divine descent also opened a rift between him and the older Macedonians. They could not accept Alexander's view of his special tie to a "barbarian" god and the implied slight to Philip, the king they believed responsible for Macedonian greatness.

FROM ALEXANDRIA TO PERSEPOLIS: THE KING OF ASIA (331–330 BC)

Shortly after founding Alexandria, Alexander left Egypt to seek a final confrontation with Darius III. Darius, for his part, made one last desperate effort to avoid battle, offering Alexander marriage to his eldest daughter, cession of all territory west of the Euphrates River, and an enormous ransom for his family. Darius' offer was unprecedented. It involved division of the empire, surrender of several of its richest satrapies, and permanent exclusion of Persian power from the shores of the Mediterranean.

Parmenion probably spoke for many when he advised Alexander to accept Darius' proposal. Alexander, however, would have none of it, curtly observing that he would accept it, too—if he were Parmenion! Faced with Alexander's refusal, Darius hastily assembled another army to face the Macedonians. The two armies finally met on October 1, 331 BC, at Gaugamela in northeastern Iraq. Thanks to the capture of the Persian plans in Darius' headquarters after his defeat, the **Battle of Gaugamela** is the best documented battle in Greek history.

The Battle of Gaugamela (331 BC)

Learning from his defeat at Issus the previous year, Darius carefully chose a battle-field that suited the strengths and weaknesses of his army. Because his new army was particularly strong in cavalry, but weak in first-line infantry, Darius hoped that the broad plain of Gaugamela would allow the Persian cavalry to envelop Alexander's Macedonians, and terror weapons such as scythed chariots and elephants would confuse and disrupt the superior Macedonian infantry. Despite Darius' careful preparations, however, the battle of Gaugamela ended just like the battle of Issus with an attack by Alexander and the companion cavalry on the center of the Persian army. Darius fled the battlefield and sought refuge in eastern Iran. Although Alexander failed to capture Darius, the heartland of the Persian Empire was now his for the taking. With justification, his troops saluted him as king of Asia.

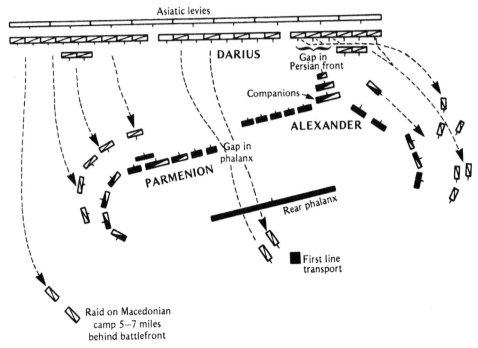

Figure 11.6. Plan of the Battle of Gaugamela.

Alexander captured Babylon, Susa, and Persepolis in rapid succession, but he treated his three great prizes differently. Alexander entered Babylon in triumph in mid-October 331. As in Egypt, he sought to conciliate the influential Babylonian priesthood, offering sacrifice to Babylon's chief god Marduk and ordering the reconstruction of his temple that the Persians had destroyed a century and a half earlier as punishment for a Babylonian rebellion. He rewarded the satraps who had surrendered Babylonia and Susa by leaving them in their positions. Far different, however, was the fate of **Persepolis** and its citizens.

Persepolis was the spiritual center of the Persian Empire where major rituals of Persian rule such as the new year's festival and the ceremonial presentation of their tribute to the Great King by his subjects took place. There also Greek ambassadors had abased themselves before Persian kings since the reign of Darius I. Persepolis was therefore identified with Persian rule in the eyes of Greeks and Persians alike, and its treatment would send a clear message to both peoples. The message Alexander chose to send was vengeance for the destruction wrought during the Persian wars of the early fifth century BC. Just before leaving Persepolis in April 330 BC, the Macedonians torched the city's palaces.

A large entourage of noncombatants including slaves, women, children, and entrepreneurs of all types accompanied the army. It was said that during a drunken revel, Thaïs, an Athenian courtesan, suggested to Alexander and his

Figure 11.7. Palace of Persepolis, 518–330 BC.

friends that Persepolis be burned in revenge for the Persians' destruction of Athens in 480. Thaïs may have inspired the actual burning of Persepolis, but Alexander clearly had decided at the time of its capture that the city was to be destroyed. Despite its surrender, Persepolis suffered the same fate as Thebes and Tyre. In the twentieth century, American archaeologists excavated Persepolis and the last Shah of Iran restored the site. The excavations have also revealed that its palaces were completely stripped of their treasures, the accumulated wealth of two centuries of Persian imperial rule, before they were set on fire. With the flames rising over the ruins of Persepolis, Alexander unmistakably signaled the triumphant end of the Greek crusade.

THE HIGH ROAD TO INDIA: ALEXANDER IN CENTRAL ASIA

As Alexander watched Persepolis burn, he could not know that the next four years would be the most difficult of the campaign. At first, his good fortune seemed to continue unabated. Darius had fled eastward from Media, leaving Ecbatana (the last of the Persian capitals) to fall into Alexander's hands with its treasures intact. Having secured Persia and Media, Alexander discharged his remaining Greek troops. All that remained was to capture Darius III himself and put an end to the long line of Achaemenid rulers.

The Death of Darius (330 BC)

Leaving Parmenion behind at Ecbatana to secure his communications with the west, Alexander raced after Darius. He hoped to intercept him before he could reach Bactria, modern Afghanistan, and continue resistance from there. Before Alexander could overtake the fleeing Great King, however, he learned that a cabal of eastern satraps headed by **Bessus**, the satrap of Bactria, had assassinated Darius III in July 330 BC. Worse yet, Bessus had escaped to Bactria, where he had assumed the throne of Persia as Artaxerxes IV.

The assassination of Darius III changed the dynamics of the campaign. Alexander had hitherto acted in Persia as the avenger of past Persian misdeeds. It was a stance that was popular with Greeks but hardly calculated to attract Persian support. Darius' assassination allowed Alexander to escape from this dilemma by assuming the role of his successor and acting as defender of Achaemenid legitimacy against the regicides. To symbolize his new role Alexander adopted a style of dress that combined both Macedonian and Persian royal style. Darius' body was brought back to Persia and buried with full royal honors. A rumor even spread that Darius' last wish had been that Alexander avenge him.

Alexander's strategy was clever and effective. Whereas Persian nobles and even some surviving members of the Achaemenid house joined Alexander, Bessus alienated potential supporters by failing to confront Alexander directly. As a result, resistance melted away as Alexander moved farther into eastern Iran. Finally, in the spring of 329, Bessus' fellow regicides, fearful for their own survival, betrayed Bessus to Alexander in exchange for a pardon and confirmation in their offices, just as they had betrayed Darius III before. Acting as the successor of the Achaemenids, Alexander turned Bessus over to his Persian supporters for trial and execution as a regicide.

The Struggle for Bactria and Sogdiana (330–327 BC)

As Alexander marched farther and farther east, the miraculous and romantic elements of his epic increased. It was even rumored that, like a mythical hero, he enjoyed a tryst with a mythical non-Greek woman: an Amazon queen. Unfortunately, Alexander's ignorance of conditions in eastern Iran almost cost him everything he had gained through his astute dynastic policy. Unaware of the close ties between the peoples of eastern Iran and the Scythians and the intricate network of tribal relations in the region, Alexander ignited rebellion throughout much of Sogdiana and Bactria by trying to establish a controlled border between Sogdiana and Scythia at the Jaxartes River. The revolt lasted almost three years.

By the time it ended in 327, Alexander had suffered the worst military defeats of the entire campaign and developed a new approach to controlling conquered territory.

Alexander replaced Iranian satraps with Greek and Macedonian officials. He also settled Greek mercenaries and discharged veterans in military colonies at strategic sites in Sogdiana and Bactria. Most important, however, the crisis in central Asia starkly revealed the growing tensions in the army and even within Alexander's court itself.

Macedonian Unrest

No Greek or Macedonian army had ever campaigned for so long or so far away from home, and Alexander's soldiers became more reluctant to advance farther into Asia. Alexander had barely dissuaded his troops from going home as soon as they learned of Darius' death. The miseries of the subsequent struggles in Bactria and Sogdiana only increased their longing for home. More worrisome to his officers was Alexander's abandonment of the traditional Macedonian style of kingship and the growing prominence of Iranians and Iranian practices at court. The most dramatic example of the trend was Alexander's marriage in the spring of 327 to **Roxane**, the daughter of a powerful Sogdian noble.

The marriage was politically astute, as it brought Alexander the alliance of one of the principal tribal chieftains in Bactria and Sogdiana, and then, as now, the support of such men was the key to controlling the area's fierce peoples. Nevertheless, to his officers and soldiers, the fact remained that Alexander's queen and the potential mother of his successor was not a Macedonian or even a Greek but an Iranian! Of course, Alexander's own mother also was not Macedonian but from Epirus, and his rivals in Macedonia had tried to use his hybrid lineage as a reason to deny him the throne.

Alexander's unsuccessful demand for the ritual prostration known as *proskynēsis* on the part of all members of his court further increased tension at court. Ancient and modern writers have seen a connection between Alexander's desire for proskynesis and his claim to be son of Ammon, but they disagree regarding his intentions. According to the historian Arrian, for example, Alexander desired that by performing ritual prostration people would recognize his divine descent from Ammon; and the biographer Plutarch, on the other hand, thought that Alexander hoped to use proskynesis as a political device.

DOCUMENT 11.1

The Divinity of Alexander

He generally behaved haughtily towards non-Greeks and made it seem as though he was fully convinced of his divine birth and parentage, but kept his assumption of divinity within reasonable bounds and did not overdo it when he was dealing with Greeks. . . . When he had been wounded by an arrow and was in great pain, he said, "What you see flowing here, my friends, is blood and not ichor, which flows in the veins of the blessed gods.". . . It is clear that Alexander had not actually become affected or puffed up, but used belief in his divinity to dominate others.

(Plutarch, *Life of Alexander* 28; Waterfield)

Most modern scholars adopt a view similar to that of Plutarch, especially because Persians viewed proskynesis as an affirmation of the hierarchical order of society. Whatever Alexander's intentions may have been, he underestimated the resistance to his plans. Greeks and Macedonians saw proskynesis as a recognition of divinity and an unwelcome reminder of past Persian arrogance. They tolerated its performance by Persians at Alexander's court, but not his effort to make them also perform it. It is not surprising, therefore, that for the first time there was open resistance to Alexander's policies and even conspiracies against his life.

The first sign of trouble appeared late in 330 and involved Parmenion's son, **Philotas**, the commander of the companion cavalry, who was executed for failing to inform Alexander of an alleged plot to kill him. Whether the charges against Philotas were true or not, Alexander henceforth took seriously the possibility of conspiracies against him and acted accordingly, ordering the assassination of Philotas' father Parmenion. Alexander of Lyncestis, a son-in-law of Antipater, who had been held under arrest since the beginning of the campaign, was also executed. Alexander even instituted censorship of his soldiers' and officers' correspondence.

These measures muted the rancor at court, but they did not eliminate discontent. The most dramatic incident was Alexander's drunken murder in autumn 328 of Cleitus the Black, who had saved his life at the Granicus. Cleitus' offense was criticizing Alexander's efforts to accommodate the Persians and his belittling the contribution of his officers and soldiers to his successes. More seriously, Alexander was nearly assassinated six months later by a group of his own pages, who claimed at their trial that they hoped to free the Macedonians from Alexander's growing tyranny. As with Philotas, Alexander was implacable in the face of disloyalty by members of his personal entourage. The pages were summarily tried and executed. Callisthenes, Alexander's historian and the pages' tutor, who had publicly opposed the introduction of proskynesis, was arrested and later died under mysterious circumstances.

By the summer of 327, Sogdiana and Bactria had been secured. That happy outcome, however, had required years of hard fighting and suffering and had resulted in major changes, especially in the army. Forced to cope with a mobile and resourceful enemy, Alexander reorganized his army to allow greater flexibility. In particular, he extensively recruited Iranian units to supplement his steadily dwindling supply of Macedonian and Greek troops.

Equally important changes occurred in Alexander's court. Men personally tied to Alexander, such as Perdiccas, Craterus, Lysimachus, and Ptolemy, had replaced the Macedonian "old guard." These men would play critical roles in the turbulent events that followed Alexander's death. Finally, the relationship between Alexander and his soldiers had altered in a subtle but significant way. Their loyalty remained unchallenged, but, as events in India were to demonstrate, Alexander would never again be able to count on their unquestioning obedience.

INDIA AND THE END OF THE DREAM

When Alexander entered India in the summer of 327 BC, he believed he was approaching the end of the inhabited world. For Greeks and Persians alike, India was the land of the Indus River, essentially modern Pakistan. Aristotle believed that beyond India there was only a great desert and then ocean. Although Darius I had incorporated India into the Persian Empire, Persian rule had long since ended when Alexander entered the region. He believed he would be campaigning in a land that Dionysus, Heracles, and the legendary Assyrian queen Semiramis had failed to conquer, a land where cannibals and monstrous men and animals lived, where cloth grew on trees and ants mined gold. What Alexander actually found was almost as remarkable and at least as strange to him: a vast subcontinent occupied by a network of peoples and states who viewed him as a new piece to be played in their complex political chess game.

As the Macedonian army descended through the Khyber Pass to the plain of the Indus River in the summer and fall of 327, it encountered some of the fiercest resistance in the campaign. Opposition ended only at Taxila, whose ruler,

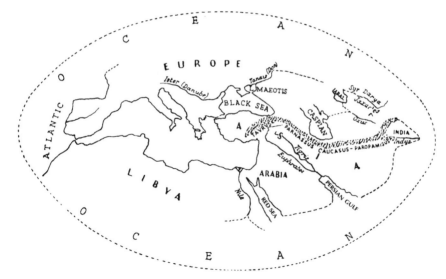

Figure 11.8. The Greek view of the inhabited world.

called Taxiles, had already solicited Alexander's aid while he was still in central Asia. Taxila was one of the principal centers of Indian religious thought. There Alexander met with a group of "naked philosophers"—ascetic Indian holy men, one of whom, Calanus, even joined his expedition.

Taxiles had sought Alexander's aid against his eastern neighbors, Abisares, the ruler of Kashmir, and especially Porus, whose kingdom included all the territory between the Jhelum and Chenab rivers. When Abisares offered his submission, Alexander moved against Porus in early 326.

The Battle of the Hydaspes (326 BC)

The two armies met at the Hydaspes River, the modern Jhelum. There Alexander found that Porus had established a strong defensive position, using his infantry and his two hundred elephants to form a living wall along the east bank of the river. Solving this difficult military problem took all of Alexander's tactical skills and involved a daring secret crossing of the flooded river. In the end, the outcome was the same as that of his earlier battles: the total destruction of his enemy's forces. (See Plate XIX.) Much to the displeasure of Taxiles, however, Alexander spared Porus. Instead, impressed by the nobility of his defeated opponent, who asked only to be treated "like a king," Alexander restored his kingdom to Porus and even added new territories to it.

Although Alexander did not realize it at the time, the **Battle of Hydaspes** was to be his last pitched battle. As the army marched farther eastward, morale dropped steadily. The crisis came when Alexander reached the river Hyphasis, the modern Beas. Exhausted by the stresses of fighting and marching during the endless rains of the summer monsoon, terrified by rumors of yet another great

Figure 11.9. Silver five-shekel coin from Babylonia, c. 326–323 BC. Obverse: Alexander attacking Porus on his elephant. Reverse: Alexander holding a scepter and thunderbolt, attributes of Zeus. London, The British Museum.

river valley occupied by great kingdoms possessing thousands of war elephants, and doubtful that they would ever return home, the army mutinied. This time not even Alexander could persuade his soldiers to go on. Ultimately, Alexander yielded, defeated by his own army, and agreed to return to the Indus, where he had already ordered the construction of a great fleet.

The End of the Campaign

As Alexander kept his plans to himself, ancient and modern historians have speculated about his ultimate goals. After he had defeated Darius and taken control of the Persian Empire, why did he continue to push ever eastward? Did he have a master plan for world conquest when he left Macedonia, or did his ambitions grow with each new success? No definitive answer is possible. Whatever Alexander's ultimate intentions may have been, his army forced him to adopt a more modest goal: the conquest of the Indus River Valley to its mouth.

From early winter 326 to midsummer 325, Alexander's army moved steadily southward against heavy resistance. The tale of slaughter told in the ancient sources is unparalleled elsewhere in the campaign. Finally, in July 325, the army reached the mouth of the Indus. On an island near its mouth, Alexander made offerings to gods for whom his father Ammon had ordered sacrifices; then he sailed out onto the Indian Ocean to pray to Poseidon for a safe voyage to Babylonia. The preparations for the journey home had begun.

Results of the Indian Campaign

Alexander's invasion was the first major incursion into India from the west since the reign of Darius I almost two centuries earlier. Like that of Darius, Alexander's campaign produced a flood of new information about India and its peoples. Also like the Persians, the Macedonians were to remain only briefly in India. Little more than a decade after Alexander's death, the Macedonian presence had disappeared from the Indian landscape and from Indian consciousness. Greek and Indian artistic traditions mingled to produce Gandara art and to establish a stylistic vocabulary for expressing Buddhist traditions in human form, but Indian culture forgot the historical Alexander and remembered only the romantic Alexander of legend.

The ephemeral character of Alexander's achievements in India suggests to some historians that he lost interest in the area once his army's mutiny halted his advance to the Ganges Valley, but this is to confuse results with intentions. Alexander's political arrangements in India indicate that he intended to maintain control of his Indian conquests after his return to the west. Three Macedonian satraps supported by strong detachments of mercenary troops governed the Indus Valley. Loyal local rulers such as Taxiles retained their thrones under the supervision of one of the Macedonian satraps. Three new Greek cities were founded in the northern satrapy, and several foundations were also planned for the other satrapies. Finally, the expanded kingdom of Alexander's ally, King Porus, protected the Macedonians' eastern flank. Alexander had planned carefully for his Indian domain, but the resources available to his agents proved inadequate to maintain Macedonian rule in this remote part of his empire.

RETURN TO THE WEST

Alexander left India for Persia in late August 325. He intended to lead his army through Gedrosia, an arid region in southwestern Pakistan. His purpose was to establish supply depots for his fleet, which was to follow the time-honored route along the north coast of the Indian Ocean from the mouth of the Indus River to the Persian Gulf. Nearchus, the commander of Alexander's fleet and one of his closest friends, later claimed that Alexander, ever the competitor, was also determined to surpass Semiramis and Cyrus the Great of Persia, who lost their armies in Gedrosia. For almost two months, Alexander's men struggled through the arid wastes of Gedrosia. Including the wives and children of his soldiers and camp followers, possibly as many as eighty thousand souls made up what was virtually a moving city. Before the army finally reached Carmania and safety, thousands died, including most of the soldiers' families, who were swept away together with the bulk of their possessions in a flash flood. Only news of the safe arrival of the fleet at the head of the Persian Gulf in December 325 BC, after an adventure-filled voyage that included encounters with whales and exploration of a "haunted" island, lessened Alexander's sense of having barely escaped total disaster.

Reorganization of the Empire

Alexander's return from India sparked turmoil throughout his empire. Eight satraps and generals—both Macedonians and Iranians—were quickly deposed and executed. One of Alexander's oldest friends, the royal treasurer, Harpalus, fled to Athens with a huge fortune looted from the king's funds and a private army of six thousand mercenaries. The ancient sources argued that the upheaval was caused by the deterioration of Alexander's character. Modern admirers cite his outrage at the reports of corruption and oppression by his officials. The truth is more complex. Some victims of the king's wrath, such as the governors of the satrapies along his line of march through Gedrosia, clearly were scapegoats for a disaster that was largely of Alexander's own making. Others were victims of court politics and jealousies, but as the Roman historian Curtius Rufus (10.1.7) perceptively noted, most were guilty of the one unforgivable crime: They had assumed Alexander would not survive and had begun to exploit his empire for their own personal benefit.

Alexander's actions were not limited to punishing overly ambitious and corrupt subordinates. He also attempted to prevent similar problems in the future. All satraps were ordered to disband their mercenary forces. When roving bands of penniless cashiered soldiers threatened the security of his Asian realm, Alexander ordered the cities of Greece to permit their exiles to return home. Fully twenty thousand exiles are said to have heard Aristotle's son-in-law Nicanor read the royal decree at Olympia in the summer of 324 BC. Reintegrating them into their various cities was to cause turmoil in Greece for years to come, sparking a last desperate attempt by the Greek cities to free themselves from Macedonian rule after Alexander's death.

Uniting Greek and "Barbarian"

Almost as serious a threat to Alexander was the dismay of his veteran Macedonian troops at the changes in their relationship to their king. In the early spring of 324, Alexander celebrated the conquest of India in grand style. Decorations were distributed to officers of the army and fleet. The climax of the celebration was a grand marriage ceremony in which Alexander himself took as wives daughters of Artaxerxes III and Darius III, although he was already married to Roxane, following the precedent set by his father Philip II, who had married at least seven women from territories he had conquered. In the same ceremony ninety of Alexander's principal officers married noble Persian and Median wives. Gifts also were distributed to ten thousand of his soldiers who had followed Alexander's example and married Asian women, and the king paid their debts.

The good feelings quickly dissipated when Alexander introduced into the army thirty thousand young Iranian troops trained to fight in Macedonian style, whom he referred to as his "Successors." Their name suggested that they were eventually to replace his Macedonians. It is not surprising, therefore, that when Alexander announced at Opis in the summer of 324 that he intended to discharge and send home veterans who were too old or too ill to fight, the army mutinied. The soldiers demanded that the king discharge them all and sarcastically urged that he henceforth rely on his father Ammon. Only after Alexander reassured them that his Macedonians were his only true "companions" did the mutiny subside.

His veterans' victory was only symbolic. Although Macedonians occupied seats of honor at a great banquet Alexander held at Opis to celebrate the end of the mutiny, he remained steadfast in carrying out his original plans. He discharged the veterans shortly thereafter and sent them back to Macedon while retaining the children produced by their marriages to Asian women with him as the nucleus of a new generation of soldiers loyal only to himself. In the meantime, the integration of Iranian units into the army continued.

Death in Babylon

The final year of Alexander's reign was full of activity and unfulfilled plans. It began with a personal tragedy. In November 324, Hephaestion, Alexander's most intimate friend, drank himself to death. The grief-stricken king executed Hephaestion's doctor and ordered a monstrous ziggurat-like monument to Hephaestion to be built at Babylon. When he believed he had received approval from Ammon, he ordered the Greek cities to grant his dead friend heroic honors. It may also have been at this time that Alexander also demanded that the Greeks worship him as a god.

On his arrival at Babylon in the spring of 323, Alexander received delegations bearing congratulations and petitions from the Greeks and other peoples of the Mediterranean. He also began to formulate plans for his next major project, the conquest of the Arabians, who, he claimed, had not sent an embassy to honor him. But omens of his impending death were already being bruited about. In desperation, the Babylonian priests even revived the ancient substitute-king ritual: A criminal was seated on the king's throne dressed in the royal regalia, then executed in the hope of averting the doom threatening the king.

This frantic effort was to no avail. On May 29, Alexander fell ill at a party hosted by one of his officers. After suffering from fever and delirium for almost two weeks, he died on June 10, 323 BC. According to later legends, he was the victim of a plot concocted by Aristotle and Antipater, whom he had decided to replace as his regent in Europe. More likely, his body, exhausted by the strain of constant campaigning and numerous wounds, was unable to fight off a disease, possibly malaria, that he contracted while at Babylon. He was not yet thirty-three years old.

THE ACHIEVEMENTS OF ALEXANDER

Hero or villain, the world was not the same after Alexander had passed through it. From the Mediterranean to India, Eurasia had been linked together and would remain so until the end of antiquity. Alexander's plans for his empire are not known, partly because Alexander did not expect to die when he did. There is, however, a more fundamental reason. When the Roman emperor Augustus was told that at the time of his death, Alexander was perplexed about what he should do next, he expressed his surprise that Alexander did not consider governing his empire a greater challenge than conquering it. Not surprisingly, his papers contained only schemes for grandiose monuments and future campaigns, not plans for the governance of his empire. He may have thought it sufficient to simply replace the top echelon of Persian administrators with Macedonians, Greeks, and native rulers loyal to him. It would be his successors who would shape the details of the new political order that would replace the Persian Empire and provide the framework for social and cultural relations in much of western Asia for the rest of antiquity.

KEY TERMS

Alexander the Great	Battle of Issus	Parmenion
Alexandria	Bessus	Persepolis
Antipater	Callisthenes	Philotas
Battle of Gaugamela	Darius III	proskynēsis
Battle of Granicus	Gordian knot	Roxane
Battle of Hydaspes	Great King	Zeus-Ammon

SUGGESTED READINGS

Badian, Ernst. 2012. *Collected Papers on Alexander the Great*. London: Routledge. Brilliantly written articles on all aspects of Alexander's reign by a master historian.

Bosworth, A. B. 1988. *Conquest and Empire: The Reign of Alexander the Great*. Cambridge, UK: Cambridge University Press. Unsentimental and clearly written political and military history of Alexander's reign.

———. 1996. *Alexander and the East: The Tragedy of Triumph*. Oxford: Clarendon Press. A revealing study of Alexander's Indian campaign and its treatment by ancient and modern historians.

Briant, Pierre. 2010. *Alexander the Great and His Empire*. Trans. A. Kuhrt. Princeton, NJ: Princeton University Press. Brilliant account of Alexander's reign from the perspective of the Persians.

Green, Peter. 1991. *Alexander of Macedon, 356–323 B.C.: A Historical Biography*. Berkeley and Los Angeles: University of California Press. Vivid and scholarly biography of Alexander the Great.

Heckel, Waldemar. 2006. *Who's Who in the Age of Alexander the Great*. Oxford: Blackwell Publishing. Comprehensive biographical dictionary of the reign of Alexander.

Holt, Frank L. 2005. *Into the Land of Bones: Alexander the Great in Afghanistan*. Berkeley and Los Angeles: University of California Press. Vivid account of Alexander's central Asian campaign and its significance for the establishment of Greek culture in Bactria.

Mossé, Claude. 2001. *Alexander: Destiny and Myth*. Trans. Janet Lloyd. Baltimore: Johns Hopkins University Press. Lucid survey of interpretations of Alexander from antiquity to the present.

Roisman, Joseph and Ian Worthington, eds. 2010. *A Companion to Ancient Macedonia*. Oxford: Wiley-Blackwell. Twenty-seven accessible, wide-ranging, and first-rate essays on Macedonian history by leading scholars.

Stewart, Andrew. 1993. *Faces of Power: Alexander's Image and Hellenistic Politics*. Berkeley and Los Angeles: University of California Press. Detailed study of the development and use of the best-known royal portrait image in antiquity.

Stoneman, Richard. 2008. *Alexander the Great: A Life in Legend*. New Haven: Yale University Press. Illuminating analysis of the Alexander Romance and its influence in world literature.

Wheeler, Mortimer. 1968. *Flames over Persepolis: Turning-Point in History*. New York: Reynal. Pioneering survey of the archaeological evidence for Alexander's campaign.

Worthington, Ian. 2012. *Alexander the Great: A Reader*. 2nd ed. London: Routledge. Valuable anthology of primary and secondary sources dealing with the principal historical issues of Alexander's reign.

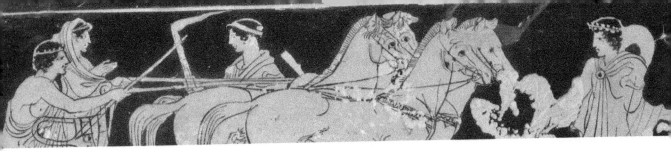

The New World of the Hellenistic Period

Alexander's conquests changed forever the world the Greeks knew. Formerly citizens of minuscule city-states on the fringes of the Persian Empire, the Greeks came to share the rule of a vast territory that stretched from the Mediterranean to India. This enormous "cosmopolis" (literally, "a city-state comprising the world") was unified only by the use of Greek as the common language of government and culture and by the creation of islands of Greek culture in settlements scattered in the region. Against this revolutionary backdrop, Greeks and non-Greeks tried to retain traditional values while living in a world vastly different from that of their grandparents. Although the modern world owes much to the classical polis and the culture it nurtured, in many respects its closest affiliation is with this new era that historians call Hellenistic.

The **Hellenistic period** spans the three centuries from the death of Alexander in 323 BC to the death of **Cleopatra VII** of Egypt in 30 BC. In many ways, the Hellenistic age anticipated the problems faced by modern imperial powers in ruling large multiethnic states. Most of the popular Hellenistic philosophies like **Stoicism, Epicureanism, Cynicism,** and **Skepticism** spoke to the needs of people with many of the same interests and anxieties as people today. In the arts also the repertoire of themes and styles expanded far beyond that typical of the Classical period to include depicting with sympathy the emotions of defeated athletes; the ravages of old age; and the lives of children, women, and even non-Greeks.

Figure 12.1. Traditionally called the Old Market Woman, this statue of an old woman carrying chickens probably represents an elderly peasant, wearing her finest dress and an ivy wreath around her head, participating in a religious festival of Dionysus. Roman marble copy of Hellenistic original of the third or second century BC. New York, The Metropolitan Museum of Art.

THE STRUGGLE FOR THE SUCCESSION

When Alexander died suddenly in 323 BC, the Persian Empire had disappeared, but no regime had emerged to replace it. Only Alexander's charismatic personality had held his empire together. A new king had to be chosen quickly, but there was no heir. Although his wife Roxane was pregnant, only Alexander's mentally deficient half-brother Arrhidaeus survived of his family. A regency, therefore, was inevitable; but who would lead it and in whose interest?

On his deathbed Alexander had given his signet ring to his chief minister, **Perdiccas**, and his bodyguards and the cavalry supported Perdiccas' proposal to wait for the birth of Roxane's child. The Macedonian infantry, however, mutinied and demanded that Arrhidaeus become king. Only a bizarre compromise averted civil war: If Roxane's child were male, he and Arrhidaeus would be joint kings. When Roxane gave birth to a son, he and Arrhidaeus were proclaimed kings as Alexander IV and Philip III. Although the immediate crisis was over, events were to prove the truth of Alexander's prophecy that there would be great "funeral games" over his corpse.

For almost a half-century, Alexander's successors fought over his empire. Only when the last of them died in 280 BC did a new political system emerge dominated by three kingdoms, each ruled by a Macedonian dynasty: the Ptolemies in Egypt, the Seleucids in western Asia, and the Antigonids in Macedon and northern Greece. This arrangement formed the framework for political and social life in Egypt and western Asia for more than two centuries and nurtured a vibrant culture that endured through later antiquity and the middle ages.

THE REGENCY OF PERDICCAS

More was at stake after Alexander's death than the selection of his successor. Decisions also had to be made concerning the goals of the new imperial government. Conquest and expansion characterized Alexander's reign, and on his deathbed Alexander was planning to invade Arabia. Perdiccas had no interest in such projects. The exhausted soldiers demanded that Alexander's final plans be abandoned. The fantastic career of conquest that had begun a decade earlier was over. The time for consolidation of Macedonian rule and enjoyment of the fruits of victory had arrived, or so the soldiers thought.

With the succession settled, Perdiccas quickly organized the regency, beginning by reallocating the satrapies of the empire. The sources anachronistically highlight the satrapies assigned to Alexander's successors: Cappadocia to Eumenes, Egypt to **Ptolemy I**, Thrace to **Lysimachus**, and much of western Anatolia to **Antigonus the One-Eyed**. Cappadocia, however, had yet to be conquered; the corrupt satrap Cleomenes of Naucratis held Egypt; and much of Thrace had been lost in a Thracian rebellion. Perdiccas understandably needed to avoid alienating the powerful Macedonian satraps in Asia to survive, and such appointments met this need.

At the same time, however, revolts broke out at both the eastern and western ends of the empire. Alexander's Asian subjects had remained quiet during the crisis after his death; not so the Greeks. The Greek settlers in Bactria revolted first, but their rebellion was quickly suppressed. Far more serious was the almost simultaneous revolt of the European Greeks. The roots of the European uprising lay in the decree of 324 BC concerning the return of exiles, which threatened many Greek cities with social and political upheaval, but none more so than Athens and Aetolia. Victory initially seemed to be almost within the Greeks' grasp. Antipater was besieged in the Thessalian city of Lamia, from which the revolt gets its name, the Lamian War (323–322 BC). But then events turned against them. The Athenian fleet was decisively defeated at the Battle of Amorgus, and Macedonian reinforcements from Asia enabled Antipater to defeat the Greek army at Crannon in

Thessaly in 322. Antipater intended that there should be no further revolts. He dissolved the League of Corinth, thereby ending the fiction that the Greeks were allies and not subjects. He also dismantled Athens' democracy. Demosthenes committed suicide, and other democratic leaders were executed. Twelve thousand poor Athenians were disfranchised. Athens was again ruled by an oligarchy maintained in power by a foreign garrison.

The Death of Perdiccas

While Antipater was occupied with the Lamian War, Perdiccas was struggling to control the satraps in Asia, especially Antigonus the One-Eyed, the satrap of Phrygia, who had refused to help Eumenes take control of his satrapy of Cappadocia. To save himself, Antigonus fled to Macedon with the news that Perdiccas was planning to marry Cleopatra, Alexander's sister. Antigonus' news outraged Antipater and split the regency, but Ptolemy ignited the wars of Alexander's successors by diverting Alexander's funeral cortege to Egypt. Perdiccas could not ignore so direct a challenge to his authority, but his invasion of Egypt in 321 failed when Ptolemy opened the Nile dikes, drowning thousands of Perdiccas' soldiers. Demoralized by defeat and seduced by Ptolemy's promises, Perdiccas' officers assassinated him.

The victors quickly met at Triparadeisus in Syria to reorganize the regency. Antipater replaced Perdiccas as regent for the kings, and the satrapies were reassigned yet again. Ptolemy and Lysimachus retained their satrapies, and **Seleucus** received Babylon as his satrapy. Eumenes was condemned to death, and Antigonus the One-Eyed, appointed strategos in Asia, was ordered to hunt him down. Antipater himself returned to Macedon with the two kings.

For the first time since Alexander had crossed into Asia over a decade earlier, a king would occupy the royal palace at Pella. Appearances, however, were deceptive. Perdiccas had failed to control the Asian satraps, and Antipater was unlikely even to try. The person best suited to exploit the new situation was Antigonus the One-Eyed, who controlled all royal forces and resources in Asia.

THE PRIMACY OF ANTIGONUS THE ONE-EYED

Antigonus' rise to preeminence in Asia was rapid. He quickly expelled Eumenes from Cappadocia and was on the verge of subduing him when Antipater's sudden death in 319 BC set off a new round of conflict. Antipater's son Cassander refused to accept his father's choice of Polyperchon—another survivor from Philip II's reign—as regent for the two kings and fled to Antigonus, precipitating the formation of a grand alliance of Antigonus, Cassander, Ptolemy, and Lysimachus against the new regent.

The struggle lasted for three years, ending with the collapse of the royal cause in both Europe and Asia and the destruction of the Argead house itself. Polyperchon enjoyed a brief period of success when Olympias joined the struggle on his side—but her passion for her grandson Alexander IV led to the murder of

Philip III and his queen Eurydice and the alienation of much of the Macedonian aristocracy, which rallied to Cassander. Shortly after the death of Philip III, Olympias was executed, leaving her grandson and Macedon in the hands of Cassander. Although Cassander claimed to be regent for Alexander IV, he was in reality the new ruler of Macedon. Alexander IV and Roxane were confined under house arrest in Amphipolis, never to be seen in public again.

A similar fate befell the royal cause in Asia. After three years of struggle, Eumenes was betrayed in 316 by his own soldiers to Antigonus, who executed him. As in Europe, so in Asia, a victory won in the name of the heirs of Alexander resulted instead in the usurpation of Argead rule. Antigonus quickly appointed his supporters to key satrapies. Although officially only strategos in Asia for Alexander IV, Antigonus actually controlled the child-king's vast Asian territories as securely as Cassander did his European ones.

The "Freedom" of the Greeks

Antigonus' triumph was brief. In 315 his allies demanded that he share the territories that he had captured. Antigonus responded with an ultimatum of his own demanding that his rivals recognize all Greek states as free. Although these ultimatums were propaganda, Antigonus' invocation of **Greek freedom** was a shrewd attempt to build Greek support. Antigonus never freed the Greek cities he controlled, but he was right to believe that his proclamation would be well received in Greece. Already in 319, when Athens had rebelled, Polyperchon promised to restore democracy and freedom to the Greeks. Antigonus hoped that his proclamation would have a similar effect among Cassander's other embittered Greek subjects when he invaded Macedon. Antigonus' invasion of Macedon, however, never materialized. Ptolemy defeated Antigonus' son **Demetrius** at Gaza in 312, and helped Seleucus return to Babylon, where he incited defections among the eastern satraps. In 311, with his southern and eastern fronts in ruins, Antigonus made peace with his former allies.

In the Peace of 311 Antigonus admitted that his attempt to gain control of all of Alexander's empire had failed. The treaty provided that Cassander would remain as strategos in Europe, Antigonus would continue as strategos over all Asia, Ptolemy and Lysimachus would retain their satrapies, and the Greek cities would be free. In return for an empty pledge to support the principle of Greek freedom, Antigonus had accepted the division of the empire as it had existed at the beginning of the war.

Antigonus' Last Gamble

The Peace of 311 was merely a truce that Antigonus and his rivals used to rebuild their strength. War resumed in 307 when Demetrius invaded Greece with a mandate "to free all the cities of Greece." Success was immediate. Demetrius liberated Athens from Cassander and restored the democracy. The next year he occupied Cyprus, seizing Salamis in the first of the epic sieges that would gain him the sobriquet Poliorcetes ("the Besieger"), and inflicted a crushing defeat on the fleet Ptolemy sent to relieve the city. Demetrius' victory transformed the political world. Alexander's successors had maintained they were only agents of the child-king Alexander IV even after his death in 310, but when the news of Demetrius' victory reached Antigonus' army in Syria, his soldiers acclaimed Demetrius and Antigonus as kings, thereby publicly admitting the end of the Argead dynasty.

Like Homer's heroes, Macedonian kings were military leaders, and it was the glory of Demetrius' victory at Salamis that justified the acclamation of his father and himself as king. Within a year Cassander, Lysimachus, Ptolemy, and Seleucus also assumed the title "King," thus affirming their independence. The struggle for control of Alexander's legacy that had been interrupted by the Peace of 311 had begun again. The end came in 301, when Lysimachus and Seleucus defeated Antigonus and Demetrius at Ipsus in central Phrygia. Antigonus was dead, trampled by Seleucus' elephants; and Demetrius was in headlong flight, their dreams of empire in ruins.

BIRTH PANGS OF THE NEW ORDER (301–276 BC)

After his death, Antigonus' enemies divided his territories in Asia. Lysimachus received Anatolia north of the Taurus Mountains; and Seleucus added to Babylonia and Iran the coastal regions of southern Anatolia, Syria, and Mesopotamia. The division of western Asia into two huge kingdoms should have created tension along their mutual borders, and it would have except for an unforeseen development. In 301, Ptolemy had occupied Judaea, Phoenicia, and southern Syria. To protect himself, he formed an alliance with Lysimachus that was sealed by the marriage of Lysimachus to Ptolemy's daughter Arsinoë (the future queen Arsinoë II of Egypt), and of Ptolemy's younger son, the future **Ptolemy II**, to Lysimachus' daughter. Seleucus responded by allying with Demetrius, the son of Antigonus the One-Eyed, who now ruled a "sea empire" comprising his father's fleet and a handful of ports in the Aegean. The renewal of war seemed imminent, but it was delayed for over a decade.

During the 290s, the kings concentrated their efforts on the development of their kingdoms. Lysimachus fought against the Getae, who lived across the Danube, while founding or reorganizing several cities in Anatolia, including Ephesus. Ptolemy designed the administration of Egypt; but the most active king was Seleucus, who founded numerous cities and military settlements in Syria, including his great new capital of Antioch near the mouth of the Orontes River. As thousands of Greeks emigrated to Egypt and western Asia, the new cities grew and prospered, acquiring large populations and splendid public buildings and amenities unknown in Aegean Greece. Little is known of Hellenistic Antioch, but the discovery of the sunken remains of the Pharos lighthouse and the palaces of the Ptolemies in Alexandria harbor is finally beginning to reveal the glory of ancient Alexandria.

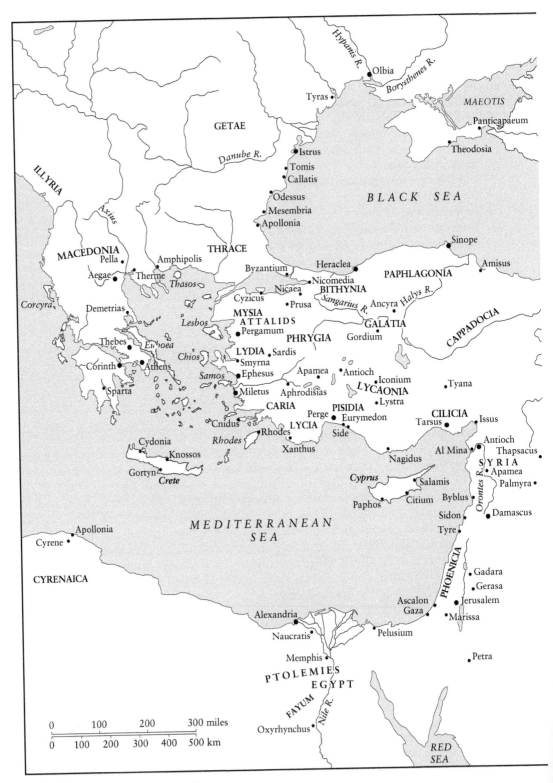

Figure 12.2. The Hellenistic world.

ARAL
SEA

Tanais

Hypanis R.

COLCHIS

Phasis

Trapezus

CASPIAN
SEA

CHORASMIA

ARMENIA

Araxes R.

Lake
Van

Lake
Urmia

HYRCANIA

PARTHIA

Samosata

Nisibis

MEDIA

Carrhae

Gaugamela

Tigris R.

Arbela

MESOPOTAMIA

Ecbatana

Seleucids

Dura-
Europus

Euphrates R.

Antiochea

Seleucia

Cunaxa

Susa

Babylon

Pasargadae

Persepolis

PERSIAN
GULF

The Final Struggle

Demetrius Poliorcetes possessed a "kingdom" without a territorial base. In 294 he remedied that deficiency, seizing Macedon from the feuding sons of Cassander. His success, however, was brief. For Demetrius, Macedon was only a stepping stone to Asia, but before his invasion was ready, his rivals struck. Lysimachus and Pyrrhus, the king of Epirus, invaded Macedon and forced Demetrius into prematurely launching his Asian campaign in 286. The result was inevitable. Outnumbered and ill, Demetrius surrendered to Seleucus and lived out the last few years of his life under house arrest near Antioch.

Demetrius' conquerors did not long survive him. Taking advantage of a bitter succession crisis in Thrace, Seleucus invaded Lysimachus' kingdom. The forces of the two aging monarchs—both were over eighty—met in early 281 at Corupedium (the "Field of Plenty") in Phrygia. At the end of the battle, Lysimachus lay dead on the field, and Seleucus, it seemed, finally had achieved the dream that had haunted Alexander's successors: rule of the whole empire. Seleucus did not long enjoy his triumph, being assassinated by an exiled son of Ptolemy, Ptolemy Ceraunus ("the Thunderbolt"). The Thunderbolt's moment of glory also passed quickly. In 279, he fell in battle, defending Macedon against Gauls, whose migration from their western Europe home had begun in the early fourth century.

The Gallic threat was brief, but it had significant consequences. The Gauls soon transferred their terror to Anatolia, but only after being defeated at Delphi and Lysimacheia by the Aetolian League (the organization of the city-states of central Greece) and Antigonus Gonatas ("Knockknees"), the son of Demetrius Poliorcetes. Their victories over the Gauls transformed the position of both the Aetolians and Antigonus, legitimizing the emergence of the former as the preeminent power in central Greece and the protector of Delphi and the latter as king of Macedon. The final pieces of the new political system that had so gradually and painfully emerged from the wreckage of Alexander's empire had fallen into place.

THE POLIS IN THE HELLENISTIC WORLD

Although the emergence of the new Macedonian kingdoms changed the character and shape of the world the Greeks knew, one aspect of Greek life remained largely unchanged: The polis continued to form the basic framework for the life of most Greeks. Old poleis such as Athens, Syracuse, and Ephesus grew and prospered. At the same time, while wars between poleis continued, cities increasingly attempted to peacefully settle international disputes by arbitration and to insulate themselves against attack by gaining recognition for themselves as *asylos*, "inviolate," from other Greek cities and kings.

Even the notorious particularism of the classical polis was partially overcome by the creation of strong federal states by the Aetolians and Achaeans. The Aetolian and Achaean leagues were alliances of cities governed by councils

of city representatives, assemblies of league citizens, and elected league officials. In the Hellenistic period both leagues expanded their membership to
include cities outside their traditional homes in central Greece and the northern
Peloponnesus. By the late third century BC, the **Achaean League** included most of
the Peloponnesus except Sparta; and the **Aetolian League** and its allies reached
all the way to the borders of Attica. Not surprisingly, the two leagues were able to
deal with Macedon and the other Macedonian kingdoms on a roughly equal basis
for much of the third century BC.

The growing influence of Rome in Greece ended the heyday of Greek federal-
ism. Although common enmity toward Macedon induced both leagues to become
Roman allies, Rome's support of polis autonomy under the guise of "Greek
Freedom" drove them apart. By 189 BC Rome had decisively defeated the Aetolian
League. The Achaean League met a similar fate two generations later in 146 BC
when Rome crushed a revolt led by the league and established direct rule in
Greece. Unlike the polarizing Athenian and Spartan leagues of the Classical era,
the federal leagues of the Hellenistic Age were remembered despite their ultimate
failure. Eighteenth-century students of federalism such as the French political
theorist Montesquieu and James Madison and other intellectuals of revolutionary
America even studied them as possible models for new federal states.

Political trends that had appeared in the fourth century BC intensified in the
Hellenistic period. Virtually all Greek cities now claimed to have democratic

Figure 12.3. This Roman bronze statuette
reflects the colossal lost statue of the Tyche
(Fortune) of the city of Antioch in Syria, the
capital of the Seleucid kingdom. The statue was
created by Eutychides (c. 300 BC) and shows
Tyche, the city's protective goddess, personified
as a goddess wearing a crown representing
the city wall seated on a swimming boy
representing the Orontes River. New York, The
Metropolitan Museum of Art.

governments, although increasingly democracy signified only that a city-state was not ruled by a tyrant. Meanwhile, the average citizen's role in government declined as aristocratic oligarchies increasingly managed affairs from behind the scenes. Wealthy men and women made generous gifts to their cities, including aqueducts, feasts, schools, and various types of charities. Numerous inscriptions documenting their generosity and public service attest to the patriotism of these new leaders as well as the poleis' need for such men and women to rescue them from recurrent financial, diplomatic, and social crises.

Athens and Sparta

Although the democracy was never fully restored, Athens flourished as the cultural center of mainland Greece. Hellenistic Athenian culture differed greatly from that of the classical city. The change is most obvious in drama, where the grand tragedies and biting political comedies of the Classical era were replaced by a lighter genre known as New Comedy. The plays of **Menander** (344–c. 292 BC), its most famous practitioner, reflect the new political order and the interests of its upper-class audience.

Menander had been a pupil of Theophrastus, Aristotle's successor as head of the Lyceum, and a friend of Demetrius of Phaleron, Cassander's governor of Athens. A Hellenistic critic wrote, "O Menander and O life, which one of you has imitated the other?" Menander's plays depict a Greece populated by swaggering mercenaries, impoverished citizens living next door to wealthy people, courtesans and pimps, spendthrift youths, and respectable young women whose destiny is marriage. Menander's characters are engrossed in their private worlds, as though weary of war and political upheaval.

Slaves are ubiquitous in New Comedy and in Hellenistic Athens. Constant warfare had reduced many people to slavery, and slave dealers took advantage of the practice of exposing unwanted newborns. Infant exposure forms the theme of several of Menander's plots (with happier destinies for their children than those that awaited them in real life). Significantly, the chief divinity in New Comedy is Tyche ("Fortune"), a fitting emblem of this chaotic era.

The altered temper of the times manifested itself also in philosophy. Plato and Aristotle had directed their teachings to affluent men interested in the political life of the autonomous poleis. Hellenistic philosophies, however, aimed to help people cope with a vast world over which they had little control. Two of the most important schools of Hellenistic thought flowered in Athens: Stoicism and Epicureanism. Born in Cyprus, **Zeno** (335–263 BC), the founder of Stoicism, was a friend of Antigonus Gonatas and lived in Athens, teaching at the Stoa Poikile ("Painted Porch"). For this reason his followers received the name of Stoics (i.e., "Porchers").

Zeno's philosophy reflected the new political order. The earth stood at the center of the universe with Zeus as its prime mover. Just as cosmic motions never changed and Zeus remained king of the gods, so monarchy was the divinely ordered system of government. Revolution, consequently, violated the natural organization of the world, whereas patriotism and public service harmonized with the cosmic order. Serenity could be achieved only by those confident that they had fulfilled their duties to their communities. Stoicism, thus, entailed a large dose of humanitarianism and public service.

Zeno urged his followers to seek an inner tranquility that was proof not only against agonizing pain but against excessive pleasure as well. He did not, however, advocate withdrawal from social and political life. Stoics were to uphold justice but not to engage in any serious attempts at reform. Stoics consequently considered slaves spiritually as free as their owners, but they did not try to abolish slavery. In keeping with their belief in an orderly universe, Stoics thought life was rational and could be planned. **Epicurus** (341–270 BC) taught a very different philosophy in the school he established in his home in Athens called "The Garden," including women among his students. Adopting the atomic theory of Leucippus and Democritus, he rejected their determinism. Although he agreed that atoms fell in straight lines from the sky, Epicurus argued that the multiplicity of substances in the universe arose from periodic swerves in the atoms' paths, causing them to collide at a variety of angles. The universe, in short, was created by chance combinations, and would perish and regenerate by chance.

The gods had little role in this philosophy. Epicurus deduced that gods exist because people saw their images in dreams, but they had no interest in humans, living, instead, serene, untroubled lives, indifferent to prayers, offerings, and rituals. (The good news was that the horrific punishments associated with the underworld were fictions; the bad news was that the gods were not interested in listening to complaints, offering solace, or avenging injustices.) After death, the atoms that had composed the soul and body of each person merely dissolved and recombined to form new entities.

Understandably, Epicurus viewed happiness on Earth as the purpose of life. He defined happiness as the attainment of *ataraxia,* an untroubled state free from excessive pleasure and pain, much like the serenity advocated by Zeno. Unlike Zeno, however, Epicurus advocated withdrawal from activities that might bring pain, both the quest for love or money (which Stoics also saw as problematic) and participation in politics (which Stoics praised). For Epicureans, anything that might threaten ataraxia was to be avoided. Although today "Epicurean" connotes indulgence in pleasure, particularly fine dining, Epicurus actually counseled moderation in food and drink to avoid indigestion and hangovers. Epicureans also approved of sex, provided love with all its pitfalls was avoided.

Despite their differences, Stoics and Epicureans shared a common goal: attaining tranquility in a turbulent world. A similar aim characterized two other philosophical schools popular in the Hellenistic period: Cynicism and Skepticism. The principal theorist of the Cynic movement, Diogenes of Sinope (c. 400–325 BC), maintained that civilization was unnatural. Denying that humans had needs different from those of animals, Diogenes scandalized contemporaries and earned the name of the Cynic ("dog," *kuōn* in Greek) by brazenly maintaining that people should follow instincts just as animals do, even urinating and masturbating in public. The Skeptics also shared the Cynics' and Epicureans' disillusionment with Greek public life. Skepticism became popular around 200 BC. Stressing the impossibility of certain knowledge, Skeptics urged withdrawal from the world. The quest for truth and power, after all, was hopeless. Today, the words "skeptical" and "cynical" suggest people who are not easily persuaded. In this, Hellenistic philosophies contrast sharply with those of Plato and Aristotle, who believed that knowledge was possible and could be gained through education.

Although Athens continued to attract intellectuals, the center of philosophical speculation in the Hellenistic era shifted not only away from Athens but also away from mainland Greece in general. Stoic thinkers came from places like Cyprus and Syria, and Tarsus and Rhodes became the most famous Stoic university towns. Stoicism ultimately took root in the Roman Empire, fortifying the minds and souls of men and women seeking to cope with and participate in the government.

Almost as remarkable was the fate of Sparta. After a century-long decline in which the number of Spartan citizens dwindled to fewer than a thousand and tensions between rich and poor became acute, two reformer kings, Agis IV (262–241 BC) and Cleomenes III (235–222 BC), revived Sparta's "Lycurgan" institutions. Debts were canceled, land was redistributed, and the traditional Spartan educational system, the *agōgē*, was reestablished. Sparta briefly became the Stoic model state. The Stoic notion that individual suffering is part of some great natural scheme and should be endured attracted Spartans, as did the idea that austerity was preferable to self-indulgence. For a few years, Spartan arms were invincible and the city seemed on the verge of dominating the Peloponnesus again. Greek intellectuals celebrated the Lycurgan system. Their dreams of Greek renewal were shattered when the joint forces of Macedon and the Achaean League crushed the Spartans at Sellasia in 222 BC. As the fate of Sparta revealed, not even the strongest polis could resist the power of the Macedonian kingdoms.

THE MACEDONIAN KINGDOMS

Greek literature contains little information about the organization of the new Macedonian kingdoms. Fortunately, archaeological evidence in the form of inscriptions and **papyri** has remedied this deficiency, revealing that the Hellenistic kingdoms were conquest states based on two fundamental principles: first, that the kingdom and its population belonged to the king; and second, that the king's business took precedence over all other considerations. These two principles were common to all the Macedonian kingdoms, but their implementation depended on local conditions.

Seleucus' kingdom extended from the Mediterranean to the borders of India, embracing the bulk of the old Persian empire. Not surprisingly, they retained much of the existing Persian governmental structure. The king's principal advisors and officials, including the satraps who governed the various regions of the empire, were largely Greeks and Macedonians. The subjects of the Seleucid's huge multiethnic empire, however, lived in many different forms of societies, including city-states, temple estates, petty kingdoms, and autonomous tribal confederations. Like the Persians before them, therefore, the Seleucids followed a policy of toleration, respecting local institutions and customs and not attempting to impose Greek culture on their subjects. Cuneiform tablets, for example, reveal Seleucid kings claiming to be King of Babylon and fulfilling the Babylonian king's traditional role of protector and supporter of the temples. Similarly, Seleucid royal decrees granted the Jews the right to live according to their ancestral laws. Although the sources allow historians to reconstruct the main features of the Seleucid state only in outline, the rich papyrological evidence provides scholars with a detailed picture of the actual operation of the government and society of Hellenistic Egypt.

Ptolemaic Egypt

Egypt's wealth lay primarily in its agricultural land, which, as heirs of the Pharaohs, the Ptolemies claimed to own. For practical purposes, however, the Ptolemaic government divided Egyptian land into two categories: royal land for basic agricultural production and "released land," which was used to provide soldiers with land grants, reward government officials, and support Egypt's numerous temples. The rest of the economy was also tightly organized. Activities such as textile, papyrus, and oil production were state monopolies, intended to generate the maximum revenue for the king from fees and taxes. The system was managed by a bureaucracy headquartered in Alexandria but with agents—both Greek and Egyptian—in even the smallest villages. The king managed the whole system as an autocrat whose word was law. The institution of a cult of the living ruler, his wife, and his ancestors legitimized royal rule and offered subjects a public means of demonstrating their loyalty and gratitude for the "benefits" provided them.

Egyptian and cuneiform texts indicate that there was continuity between Egyptian and Persian administrative practices and Hellenistic state organization. Ptolemaic Egypt and Seleucid Asia, for example, maintained many of their traditional administrative structures, together with many of their key institutions, and

Figure 12.4. This gold octodrachm showing the deified Ptolemy II and Arsinoë II was minted by Ptolemy III (246–221 BC). Arsinoë's appearance on the front of the coin indicates her prominence in the government. New York, American Numismatic Society.

remained divided into their traditional subdivisions, such as nomes and satrapies. Not surprisingly, the Greek terminology of many of our sources often proves on analysis to be a facade, hiding traditional preexisting institutions.

In Hellenistic Egypt and Asia, the temples still played major roles in the social and economic lives of their peoples. Egyptian priests used the names of the Greek gods, equated the Macedonian and Egyptian calendars, and translated royal titles into Greek to give a Hellenic cast to Egyptian religious traditions. This continuity is not surprising, as the Ptolemies and Seleucids were both Macedonian kings and also pharaohs and kings of Babylon, whose responsibilities had included support of traditional institutions. (See Plate XXIII.)

Epigraphical and papyrological evidence has revealed "irrationalities" and inefficiencies in the kingdoms' operations. Ptolemaic Egypt and Seleucid Asia were personal autocracies. Official documents describe their governments as consisting of the "king, his friends" (the king's personal entourage), "and the army." Their power was restrained only by fear of losing the support of their armies and generals, who could unseat a king if provoked too far. Government officials were political appointees with often multiple and even conflicting responsibilities, who filled posts assigned them by the king irrespective of their experience and qualifications.

Instead of smoothly functioning bureaucratic machines, Hellenistic governments were inefficient and often arbitrary instruments, primarily designed to extract the maximum revenue from their rulers' subjects. Documents such as the letters of Ptolemy II (282–246 BC) forbidding lawyers from assisting individuals in disputes concerning taxes bear witness to the kings' insatiable need for money to support their ambitious foreign policies and grandiose domestic projects. Similarly, the numerous royal orders forbidding government officials from exploiting the king's subjects for personal gain and amnesties for unfulfilled obligations to the government highlight the inherent inefficiency and corruption of these systems in actual practice.

HELLENISTIC SOCIETY

The new Macedonian monarchies not only posed a threat to the independence of the cities of Aegean Greece, they also created unprecedented opportunities for individual Greeks. Whatever Alexander's plans for the governance of his empire may have been, his successors clearly decided to rely on Greek immigrants to staff the upper levels of their governments.

New Opportunities in a Colonial World

The resulting opportunities were greatest for Greek men, who quickly formed an influential class of expatriate civilian and military officials. Inscriptions and papyri document the wealth and influence of members of this new governing class—such as Apollonius, the chief financial officer of Ptolemy II, and Zenon, the Carian immigrant who managed his estate. Less glamorous, but equally real and far more numerous, were the multitude of minor, but potentially lucrative, administrative jobs required to govern the new kingdoms. The court poet **Theocritus** spoke the literal truth when he described Egypt as a land of opportunity for immigrants and characterized Ptolemy II as a "good paymaster."

DOCUMENT 12.1

Letter of King Ptolemy II to Apollonius concerning the revenues of Egypt (259 BC)

King Ptolemy to Apollonius, greeting. Since some of the advocates listed below are intervening in fiscal cases to the detriment of the revenues, issue instructions that those advocates shall pay to the crown twice the additional tenth and that they shall no longer be allowed to serve as advocates in any matter. And if any of those who have harmed the revenues be discovered to have served as advocate in some matter, have him sent to us under guard and have his property assigned to the crown.

(Papyrus Amherst 33 Burstein 121–122)

Opportunities expanded also for women, although not to the same extent. As in the case of men, they were greatest for women of wealth. Queens like Arsinoë II and Cleopatra VII of Egypt stand out in the ancient sources, but some Greek cities allowed women to hold minor public offices in return for their willingness to use their wealth for civic purposes. Some educated women even pursued careers, such as the Cynic philosopher Hipparchia and the professional musician Polygnota of Thebes, who won honors at Delphi. More women, however, benefited from the modest changes in their rights that occurred in the colonial society of the Macedonian kingdoms, where marriage contracts and other legal documents reveal women capable of conducting their own business and seeking legal redress for their husband's misconduct. Not surprisingly, the explosion of new opportunities and royal patronage made the Hellenistic period one of the great creative ages of Greek civilization.

DOCUMENT 12.2

Marriage contract of Heracleides and Demetria (311 BC)

The improved legal position of married women in the Hellenistic period is clear in this marriage contract from Egypt. The diverse origin of Greek immigrants to Egypt is evident in the variety of ethnics among the witnesses to Heracleides' and Demetria's marriage contract.

Seventh year of the reign of Alexander, the son of Alexander, fourteenth year of the satrapy of Ptolemy, month of Dius. Marriage contract of Heracleides and Demetria. Heracleides, a free born man, takes as his lawful wife Demetria, a free born woman from Cos, from her father Leptines from Cos, and from her mother Philotis. Demetria will bring with her clothing and ornaments worth 1,000 drachmas. Heracleides will furnish to Demetria everything that is appropriate for a free woman. We shall live together in whatever place seems best in the common opinion of Leptines and Heracleides.

If Demetria shall be detected devising something evil for the purpose of humiliating her husband Heracleides, she shall be deprived of everything she brought to the marriage. Heracleides shall declare whatever charge he may make against Demetria before three men whom both approve. Heracleides may not introduce another woman into their home to insult Demetria, nor have children from another woman, nor devise any evil toward Demetria for any reason. If Heracleides shall be detected doing any of these things and Demetria declares this before three men whom both approve, Heracleides shall return to Demetria the dowry of 1,000 drachmas which she brought, and he shall pay to her in addition 1,000 silver Alexandrian drachmas. Demetria, and those with Demetria, shall be able to exact payment, just as though there were a legal judgment from Heracleides himself, and from all of Heracleides' property on both land and sea.

This contract shall be wholly valid in every way wherever Heracleides produces it against Demetria, or Demetria and those with Demetria produce it against Heracleides, in order to exact payment. Heracleides and Demetria each have the right to preserve their contracts and to produce the contracts against each other. Witnesses: Cleon of Gela, Anticrates of Temnos, Lysis of Temnos, Dionysius of Temnos, Aristomachus of Cyrene, Aristodicus of Cos.

(*Papyrus Elephantine* 1 lines 1–18)

ALEXANDRIA AND HELLENISTIC CULTURE

Alexandria was the most famous and enduring of Alexander's foundations and the site of his tomb. The first three Ptolemies transformed it into the foremost city of the Hellenistic world with a multiethnic population including Macedonians,

Figure 12.5. Tetradrachm of the Roman emperor Commodus (AD 180–192) minted at Alexandria, showing ship(s?) passing the Pharos. London, The British Museum.

Jews, Greeks, and Egyptians. The clearest symbol of Alexandria's dynamism and originality was its signature monument, the **Pharos**. Built by Ptolemy II, the Pharos was the first skyscraper, a 300-foot-high polygonal tower topped by a statue of Zeus Soter ("Savior") whose beacon fire guided ships to Alexandria. The Ptolemies also made Alexandria the cultural center of the Greek world. Like Alexander, Ptolemy I and his immediate successors encouraged prominent Greek scholars and scientists to come to Egypt. With the enormous wealth of Egypt at their disposal, they could afford to subsidize intellectuals, encouraging artistic and scientific work by establishing cultural institutions of a new type.

The Ptolemies' principal cultural foundation was the **Museum**, so named because of its dedication to the nine Muses, the patron goddesses of the arts. There distinguished scholars, supported by government stipends, could pursue their studies in congenial surroundings including dormitories, dining facilities, and pleasant gardens. To assist the Museum's scholars, Ptolemy I established (with the aid of Demetrius of Phalerum) a **library** intended to contain copies of every book written in Greek. The library's collection is said to have ultimately reached 700,000 papyrus rolls.

The Ptolemies' passion for their library was legendary. Ptolemy II supposedly sponsored the Greek translation of the Jewish Bible, the *Septuagint,* and Ptolemy III allegedly stole the official Athenian copy of the works of the three canonical

Figure 12.6. The new library of Alexandria, now a symbol of Egyptian national pride.

tragedians. Even the books of visitors to Egypt were seized—the owner received a cheap copy—if the library lacked them. The library offered unprecedented resources for scholarly research in every field of intellectual endeavor (despite sneers at the occupants of Ptolemy's "bird coop" who were expected to earn their keep). Doctors and writers receiving government stipends served as physicians and tutors to the royal family and celebrated its achievements. The scholar and poet **Callimachus** catalogued the library in 120 books, thereby laying the foundation for the history of Greek literature. In his poem *The Lock of Berenice,* Callimachus also celebrated the transformation into a comet of a lock of hair dedicated by Berenice II in 246 BC to commemorate the beginning of the Third Syrian War. In a similar vein, Theocritus' seventeenth *Idyll* extravagantly praised the first decade of the reign of Ptolemy II, comparing the king and his sister-wife Arsinoë II to Zeus and Hera.

The work of Alexandrian intellectuals was not limited, however, to satisfying the whims of their royal patrons. Alexandrian writers made important innovations in Greek literature. In his *Idylls,* brief dialogues or monologues set in an idealized countryside, Theocritus introduced the pastoral mode into Western literature, while poets such as Posidippus of Pella transformed the epigram, originally a short commemorative poem inscribed on stone, into a flexible literary form that could be used equally for trivial subjects such as the death of a pet bird and for serious topics such as celebrating the achievements of the Ptolemies. A good example is this recently discovered elegant poem by Posidippus in which he celebrates a victory in a chariot race by Ptolemy III's wife, Berenice II, as the most recent example of such victories in Panhellenic games by the Ptolemies.

> Speak, poets all, of my renown, [if ever you enjoy]
>   saying what's known: my glory's [not of yesterday],
> my grandfather [Ptolemy (I) won] in the chariot,
>   driving his steeds over the courses at Pisa,
> and Berenice [I], mother of my father [Ptolemy II], and my father
>   again in the chariot, triumphed, king after king,
> Ptolemy after Ptolemy; and Arsinoë [II] won all three
>   harness victories at a single [competition].
> [. . .] sacred line [. . .] of women
>   [. . .] maiden [. . .]
> Olympia witnessed [all these exploits] of a single house,
>   the children and *their* children winning in the chariot.
> Sing then, O women of Macedon, of the garland taken by royal
>   Berenice in the chariot drawn by full-grown horses!
>   (Posidippus 78; Nisetich)

At the same time, Callimachus inaugurated the tradition of "learned" poetry in works such as his *Hymns* and *Aetia,* in which he retold in elegant verse obscure myths and the origins of strange customs and festivals collected from all over the Greek world. Callimachus' younger contemporary and rival **Apollonius of Rhodes** reinvigorated the old epic genre with his acute psychological portraits of Jason and Medea in his vivid retelling of the story of Jason and the Argonauts, the *Argonautica*. **Euhemerus**, an ambassador of Cassander to Ptolemy I, used the utopian travel romance to propound in his *Sacred Tale* the radical idea that the gods had once been great rulers worshiped after their deaths for their gifts to humanity like contemporary kings.

The Visual Arts

The visual arts reflect the combination of old and new that is a distinctive feature of the Hellenistic Age. Classical artists had perfected a limited number of artistic genres or types such as the idealized figure of an unemotional youthful nude male. This type of figure continued to be sculpted as a heroic representation of Hellenistic kings. Hellenistic art is, however, characterized by variety and experimentation, providing dramatic renderings of a cross-section of humanity experiencing a variety of emotions under extreme stress, as in the case of the Laocoön, where the doomed effort to escape a horrible death is captured in stone; or the Boxer, where the pathos of defeat is equally vividly depicted in bronze. Sculptors particularly delighted, however, in depicting the female nude, as illustrated by the various portrayals of Aphrodite at her toilette. (See Plate XVI.) Sculpture thus provides strong evidence of the new focus on the individual as special and unique rather than only a citizen of a polis.

The production of small terra-cotta figures began in the fourth century and flourished in the Hellenistic period. These mold-made figurines were relatively inexpensive and popular throughout the Greek world. They are our best evidence for the visual arts as a reflection of reality, portraying people of all ages, every social status, and a range of ethnicities, including chubby children; stooped, stout, and wrinkled elderly people; elegant and graceful society women; and members of the lower classes. (See Plate XXII.) Small bronze sculptures, although more expensive, also depict a broad variety of people.

Portraiture on coins and in sculpture was also fostered by interest in the individual and in the personality. Hellenistic portraits sought not only to portray the actual features of the subject but also to influence the viewer's perception of the character. Like Alexander, who encouraged belief in his own divinity and was worshiped as a god after his death, Hellenistic rulers manipulated religion to legitimize their use of absolute power. Members of the ruling dynasties were portrayed on coins and in sculpture with the attributes and epithets of gods and heroes. The political and propagandistic value of sculpture is obvious in the image of Alexander in the company of Egyptian divinities (Chapter 11, Figure 11.5) and in the sculpture of Arsinoë II portraying her as an Egyptian goddess (Figure 12.9). Viewers would immediately understand that Alexander and his successors were not mere mortals but incarnations of divinities, and the rightful rulers of Egypt and the Greek world.

a

Figure 12.7a. Laocoön. Dramatic representation of the Trojan priest Laocoön and his two sons being killed by sea serpents as punishment for advising the Trojans not to bring the Trojan horse into the city; c. 150–100 BC. Vatican City, Vatican Museum.

b

Figure 12.7b. Bronze Boxer. Brilliant study of an aging athlete. Cleaning has revealed that his body is covered with wounds represented by red copper inlays; c. 70–50 BC. Rome, Museo Nazionale delle Terme.

c

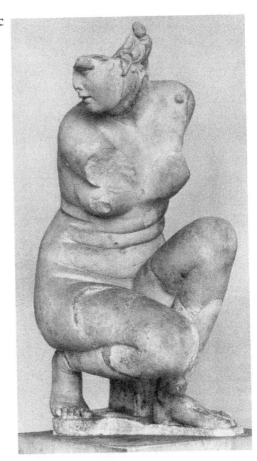

Figure 12.7c. Crouching Aphrodite (Rome). The goddess Aphrodite represented as a beautiful woman interrupted by an unseen viewer as she washes her shoulder and neck; c. 250–240 BC. Rome, Museo Nazionale delle Terme.

Many monuments Hellenistic rulers commissioned are now known only through images on coins, Roman copies, and verbal descriptions. These convey a vivid impression of the wealth and power of the monarchs and proud cities who constructed them. Artists traveled wherever such patrons beckoned. Bravura characterizes many major Hellenistic sculptures such as the Victory (Nike) of Samothrace dedicated by the Rhodians to commemorate their victories over Antiochus III of Syria (222–187 BC). Victory is portrayed alighting on the prow of a ship. Her wet and windblown dress reveals the contours of her body; while the cloth, flaring out behind the goddess, illustrates the drama and restlessness characteristic not only of the art but also of Hellenistic life. Her raised wings also suggest that her presence is not necessarily permanent. Like the goddess **Tyche** (Fortune), Victory can be fickle.

Figure 12.8a–c. Miniature Hellenistic sculptures. (a) Terra-cotta figurine of old nurse and child; late fourth century BC. New York, The Metropolitan Museum of Art. (b) Terra-cotta figurine of schoolgirl reading papyrus roll. Hamburg, Museum für Kunst und Gewerbe. (c) Bronze statuette of black youth in craftsman's garb; third to second century BC. New York, The Metropolitan Museum of Art.

The visual arts also reveal nostalgia for a safer and more secure past. Portraits of philosophers, poets, and other historical figures decorated public areas and private enclosed spaces such as libraries (cf. Demosthenes, Chapter 10, Figure 10.6). For example, portrait busts of Homer (about whose appearance nothing was known) were common, no doubt because the *Iliad* was the most widely read book in the Greek world and was used as a text in school. Nevertheless, despite the reverence for the past, the visual arts allowed Hellenistic Greeks no doubt that the world had changed drastically since the time of Homer.

Scholarship and Science

Hellenistic intellectuals also made fundamental contributions in literary scholarship and applied science. Callimachus and philologists such as Zenodotus and

Figure 12.10. Victory (Nike) of Samothrace. The colossal statue depicts a winged goddess of victory alighting on the prow of a warship, possibly commemorating a Rhodian naval victory of c. 200 BC. Paris, The Louvre.

Figure 12.9. Limestone statue of Arsinoë II in Egyptian style. A hieroglyphic inscription on the back pillar of Arsinoë's portrait indicates that the figure was dedicated not long after her death and deification in 270 BC. The stiff pose, with one foot forward, the dress clinging to her body, and the features of her face—including high-arched brows; large, wide-open eyes; and full curved lips—are depicted in Egyptian style; but the queen carries a double cornucopia, an attribute of Greek goddesses such as Demeter that symbolizes their powers of fertility. Her corn curls were painted black, and her face and the exposed flesh of her body were originally gilded and painted. New York, The Metropolitan Museum of Art.

Aristarchus founded the critical study of Greek language and literature, preparing texts of Homer and other poets that are the ancestors of those we still use. The mathematician and geographer **Eratosthenes** established the principles of scientific cartography and produced a strikingly accurate estimate of the circumference of the earth. The physicist Ctesibius pioneered the study of ballistics and the use of compressed air as a source of power, and other scientists experimented with the use of steam to operate simple machines. More mundanely, an unknown Ptolemaic

Figure 12.11. Sculpted relief of the Apotheosis of Homer by Archelaus of Priene, found in Bovillae, Italy, late third- to late second century BC. The deified poet, seated at the lower left, holding a scroll and scepter, is crowned by Oecumene (the World) and Chronus (Time). The other figures include Zeus and Mnemosyne (Memory) and their daughters, the Muses. A Hellenistic poet may have dedicated this relief to the Muses. London, The British Museum.

technician invented the *saqqiyah,* an animal-powered waterwheel still used in Egypt and the Sudan. New discoveries such as the so-called **Antikythera Mechanism** reveal, however, that the literary sources provide only an incomplete picture of the achievements of Hellenistic mathematics and technology. Long after this remarkable object was discovered by sponge divers in 1901 in the wreckage of a ship that was probably taking Greek art treasures to Rome, scientific analysis—using X-rays and digital photography—revealed that the Antikythera Mechanism was an astronomical calculator that allowed a person to simultaneously represent the motion through the zodiac of the sun and the moon, calculate leap years, determine the dates of the principal Greek athletic festivals, and even predict eclipses by turning a crank that was connected to a system of gears that is unparalleled for its complexity before the fourteenth century AD.

The doctors Herophilus and Erasistratus made fundamental discoveries concerning the anatomy and functions of the human nervous, optical, reproductive, and digestive systems by dissecting corpses and even vivisecting criminals provided by the government for the "advancement of science." The Hippocratic Oath also dates to the Hellenistic period and enjoins physicians to promise to respect their teachers and to hand on their knowledge only to their teachers' sons and apprentices. Doctors are to swear to abstain from harming any person and to refrain from practicing abortion and euthanasia and from divulging what patients tell them in confidence. Because there was no consensus about the ethical role of physicians in antiquity, the oath was not adhered to by all

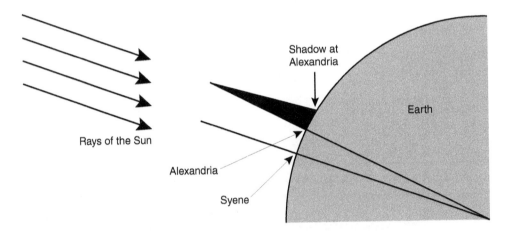

Figure 12.12. Eratosthenes' calculation of the circumference of the Earth. Eratosthenes measured at Alexandria the shadow cast by a pointer at noon of the summer solstice when the sun was directly overhead at Aswan. By applying two simple geometric theorems—the angles of similar triangles are equal and equal angles sweep out equal arcs—he concluded that the 5,000-stade distance between Alexandria and Aswan represented 1/50 of a sphere with a circumference of approximately 250,000 stades, a little over 31,000 miles (assuming a stade equaled eight miles).

Greek physicians, as is obvious from medical texts that discuss abortion, and from the use of vivisection. Royal patronage did, however, have a drawback. Areas that did not receive royal largess tended to stagnate. Thus, apart from the *Elements* and *Optics* of the mathematician Euclid, the Alexandrian contribution to the theoretical sciences and philosophy, which were of limited interest to the Ptolemies, was undistinguished.

SOCIAL RELATIONS IN THE HELLENISTIC WORLD

Greek cultural preeminence tends to obscure the fact that Greeks were a minority in the Hellenistic world, even in cities like Alexandria and Antioch. Not surprisingly, therefore, historians differ in their interpretations of relations between immigrant Greeks and the native populations, some seeing the Hellenistic cities as "melting pots" in which Greek and non-Greek cultures and peoples blended into a new cosmopolitan civilization and others as capitals of segregated societies in which social status and privilege were determined primarily by ethnicity and in which the ethnicities that counted were Macedonian and Greek. A considerable degree of social and cultural segregation was, of course, inherent in the demography of the Hellenistic kingdoms because of the predominantly urban character of Greek settlement. Studies of Egyptian villages have revealed an almost total absence of either Greek residents or Greek influence on daily life.

Segregation was not limited, however, to the countryside. Non-Greeks were not citizens of the Hellenistic cities and lived in separate residential quarters. Greeks, Egyptians, and Jews even used separate legal systems in Egypt. Ethnic prejudices and tensions are also well documented by papyrological evidence. Theocritus characterizes petty street crime as "an Egyptian game," and an agricultural worker complains of being treated with contempt "because I am a barbarian." Prophecies of the end of Macedonian rule are common in both Hellenistic Egyptian and Jewish literature, and Hellenistic history is replete with rebellions intended to achieve that goal.

The Place of Non-Greeks

Nevertheless, the picture of the Hellenistic kingdoms as totally segregated societies distorts ancient reality. Greek translations of Egyptian literature prove that at least some Greeks were interested in contemporary Egyptian culture. More important, the native populations of the Hellenistic kingdoms were not united in their reaction to Macedonian rule.

As in the past, the security of the Hellenistic kingdoms depended on the support of the local gods and their priesthoods. Although the Ptolemies strictly supervised the temples of Egypt, they also generously subsidized them and their priests, as is illustrated by the extensive temple building they sponsored. Egyptian papyri document the prosperity of priestly families, who acquired estates and spent large sums on lavish tomb furnishings and dedications to the gods. Their prosperity also provided the basis for a vigorous revival of Egyptian culture,

Figure 12.13. Antikythera Mechanism. (a) Reconstruction of front with dial representing motions of sun, moon, and planets. Photo: Dr. T. Freeth. (b) Main gear. Athens, National Archaeological Museum. (c) Reconstruction of rear with calendrical dials. Photo: Dr. T. Freeth.

resulting in the production of numerous new literary and artistic works. It is not surprising, therefore, that Egyptian priests congratulated Ptolemy V for suppressing a native rebellion that threatened them as much as him.

Opportunity was not limited to the religious elite. Village officials also prospered by exploiting their role as intermediaries between the Greek-speaking central gov-

Figure 12.14. The Rosetta Stone. March 27, 196 BC. Fragment of a black granite stele found at the Rosetta mouth of the Nile containing a trilingual (Greek, Hieroglyphic [Middle Egyptian], and Demotic [vernacular late Egyptian]) inscription recording a decree passed by a synod of the priests of Egypt commemorating the coronation of Ptolemy V (204–180 BC) as king of Egypt. Study of this stone enabled champollion to decipher Hieroglyphics in 1822. London, The British Museum.

ernment and its Egyptian subjects. Not surprisingly, priests and local officials both were singled out for reprisal during native uprisings. Similar patterns of royal patronage of temples and priestly prosperity characterize Seleucid Asia, where the Seleucid monarchs subsidized Babylonian temples and the temple of Yahweh at Jerusalem and received the loyal support of their respective priesthoods.

Demography also moderated ethnic segregation in the Hellenistic kingdoms. Although the Ptolemies encouraged Greek immigration with generous rewards including grants of land, the actual extent of immigration was limited and mostly male in character because most immigrants were soldiers. The number of ethnic Greeks in the Hellenistic East was, therefore, probably small; and intermarriage was not uncommon, so that over time Greeks assimilated somewhat to the social and cultural mores of their non-Greek neighbors. This was particularly true in the area of religion, as Greeks, like other polytheists, were already predisposed to honor the gods of countries in which they lived.

Hellenistic Religion

Greek religion underwent a profound change in the Hellenistic kingdoms. Paganism and polytheism were flexible, nondogmatic religious systems, open

Figure 12.15. Altar of Pergamum. This monumental altar dedicated to Zeus was built by Eumenes II (197–158 BC). The great frieze, marked by swirling forms carved in high relief, represents the battle between the gods and the giants. Berlin, Pergamon Museum.

to new divinities and to the reshaping of old ones with the result that the powers of the old Olympian gods were often redefined, as they could no longer be conceived as defending Greeks against non-Greeks. In Egypt, for example, Ptolemy I ordered the creation of a new god to serve as Alexandria's new patron deity. The new god, **Sarapis**, was a synthesis of Egyptian and Greek elements, combining aspects of Hades, Dionysus, Zeus, and Osiris. Outside Alexandria, Greeks worshiped traditional Egyptian gods such as **Isis** and Osiris, aided by the traditional Greek practice of identifying their own gods with those of other peoples (syncretism).

In the process, Egyptian gods also changed. Practices alien to Greek religious traditions, such as animal worship or mummification, were purged from the new Hellenized cults, and the Egyptian gods assimilated to the Greek gods with whom they were identified. Isis, for example, was originally the wife of Osiris and mother of Horus in the charter myth of the Egyptian monarchy; but through her identification with Aphrodite, Demeter, and Athena, she assumed a character unprecedented in Egyptian tradition: queen of the universe, benefactress of all people, and creator of civilization. Thus accommodation between Greek and non-Greek culture occurred.

DOCUMENT 12.3

The Praises of Isis (first century BC or first century AD)
The Hellenization of Egyptian religion is evident in this inscription from the city of Cyme in northwest Anatolia with its universalization of Isis' power and identifications of Greek and Egyptian gods (Hephaestus: Ptah, the creator god of Memphis; Hermes: Thoth, god of wisdom and inventor of writing; and Cronus: Geb, god of the earth and father of the royal gods of Egypt).

Demetrius, the son of Artemidorus, who is also called Thraseas, a Magnesian from Magnesia on the Maeander, an offering in fulfillment of a vow to Isis. He transcribed the following from the stele in Memphis which stands by the temple of Hephaestus.

I am Isis, the tyrant of every land; and I was educated by Hermes, and together with Hermes I invented letters, both the hieroglyphic and the demotic, in order that the same script should not be used to write everything. I imposed laws on people, and the laws which I laid down no one may change.

I am the eldest daughter of Cronus. I am the wife and sister of King Osiris. I am she who discovered the cultivation of grain for people. I am she who is called goddess by women. By me the city of Bubastis was built. I separated Earth from sky. I designated the paths of the stars. The sun and the moon's course I laid out. I invented navigation.

I caused the just to be strong. Woman and man I brought together. For woman I determined that in the tenth month she shall deliver a baby into the light. I ordained that parents be cherished by their children. For parents who are cruelly treated I imposed retribution. Together with my brother Osiris I stopped cannibalism.

I revealed initiations to people. I taught people to honor the images of the gods. I established precincts for the gods. The governments of tyrants I suppressed. I stopped murders. I compelled women to be loved by men. I caused the just to be stronger than gold and silver. I ordained that the true be considered beautiful. I invented marriage contracts. Languages I assigned to Greeks and barbarians. I caused the honorable and the shameful to be distinguished by Nature. I caused nothing to be more fearful than an oath. Anyone who unjustly plotted against others I gave into the hands of his victim. On those who commit unjust acts I imposed retribution. I ordained that suppliants be pitied. I honor those who justly defend themselves. With me the just prevails.

I am mistress of rivers and winds and the sea. No one becomes famous without my knowledge. I am the mistress of war. I am the mistress of the thunderbolt. I calm and stir up the sea. I am in the rays of the sun. I sit beside the course of the sun. Whatever I decide, this also is accomplished. For me everything is right. I free those who are in bonds. I am the mistress of sailing. The navigable I make unnavigable whenever I choose. I established the boundaries of cities.

I am she who is called Thesmophoros. The island from the depths I brought up into the light. I conquer Fate. Fate heeds me. Hail Egypt who reared me.

(*Inscriptiones Graecae* 12.14; Burstein)

Over time the lack of rigid barriers between Greek and local societies resulted in situations in which many individuals, who are referred to as "Greeks" in Hellenistic sources, were not so much persons of Greek birth as of Greek culture—people, that is, who had received a Greek education, adopted a Greek lifestyle (and frequently a Greek name), and worshiped their old gods under Greek names.

Likewise, many "Greek cities" in the Near East were simply renamed local settlements with citizen bodies composed of such acculturated non-Greeks. Some Jews sought to transform Jerusalem into such a Greek polis in the early second century BC, but other Jews led by the Maccabees vigorously opposed them. The conflict escalated when Antiochus IV forbade the Jews to carry on their traditional religious practices and in 167 BC had the temple of Yahweh rededicated to Zeus. The festival of Chanukah commemorates the Maccabees' triumph over Antiochus and his supporters. The books of *First* and *Second Maccabees* in the *Apocrypha* illuminate the Hellenistic world from the viewpoint of a subject people and reveal that much of the population of the Hellenistic kingdoms resisted Hellenization.

Macedonian rule in Egypt and western Asia lasted for almost three centuries. Scholars evaluate its significance differently, some emphasizing the spread of Greek culture in the region and others viewing it as a transitory period of colonial rule in which Greek culture was little more than a veneer with limited influence. Not surprisingly, the truth is more complex. Hellenization did occur, but primarily in the major urban centers of the region. Likewise, native traditions endured and even flourished, but their vigor was short-lived, surviving often exclusively among women. Education, culture, and elite status had always been closely connected in the region. The privileged position enjoyed by Greek culture, however, severed that link, encouraging native aristocrats to abandon their traditional cultures and Hellenize. The establishment of the Macedonian kingdoms, therefore, marked the beginning of the end of the ancient civilizations of Egypt and the ancient Near East.

KEY TERMS

Achaean League	Eratosthenes	Pharos
Aetolian League	Euhemerus	Ptolemy I
Antikythera Mechanism	Greek freedom	Ptolemy II
Antigonus the One-Eyed	Hellenistic period	Sarapis
Apollonius of Rhodes	Isis	Seleucus
Callimachus	library [of Alexandria]	Skepticism
Cleopatra VII	Lysimachus	Stoicism
Cynicism	Menander	Theocritus
Demetrius	Museum	Tyche
Epicureanism	papyri	Zeno
Epicurus	Perdiccas	

SUGGESTED READINGS

Bagnall, Roger S. 1995. *Reading Papyri, Writing Ancient History*. London: Routledge. Masterly introduction to the use of papyri to write social and economic history.

Burstein, Stanley M. 1985. *The Hellenistic Age from the Battle of Ipsos to the Death of Kleopatra VII*. Cambridge, UK: Cambridge University Press. Standard collection of nonliterary sources for Hellenistic history.

Cribiore, Raffaella. 2001. *Gymnastics of the Mind: Greek Education in Hellenistic and Roman Egypt*. Princeton, NJ: Princeton University Press. Detailed account of Hellenistic education based on intensive study of the papyrological evidence.

Empereur, Jean-Yves. 1998. *Alexandria Rediscovered*. New York: George Braziller, Inc. Lavishly illustrated account of archaeological discoveries in Alexandria, Egypt.

Erskine, Andrew, ed. 2003. *A Companion to the Hellenistic World*. Oxford, UK: Blackwell. Valuable collection of articles on all aspects of Hellenistic history.

Holt, Frank L. 1999. *Thundering Zeus: The Making of Hellenistic Bactria*. Berkeley and Los Angeles: University of California Press. Pioneering history of the Greek experience in central Asia based on numismatic and archaeological evidence.

Lewis, Naphtali. 1986. *Greeks in Ptolemaic Egypt*. Oxford, UK: Clarendon Press. Account of life in Ptolemaic Egypt as reflected in the careers of eight Greeks and Egyptians.

Lichtheim, Miriam. 1980. *Ancient Egyptian Literature: A Book of Readings. Volume III: The Late Period*. Berkeley and Los Angeles: University of California Press. Standard anthology of Egyptian literary texts composed in the first millennium BC.

Manning, J. G. 2010. *The Last Pharaohs: Egypt Under the Ptolemies, 305–30 BC*. Princeton, NJ: Princeton University Press. Perceptive analysis of Ptolemaic Egypt based on both Greek and Egyptian sources.

Momigliano, Arnaldo. 1975. *Alien Wisdom: The Limits of Hellenization*. Cambridge, UK: Cambridge University Press. Pioneering study of cultural interaction in the Hellenistic period.

Pollitt, J. J. 1986. *Art in the Hellenistic Age*. Cambridge, UK: Cambridge University Press. Standard treatment of Hellenistic art.

Pomeroy, Sarah B. 1989. *Women in Hellenistic Egypt: From Alexander to Cleopatra*. Detroit, MI: Wayne State University Press. Wide-ranging survey of the social, economic, and legal status of women in Ptolemaic Egypt.

Shipley, Graham. 2000. *The Greek World After Alexander: 323–30 BC*. London: Routledge. Comprehensive account of all aspects of Hellenistic history with full discussion of sources and contemporary scholarship.

Walbank, F. W. 1992. *The Hellenistic World*. Rev. ed. Cambridge, MA: Harvard University Press. Lucid brief history of the Hellenistic kingdoms from their foundation until the Roman conquest.

Waterfield, Robin. 2011. *Dividing the Spoils: The War for Alexander the Great's Empire*. Oxford, UK: Oxford University Press. Vivid account of the wars of Alexander's successors.

Epilogue

In many ways the early third century BC was the climax of ancient Greek history. Macedonian power and Greek culture reigned supreme in western Asia. New Greek cities were founded throughout the region, and a person could travel almost to India speaking only Greek. The heyday of the Hellenistic kingdoms, however, was brief, as their survival itself was called into question shortly after their founding.

The Seleucids' kingdom proved the most vulnerable. From Antioch the Seleucids struggled to maintain control of the Asian territories of Alexander's empire. Seleucus I (311–281 BC) gave up his claims to Alexander's conquests in India to Chandra Gupta (c. 324–300 BC), the founder of the Maurya dynasty, who had already conquered northern India. Further territorial losses followed in the third century BC. The catalyst was Ptolemy I's seizure of Coele Syria—southern Syria, Lebanon, and Palestine—in 301 BC. Although Seleucus I forbore contesting Ptolemy's coup, his successors did not, fighting five so-called Syrian wars between the 270s and the end of the century before Antiochus III finally reestablished Seleucid control of the region in 198 BC. Unremitting warfare against the Ptolemies, however, undermined dynastic unity. The critical event, the Third Syrian War (245–241 BC), had originated in a bitter dispute between the families of Antiochus II's two wives over the succession to the throne. The conflict opened a civil war between the sons of Antiochus that lasted more than a decade. While Seleucus' successors fought over the royal succession, enemies attacked their western and eastern frontiers. In the west, the Attalids of Pergamum seized control of much of Anatolia; in the east, the Parthians (Iranian-speaking nomads) and rebellious Greek settlers carved out kingdoms for themselves in eastern Iran and Bactria.

The Ptolemies' hold on Egypt was more secure. Not until 170 BC did an enemy succeed in breaching Egypt's defenses. Ptolemy II (282–246 BC) and Ptolemy III (246–222 BC) extended Egyptian power around the fringes of the Seleucid kingdom, occupying Crete, Cyprus, most of the Aegean islands, and the Greek cities of southern and western Anatolia. For almost three-quarters of a century, Ptolemaic Egypt was the preeminent naval power in the eastern Mediterranean. Nevertheless, Ptolemaic authority in Egypt also weakened significantly in the third century BC. Native rule was reestablished in southern Egypt in the last decades of the century, even as succession crises sapped the dynasty's strength. By 200 BC, the Ptolemies ruled only Lower and Middle Egypt. With the total collapse of the Hellenistic state system in sight, Antiochus III (223–187 BC) and Ptolemy V (204–180 BC) launched vigorous counteroffensives that seemingly restored their dynasties' authority. Before the Seleucids and Ptolemies could fully consolidate their power, however, disaster struck in the form of the Romans. Roman expansion into the eastern Mediterranean was so dramatic and unexpected that the historian Polybius could justifiably ask the deceptively simple question: How could anyone not be interested in knowing how the Romans overthrew the world created by Alexander in less than half a century?

Although Roman relations with Egypt dated to the 270s BC, Rome first intervened in the political life of the eastern Mediterranean only in the early second century BC, defeating Philip V of Macedon and Antiochus III. The Romans did not annex any territory after their victories, preferring instead to pose as the defenders of Greek freedom. The Roman Senate's refusal to brook potential rivals to Roman preeminence in the region, however, effectively undermined all the Hellenistic kingdoms. By the mid-second century, the kingdom of Macedon had disappeared. Defeated in the Third Macedonian War (171–168 BC), Macedon became a Roman province. It was the Achaean League's turn next. In 146 BC, the League was dissolved, and the ancient city of Corinth was sacked and its citizens sold into slavery. A generation later, Roman power expanded across the Aegean when Attalus III, recognizing the inevitability of Roman rule, willed the kingdom of Pergamum to Rome in 133 BC in the hope of preserving a privileged status for the Greek cities of his realm. Only one final obstacle stood in the way of total Roman domination of the eastern Mediterranean: Mithridates VI (120–63 BC), the king of Pontus in northern Anatolia, who claimed descent from the Achaemenid kings of Persia and Alexander the Great and ruled an empire encompassing the entire Black Sea basin. In three great wars between 89 and 63 BC, he sought to rally the peoples of Anatolia and Greece against Rome, only to be finally defeated by the Roman general Pompey, who pursued him to the Crimea, where he committed suicide.

Meanwhile, the Seleucids, weakened by dynastic rivalry and subversion often abetted by Rome, were locked in a losing struggle with the Parthians. This struggle gradually reduced their kingdom to a few cities in Syria that Rome finally occupied in 63 BC. Pompey also occupied the kingdom of Judaea the same year. Of the successor states of Alexander's empire, only Egypt remained independent. The Ptolemies survived their Seleucid rivals by a generation, but only because the Senate could not agree on which senator would take credit for the annexation

Figure E.1. Coin portrait of Cleopatra VII, wearing diadem. She ruled Egypt from 51 to 30 BC. London, The British Museum.

of Egypt. That debate ended in 31 BC when Octavian, the grandnephew of Julius Caesar and the future emperor Augustus, defeated Antony and Cleopatra VII at Actium in northwest Greece. With Cleopatra's suicide in 30 BC, the three-century-long history of Alexander's successors finally ended.

Rome and Parthia turned out to be the ultimate heirs of Alexander's legacy, having extinguished the kingdoms of his successors. The demise of the Hellenistic state system did not mark the end of Greek civilization, but it did change its character and role. In the eastern portions of Alexander's empire, Greek civilization gradually disappeared. Macedonian and Greek rulers were responsible for the flowering of Greek culture in the Hellenistic East, and their patronage ended with the disappearance of their kingdoms. Deprived of a political base, Greek culture withered as the new Parthian rulers of the Middle East sought to rally support from the non-Greek elites of their territory by favoring local traditions. In the west, however, Greek culture flourished thanks to Roman interest.

Although the Roman conquest of the eastern Mediterranean was marked by brutality that belied the promise of "freedom" the Romans had made to the Greeks in 196 BC after the defeat of Philip V, it was not the whole story. The Romans were no strangers to Greek culture. Greek influence on Roman culture dated from the beginnings of Roman history and continued long after Greece had become merely a minor province of the Roman Empire. Greek literature and art were familiar to many upper-class Romans. Some senators, like Fabius Pictor (c. 220 BC), the father of Roman history, even wrote books in Greek. By the first century BC, Roman culture was saturated with Greek influence. Rome's gods and myths had been recast in terms of Greek mythology. Latin writers constantly echoed their Greek predecessors, so that a work like Virgil's *Aeneid*, Rome's national epic, has to be read against the background of the *Iliad* and the *Odyssey* to be fully appreciated. Virgil's contemporary, Horace, was only recognizing reality when he wrote that "Greece, though a captive, captured her fierce conqueror, and brought the arts to rustic Latium" (*Epistles* 2.1).

Because of the Hellenization of the Roman upper class, the Romans made the support of Greeks and Greek culture the linchpin of their rule of the eastern Mediterranean. Greeks enjoyed privileged status, and Greek cities provided the framework for Roman provincial administration.

The result was a remarkable renaissance in the cultural life of the Greek cities during the first two centuries AD. Evidence of this renaissance is visible in the honorary statues that nowadays crowd our museums and in the ruins of the splendid public buildings that everywhere in the eastern Mediterranean dominate the remains of Greek cities. Greek writers, such as the historian Appian and the orator Aelius Aristides, celebrated the benefits of the *Pax Romana* ("Roman Peace"). Science and philosophy also flourished. Galen's medical works and Ptolemy's syntheses of astronomy and geography remained authoritative for more than a millennium. The Egyptian-born Neo-Platonist Plotinus created the last great philosophical system of antiquity, a philosophical mysticism—loosely based on the works of Plato—that was Christianity's most formidable intellectual rival. Only in one area of Greek life was there no renaissance: the civic and political culture of the Greek cities themselves. Instead, during these same two centuries, the last vestiges of the polis tradition of self-government disappeared. As the moralist and biographer Plutarch candidly observed, "Nowadays, when the affairs of the cities no longer include leadership in wars or the overthrowing of tyrannies or acts of alliances, what opening for a conspicuous and brilliant public career could a young man find?" Plutarch answered his own question by pointing out that "there remain the public lawsuits, and embassies to the Emperor" (*Precepts of Statecraft* 805a–b Fowler). Not surprisingly, men such as Arrian, who was governor of Cappadocia under the emperor Hadrian (AD 117–138) and a historian of Alexander, abandoned their poleis and found rewarding careers in the service of Rome.

Whereas Greeks and Greek culture prospered under Roman rule, the same was not true of the non-Greek cultures of Egypt and the Near East. Roman patronage heightened the value of Greek culture and Roman citizenship. Non-Greek cultural traditions and institutions were not repressed, but they were devalued. In the second century AD, the Syrian writer Lucian expressed the cultural priorities of the new regime in his autobiographical essay *The Dream*, stating that without a Greek education a man could only be an "artisan and commoner, always envying the prominent and fawning on the man who was able to speak"; whereas the educated man was "honored and praised, in good repute among the best people, well regarded by those who are preeminent in wealth and breeding . . . and considered worthy of public office and precedence" (*The Dream* 9–11). Lucian's calculation was correct. His Greek education and literary skill brought him fame and a lucrative post on the staff of the Prefect of Egypt.

The process of assimilation was not always free of friction. Complaints of Greek prejudice and cultural chauvinism are frequent in the writings of Hellenized non-Greeks such as, for example, the Hellenized Syrian rhetorician Tatian, who urged Greeks not to despise non-Greeks and their ideas because most Greek practices "took their origin from barbarian ways" (*Address to the Greeks* 1.1). Nevertheless, by late antiquity, a significant portion of the social and intellectual elite of the eastern provinces of the Roman Empire consisted of Hellenized non-Greeks. The local languages of the region survived in the vernacular speech of the urban lower classes and the countryside and even found new written expression in the literatures of Syriac and Coptic Christianity. But the traditional cultures of Egypt and the Near East died, as the native elites who had patronized them for millennia gradually deserted them. Meanwhile, the dominant strand in the intellectual life of the eastern Mediterranean basin became what scholars call Hellenism, essentially a cosmopolitan form of Greek culture loosely based on Classical Greek literature. In this form, Greek culture continued to flourish in the lands conquered by Alexander the Great and influenced the medieval civilizations of Byzantium and Islam and through them the culture of Europe and the Americas.

SUGGESTED READINGS

Bowersock, G. W. 1990. *Hellenism in Late Antiquity*. Ann Arbor: University of Michigan Press. Important analysis of the transformation of Greek culture in the Roman Empire.

Burstein, Stanley M. 2007. *The Reign of Cleopatra*. Norman: The University of Oklahoma Press. Clearly written brief biography of Cleopatra VII emphasizing the Egyptian context of her reign and containing an extensive selection of useful primary sources.

Errington, R. M. 1972. *The Dawn of Empire: Rome's Rise to World Power*. Ithaca, NY: Cornell University Press. Lucid history of Rome's wars with Carthage, Macedon, and the Seleucid kingdom.

Gruen, Erich. 1992. *Culture and National Identity in Republican Rome*. Ithaca, NY: Cornell University Press. Brilliant discussion of the interaction of Greek and Roman culture in the Roman Republic.

Kleiner, Diana E. E. 2005. *Cleopatra and Rome*. Cambridge, MA: Harvard University Press. Lucid and beautifully illustrated analysis of the Roman image of Cleopatra.

Plutarch. 1999. *Advice to the Bride and Groom and Consolation to His Wife*. Sarah B. Pomeroy, ed. New York: Oxford University Press. Multiauthored essays on marriage, gender relations, childhood, and parenthood in Greece under Roman domination including English translations, commentary, and bibliography.

Pomeroy, Sarah B. 2007. *The Murder of Regilla*. Cambridge, MA: Harvard University Press. A vivid biography of a Roman woman in second-century Greece grounded in an analysis of justice, society, culture, and marriage.

Roller, Duane W. 2010. *Cleopatra. A Biography*. New York: Oxford University Press. A well-researched easy-to-read biography of Cleopatra written using only ancient sources.

Walker, Susan and Averil Cameron, eds. 1986. *The Greek Renaissance in the Roman Empire: Papers from the Tenth British Museum Classical Colloquium*. London: University of London, Institute of Classical Studies. An early collection of papers in an area that has become a current focus of scholarly interest, including articles on art, literature, and religion.

GLOSSARY

ACROPOLIS Literally, the "upper city," the citadel of a city or town. Many citadel hills had been the sites of Mycenaean palaces and remained as special places in *polis* life. The most famous is the Acropolis of Athens, the religious center of the city, which was magnificently adorned with temples in the fifth century.

AGORA In Homer, the term for the "place of gathering," the assembly of the people. In the city-state period it denoted the public space of a city or town, being both the marketplace and civic center. Lingering in the agora was the best way to inform oneself about public affairs, make business contacts, and collect gossip.

AMPHICTYONIC COUNCIL The governing body of an ancient league of Delphi's neighbors, the Delphic Amphictyony, that administered the oracle. It also conducted the Pythian games and dealt with transgressions against the oracle and its territory. The members were *ethnē*, of which the most important were the Thessalians, Phocians, Boeotians, Dorians, and Ionians. Votes were unequally divided among the members, so that Philip II's acquisition of the twelve Thessalian and two Phocian votes gave him a majority of the council's twenty-two votes and control of the Amphictyony.

ARCHON A common title (meaning "leader") for the highest-ranking magistrate in the early city-states. During the Classical period, even when the *strategoi* had become the most important officials in Athens, nine archons continued to be chosen (by lot) to serve judicial and administrative functions.

ARISTOCRACY The term *aristokratia* ("power in the hands of the best men") was coined, probably in the fifth century, possibly to describe the rule of the elite in preference to the less noble-sounding *oligarchia*. Aristocratic power and exclusiveness were strongest in the early Archaic period and gradually weakened as strong democratic sentiments emerged in the city-states.

ASSEMBLY One of the two primary elements of Greek governance (see *boule*). From the Dark Age on it was made up of the free adult males of the community who met the minimum qualifications for citizenship, usually membership in a household and ability to perform military service. In the Dark Age, the assembly (which met in the *agora* in Homer) had limited power vis-à-vis the chiefs, although its concurrence was crucial. By the Classical period it had become the deciding body of state policy. In Athens, the assembly or *ecclesia* met in the open air on the hill called the Pnyx about forty times a year.

BARBAROS Term for all people who were not Greek in language and culture, so that the highly civilized and generally admired Egyptians and Persians were *barbaroi*. Increasingly from the fifth century on, however, barbaroi came to be stigmatized as the inferior "others," lacking the mental and moral capabilities that belonged naturally to Hellenes.

Basileus The term for the legitimate monarch, the "king." In Mycenaean society, the title *pasireu* denoted a village or district administrator; in the Dark Age *basileis* were the warrior chiefs who ruled the villages and districts. The hierarchy of basileis was replaced in the Archaic Age by oligarchies of landed aristocrats.

Boule Term for the "council," which was one of the two primary governing institutions of the Greeks (see "assembly"). Composed of the chiefs and other influential men in the Dark Age, it became the major organ of aristocratic power in the Archaic Age. In Classical Athens, the *boule* consisted of five hundred men chosen by lot; it prepared business for the assembly and also tried certain court cases.

Cella The inner shrine of a temple. A gold and ivory statue of Athena, over 38 feet high and now lost, stood in the cella of the Parthenon.

City-State See polis.

Currency, Athenian The basic units of Athenian currency were the obol and the drachma (= six obols). For accounting purposes, drachmas could also be collected into larger groups; so one hundred drachmas made a mina, and sixty minas added up to a talent. In fifth-century Athens, a silver drachma coin was considered good pay for a day's labor by an unskilled worker and was probably a living wage for a small family. A drachma was the standard daily pay for a rower in the fleet. Maintaining a trireme cost a talent a month.

Demagogos Literally, a "leader of the people." Term used by some Athenians to categorize democratic politicians, particularly after Pericles' death. Usually it had negative connotations and suggested that such a man was self-interested, unlike a true statesman, who cared for the welfare of the state.

Democracy A form of government in Classical Greece that permitted all free male citizens some degree of participation in politics, regardless of wealth or family background. Despite ideologies of equality, economic inequalities prevailed and generally brought political inequalities with them. Athens encouraged democratic governments in its allies.

Demos A territory and the people who live in it; thus, "the land" and "the people." It occurs in the Linear B tablets in the form *damo*, meaning, possibly, a village community and its free inhabitants. Although always retaining its official meaning of "the (whole) people," aristocrats increasingly used it as an exclusive term for the "commoners," or the "masses."

Dicasteries (*dikasteria*) Democratic courts at Athens. A dicasterion was composed of hundreds of adult male citizens chosen by lot from those belonging to the pool of jurors known as the heliaia. Both the last-minute element of the choice and the large size of the juries discouraged bribery, especially because Athenian court cases had to be decided in a single day and there was no appealing its decisions. Beginning around the middle of the fifth century, jurors received a small amount of pay for their services.

Dokimasia The scrutiny Athenian citizens had to undergo before assuming a position in the government. Political enemies often used this procedure as a means of keeping a man out of public office.

Drachma See currency, Athenian.

Ecclesia See assembly.

Ephor (*ephoros*) "Overseer," an office found in Sparta and in other Dorian states. In Sparta a board of five ephors was elected annually by the assembly; the senior ephor gave his name to the year. The ephors had great power in the Spartan state, including general control over the kings' conduct.

Epikleros A brotherless Athenian girl compelled to marry her nearest male relative to produce a son to inherit her father's property. Although often translated "heiress," the epikleros could not herself inherit but only transmit property.

ETHNOS Term for a group of people who shared a common identity and territory, but were not politically united, preferring local self-government. From the sixth century BC on Greek *ethnē* acted as unified states by forming federations of local and regional segments of the *ethnos*. By the fourth century, ethnic confederacies and leagues played a prominent role in the geopolitics of Greece.

GENOS A category of families claiming descent from a single male ancestor. A *genos* was led by its most prominent family and played a prominent part as a political group in the Archaic Age. In the Classical period *genos* membership continued to confer social prestige on their constituent families.

GEROUSIA The "council of elders" (from *gerōn* "old man"). Term used at Sparta and in other *poleis* for the aristocratic council. The Spartan *gerousia* consisted of the two kings plus twenty-eight men over age sixty who served for life.

GRAPHE PARANOMON Athenian procedure used from the late fifth-century BC to indict a man for making an illegal proposal in the assembly. Because there was no Athenian constitution and illegality was difficult to determine, the procedure could be used as a form of political attack. Those convicted were generally fined; three convictions barred a citizen from making further proposals.

GUEST FRIENDSHIP (*xenia*) A form of ritual friendship, whereby a "stranger" (*xenos*) entered into a hereditary relationship of mutual friendship with a man from another *demos*, each obliged to offer hospitality and aid when they visited each other's community. A prominent feature of Homeric society, *xenia* continued throughout antiquity, eventually becoming the more formal diplomatic relationship of proxeny.

HEGEMON A state or individual who headed an organization of states. Athens, for example, was the hegemon of the Delian League, Sparta of the Peloponnesian League. A hegemon was said to exercise hegemony, hence the period of Theban ascendancy in the 360s BC is known as the Theban hegemony.

HEKTEMOROI A term used in Solonian Athens meaning "sixth-parters," referring, presumably, to poor farmers who had fallen into debt to wealthy landowners and had to hand over to them perpetually a sixth of their produce under threat of enslavement as payment for their debt.

HELIAIA The body of prospective jurors from which *dikasteria* were selected at Athens. Any adult male citizen might present himself for participation.

HELLENES Greek name for themselves. They had a myth of an eponymous ancestor, Hellen, who was the son of Deucalion, the Greek Noah, and the father of the eponymous ancestors of the Dorians, Ionians, and Aeolians. The common name (and the supporting myth) probably arose relatively late, perhaps in the eighth century BC.

HELOTS Term for groups of conquered people in Greece forced by their conquerors to work as serfs on their former lands. It is most commonly associated with Sparta, where helots probably outnumbered citizens by a ratio of seven to one. The Spartan way of life both depended on and was formed by the state's ownership of thousands of helots in Laconia and Messenia. Fear of helot uprisings often discouraged Sparta from engaging in distant campaigns.

HETAIRA Term meaning literally "female companion" and normally used for courtesans in Classical Athens. *Hetairai* were usually metics. Often more cultivated than citizen women, they were trained to be entertaining and interesting rather than to be thrifty managers of households. Because Pericles' citizenship laws of 451–450 made it difficult for a man to marry a metic woman, some Athenian men formed long-term associations with hetairai simultaneously with their legal marriages to Athenian women.

Although some hetairai functioned as entrenched mistresses or even common-law wives, others were essentially prostitutes.

HETAIREIAI The military systems of some cities such as those in Crete grouped men in *hetaireiai* or "bands of companions," but the word is most commonly associated with hetaireiai or social clubs with political overtones, often of an antidemocratic nature, in Athens. The mutilation of the herms in 415 BC was allegedly the work of such a hetaireia, and hetaireiai probably played a part in the oligarchic revolutions of 411 BC and 404 BC.

HETAIROS "Companion" or "comrade." In the Dark Age, follower bands of *hetairoi* formed the military and political support of the chiefs who recruited and rewarded them. For associations of hetairoi in the city-states, see *hetaireiai*. In Macedonia, the hetairoi were an elite band of warriors and advisors who formed the retinue and personal bodyguard of the kings.

HOPLITE *hoplitēs* The heavily armored infantryman, named from his distinctive shield (*hoplon*). Hoplites were the dominant military arm in Greece from the seventh century on, gradually undergoing changes in weaponry and tactics. Because Greek governments did not issue arms to their soldiers, hoplites tended to come from the middle class, men able to afford armor and swords.

KLEROS An allotment of farmland sufficient to support a citizen-family; it was passed on in perpetuity in the male line. In oligarchic states, full citizenship was frequently tied to the possession of a certain amount of land.

KORE "Maiden." Term for the life-size or larger marble Archaic statues of clothed females, made as cult offerings or grave markers. The term *kouros* ("youth") is used of the corresponding nude male statues.

LITURGIES An indirect system of taxation at Athens whereby the rich were required to use their own money to finance public services such as the training of a chorus for dramatic performances or sending a delegation to a religious festival in another state. The trierarchy was the most expensive, requiring a man to maintain a trireme for a year and to equip and train its crew.

MEGARON A large rectangular building that served as the focal point of Mycenaean palaces. Its function as the "great hall" of the ruler continued in the reign of the Dark Age chiefs. In the city-states the ancient *megaron* achieved immortality as the basic plan of the Greek temple.

METICS Resident aliens in a Greek state. We know most about metics in Athens. Although they lacked citizenship, metics mingled comfortably in Athenian society and were called on for help in wartime, but they were not permitted to own property or represent themselves in court.

METROPOLIS "Mother-city." Term for a *polis* that founded a colony. The relationship between the mother-city and the new *polis* was normally very close, combining economic, political, and spiritual ties.

MINA See currency, Athenian.

MYTH All cultures possess myths, traditional tales that treat aspects of life that are important to the collective group (e.g., marriage, initiation, food, cultural institutions, human–divine relations, etc.). The Greeks knew many such orally transmitted stories going back to the second millennium BC and continually enriched by additions from the mythologies of the Near East. Greek historians depended on myths to reconstruct the preliterate past. Modern researchers attempt to glean from them evidence for historical or psychological realities.

NOMOS Custom or law. Sometimes it corresponds to the English word "mores," connoting a way of doing things that is deeply embedded in a value system. It can also be used, however, in a legal context; thus, for example, the rules laid down by Solon were called his *nomoi*.

NOMOTHETAI A body of Athenian officials established after the restoration of the democracy in 403 BC. The *nomothetai* reviewed and ratified proposed Athenian laws in a trial-like procedure. The number of *nomothetai* varied depending on the significance of the proposed law, but it could be as high as 1,001.

OBOL See currency, Athenian.

OIKIST The *oikistēs* (note the root of *oikos*) was the "founder" and the leader of a colony sent out by a mother-city (*mētropolis*). The *oikistēs* had great authority in the new settlement and was often deified after his death.

OIKOS "Household." The fundamental social and economic unit in Greek society, comprehending the family group, its house, land, animals, and property, including slaves.

OLIGARCHY *Oligarchia* ("rule by a few men") replaced the system of ranked chieftains as the standard form of government in the early city-states. Opposition from below the narrow ruling circle caused most oligarchies to broaden inclusion in state affairs. Democratic *poleis* were subject to oligarchic revolutions, as in Athens in 411 BC and again in 404 BC. Throughout the fifth and fourth centuries, tension between oligarchs and democrats—which often added up to tension between rich and poor—was a constant factor in Greek political life and sometimes erupted in bloodshed.

PARAMOUNT An anthropological term referring to the highest-ranking leader of a community or group. The major warrior heroes of the Homeric epics, who rule over other leaders as a "first among equals," represent the paramount chiefs who ruled during the tenth to eighth century BC.

PEDIMENT The elongated triangular spaces that sat on top of the columns on the front and back of Greek temples. They were frequently adorned with elaborate relief sculpture.

PELTASTS Lightly armed Greek soldiers who carried light throwing spears and small, round shields. They were deployed as skirmishers either alone or in concert with hoplites. Although used during the Peloponnesian War, their importance increased dramatically in the fourth century.

PENTAKOSIOMEDIMNOI The highest of the four property classes in the Solonic system. To qualify for membership, the *pentakosiomedimnoi* or "500-measure men" each needed an estate that produced at least 500 *medimnoi* (bushels) of produce in any combination of oil, wine, or grain.

PERIOECI "Those who dwell about," the term used for neighboring peoples subordinate to a dominating *polis*. The chief example is Sparta, which treated the people of the perioecic communities of Laconia and Messenia as half-citizens who possessed local autonomy and were obligated to military service but had no say in the conduct of policy.

PHALANX The tactical formation of a hoplite army, consisting in the Archaic and Classical periods of ranks of heavy infantry, usually eight deep. The phalanx introduced by Philip II of Macedon consisted of six brigades of 1,500 men each. Each phalangite was armed with a short sword, a small round shield, and a pike (*sarissa*) up to 18 feet long, and they fought in rectangular formations sixteen men deep.

PHRATRY A subdivision of the tribe (*phylē*) and, theoretically, a kin group. In Classical times phratries were well-defined social groups concerned with defining descent and, therefore, citizenship. Every citizen family in Athens belonged to a phratry.

PHYLAI "Tribes." The term for the large descent groups into which a *dēmos* was divided. Ionian communities had four such "tribes"; Dorian communities had three. The tribes functioned as organizational units in the city-states. In his reform of the Athenian government, Cleisthenes bypassed the four traditional tribes and divided Attica politically and militarily into ten new *phylai*.

POLEMARCH The office of *polemarchos* ("war leader") was common to many early city-states. As army commander for a specified term, usually a year, and subject to the policy of the aristocratic council, the polemarch was limited in his power. Circa 500 BC, the military functions of the Athenian polemarch were transferred to the board of ten *strategoi* (see *strategos*). After 487 BC, when the polemarch became appointed by lot, his functions became mainly legal and ceremonial.

POLIS "City," "town." From the eighth century on, *polis* designated a political community, composed of a principal city or town and its surrounding countryside, which together formed a self-governing entity: the "city-state." The small polis was the principal form of Greek state, numbering in the high hundreds by the fifth century BC.

PROBOULEUTIC The term for the council's (*boulē's*) function of preparing state business for consideration in the assembly.

PROSKYNESIS Greek name for the Persian ritual greeting offered by social inferiors to their superiors and by all Persians to the Persian king. In its simplest form, *proskynēsis* involved merely blowing a kiss. Proskynesis to the Persian king, however, required full prostration before the ruler. Although Persians did not believe that their king was divine, Greeks and Macedonians considered proskynesis appropriate only to deities and resented attempts to make them perform it.

PROXENY The term used for a diplomatic arrangement whereby citizens in one state, called *proxenoi*, looked after the interests of other states in their communities. The *proxenos* was highly honored by the foreign state he represented. The system of proxeny (*proxenia*) developed from an earlier system of *xenia* or private "guest-friendship."

PRYTANIS One of the titles for the presiding magistrate (or a college of magistrates) in a city-state. In the reorganization of the Athenian *boulē* (508 BC), ten boards of fifty *prytaneis* each, chosen by lot from the ten new "tribes" (*phylai*), took turns as the officials in charge of the daily business of the *boulē* and *ecclesia* for a tenth of the year. Each group of fifty men comprised a prytany.

REDISTRIBUTIVE SYSTEM The term for the kind of economic and political arrangements found in the Bronze Age kingdoms of the Near East and Greece where most of the agricultural and manufactured production of a region was controlled from the center (the king and his palace), which redistributed the resources as it saw fit. In the Greek city-states, by contrast, the government exercised only limited control over production and distribution. See liturgies.

RHETORES The men who chose to involve themselves intensively in Athenian politics during the fourth century, proposing decrees and making speeches in the assembly. It is often translated "politicians," although technically the term referred to their skill as public speakers.

SATRAP Title of the governors of the principal territorial subdivisions of the Persian Empire, then of Alexander III's empire, and later of the Seleucid kingdom.

SATRAPY Originally a province of the Persian Empire. Alexander III retained the satrapal system of the Persian Empire as the administrative framework of his empire. After the division of Antigonus the One-Eyed's empire in 301 BC, the term was used to designate the largest territorial subdivisions of the Seleucid kingdom.

SOPHISTS Itinerant intellectuals who taught and gave speeches during the latter part of the fifth century BC. Some were primarily teachers of oratory, while others engaged in thoughtful speculation about society that challenged entrenched conventions. Plato made the discrediting of the sophists an important part of his dialogues, accusing them of substituting showy rhetorical displays for real wisdom such as Socrates possessed.

Stasis The term first for a group of men who take the same "stand" in a political dispute— a faction—and then by extension the act itself of taking sides. In the city-states *stasis* (civil strife) occurred between oligarchical factions and between the rich and the poor. At its worst, stasis entailed bloodshed; thus, containing it within nonviolent bounds was a principal objective of the city-states.

Stele A stone slab inscribed with a text, a decoration, or both. Stelae could be used to indicate graves, military victories, or property boundaries. Important texts such as legal decrees and treaties might also be inscribed on them.

Strategos The common term for a "military leader." In Athens, after 487 BC, the ten strategoi were the only elected high officials; thus most influential fifth-century politicians were strategoi. In the early Hellenistic era, *stratēgos* (general) was the title of the highest-ranking Macedonian military commander in Europe and Asia. The four attested strategoi of this period were Antipater, Polyperchon, and Cassander in Europe and Antigonus the One-Eyed in Asia.

Symposium In Archaic and later periods, the after-dinner "drinking party," made up of a small number (between fourteen and thirty) of men, was a frequent event in adult male social life, primarily among the elite. The *symposium* was an important bonding ritual among young aristocrats and (like the *hetaireiai*) was often the occasion of factional plotting.

Synedrion A representative council such as that of the Second Athenian Confederacy or the Corinthian League. The synedrion of the Second Athenian Confederacy was composed of a single representative from each member state and ruled the confederacy jointly with the Athenian assembly; policy decisions had to be ratified by both bodies. The synedrion of the Corinthian League consisted of representatives of the member cities and *ethnē* of the league. The latter synedrion was responsible for upholding the Common Peace that established the Corinthian League and was empowered to arbitrate disputes among its members and to try individuals accused of betraying its goals.

Synoecism (*synoikismos*) The term used for the process whereby several separate communities were formed into a single political union. Synoecism also referred to the actual movement of people from several communities into a new composite settlement.

Talent See currency, Athenian.

Thes The term for a free man who was forced by his poverty to hire out as a laborer for wages. In Athens, according to the economic divisions attributed to Solon (c. 600 BC), the *thētes* (plural) formed the lowest class of citizens.

Tholos (plural tholoi) A type of monumental above-ground stone tomb (shaped like a beehive) favored by the elites of the Late Bronze Age. In the Classical period, circular structures, also called *tholoi*, served as temples and public buildings.

Trireme Term for the standard form of Greek warship (*trieres*) in the Classical period. Propelled by three banks of oars, and attaining speeds of nine knots, the trireme used its bronze ram to disable enemy ships.

Tyranny (*tyrannis*) The illegal seizure and control of governmental power in a *polis* by a single strong man, the "tyrant" (*tyrannos*). Tyranny occurred as a phase in many city-states during the Archaic period and is often seen as an intermediate stage between narrow oligarchy and more democratic forms of polity. In the late fifth and the fourth century, a new kind of tyrant, the military dictator, arose, especially in Sicily.

Wanax "Lord," "master." The title of the monarchical ruler of a Mycenaean kingdom. In the form *anax* it appears as the title of gods and high-ranking chiefs in Homer.

Xenia See guest-friendship.

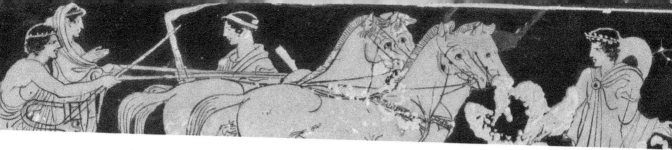

ART AND ILLUSTRATION
CREDITS

1.1   A papyrus of Homer, *Iliad* 24, lines 693-711. London, The British Museum (Papyrus 114). Used with permission of the British Library.

1.1a   Heinrich Schliemann. Photo: Library of Congress.

1.1b   Sophie Schliemann adorned by the "Treasure of Priam." Photo: akg-images/ullstein bild.

1.1c   Gold mask from shaft graves, Mycenae. Athens, National Archaeological Museum, Inv. no. 3928. Photo: Museum.

1.1d   Gold mask from an early shaft grave at Mycenae. Athens, National Archaeological Museum. Photo: Foto Marburg/Art Resource, New York.

1.2   Cycladic marble figurine of a male figure playing double pipes from Keros (c. 2500-2200 BC). Athens, National Archaeological Museum. Nimatallah/Art Resource, NY.

1.5a   Inlaid dagger. Athens, National Archaeological Museum. Photo: Hirmer Fotoarchiv, Muenchen.

1.5b   Plan and cross-section of a Mycenaean tholos tomb. Photo: British School, Athens.

1.5c   Interior vault of a tholos tomb at Mycenae. Photo: Hirmer Fotoarchiv, Munich.

1.6b   The megaron hall at Pylos. Photo: Alison Franz, American School of Classical Studies at Athens: Agora Excavations.

1.6c   The "Lion Gate." Photo: Bildarchiv Preussischer Kulturbesitz, Berlin.

1.7a   A chariot table from Mycenaean Cnossus. After J. Chadwick, *The Decipherment of Linear B*, 2nd ed. (Cambridge: Cambridge University Press, 1976).

1.7b   Linear B tablet from Mycenaean Knossos. After J. Chadwick, *The Decipherment of Linear B*, 2nd ed. (Cambridge: Cambridge University Press, 1976), p. 108.

1.8a   Gold ring from Knossos. Herakleion, Archaeological Museum. Photo: Hirmer Fotoarchiv, Munich.

1.8b   Scene on a gold ring from Late Bronze Age Mycenae. From Donald Preziosi and Louise A Hitchcock, *Aegean Art and Architecture* (New York: Oxford University Press, 2000), p. 139, fig. 87. Reprinted by permission of the publisher.

1.9a   Bronze plate armor and boar's tusk helmet from Dendra in Argolis (c. 1400 BC). Nauplion, Museum. Photo: German Archaeological Institute, Athens.

1.9b   Vase showing line of soldiers on the march, Mycenae. Athens, National Archaeological Museum. Photo: Hellenic Ministry of Culture/Archaeological Institute, Athens.

2.1   Late Protogeometric vase. Athens, Kerameikos Museum K2616. Photo: German Archaeological Institute, Athens.

2.3   Gold jewelry from the cremation grave of a wealthy Athenian woman (c. 850 BC). Athens, Agora Museum. Photo: American School of Classical Studies at Athens: Agora Excavations.

2.4   Blind Homer. Boston, Museum of Fine Arts. Photograph © 2006 Museum of Fine Arts, Boston.

2.6b   Late Geometric vase from the Dipylon cemetery. Athens, National Archaeological Museum NM192. Photo: The Art Archive/National Archaeological Museum Athens/Gianni Dagli Orti.

2.7a   Middle Geometric crater from Athens. Paris, The Louvre. Photo: Herve Lewandowski, Réunion des Musées Nationaux/Art Resource, NY.

2.7b   Large Late Geometric grave amphora. Athens, National Archaeological Museum. Photo: The Art Archive/National Archaeological Museum Athens/Gianni Dagli Orti.

2.9   Clay model of a house or temple from Argos. Athens, National Archaeological Museum. Photo: The Art Archive/National Archaeological Museum Athens/Gianni Dagli Orti.

3.2a   Corinthian vase with depiction of a hoplite battle. Rome, National Etruscan Museum of the Villa Giulia. Photo: The Art Archive/Museo di Villa Giulia Rome/Gianni Dagli Orti.

3.2a   Statue of an Egyptian nobleman. Boston, Museum of Fine Arts 07.494. James Fund Purchase and Contribution, August 8, 1907. Photograph © 2009 Museum of Fine Arts, Boston.

3.2b   Bronze votive offering. Museum of Fine Arts, Boston. Fracs Bartlett Donation of 1900, 03.997.

3.3   Athenian amphora. Boston, Museum of Fine Arts 01.8037. Henry Lillie Pierce Fund. Photograph © 2009 Museum of Fine Arts, Boston.

3.4   Statue of an Egyptian nobleman. Boston, Museum of Fine Arts 07.494. James Fund Purchase and Contribution, August 8, 1907. Photograph © 2009 Museum of Fine Arts, Boston.

3.5   Marble kouros. New York, The Metropolitan Museum of Art 32.11.1. Fletcher Fund. Image © The Metropolitan Museum of Art.

3.6   Marble kouros. Athens, National Archaeological Museum NM3938. Photo: Hellenic Ministry of Culture/Archaeological Receipts Fund.

3.7   Late Archaic kore from the Acropolis. Photo: German Archaeological Institute, Athens.

3.8   Electrum coin from eastern Greece. Athens, Numismatic Collection. Photo: Hirmer Fotoarchiv, Munich.

4.1   View of Sparta. Photo: Ulrich Tichy.

4.3   Bronze statuette of a Spartan girl running. London, The British Museum. Courtesy of the Trustees of The British Museum.

4.4   Laconian bronze mirror. New York, The Metropolitan Museum of Art 38.11.3. Image © the Metropolitan Museum of Art.

4.5   Laconian cup. Paris, The Louvre. Photo: Réunion des Musées Nationaux/Art Resource, NY.

4.6   Hilaire Germain Edgar Degas' painting, "Young Spartans Exercising." London, The National Gallery. Photo courtesy of the museum.

5.1   Detail of Attic red-figure cup by Epictetus. London, The British Museum. Courtesy of the Trustees of The British Museum.

5.2   Water jar from Athens by the Priam Painter. Toledo Museum of Art 1961.23, Purchased with funds from the Libbey Endowment, Gift of Edward Drummond Libbey. Photo: Museum.

5.3   Tetradrachm, Athens. New York, American Numismatic Society 1957.172.1033. Photo: The American Numismatic Society.

5.4   Attic red-figure psykter. New York, The Metropolitan Museum of Art 1989.281.69. Gift of Norbert Schimmel Trust, 1989. Image © The Metropolitan Museum of Art.

5.5   Statues of Harmodius and Aristogiton. Naples, National Museum. Photo: Hirmer Fotoarchiv, Munich.

5.7   Delegations bringing tribute to the Persian king. Berlin, Preussischer Kulturbesitz. Photo: bpk Berlin.

5.9   The tumulus for the Athenian dead at Marathon. Photo: akg/ De Agostini Picture Library

5.10   Ostraka discovered in the Athenian agora. American School of Classical Studies at Athens: Agora Excavations.

5.11   A trireme at sea. Photo: © The Trireme Trust

6.1   Section of the Athenian Tribute List inscription. Athens, Epigraphical Museum. Photo: Epigraphical Museum.

6.3   Bronze charioteer. Delphi, Delphi Museum. Photo: Erich Lessing/Art Resource, NY.

6.4   Roman copy of the discobolus Rome, National Museum. Photo: Hirmer Fotoarchiv, Munich.

6.5a–b   Reconstructions of the pediment of the temple of Zeus at Olympia. From Bernard Ashmole, *Architect and Sculptor in Classical Greece* (New York: New York University Press, 1972), p. 25.

6.5c   Seer from east pediment. Olympia Museum. Photo: Olympia Archaeological Museum.

6.6   Marble relief depicting girl with doves. New York, The Metropolitan Museum of Art 27.45. Fletcher Fund, 1927. Image © The Metropolitan Museum of Art.

6.7a–b   Attic vase c. 470 BCE. Boston, Museum of Fine Arts, 63.1246. William Francis Warden Fund. Photograph © 2009 Museum of Fine Arts, Boston.

6.8   Attic vase depicting craftspeople at work. Boston, Museum of Fine Arts, 01.8035. Henry Lillie Pierce Fund. Photograph © 2009 Museum of Fine Arts, Boston.

6.9   Attic red-figure chous depicting a little boy. Boston, Museum of Fine Arts. Photograph © 2009 Museum of Fine Arts, Boston.

6.10   Detail of Attic red-figure wedding bowl by the Washing Painter. Munich, Staatliche Antikensammlungen und Glyptothek. Photo: Museum.

6.11   Attic red-figure pyxis (cosmetic box), c. 430 BC, attributed to the Marlay Painter. London, The British Museum. Courtesy of the Trustees of The British Museum.

6.12   Attic black-figure jar attributed to the Amasis Painter. New York, The Metropolitan Museum of Art 31.11.10. Fletcher Fund, 1931. Image © The Metropolitan Museum of Art.

7.2   Roman copy of the head of Pericles. Munich, Staatliche Antikensammlungen und Glyptothek. Photo: Bildarchiv Preussischer Kulturbesitz/Art Resource, NY.

7.3   Model of Periclean Acropolis. Toronto, The Royal Ontario Museum 956.118. With permission of the Royal Ontario Museum © ROM.

7.6   The Parthenon today. Photo: Gjon Mili Time Life Pictures/Getty Images.

7.7   Parthenon east frieze, slab V. London: British Museum. Photo: Foto Marburg/Art Resource, New York.

7.9   Erechtheion (426–406 BC), Athens Acropolis. Photo: The J. Allen Cash Photo Library, London.

7.11   Medea Vase. Photo: © Cleveland Museum of Art

7.12   Drinking cup. Oxford, The Ashmolean Museum (1967.304). Photo: Museum.

8.2   Attic red-figure stamnos. London, The British Museum. Courtesy of the Trustees of The British Museum.

8.4a   Bronze shield with graffiti. Athens, Agora Museum. Photo: American School of Classical Studies at Athens: Agora Excavations.

8.5a–b   Attic red-figure chous. Paris, The Louvre. Photo: Réunion des Musées Nationaux/Art Resource, NY.

8.6   Fragmentary fifth-century herm. Athens, Agora Museum. Photo: American School of Classical Studies at Athens: Agora Excavations.

9.1   Head of a Greek statue of Socrates, Roman copy. Paris, The Louvre. Photo: Giraudon/Art Resource, NY.

9.2a   Monument commemorating the death of Dexileus. Athens, Ceramicus, Oberländer Museum. Photo: The Art Archive/Kerameikos Museum, Athens/Gianni Dagli Orti.

9.2b   The Street of the Tombs in the Ceramicus cemetery. Photo: The Art Archive/Gianni Dagli Orti.

9.3   Remains of the walls built by the Athenians after the Battle of Cnidus, Piraeus. Photo: Larry Tritle.

9.4   Hypothetical reconstruction of the Mausoleum. Photo: Bridgeman Art Library.

9.5   Fragment of the *kleoterion*. Athens, Agora Museum. Photo: The American School of Classical Studies at Athens: Agora Excavation.

9.6   *Klepsydra* ("water clock"). Athena, Agora Museum. Photo: The American School of Classical Studies at Athens: Agora Excavation.

9.7   Reconstruction of gastraphetes. From John Warry, Warfare in the Classical World, An Illustrated Encyclopedia (paperback) (Salamander Books, 1995), p. 78.

10.1   Gianni Dagli Orti / The Art Archive at Art Resource, NY

10.3a   Silver tetradrachm of Philip II (359–336 BC). Obverse: Head of Zeus. Reverse: Mounted Macedonian king—probably Philip II—wearing Macedonian hat and cape. Oxford, The Ashmolean Museum, Plate 28, No. 513. Photo: Museum, Herberden Coin Room.

10.3b   Silver tetradrachm of Philip II (359–336 BC). Obverse: Head of Zeus. Reverse: Jockey commemorating the victory of Philip's horse at Olympia in 356 BC. Oxford, The Ashmolean Museum, Plate 28, No. 513. Photo: Museum, Herberden Coin Room.

10.5   Macedonian infantry sarissa (modern reconstruction). Photograph used by permission of Professor W. Heckel.

10.6   Portrait of Demosthenes. Braccio Nuovo, Vatican City, Vatican Museum. Photo: Scala/Art Resource, NY.

10.7   Burial monument at Chaeronea. Photo: SEF/Art Resource, NY.

10.8   Theater at the Macedonian capital, Aegae, modern Vergina. Photo: Vergina Museum.

11.1   Alexander. Photo: Erich Lessing/Art Resource

11.3   The Alexander Sarcophagus. Istanbul, Archaeological Museum. Photo: Time & Life Pictures/Getty Images.

11.4   Alexander coin. London, The British Museum. Courtesy of the Trustees of The British Museum.

11.5   Alexander as Pharaoh. Chicago, The Oriental Institute of the University of Chicago P.38387/N.43812/CHFN9246. Photo: Museum.

11.7   Palace of Persepolis. Photo © Lloyd Cluff/CORBIS.

11.9   Silver five-shekel coin from Babylonia. London, The British Museum. Courtesy of the Trustees of The British Museum.

12.1   Statue of old market woman. New York, The Metropolitan Museum of Art 09.39. Rogers Fund 1909. Image © The Metropolitan Museum of Art.

12.3   Roman bronze statuette copy of the Tyche of Antioch by Eutychides. New York, The Metropolitan Museum of Art 13.227.8. Rogers Fund, 1913. Image © The Metropolitan Museum of Art.

12.4   Gold octodrachm. New York, American Numismatic Society. 1977.158.112. Photo: The American Numismatic Society.

12.5   Tetradrachm of Commodus. London, The British Museum. Courtesy of the Trustees of The British Museum.

12.6   Alexandria Library. Photo courtesy of James Willis.

12.7a   Laocoön. Vatican City, Vatican Museum. Photo: Nimatallah/Art Resource, NY.

12.7b   Bronze boxer, Rome. Rome, Museo Nazionale della Term. Photo: Scala/Art Resource, NY.

12.7c   Crouching Aphrodite, Rome. From John Boardman, The Oxford History of Classical Art (New York: Oxford University Press, 1997), p. 192, fig. 190. Rome, National Museum of the Terme.

12.8a   Terra-cotta figurine of old nurse and child. New York, The Metropolitan Museum of Art 10.210.38. Rogers Fund, 1910. Image © The Metropolitan Museum of Art.

12.8b   Terra-cotta figurine of schoolgirl reading papyrus roll. Hamburg, Museum für Kunst und Gewerbe. Photo: Museum.

12.8c   Bronze statuette of black youth in craftsman's garb. New York, The Metropolitan Museum of Art 18.145.10. Rogers Fund, 1918. Image © The Metropolitan Museum of Art.

12.9   Limestone statue of Arsinoë II. New York, The Metropolitan Museum of Art 20.2.21. Rogers Fund, 1920. Image © The Metropolitan Museum of Art.

12.10   Nike of Samothrace. Paris, The Louvre. Photo: Réunion des Musées Nationaux/Art Resource, NY.

12.11   Sculpted relief of the Apotheosis of Homer. London, The British Museum. Photo: Werner Forman Archives/Art Resource, NY.

12.13a–c Antikythera Mechanism. Photo: © 2008 Tony Freeth, Images First Ltd.

12.14   The Rosetta Stone. London, The British Museum. Photo: bpk Berlin.

12.15   Altar of Pergamum. Berlin, Pergamon Museum. Photo: © Wolfgang Kaehler/CORBIS.

E.1   Coin portrait of Cleopatra VII. London, The British Museum. Photo: Museum, courtesy of the Trustees of The British Museum.

Plates

Plate Ia   Excavations at Uluburun. Photo: Institute of Nautical Archaeology.

Plate Ib   Excavations at Uluburun. Photo: Institute of Nautical Archaeology.

Plate II   Golden diadem from the "Treasure of Priam." Photo: akg-images/ullstein bild

Plate III   Bridgeman Art Library.

Plate IV   Terra-cotta chest, surmounted by a lid with five model granaries. Athens, Agora Museum. Photo: American School of Classical Studies at Athens: Agora Excavations.

Plate V   L.H. Jeffery Archive at the Centre for the Study of Ancient Documents

Plate VIa   Scala/Art Resource, NY

Plate VIb   Getty Images.

Plate VIIa   Bridgeman Art Library

Plate VIIb   De Agostini Picture Library / G. Dagli Orti

Plate VIII   Archaic poetry on Hellenistic papyrus. Photograph courtesy of the Egypt Exploration Society and the Imaging Papyri Project, University of Oxford.

Plate IX   Procession of life-size guards from the palace of Darius the Great, Susa, Iran. Erich Lessing/Art Resource, NY.

Plate Xa   Francois Vase. C.M. Dixon/Ancient Art & Architecture Collection Ltd.

Plate Xb   Francois Vase detail depicting Thetis. C.M. Dixon/Ancient Art & Architecture Collection Ltd.

Plate XIa   Attic red-figure calyx-*krater* attributed to Euphronius. Munich, Staaliche Antikensammlungen. Photo: Museum.

Plate XIb   Libation phiale. Boston, Museum of Fine Arts, 65.908 Edwin E. Jack Fund. Photograph © 2009 Museum of Fine Arts, Boston.

Plate XIIa   Peplos kore. Athens, The Acropolis Museum. Photo: The Art Archive/Acropolis Museum Athens/Gianni Dagli Orti.

Plate XIIb   Painted reconstruction of the Peplos kore. Museum of Classical Archaeology, Cambridge. Photo: Museum.

Plate XIII   Louvre Museum; Paris, 1999.

Plate XIV   Bronze charioteer. Delphi Museum. Photo: Erich Lessing/Art Resource, NY.

Plate XV   Temple of Apollo at Delphi. Amon Carter Museum, Fort Worth, Texas, Bequest of Eliot Porter.

Plate XVI   Aphrodite of Cnidus. Photo: Scala/Art Resource, NY.

Plate XVII   akg/Bildarchiv Monheim

Plate XVIII   The Derveni Krater. Archeological Museum of Thessaloniki. Photo: The Art Archive/ Archaeological Museum Salonica/Gianni Dagli Orti.

Plate XIX   Gold double Daric medallion minted by Alexander the Great. O. Bopearachchi and P. Flandrin, *Le Portrait d'Alexander le Grand: Histoire d'une découverte pour l'humanité* (Monaco: Éditions du Rocher, 2005). Photograph courtesy of Osmund Bopearachchi

Plate XXa   Royal tomb at Aegae, modern Vergina. Photo: Vergina Museum.

Plate XXb   Silver hydria discovered in the Macedonian tomb in Plate XIXa. Photo: Vergina Museum

Plate XXI   The Alexander mosaic from Pompeii. Naples, National Archaeological Museum. Photo: Erich Lessing/Art Resource, NY.

Plate XXII   Hellenistic terra-cotta depicting two women talking. London, The British Museum (Cat. No. C 529). Photo credit : British Museum/Art Resource, NY.

Plate XXIII   Basalt statue of Cleopatra VII. Photo: © State Hermitage Museum, St Petersburg.

INDEX